Keyingham and its People

The Story of a Millennium

Editor: M H Smith

Keyingham Local History Group
Keyingham Millennium Book
2000

Published by
Keyingham Millennium Book
21 Eastfield Road, Keyingham,
East Yorkshire, HU12 9RY

ISBN 0 9536486 0 5

Produced by
Burstwick Print and Publicity Services
13a Anlaby Road, Hull, HU1 2PJ

Front Cover: ***Keyingham Main Street, circa 1905.*** *The saddler's shop, with a horse collar hanging outside the door, is on the left. The saddler later moved to the opposite side of the street. The white house with the bay windows is where Dr Compton lived.*

Courtesy of Peter McCurdy

Back Cover: ***Planting the Millennium Yew tree in the school grounds, October 1999.*** *Ken Suddaby plants a yew sapling provided by Yews for the Millennium, a project launched by the Conservation Foundation with the aim of providing every parish in the country with a yew, a tree that can survive for several hundred years. The tree had been previously blessed by the Archbishop of York at a special service conducted at Northallerton, from where Ken and Joan Suddaby collected it. Watching Ken are, from left to right: Samual Moss, John Moss, Mrs Joan Suddaby, Mrs Dawn Huntley, Rebecca Huntley, Mrs Debbie Norman, Jonathan Norman, Luke Overvoorde, James Norman and George Harrison.*

Photo: Mrs M R Smith

Preface

The idea of commemorating the Millennium in Keyingham with a book covering the last thousand years of the village's history was first suggested by Mike Smith in the Keywatch magazine in 1997. The book was to be in three sections: one dealing with the history from the year 1000 to the year 1900, one with the history of the last century and one giving detailed information on the village as it is today. The suggestion was taken up by the Keyingham Parish Council, who not only gave the project their backing but also gave a donation of £200 towards the cost of production. In the spring of 1998 a Workers' Educational Association class was formed with the intention of collecting material for the book. The tutor, Mike Smith, who had already gathered much information on the early years of the village during 30 years of teaching local history, was to deal with the first section, and the class was to compile the other two sections, using not only written records, but also using photographs and information and recollections gathered from the people of Keyingham. Unfortunately, the class was unable to continue after the first term because of lack of the requisite numbers, and the work was carried on by a group of people, all of whom were villagers of long standing, meeting at intervals in each other's houses. The group - Gladys Beadle, Ann Braithwaite, Robert and Barbara Brown, Audrey Foster, Leonard and Rosalie Haxby, Violet Roydhouse and Mike Smith - put in a lot of hard work, but it was a lengthy task, which has taken longer to complete than expected, and in order to have the book published in the magic year 2000, it was decided to abandon the section dealing with Keyingham as it is today.

The text was written by Audrey Foster, Ros Haxby and Mike Smith. Ann Braithwaite undertook the research of records at the Hull Central Library and the Beverley Record Office, Barbara Brown chronicled the parish council minutes and Rob Brown gathered useful information from the Internet, but everyone in the group played their part in gathering and checking information and discussing what should be included - or left out! The work has been a real team effort.

The book is divided into two sections, the first dealing with the history of Keyingham up to 1900, and the second with the village in the 20th century. The first section will give the reader an indication of the wealth of documentary evidence that relates to Keyingham, and the second will indicate what a vast amount of assistance we have had from past and present residents of the village. No one has refused to give us information where they could, and many have lent us photographs for use as illustrations. We are very grateful to them and apologise for not being able to give a list of all their names. We have acknowledged the source of the photographs; those with no acknowledgement were taken by the editor. On the technical and practical side we have been greatly assisted by Ian Lanham, who prepared some of the maps, David Mitchell in designing the cover, and Hazel Gibson, who did the proofreading. All three are Keyingham people by birth or adoption.

In the preparation of the book the group has been encouraged by the financial assistance it received, and we express our thanks to the Keyingham Parish Council, the Keyingham Gala Committee, the WEA, the Patrington Local History Group, BP Chemicals and, above all, the

Millennium Festival Awards-For-All, who made a generous grant of £3,000 towards the project. We have also been encouraged by the advance orders for 250 books - in fact, encouragement has come pretty steadily from that quarter, especially from those who paid in advance!

As already mentioned, the nine authors have worked hard, and the reason for the delay in producing this work has been a striving for accuracy and, as near as possible, completeness. We know we will not have achieved either and we know the pitfalls of writing about events within living memory! However, despite any shortcomings the book may have, we can only say that we have enjoyed compiling it and meeting the many people who have helped with the work. We hope that reading the book brings as much pleasure.

M H Smith, August 2000

Contents

Maps

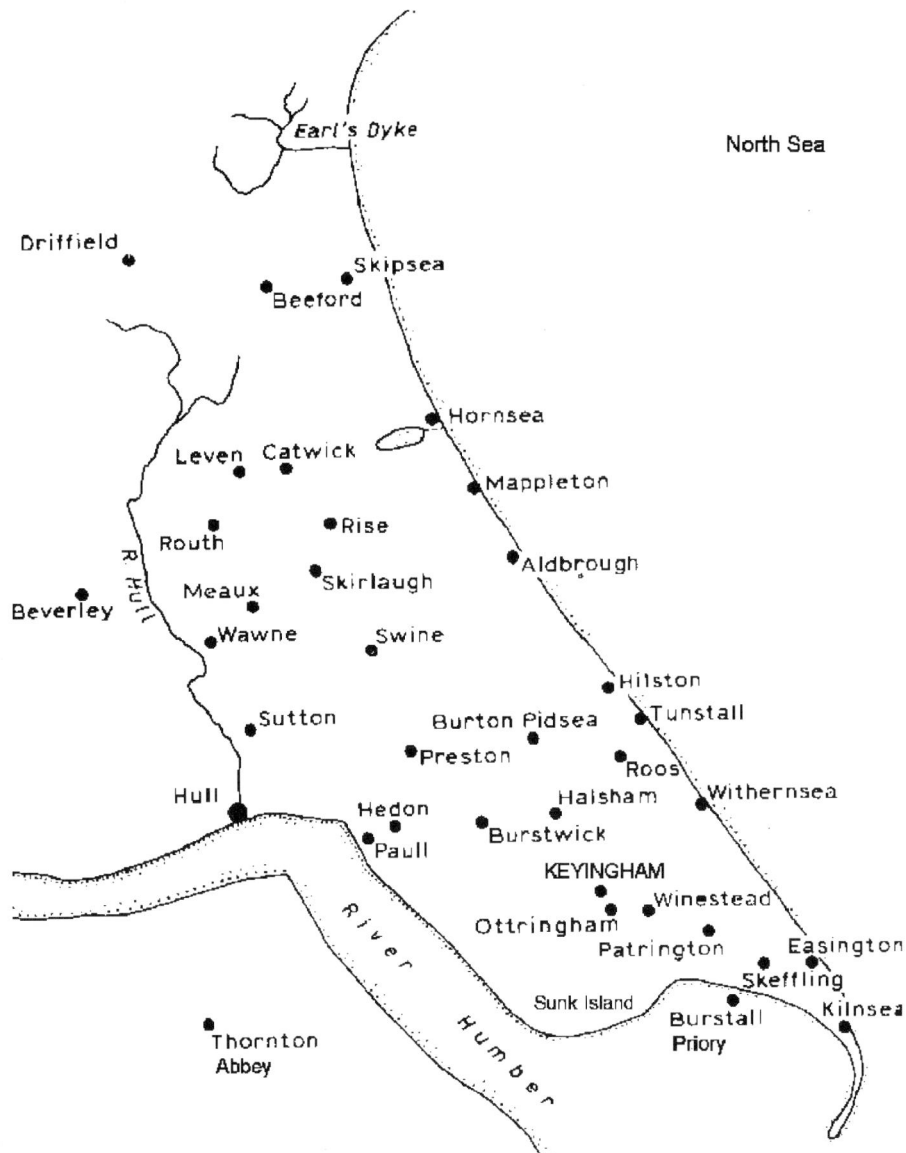

Holderness, showing the location of Keyingham and other places mentioned in the text. Geographically, Holderness is the area bounded by the River Hull, Earl's Dyke, the River Humber and the North Sea.   *Map by Len Haxby*

1 - Dawn of a Millennium - Invasions, Wars and Taxes

A thousand years ago it is highly unlikely that the villagers of Keyingham were looking forward with hope to the dawn of the second millennium. More probably they were anticipating with dread the ending of the first. The local priest would no doubt have instilled into them the message of the Book of Revelations, that after Christ had reigned a thousand years he would come to judge both the living and the dead, and for those judged guilty of sin the punishment was to be cast into the lake 'burning with fire and brimstone'. This message of the Day of Judgment, or Day of Doom, may well have been repeated in paintings on the walls of the church, 'so that everyone who entered, even if they could not read, having before their eyes the perils of the Last Judgment, might examine their hearts the more strictly on that account'. So wrote the Venerable Bede in the eighth century when describing the interior of a Northumbrian church.

Events in England at the end of the tenth century seemed to herald doom. The country had been united under one king for only fifty years. In the early years of the Anglo-Saxon settlement, Keyingham had been part of Northumbria (the lands to the north of the Humber), which was one of more than half a dozen kingdoms that made up the land of the English. In the ninth century had come the invasions and eventual settlement of the Danish Vikings, to which Northumbria had succumbed. Only the kingdom of Wessex, under Alfred the Great, had held out against the Danish attacks and in 886 had come to an agreement with the invaders to partition the country between English and Danish rule. To the southwest of a line running roughly from London to Chester, govern-

ment was to be by the house of Wessex; to the northeast, was to be the Danelaw, of which Keyingham was part. It was a situation which did not last; by 954, under the leadership of Alfred's descendants, the whole of the country had been regained by the house of Wessex, and Keyingham was once more subject to the rule of an English king, this time one who ruled the whole of the land. Twenty-five years of peace had followed. It was then that the infamous Ethelred the Unready had come to the throne, and it was he who was king as the thousandth year of Christ's reign approached.

Ethelred's rule is generally considered as a disaster for the English. His weakness encouraged fresh waves of Viking adventurers to descend on the country's shores. Lands were ravaged, villages pillaged and people massacred, particularly in the south of the country. Ethelred's sole solution was to buy off the invaders with vast amounts of gold and silver. In 991 and 994, sums totalling £38,000 were paid, equivalent to three or four times the annual income of the nation. The money was raised by a tax, later known as the Danegeld, the burden of which was felt in every region of the country but whose effect was simply to encourage new armies of Danes to try their luck. The English must have considered all this as portents of worse to come as the Day of Judgment approached.

The end of the first millennium came but divine judgment did not befall. Sinners and the righteous had to await their deserts. In England the account of the sinners mounted, with treachery and atrocities committed by both Danes and English. The Danegeld continued to be exacted. In 1002 £24,000 of silver was paid, in 1006 £36,000 and in 1012 the final tribute of £48,000 was handed over with the Danes holding Alphege, Archbishop of

Canterbury, as hostage. In an act, typical of the times, they slew him after the ransom had been paid. The following year, Sweyn, King of Denmark, entered the country. He was quickly accepted by the people of the former Danelaw, and eventually proclaimed King of England. Once more Keyingham was subject to Danish rule. Ethelred fled across the Channel for refuge with Richard, Duke of Normandy, whose sister, Emma, he had married.

Sweyn died and in 1016 his younger brother, Canute, became King of England. Although he was also King of both Denmark and Norway, he chose to make his home in this country. He married Emma of Normandy, widow of Ethelred. He was succeeded in turn by his two sons, one of whom was by Emma, and then in 1042 by Edward the Confessor, son of Ethelred and Emma. Emma thus had the distinction of being wife to two kings of England and mother to two. In 1066 her great-nephew, William the Conqueror, was also to do well for himself.

The period from Canute's accession in 1016 to the death of Edward in 1066 was one of comparative peace, but not of freedom from taxes. Gelds continued to be imposed up to the year 1051 in order to maintain a fleet and a standing military force in the king's service. In the event of any serious threat of invasion, however, all men capable of carrying arms were called on to defend their country. This obligation to serve in the militia, or fyrd, had been a feature of Anglo-Saxon society from early times. In 1066 the local fyrds were to be called into urgent action, as another period of English misery began.

Canute, in order to assist in the ruling of his kingdom, had set up a number of earldoms. One of his earls, Godwin, Earl of Wessex, came to exercise great power, particularly during the reign of Edward the Confessor. When Godwin died in 1053

he was succeeded as earl by his son Harold. Two years later, the power of the family was extended further when another of Godwin's sons, Tostig, half-brother to Harold, was made Earl of Northumbria. However, in 1065, probably because of continual absence from his earldom, not to mention a few atrocities inflicted on his opponents, Tostig was driven out by the Northumbrians. The king sent him into exile, and he was replaced by Earl Morcar. Harold, Tostig and Morcar, who played principal parts in the events of 1066, all held important estates in Holderness.

Edward died childless on 5 January 1066. The following day, Earl Harold was crowned King of England. But the complexity of Edward's antecedents meant that there were other claimants to the English throne. Edward, who had spent the 25 years of his life before his accession in the court of the Duke of Normandy, was said to have promised the crown to Duke William. In Scandinavia, Harold the Ruthless, King of Norway, laid claim because of his connexions with Canute. The new king awaited invasion by both parties. In September, Harold of Norway, with 300 ships and the exiled Tostig as a vengeful ally, sailed up the Humber. They threw off the attempted boarding-parties of the local fyrd, which no doubt included men from Keyingham, and continued up the River Ouse towards York. Two miles below York on 20 September they defeated Earl Morcar and his brother, Edwin, Earl of Mercia, at the Battle of Fulford. York surrendered and the Norwegians moved into encampment near Stamford Bridge. Meanwhile, Harold of England, who had heard of the Norwegians' approach as they sailed towards the Humber, had marched swiftly north gathering the fyrds as he went. At York he learnt of the invaders' position and took them by surprise on the morning of the 25th. At the end of a long battle, both Harold of Norway and Tostig lay dead, and the English had won the day. The Norwegian survivors were allowed to return to their own country. Twenty-four ships sufficed to carry the survivors, 'their prows', as the saga puts it 'by Spurn Head treading the watery way'. Harold had little time to rejoice in victory: on 28 September, William of Normandy and his troops disembarked on an undefended Sussex shore.

The Battle of Hastings was fought on 14 October. Harold was slain and on Christmas Day William was crowned King of England at Westminster Abbey. But the country was not completely subjugated. In 1069, there was a major uprising in the North. The rebels captured York. William came north, and put down the rebellion with ruthless efficiency. The rebels surrendered, but William was determined to teach the Northerners a lesson. He laid waste to the countryside, and bands of his raiders were sent out on terrible errands of destruction. Starvation and death ensued. William's 'Harrying of the North', as it was called, finally brought Northumbria under Norman control, a control maintained by the setting-up of castles at strategic points in the subjugated countryside. One such castle was at Skipsea in North Holderness.

William spent the remainder of his life between England and Normandy, protecting his new kingdom and his old dukedom. For England there was always the threat of invasion from Scandinavia and, when such a threat arose from the Danes in 1085, William ordered a 'scorched earth' policy for the eastern counties in order to prevent the invaders finding any means of sustenance on landing. Though the Danish fleet in the end failed to set sail it is highly likely that villages, like Keyingham, still struggling to recover from the terrible harrying of 1069 and '70, would have suffered further

privation as their crops were burned and livestock driven away. To add insult to injury, William reimposed the Danegeld and is known to have exacted four such taxes during his 20-year reign.

One of the Conqueror's last great acts in England was the ordering of the compilation of the Domesday Book. The decision was taken at the King's court held at Christmas 1085. The results of what was a truly monumental survey, covering practically the whole of England, were brought to William within 18 months. A month later, at Rouen, he died of a wound sustained whilst defending his Norman possessions.

The Domesday Book was so called because it became the ultimate authorative document in judging any disputes over the possession of land or its geld assessment. But some said it was because its searching nature was a judgment on the people. It is perhaps an insight into the medieval mind that after nearly a century of intermittent invasions, starvation and atrocities the term Domesday should be reserved for a piece of Norman bureaucracy. It is with this monument to bureaucratic endeavour that we have our first recorded account of the village of Keyingham.

Overleaf: Conjectural map of Keyingham at the beginning of the Second Millennium. Sea levels are still high on the eastern seaboard of England and the Humber was probably lapping up to the southern end of Ings Lane. However, mud flats are beginning to appear and two are shown to represent what by the 12th century had expanded and become Keyingham Marsh and Saltaugh Grange. Keyingham Fleet winds its way through a shallow marshy valley that forms the northwest boundary of the manor. The high ground is almost fully taken up by the two great arable fields, West Field and East Field, with their 'falls' of ridge and furrow. Between the two fields runs the village street with the houses and closes of the villagers along it. A simple church is in existence. Map by I Lanham

KEYINGHAM   AD 1000

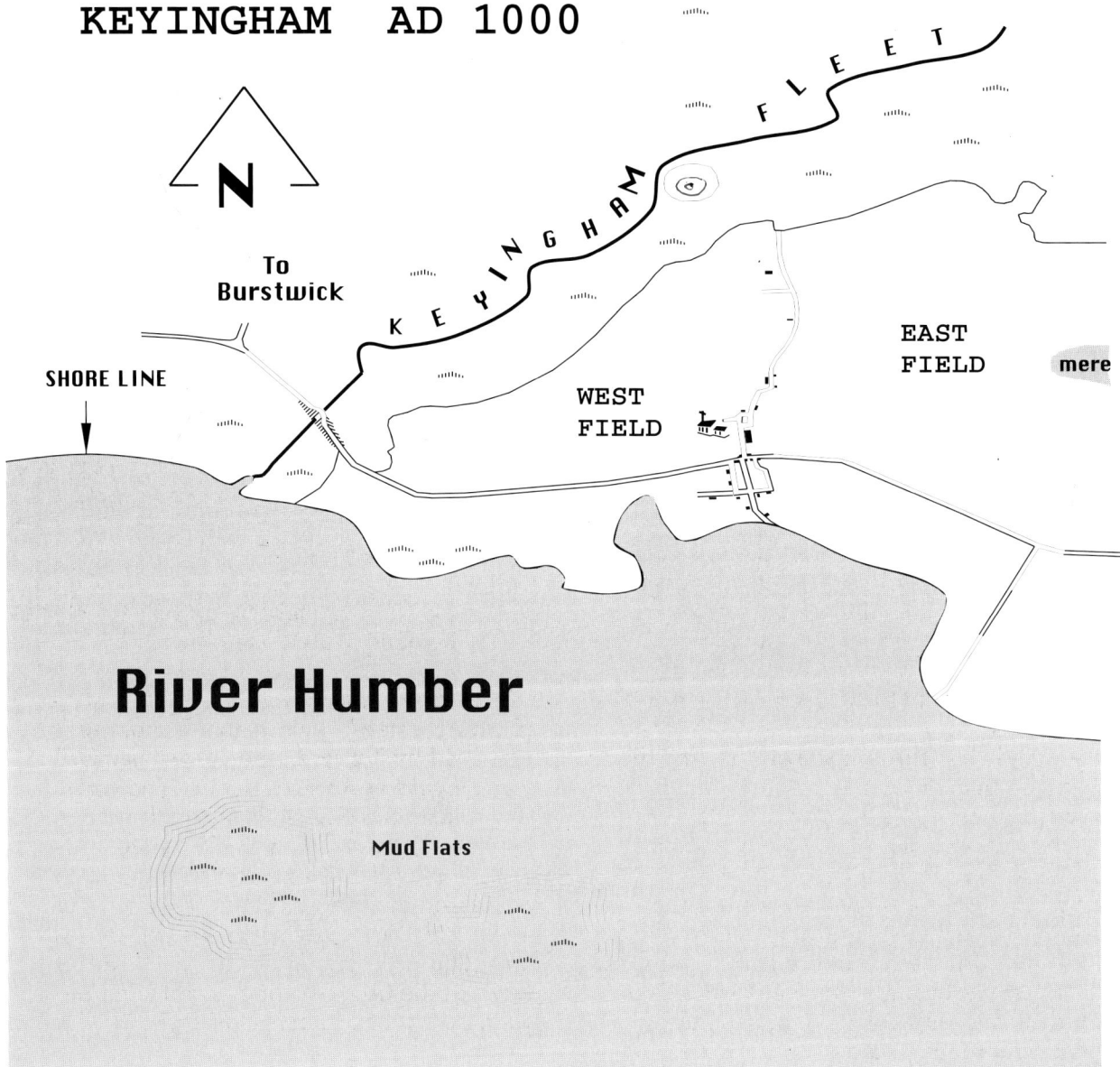

N

To
Burstwick

SHORE LINE

KEYINGHAM FLEET

OTTRINGHAM

WEST
FIELD

EAST
FIELD

mere

River Humber

Mud Flats

2 - The Growth of Keyingham

The entry in the Domesday Book is the first written reference to Keyingham and its inhabitants. There were, however, people occupying the site long before the 11th century. Romano-British pottery and a coin dating to the first century, discovered on the southern edge of Berrygate Hill by Jan Overvoorde, indicate occupation by a British tribe during Roman times. At this time, sea levels on the east coast were higher than they are now, and the dwellings of these people were probably at the very edge of the Humber, which would have covered the whole of Keyingham Marsh from the bottom end of Ings Lane southwards. Humber tides ebbed and flowed along a wide fenny river that came to mark the northwest boundary of Keyingham. This river was later known as the Keyingham Fleet and, in much later times, was deepened and straightened to form the Keyingham Drain.

The marshy nature of the district was still very much in evidence when the Anglo-Saxons began to settle on the higher and drier ground of Keyingham. This new settling of Keyingham is believed to have begun very early in the Anglo-Saxon period, probably in the fifth or sixth century, when the suffixes 'ham', 'ing' and 'ingham' were commonly used by the new settlers in the formation of settlement names. After that it is generally held that other suffixes, particularly 'ton', came into favour with the Anglo-Saxons in the naming of their habitation sites.

The English settlers, perhaps continuing a process begun by the British, gradually cleared the trees which would have covered the higher ground, and slowly brought the land under the plough. From the end of the ninth century onwards the community came to be joined by Danish invaders-turned-settlers, although the Danes also founded completely new settlements on land not yet occupied by the English. Such settlements, of which there are a few in Holderness, are indicated by the Danish place-name endings 'by' and 'thorp'.

During the 10th and 11th centuries, as we have seen, Keyingham had been alternately subject to rule by English and Danes. On the eve of the Norman Conquest the village was inhabited by people of both Anglo-Saxon and Danish descent who had taken on something of the speech, laws, practices and organisation of both races. Furthermore they had become used to being assessed for, and paying, English and Danish taxes. With the Norman Conquest, they were to come under a different rule, different methods of organisation and a new set of tax collectors.

- o -

The entry for Keyingham in the Domesday Book may be paraphrased as follows:

'Keyingham consists of a single manor [farming estate]. Before the Conquest it was held by Torverd, and it was assessed for the geld at 8 ploughlands. The estate could keep 8 ploughs occupied. It is now held by Drogo, who has 30 villein tenants with 3 ploughs. There is a priest and a church on the estate. There are 24 acres of meadow. The whole estate is 2 leagues long and 1 league wide. In the time of Edward the Confessor it brought in £8 per year; now it brings in 30 shillings.'

This entry was written in abbreviated Latin by Norman-French scribes taking their information from local witnesses speaking an Anglo-Danish dialect. This led to some confusion, particularly in the recording of proper names and place-names. For example, the French did not have a 'th' sound and so what is thought to be the Danish name of the pre-Conquest holder of Keyingham, 'Thorfrothr', went into Domesday as 'Torverd'. Whatever his name, he troubles the historian no further, although one could well imagine him and his tenants joining the fyrd in trying to repel the Norwegian fleet sailing up the Humber in the September of 1066, or joining in the uprising against the Normans in 1069.

Thorfrothr appears to have been only a minor landholder, although a man, or men, with the same name held Oubrough (now a single farm on the road between Coniston and Skirlaugh) as well as one of the eight small manors at Preston. Thorfrothr, however, had powerful neighbours. Tostig, the exiled Earl of Northumbria, slain at Stamford Bridge, held Burstwick. King Harold, slain at Hastings, held a large estate near Skipsea. Morcar, Tostig's successor as Earl, held the important coastal manors of Hornsea, Mappleton, Withernsea, Easington and Kilnsea. At the time of the Domesday survey he was languishing in a Norman gaol. The Archbishop of York was lord of the manor of Patrington, which included Winestead and parts of Halsham and Welwick. He also held a large tract of land in the Swine area.

Thorfrothr's successor at Keyingham was also powerful. He was Drogo, a Flemish knight who had accompanied William in his conquest of England. He had, like most of William's followers, been well rewarded for his support. But, whereas William had tended to grant most of his tenants-in-chief estates scattered over all the country in order to prevent them ever building a power base against him, he had favoured Drogo by granting him the compact estate of Holderness as well as lands on the other side of the Humber in Lincolnshire. Drogo also received manors in Leicestershire, Northamptonshire, Norfolk and Suffolk. In Holderness he was granted almost every manor, those which had belonged to great men like Morcar and those which had belonged to lesser men like Thorfrothr. The only exceptions were those manors held before the Conquest by the Archbishop of York or by St John's minster church of Beverley. These institutions continued to hold their lands after the Conquest.

Drogo received another favour from William - the hand in marriage of one of William's female relatives. William's purpose in granting a favoured follower a compact estate on the northeast coast and along the Humber was to help protect the coast and the route up the Humber against invading Vikings. He made similar large and compact grants to trusted followers, in areas subject to inroads from the Scots and Welsh. Probably as part of this defence policy, Drogo built a castle at Skipsea and kept in his own hand all the manors along the Holderness coast rather than sub-granting them to any of his band of followers. Burstwick and Keyingham he also retained.

Drogo did not end his days in Holderness, or in England. The Domesday Book hints at his departure. The Yorkshire section ends with a summary of who owned which manor in each village. It was probably the last part of the survey written. For the Holderness villages, although the amount of land for tax assessment is given in each case, Drogo's name is omitted. His disappearance from the record is explained by an account written at Fountains Abbey more than two centuries later. According to this account, Drogo, by some mischance, killed his wife. He then went to his in-law, the king, pretending that he and his wife wished to return to Flanders and could he have the wherewithal to finance the voyage? The king obliged and Drogo fled abroad. When the king discovered the true facts he ordered Drogo to be seized but he was heard of no more.

For such misdeeds, Drogo naturally forfeited his estates, and William granted the Holderness lands to another of his in-laws, Odo, who was married to the Conqueror's sister. By right of his wife, Odo held the small county of Albemarle in Normandy. He was succeeded by his son Stephen, who inherited both his mother's and his father's titles. He was thus Lord of Holderness, as well as of other lands in England, and Count of Albemarle. The Albemarle title, commemorated in a Keyingham street name, remained linked to the Holderness estates until Stephen's line ended with the death of Isabella, dowager Countess of Albemarle, in 1293.

Returning to 1086 and the Domesday Book entry for Keyingham, it is noticeable that the value of the manor had fallen sharply between the time of Edward the Confessor and the time of the survey. In 1066, Keyingham was worth £8 a year; in 1086 the annual income was only 30 shillings (£1.50). This great drop in value is attributable to the Harrying of the North of 1069 and '70, and also, possibly, to the scorched-earth policy of 1085. Yorkshire was direly affected. It has been calculated, for example, that the total value of the Holderness manors in 1086 was only 17% of their value in 1066. Some manors, such as Hilston and Owstwick, were completely wasted, with no inhabitants and no land under cultivation. Holderness must have presented a dismal picture of largely overgrown and neglected fields, with what cultivated areas there were being worked by a greatly reduced population.

For tax purposes the manor of Keyingham was assessed at eight ploughlands. Thus, when King William had found need to emulate his Anglo-Saxon and Danish predecessors by imposing a geld on his subjects, he would have expected to receive as much from Keyingham as from Holmpton, which was also assessed at eight ploughlands, but twice as much as from Burstwick, which was assessed at four ploughlands. The Domesday entry tells us that the manor of Keyingham could keep occupied eight ploughs (and their teams of oxen). Thus, as on most of Drogo's other Holderness manors the number of geld-assessment ploughlands was the same as the number of ploughs that the manor could keep occupied. This seems logical and fair: the more land under the plough, the more tax the lord of the manor could afford to pay. One could imagine an assessor, at some time before the Conquest when the land was flourishing and under maximum cultivation, requesting landowners to inform him of how many ploughs there were on their estates so that he could give them a tax rating. It is the same today, when the size of your house is used to determine the amount of council tax you pay. However, in 1086, the land was not flourishing or under maximum cultivation. At Keyingham, for instance, only three ploughs were in use. The king's officials might have to have a rethink about the gelds they could exact. At Hilston and Owstwick they would have had to forego their dues.

The figure of eight ploughs that the Domesday Book said Keyingham could maintain presents a problem. The amount of land that could be kept under cultivation by one plough drawn by a team of eight oxen varied with the type of soil but it is generally considered to be equivalent to 120 acres.

The amount was called a ploughland. Thus, it was an actual amount of land as well as being a notional amount for tax purposes. It would seem, therefore, that Keyingham had nearly a thousand acres of land capable of arable production. But this is far more than the area of higher ground in Keyingham, the ground we would expect to be put under the plough in the Middle Ages. Even at the end of the 18th century the area of arable on Keyingham's high ground was less than 800 acres. Domesday Book seems to be giving us misleading information, especially as there is another oddity in the Keyingham entry. Drogo does not appear to be keeping any land for his own use - it is his villein tenants who have the three ploughs. The normal way for a Norman lord to run his manor was to keep some of the land for himself (his demesne land) and rent the remainder to his tenants. Thus, at Mappleton, Drogo is recorded as having one plough, with four villeins having one plough. The villeins paid the rents for their lands in kind - most of it as work services, so that at Mappleton the four villeins, besides working their own lands, also cultivated and harvested Drogo's demesne, using his plough and farming equipment. At Keyingham, with no demesne land mentioned, the question is, where were Drogo's 30 villeins doing their work services? The answer to this and the problem of the missing acres is probably supplied by the next survey of Keyingham that we know of, carried out nearly 200 years later, in 1260. In this survey, the Count of Albemarle does have demesne land in Keyingham, but all of it is in Keyingham Marsh. So what might have been happening in 1086 and before?

In the 11th century sea levels along the east coast were falling, and great areas of siltland were becoming exposed along the Humber foreshore.

Across the Humber, at South Ferriby, 260 acres of this siltland were quoted in the Domesday Book as one of the assets bringing revenue to the manor. In 1033, when King Canute granted the manor of Patrington to the Archbishop of York, it consisted of the whole of Patrington, together with Winestead, Welwick Thorpe and part of Halsham. But by 1086, the manor had expanded to include Tharlesthorpe, a completely new settlement that had emerged from the Humber mud to the southwest of Patrington. There can be no doubt that a similar emergence of profitable siltland from the marshes on the southern fringes of Keyingham had occurred or that positive efforts had been made to hasten the process by embanking and draining. The Humber silts, once the salt content has washed away, are recognised as very productive, initially as grazing land, but also as arable when conditions become drier. It would seem that the tax assessors had recognised this and put a valuation on the reclaimed land.

It would seem also that the lord of Keyingham manor had realised the value of the siltlands and claimed them as his demesne, foregoing any rights he had to land on the higher ground. Although productive, the siltlands were vulnerable and following the uprising of 1069, when William wished to punish the rebels by laying waste to their lands, it would have been an easy task at Keyingham for the wreckers to cut any primitive embankments protecting the reclaimed silts. Repairs by a population reduced by famine would have been slow, and flooding by the salty waters of the Humber would have delayed new growth. This would account for the lord of the manor having no demesne lands in Keyingham at the time of the survey, although he may still have had the burden of their tax assessment. The work services of Drogo's 30 villeins, in all probability, consisted in helping with the reclamation and tending sheep put on to the new pastures. Certainly, 200 years later, Keyingham's villeins are known to have had special responsibility for the Count of Albemarle's flocks in south Holderness.

Embanking, or re-embanking, with only spades and barrows as tools, by a workforce of two or three dozen men with their own fields to tend would have been a lengthy process. There may have been halts and reversals in the slow fall in sea level that was occurring. Progress would have been measured in generations rather in years. Shortly after the middle of the 12th century, however, progress received a boost.

At that time the Lord of Holderness was William le Gros, so called because of his corpulence. He was the son of Stephen, already mentioned. William had made a vow to join the second crusade but because of his age (he was in his 40s) and his weight (whereby he could no longer ride a horse) he asked the Pope to be absolved from his vow. This the Pope did, on condition that William founded a Cistercian monastery. William, who had already founded religious houses at Thornton Abbey and Vaudey, both in Lincolnshire, agreed, and he gave a site for an abbey in Holderness, at Meaux, just north of Wawne. The first monks arrived there from the mother abbey of Fountains in January 1151. William endowed the monks with lands with which to support themselves, and amongst his gifts was Saltaugh, in Keyingham. Saltaugh lay mostly along the eastern fringe of Keyingham Marsh, bordering Ottringham Marsh, which itself was in an advanced state of reclamation. But part of Saltaugh was on the south of Keyingham Marsh, bordering the ever-threatening Humber. Fortunately, the Cistercian Order laid strong emphasis on the work ethic. Included in their system were the lay brothers who did most of the manual work of the monastery, especially on the lands lying remote from the abbey. Here was a dedicated workforce, with no fields of their own to divert their attentions. They could devote their energies to the embanking of Saltaugh and protecting it from the force of the Humber waves. In doing so, they would be providing a shield to le Gros's lands to the north. William's generosity in granting Saltaugh may have been not untouched with self-interest.

By 1177, Meaux Abbey had built a grange at Saltaugh to house the lay brothers who tended the sheepfolds and pastures. The monks established granges on other East Riding lands that they received, including more lands on the fringes of the Humber, such as at Tharlesthorpe. In time the abbey became one of the leading wool producers in the district. From the monks' little port of Wyke, at the mouth of the River Hull, wool from their flocks was shipped, not only to the great wool fairs at places like Boston, but also abroad to Italy.

By the second half of the 13th century, reclamation of the marshlands had progressed enormously. In 1260, the death occurred of William de Fortibus, Count of Albemarle, and great-grandson of William le Gros. An inquiry was held into the annual value of his estate so that the Exchequer could calculate the amount payable by his heir on succeeding to the estate. It was found that the demesne at Keyingham Marsh then extended to about 1,200 acres. Some of this was under the plough, but the major part (over 800 acres) was either meadow or pastureland. Similarly, at Saltaugh the monks had made large gains from the Humber. Their estate had come to cover nearly 700 acres which, like the de Fortibus estate, was largely given over to stock rearing, although some of the land was tilled.

KEYINGHAM AD 1300

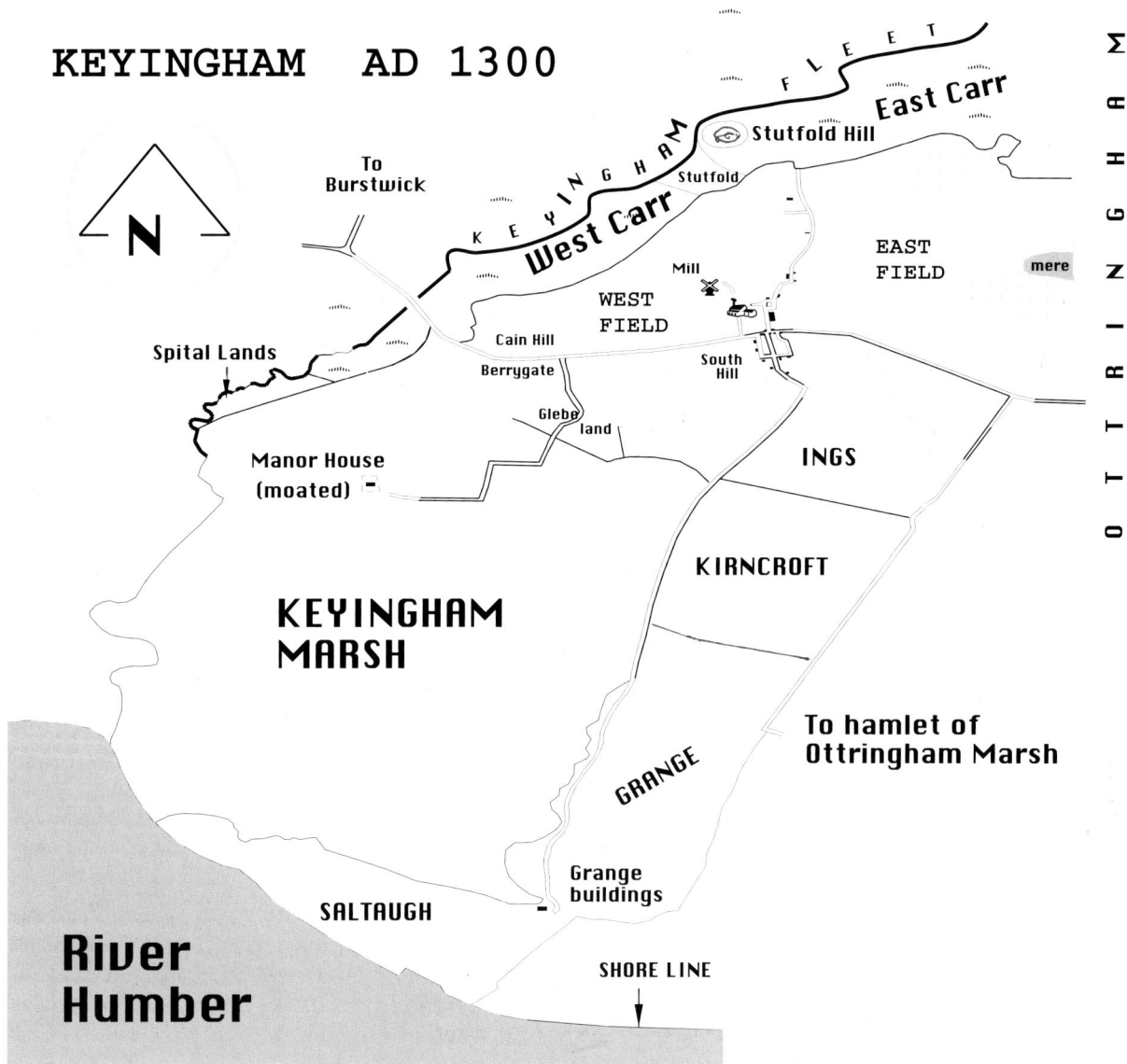

N

FLEET

KEYINGHAM West Carr

East Carr

Stutfold Hill

To Burstwick

Stutfold

EAST FIELD

mere

Mill

WEST FIELD

Cain Hill

Berrygate

South Hill

Spital Lands

Glebe land

INGS

Manor House (moated)

KIRNCROFT

KEYINGHAM MARSH

To hamlet of Ottringham Marsh

GRANGE

Grange buildings

SALTAUGH

SHORE LINE

River Humber

OTTRINGHAM

In the meantime more land was accruing to the villeins. By widening and deepening the Keyingham Fleet, an area, previously fen, began to yield rough pastures capable of feeding extra livestock, at least in the dry summer months. This carr-land, as it was known, formed a valuable part of the village economy, with every householder having some rights to pasture animals there and to take a share of the fuel it yielded in the form of turves and wood.

What was happening at Keyingham reflected to a greater or lesser degree what was happening nation-wide. More and more land was being brought under cultivation. Vast acreages of marshland were being reclaimed from England's shores - from the estuarine marshes of Devon to the fens of Lincolnshire. On the north shore of the Humber new settlements came into being. Besides Tharlesthorpe, which was in existence before 1066, Frismersk and Orwithfleet sprang up on the reclaimed silts to the south of Patrington. A new hamlet of more than 20 houses came into being in Ottringham Marsh. Keyingham Marsh, however, never became a settlement for people. Except for the monks' grange at Saltaugh and possibly a manor house from which the running of the demesne was organised, Keyingham Marsh was a landscape of sheepfolds, byres and the occasional shepherd's hut.

At the same time as land was being reclaimed along England's shoreline, thousands of acres of forest and moorland were being cleared for farming. All this was made necessary by the country's rising population and the need to feed more and more mouths. It has been variously estimated that England's population rose from between 1.1 and 2.2 million at the time of the Domesday survey to between 5 and 6 million in the early part of the 14th century. Such an increase put great pressure on the agricultural resources of the country, and this is no better illustrated than by the events at Keyingham. In the first two and half centuries of the second millennium Keyingham more than doubled its agriculturally productive area. But in the case of Keyingham and all the reclamation along England's eastern seaboard, the hand of man had been greatly assisted by Nature. Falling sea levels, coupled with a tilting upwards of the south-eastern edge of Britain, made for a natural emergence of lands. But what Nature gave she could also take away and, in the 14th century, this is what she did. That is a story for a later chapter.

Keyingham in the Year 1300. Keyingham Marsh and Saltaugh Grange have been reclaimed from the Humber. The Lord of Holderness has a manor house on his demesne land and Meaux Abbey has grange buildings at Saltaugh. The Knights Hospitaller have been granted Spital Lands out of the marsh. To the south of the high ground some of the marsh has become meadowland - the Ings. Later, a large block of the Ings was to be converted to an arable field known as Kirncroft. The fen land on the edge of Keyingham Fleet is now sufficiently well drained for it to be used as rough pasture called West Carr and East Carr. Between the two carrs is a piece of ground called Stutfold, which may have been the fold where stots, or young oxen, were kept. A mill has been built by the lord of the manor. Map by I Lanham

Keyingham's West Field and West Carr, April 1987.
View southeast from Keyingham Drain. In the foreground is the low-lying flat land of the carr. The mill and Mill House stand on the high ground of the West Field. The remaining houses of the village are over the brow of the hill. Across the centre of the picture is the bank and ditch originally marking the edge of the Keyingham Fleet but later the boundary between the West Field and the West Carr. In the centre of the picture a track runs down to the carr.

3 - Lords and Tenants

We know little about the relationship between the lord of the manor of Keyingham and his tenants between the start of the millennium and the Norman Conquest. In the second half of the tenth century the village was probably peopled by independent Danes and English, owning their lands freely and owing loyalty and dues to no-one but the king. But around the turn of the millennium, invasion by new armies of Danes and the impositions of heavy gelds by Ethelred the Unready brought the smaller landowners to desperate states of poverty. Their only remedy was to seek the protection of a wealthier and more powerful landowner. In many cases they turned their lands over to their protector and received them back under terms requiring them to pay dues, in kind and as work, to their new overlord. Thus, on the eve of the Conquest there existed in England what is known as the manorial system, whereby an estate was held by a man of some standing, whose lands on the estate were worked by his tenants in return for the lands they held. In Keyingham in 1066 the lord of the manor was Thorfrothr. He owed loyalty and dues to his king, but his land was his own, held freely. His tenants were probably in different degrees of prosperity, but they, too, were free: it was possible for them to take their lands and services to another lord. This is probably what happened at neighbouring Ottringham where, before the Conquest, the overlordship was shared amongst three lords - the minster church of Beverley and two Anglo-Danes of moderate status. Some of the villagers, however, appear to have sought stronger protection: they had put themselves and their lands under the jurisdiction of Ulf, the powerful lord of Aldbrough. Consequently, in the Domesday Book a small portion of Ottringham land is included with the manor of Aldbrough.

Following the Norman Conquest, the relationship between lord and tenant became more and more rigorously defined. Under the feudal system, which the Normans embraced and developed to a high degree, all land was held in return for services rendered. The king was ultimate owner of all the land and what he didn't keep in his own hands he granted to tenants-in-chief in return for military service and other obligations. Thus, in return for the grant of Holderness the first Norman holder, Drogo, and his successors owed the king the service of ten knights, who would have to serve in the field or help guard castles for 40 days of each year. The Domesday Book records ten knights with portions of lands in Holderness granted to them by Drogo, presumably to maintain themselves while in the service of Drogo. The lords of Holderness also sub-granted lands to other of their followers in return for military service. In theory, each grant of land, known as a knight's fee, should have been sufficient to support one knight. However, grants were subject to bargaining, and a grantee would sometimes accept smaller grants than warranted the service of one knight. Moreover, as military service became commuted to a money payment it was possible to grant fractions of knight's fees. By 1260 a small amount of land in Keyingham had been sub-granted to a number of tenants on such military terms.

Lower down the feudal scale, the villeins on a manor held their plots of land, not in return for military service, but in return for work services carried out on the demesne of the lord. They each, for example, may have had to do so many days' ploughing, mowing, reaping and carting during the year. In addition to this there were other impositions. There were payments in kind to be made to the lord at certain times of the year (eggs at Easter, fowls at Christmas). An heir could not succeed to his father's lands until he had paid a fine, usually his best beast, to the lord. The villein may have had to pay a fine to his lord when his daughter married. He had to attend at the lord's manor court, and submit to his lord's justice. The lord would own the only mill on the manor, and the villeins would have to use this mill for the grinding of their corn on payment of a fee, usually a fraction of the corn ground. Similar, but lesser, services and dues were owed by cottagers on the manor, whose holdings of land were much less than those of the villeins, perhaps only an acre or so. Cottagers were the men who acted as labourers at busy times on the lands of the lord or of the villeins. Some of them were also the craftsmen of the village. The services and dues owed by villeins and cottagers varied from manor to manor and in the course of time became commuted to money payments. But, what did not change or vary was the fact that the villein and cottager were not free; unlike tenants that held their land on military terms, they could not leave the manor and go and live elsewhere without the express permission of the lord.

The men who were the lords of Keyingham following the Conquest also happened to be the lords of Holderness. They had lands in Normandy and elsewhere in England. Some of them were important national figures. Their public and domestic affairs took them to many places, and Keyingham was not the centre of their world. Much of their time was spent on their Norman lands, and four of the eight who succeeded Drogo died abroad. However, some did reside at times in Holderness, and the people of Keyingham would be aware of their presence, especially when the seat of the estate was moved from Skipsea to Burstwick early in the 13th century.

Isabella de Fortibus. *Sculpted head at the former Augustinian priory at Christchurch, Hants., where the Earls of Devon were lords of the town.*
Courtesy of the Vicar of Christchurch

The last Count of Albemarle, William de Fortibus, died in France in 1260. The inquiry into the value of his estates for the purpose of assessing the death duties payable to the Crown by his heir has already been referred to. Under the feudal system, William's widow, Isabella de Fortibus was entitled to a third of the estates, whilst the other two-thirds was run by the king for his own profit until the heir came of age. However, Isabella and her mother, Amice, dowager Countess of Devon, bought the two-thirds for the term of the heir's minority and ran the estates jointly. As Holderness was the chief of her estates, Isabella moved into residence at Burstwick and was there from 1259 until 1263. But following the death of her brother, the Earl of Devon, Isabella, at the age of 25, succeeded to his titles and became in her own right Countess of Devon and Lady of the Isle of Wight. She then moved to the south of the country, living mostly at Carisbrooke Castle on the Isle of Wight.

Through her inheritance and her dower lands, Isabella was one of the wealthiest landowners in the kingdom, and her eldest son the heir to vast estates. However, her three sons all died before coming of age, and it was her one surviving daughter, Aveline, who became heiress. She was married off to Edmund Crouchback, one of Henry III's sons, with the intention of bringing, through their children, some strategically important lands into royal hands. She, however, died in 1274, before bearing any children. Her tomb is in Westminster Abbey. On her death the two-thirds of Holderness held by Isabella and Amice was taken back into royal hands, although Isabella continued to hold her one-third dower. She, of course, continued to hold Devon and the Isle of Wight as her inheritance. When she died in 1293, with all her children dead, the entirety of her lands passed to the Crown. What had been hoped for by the marriage of Aveline had come about by other means.

The Holderness estates were run on behalf of the Counts or Countesses of Albemarle by one of their officials, the sheriff of Holderness, assisted by bailiffs. Unlike his employer, the sheriff would be a frequent visitor to Keyingham, ensuring the proper running of the manor and collecting its receipts and dues. The usual officer on a manor for helping run the demesne - managing the lands, paying wages and other expenses, collecting monies, and passing the profits to the lord via the sheriff - was the reeve. Keyingham had such a person but, because sheep farming was so important on the reclaimed marshlands of the demesne, the manor also had a stock-keeper, who acted independently of the reeve and handled all the monies relating to sheep-rearing and wool production. Although the stock-keeper's headquarters were at Keyingham he was responsible, through a staff of half a dozen or more shepherds, for the Albemarle flocks in other parts of Holderness, such as Preston, Little Humber in Paull parish, Sutton, and Ridgemont in Burstwick.

The checking of the reeve's and stock-keeper's accounts and the collection of the manorial proceeds by the sheriff probably took place at the manor house. This was situated on the demesne lands on a three-acre site, probably near Marsh Cottage, where the remains of a moat can still be discerned. It was also at the manor house where the manor court was held, although at a later date Keyingham tenants attended at Burstwick, the seat of the Holderness estate. It was at the manor court that disputes between tenants were heard before the manor jury, presided over by the sheriff or one of his bailiffs, and where the descent of lands following the death of a tenant was decided. All fines went to the lord.

The inquiry into the value of the estates following the death of William de Fortibus in 1260, coupled with the accounts of the sheriff and his staff, particularly during the time of Isabella, give us a marvellous insight into the manor of Keyingham and its people in the second half of the 13th century.

In 1260 there were 31 villein tenants in Keyingham, only one more than at the time of the Domesday survey. There were, however, 26 cottagers, although their numbers included eight men who also had villein holdings. There were eight free tenants, that is, men holding by knight service. Thus, since 1086, the number of households in Keyingham had approximately doubled from the 30 of the Domesday Book to nearly 60 in 1260. The resources of the village should have been well able to cope with this increase since, as we have already seen, the amount of land capable of useful production had more than doubled. Compared with elsewhere in the country, Keyingham's increase in population was low. In England as a whole the increase was three- to fourfold. In the East Riding the figure has been calculated to be nine- to tenfold. It must be borne in mind, however, that some villages in the East Riding, such as Hilston and Owstwick mentioned in the previous chapter, were completely depopulated in 1086. At that time Keyingham was comparatively well populated, rather supporting the theory that, following the devastations of 1069 and later, tenants were moved from wasted and less fertile areas to more favourable sites, such as South Holderness, where the land could be brought into production more easily.

The usual holding of a villein was an oxgang, the amount of land that could be kept in cultivation by one ox. As a ploughland was the amount of land that could be kept in cultivation by one plough drawn by a team of eight oxen, and approximated to 120 acres, so an oxgang approximated to 15 acres. In 1260 Keyingham's 31 villeins held in all $31\frac{1}{2}$ oxgangs. The usual rule for inheritance of land was for it to pass to the eldest son, provided he paid the fine of entrance to his lands. However, at a time when a man's chances of reaching his majority were a good deal less than 50:50, the smooth passage of land in the male line did not always occur. If a tenant was succeeded only by daughters, his land was usually divided between them, rather than going in an undivided portion to the eldest daughter. Thus, villein holdings of less than an oxgang came into being, just as holdings of more than an oxgang did if a villein married the heiress to part of an oxgang. If a villein had no heirs or if the heir could not pay the entry fine, the land came into the lord's hands and he could sell it, perhaps to a villein already holding land, so again holdings larger than an oxgang could be formed. In Keyingham in 1260 villein holdings ranged in size from a half to one-and-a-half oxgangs.

By 1260 the lord was no longer receiving dues in kind at Keyingham. All the payments due for the holding of land had by that time been commuted to money. When a villein succeeded to his oxgang he paid to the lord, not his best beast, but 13s.4d (67p). And, instead of doing work services and presenting his lord with a chicken at Christmas, he paid him 13s.4d a year. Things were different at Burstwick. Here, besides paying money rents, the tenants did work services and owed eggs and hens to the lord. The difference in treatment is probably explained by the difference in the nature of the demesne lands on the two manors. On both there were well over 1000 acres of demesne land but, whereas at Burstwick by far the larger part was arable, at Keyingham most of the demesne was given over to meadow and pasture. Stock-rearing on grass requires far less manpower than cultivating arable land, and it would suit the lord, and give the tenant far more freedom of action, if rents were paid in money. When the lord did need men to work on the demesne he could always call on the hired labour of the cottagers.

Although villeins and cottagers were not free, it was possible for them to gain their freedom, especially if it was in the lord's interest. Towards the end of the 13th century one of the receipts passed to the lord from the reeve of Keyingham was the income from chevage. Chevage was the payment made by unfree tenants so that they could live away from their native manor. It may be that they had found a better opportunity elsewhere, perhaps by marrying the heiress of a villein who had lived in another village. As work services were no longer used in Keyingham the lord did not lose, because he still received any rents due from the absent tenant as well as the payment of chevage.

One place where opportunity beckoned the unfree man was in the towns. In the 12th and 13th centuries with the expansion of trade and the swelling of population, old towns were thriving and new ones were being established. One such new town was Hedon, which the Lords of Holderness deliberately planted during the 12th century in order to increase their revenues from such payments as market tolls and port dues. Acre for acre, they also received far higher rents in a town than they did in the country. In such circumstances it was in the lord's interest to encourage men to move from his over-populated manors to his blossoming new town. It was, in fact, possible for a man to gain his freedom from bondage if he could reside in a town for a year and a day without being claimed by his lord. We know of one native of Keyingham who, one way or the other, managed to become a resident of Hedon: the chronicler of Meaux Abbey tells us of a man called Askill, who had been born in Keyingham, later being known as Askill of Hedon. This occurred very early in the history of the town.

Not only were bondmen moving out of Keyingham, some were moving in, or at least obtaining land in Keyingham. In 1289 the reeve of Keyingham accounted for the fine of 6s.8d (33p) paid by Peter of Rise for entry into half an oxgang of land formerly held by Peter Turre. The village of Rise, 12 miles to the north of Keyingham, was held by the de Fauconberg family. At that time, the reeve, and so almost certainly a villein and resident of Keyingham, was Henry of Rise. It is apparent that men in bondage were able to move, not only between manors or towns held by the same lord, but also from the manor of one lord to that of another.

Not everyone on the Keyingham scene was a tenant of the lord. When William le Gros granted Saltaugh to the monks of Meaux Abbey soon after its foundation in 1150, he did so in free alms, that is they owed him nothing for the land but their prayers for him in this life and the next. William's grant had included the road from Keyingham to Saltaugh. This road may have followed the line of the present Saltaugh Road, although it could have followed Marsh Lane since the first grange established by the monks was further west than the present Saltaugh Grange. In the 13th century the abbey's lay brothers, dressed in their brown habits, would have been a familiar sight in Keyingham as they drove their sheep and their carts between the marshlands and Meaux Abbey.

Another religious institution, the Knights Hospitaller, also held land in Keyingham. They were an order founded at the time of the First Crusade at the end of the 11th century. They received a few acres of land, also in the Marsh. The land lay on the edge of the Keyingham Fleet, at the end of the track that now leads to the sewage works. Known as Spital (hospital) Lands in the 18th century, they became detached from the rest of Keyingham when the fleet was straightened soon after 1805, putting the bend on which they were situated on the west of the drain.

Keyingham's parson had land on the manor. He, too, was free from paying rents and services for his holding (his glebe). He owed the possession of at least some of it to the generosity of some early pre-Conquest lord of Keyingham who had built the village church and endowed it with lands to maintain a priest. In 1535 the amount of glebe was four oxgangs as well as some other property. The four oxgangs included land in the Marsh, and this may have been granted by one of the post-Conquest lords, perhaps in return for the parson acting as chaplain at the manor house, where there was certainly a chapel in 1340. Four oxgangs was a generous amount of land. The average villein had

to maintain himself and his family with the produce from one oxgang. After the 11th century, when the clergy were expected to remain unmarried, Keyingham's parson would have only himself and perhaps one or two assistant clergy and a servant or two to maintain. Before this, when the village priest may have been married with a family and was not expected to be particularly learned, he may well have been seen working his oxgangs himself.

It has been calculated that the oxgang of land held by the average villein was just about sufficient to maintain him and his family. But that was if things went right. Bad weather, a poor harvest or disease in the livestock, could all bring the family close to starvation, with early deaths amongst the weaker members. For a cottager, with only an acre or so of land and a great reliance on the wages received for working for others, life was even more precarious. If things went wrong, as they did with a vengeance in the 14th century, many could perish and a thriving village could be reduced to a community struggling to cultivate hard-won lands.

4 - The Shaping of Keyingham

Keyingham was a long village, with its chief street extending from North End Farm, along what is now called Station Road and down to the southern end of Ings Lane. In this respect it resembled many other so-called 'linear' or 'street' villages in Holderness where the houses were laid out along one principal street. Keyingham's neighbour, Ottringham, for instance stretched from another North End Farm to beyond the church at the south end of the village. This linear shape derived almost entirely from the village agricultural arrangements.

As we have seen, the usual holding of a villein tenant was an oxgang, which approximated to 15 acres of land. However, each oxgang was not a compact block of land, fenced off by the tenant and organised as he pleased. Instead, it consisted of numerous strips of arable land and shares of grassland distributed throughout the manor and organised by the community through the workings of the manor jury.

In Keyingham, as in most Holderness villages, the arable strips were divided between two great open arable fields. Elsewhere in Yorkshire and other parts of England, the division was usually into three fields and sometimes more. The two fields, called East Field and West Field in Keyingham, were divided into blocks of land, known locally as falls or flatts, roughly rectangular in shape, and a furlong (220 yards) or more in length. Within each fall, each tenant usually had a strip of land, running the full length of the fall and perhaps one chain (22 yards) or half a chain wide, giving him a one-acre or half-acre strip. According to one school of thought this layout of strips within falls probably came into being as a new settlement was gradually brought under cultivation: an area of land (corresponding to a fall) was cleared by a group of settlers and divided amongst them in strips. In time, other falls were cleared, again with a division of land amongst the cultivators. The strips were not necessarily of all the same size; the leader of the group might, for example, receive wider strips than did his followers.

The clearing of the whole territory took place over many generations. As population increased, more men may have become eligible to strips in a newly cleared fall, which would therefore contain more strips than earlier clearances. If the village overlord happened to found a church he may have funded a priest by granting him some strips (his glebe-land) in the two fields. So, side by side, in the falls lay the strips of lord, tenants and priest.

The falls were divided from each other by tracks or headlands running round their perimeters, giving access to the strips and room for the plough-teams to turn at the end of each furrow. The dividing line between each man's strips came about through the method of ploughing. The plough threw the soil to one side and as it moved up one side of a strip and down the other, the strip became built up into a ridge, known as a land in these parts, with a furrow along each side. The furrows formed the boundaries between the strips. Within each fall the strips usually lay in the direction of the slope so that the furrows acted as drains as well as boundaries.

By the beginning of the millennium all the higher, better-drained, ground in Keyingham had been cleared and had come to have the appearance of a great patchwork quilt of falls, their strips of ridge and furrow running in different directions depending on the lie of the land, and stretching from the boundary with Ottringham down to the marsy fringes of the Humber and the Keyingham Fleet. It was a huge open hedgeless terrain that was to persist into the beginning of the 19th century.

The arable fields provided the villagers with their two vital commodities: wheat for their bread and barley for their beer. These were not their sole needs, however. They needed clothing and, very importantly, power for their ploughs. Clothing came from the wool and skins of sheep and the hides of cattle; power came from the ox. These animals needed feeding. During the early years of settlement-clearance there was plenty of browsing to be had amongst the trees of the uncleared areas but, as these areas came gradually under the plough in order to provide the corn necessary for the expanding human population, only the lower, wetter, lands remained for grazing. Of these lands, the best-drained were used as meadows, or ings. They were dry enough for a crop of hay to be taken off in the summer, essential if the majority of the flocks and herds were to survive the winter. The remaining low grounds - the salt marsh next the Humber and the carrs along the Keyingham Fleet - were used as pasture whenever conditions were dry enough to allow on livestock.

In the same way that the arable land was divided out amongst the lord and his tenants, so were the meadows and pastures. In the meadows each oxgang-holder had so many acres. For the taking of the hay the ings were marked out by stones or stakes into what were sometimes called dales (meaning a dole or share), but in Keyingham seem to have been called leys. A man's dales might be scattered in different parts of the ings, just as his strips were scattered in the arable fields. Both practices ensured a fair distribution of soils of differing qualities amongst the holders of land. Allowing for this difference in quality may have

been the reason why some tenants had to change their allotment in the meadows each year. When William Tennyson died in 1739 he left his wife, Mary, lands which included one ley, called Balley Ley, in Keyingham Ings, 'abutting on and changing with the parsonage every year'. In this case the 'parsonage' was a ley held as part of the glebe.

Pasturage on the manor consisted not only of Keyingham's low grounds but of any land where crops were not being grown - the ings when the hay had been taken off and the arable fields when they were lying fallow. Thus a man's share in the pasturage was measured not in acres but in the number of animals he was allowed to put out on the different sources of pasture. This number varied from village to village depending on the proportion of grassland available. It could also vary over time as circumstances changed. In 1260 the holder of each oxgang in Keyingham had the right to pasture four cattle and eight sheep. By 1338, the rate had become four cattle and 12 sheep, presumably because, through improved drainage, more of the carr land had become available as pasture.

Thus, the oxgang was not a simple acreage of land: it was a number of strips divided between the arable fields, a share of the meadow land, and the right to pasture so many animals on land otherwise unused, either temporarily or permanently.

A system like this, where neighbours' plots lay inter-mingled and animals were let out on to lands due to be cropped, needed proper organisation. This was done through the manor jury, a group of about a dozen villeins meeting in the lord's court in the presence of his steward, sheriff or bailiff. The jury, for example, decided the dates on which livestock was allowed on to the arable fields and meadows. If you had failed to take in your corn or hay by those dates, then that was your misfortune. Similarly, the jury decided the dates when animals had to be taken off the common fields. They also decided what crops went into the arable fields. In a three-field system the usual rotation was wheat, barley, fallow. In a two-field system, such as Keyingham's, the arrangement was usually half wheat and half barley in one field while the other field lay fallow. On the face of it the two-field system looks like an inadequate use of resources. In any one year half the arable land of the village was out of commission whereas in the three-field system only one third of the land was out of use during the year. However, it should be remembered that a fallow field was not lying useless: animals were pasturing on it. A village that had passed to a money economy from the mere subsistence stage of providing corn and clothing sufficient only for its own needs might find that there was a profitable market for wool. Shifting the balance towards sheep rearing would then be worthwhile and a two-field system would provide more herbage for sheep than would a three-field system. At the same time the fields were being manured more frequently.

Whatever the advantages or otherwise of the two-field system, it was the system which predominated in Holderness. The two fields helped to give Keyingham and other linear villages their shape. When, one year ploughing and harvesting were taking place on the east of the village, and the next year on the west, the best position for the farmers to site their houses, stackyards, implements and foldyards was between the two fields. Consequently, the villagers' cottages, lying in their plots, or garths, of an acre or more, came to be on a street dividing the two fields. The street had to be bounded by hedges along its full length from the carrs in the north to the ings in the south, because, almost daily, cattle and sheep were being driven one way or the other between farmyard and pasture, and the farmyards and the standing crops in the East or West Field had to be protected from straying stock. Thus the street was a permanent feature, defined by its hedgerows and ditches, even though the simple mud-and-thatch cottages along its length might be rebuilt time and again, often on different positions within their garths.

Keyingham West Mill, February 1999. The first mill in Keyingham, recorded in the second half of the 13th century, was probably on this site. It would have been a post mill with the whole wooden body of the mill being able to rotate on a central post. Photo: J A McLeod.

27

The street was the day-to-day thoroughfare of the villagers. They used it far more frequently than the east and west roads leading to the weekly markets at Patrington or Hedon. Besides being the way along which they daily drove their cattle and sheep, it was also the way which took them to the water's edge where they could lay eel traps, capture wildfowl for the pot, gather reeds for thatching, cut osier and willow for basket- and hurdle-making or dig turves for fuel. It was the way which could take them to their boats in the Keyingham Fleet and thereby to the Humber or, in the opposite direction, to two other linear villages, Burton Pidsea and Roos, which also ran down to the fleet. The street led to the water where the villagers washed their sheep before shearing or hides before tanning. The street was *the* way of the village traffic.

In some linear villages a back lane ran behind the garths which lay along the village street. The back lane gave direct access from the garths to one or other of the arable fields. The present Chapel Lane and Beck Lane may have been such lanes. In old documents Beck Lane is frequently referred to as Back Lane and it is so marked on the Ordnance Survey map of 1855. However, the fact remains that there was a stream or beck running along Beck Lane (the winding nature of the lane gives a clue to this) and in 1584, Sir Henry Constable, the then lord of Keyingham, leased some property in an area called 'the Becke' to a Richard Kirkman. One other lane came into being in Keyingham in the Middle Ages. When the lord of the manor built the first windmill in the village in the 13th century, almost certainly on the same site as the present one on the hill near the church, where the sails would capture every wind, he required all his tenants to use it. Consequently, a lane, now called Church Lane and Mill Lane, came into being, bringing the villagers with their carts or pack-horses up to the mill with their sacks of corn for grinding.

The street was not the only place marked off by hedges and ditches. Livestock had to be prevented from straying from the carrs into the arable fields when they were under crops, or from the fallow field into the ings before the hay was cut, or from Keyingham lands into Ottringham lands. There was a village shepherd to look after the sheep and a neatherd to look after the cattle, but their jobs were made easier by the use of hurdles or more permanent barriers between the different areas to prevent there being 'sheep in the meadow or cows in the corn'.

The permanent barriers consisted of ditches and hedges, often following natural contours. Between the carrs and the two arable fields a ditch was dug and a hedge planted (or, more probably, existing trees were left in place) along what had been the edge of the Keyingham Fleet. The ditch, with a few osiers, willows, elders, hawthorn and blackthorn along it, still exists in part. An interesting viewpoint from which to see it and let your imagination wander over more than a thousand years of Keyingham's history is from the hilltop reached via Mill Lane. From there you can look down on a flat valley which was at first a muddy inlet leading into the Humber only a few hundred yards away beyond Bridge Bungalows. Then it became a fen of reeds and willows and later, when a drainage channel had been cut along the centre, wet grassland with livestock grazing in the summer months. Finally, with modern drainage, the valley became good corn land.

Besides forming a barrier to livestock, the hedges were intended to provide a variety of useful products. Osiers for basket making have already been mentioned. Ash trees provided tool handles. Any kind of nut or fruit tree was encouraged, and blackthorn, besides forming an impenetrable hedge, provided good stout sticks for flail making. These hedges, together with the thin scrubwood of the carrs, were the only source of wood in the village for either fuel or making things. Other sources had often to be turned to. Turves and whins (gorse) were used for fuel, and in 1288, when Henry Snell the stock-keeper needed to make sheepfolds on the lord's demesne, he had to obtain some of the wood from Cottingham, with all the additional costs of carriage which that necessitated.

One feature not fenced was the east-west road that took people to and from the village. It had no need to be, for it did not divide one type of land - arable, meadow or pasture - from another. The land on either side of the road was of the same type - carr land as you passed into the village from the west, then the arable lands of the West Field and the East Field. The road was not bounded by hedge and ditch until the open fields of Keyingham were enclosed in 1805. There were, however, gates across it - at the bridge that took you to Ryehill and Burstwick, at the junction of West Carr and West Field and at the boundary with Ottringham.

Some remnants of Keyingham's medieval pattern are still with us today. The long village street remains, although from either end you can reach only isolated farms. The back lanes and the lane leading to the mill are still here as are some of the ancient ditches which divided arable from carr land, meadow from marsh land, and Keyingham from Ottringham. Otherwise, we have only names, such as Eastfield Road, East Carr Road and Ings Lane, to remind us of the old-time agricultural arrangements of the village.

5 - Running the Manor

The open-field system was a communal way of farming which gave the villein a share in the lands, good and bad, in all parts of the manor. It also gave him a share in other things. The holder of an oxgang might own only one ox, but up to eight might be required to pull a plough. In the open-field system he was able to borrow oxen from his fellows and use them to pull one of the village ploughs when his turn came. Even landless cottagers had certain rights in the fields, the ings and the carrs when they were thrown open to pasture. It was a system that persisted in Keyingham up to the time of enclosure of the open fields at the beginning of the 19th century, although by that time the terms 'villein' and 'cottager' had been dropped.

A communal system such as open-field farming needs to be properly run and overseen. This was usually done through the jury at the manor court. Some time after the Lords of Holderness moved the seat of their estate to Burstwick, Keyingham business came to be transacted at the Burstwick manor court, along with the business of not only Burstwick but also of other nearby manors of the lord, such as Preston, Lelley and Burton Pidsea. Keyingham then only contributed two or three men to the manor jury, with Keyingham affairs being kept a particular eye on by the six men of the homage chosen from the village. The court met every three weeks. The homages of the different villages constituting Burstwick manor were chosen annually and sworn in at the Michaelmas court. They in turn chose officers from amongst their fellow villagers to help them - two constables to assist with matters of law and order and two aletasters to test the products of those villagers who brewed ale and baked bread for sale. When the office of reeve died out in the later Middle Ages one or more pennygraves were also chosen to collect the rents and dues owing to the lord.

On some manors the lord's demesne lands lay intermingled in the open fields with the lands of his tenants. This was the case at Skeffling, about ten miles east of Keyingham, where the Lord of Holderness was also the lord of the manor. This could prove very irksome to the lord as his lands were then subject to all the rules of husbandry decided on by the manor court jury. Following the Conquest many lords sought to separate their lands from those of the tenants. They could then enclose them or otherwise deal with them as they wished. In some cases it was a century or more before the separation was achieved, and at Skeffling, for example, it was not achieved before enclosure of all the fields of the manor in the 1760s. However, at Keyingham, as we saw in an earlier chapter, separation of the demesne lands had taken place by the time of the Domesday survey in 1086. All the siltlands reclaimed from the Humber (except Saltaugh, granted to Meaux Abbey by William le Gros) were to be the lord's demesne lands. They were run in a way much different from the way the tenants ran their lands. For example, the demesne arable lands in Keyingham were cultivated under a three-field system in 1260, whereas the tenants' lands were in two fields. Seventy-five years later a two-field system of cultivation was being used on the demesne. Several demesne fields were also separated off by fences. The rigidity of the manorial rules would have probably prevented such changes and fluidity of management on the tenants' lands.

The farming of the lord's demesne was overseen by a reeve, whose duties were similar to those of a modern-day farm manager. He also collected the rents and other dues from the lord's tenants. He was chosen from amongst the villagers and if he showed an aptitude for the job, he might have it for longer than the customary year, or be moved to a post of similar, or even greater, responsibility. Peter of Sniphou, for example, who had been the reeve of Little Humber on the demesne in Paull from 1264 to 1266, became reeve of Keyingham the following year. In 1270 he was the stock-keeper, with a staff of several shepherds, responsible for upwards of 9,000 sheep on the demesne pastures of both Keyingham and Little Humber. In 1277 he and Robert Cayr were elected by the villagers of Preston, Keyingham and Easington to be Countess Isabella's local receivers, collecting the receipts of all her Holderness manors on behalf of her sheriff.

These various posts brought small rewards with large responsibilities. The remuneration of the reeve of Keyingham amounted to being excused paying the rent on his land whilst in office. If he held an oxgang of land this was 13s.4d (67p) a year. In the course of that year, perhaps one or two hundred pounds (in silver pennies, 240 to the pound) would pass through his hands. At the end of his term of office he was personally responsible for any arrears he had failed to collect. He might be given time to pay, but this might not be enough. Some sought flight to escape their debts. In 1271 Isabella's sheriff needed to hire many men in his pursuit of Richard of Keyingham, Robert son of Isabel of Keyingham and Nicholas son of Warner the stock-keeper. They were captured 25 miles away, at North Cave, to the west of Hull. From what the records tell us Robert had been reeve of Keyingham and Nicholas's father, Warner, had been in arrears to the tune of over £80 when he left office and had died before paying off

the Countess. The debt descended on his son. The offences of the three men were compounded by the fact that they were unfree men and had left the manor without the Countess's permission.

The accounts of Keyingham's reeves and stock-keepers during the time of Isabella de Fortibus show that, on the Keyingham manor at least, the lady preferred transactions in money rather than in kind. No labour services were exacted. Wage labour was used for any work needed on the demesne although some of the wages were paid in corn. Isabella also preferred the receipts from Keyingham's windmill to be in money. Rather than taking payments in corn (a multure) from her tenants for using the mill, Isabella rented the mill out at £1.6s.8d (£1.33) a year. The tenants on the manor were still compelled to take their corn there, but paid the multure to the miller who would hope to make a profit on the rent he paid to Isabella.

The account of Henry of Rise, who was reeve of Keyingham from Michaelmas 1288 until the following Michaelmas, provides us with a good example of how busy the reeve could be on his lord's or lady's behalf. He, of course, also had his own lands to run. In Henry's case, these consisted of only half an oxgang, so that his remuneration was in effect only 33p. One imagines there were one or two unrecorded perquisites to the job: the odd peck of demesne seed-corn diverted on to Henry's strips or the occasional carting of Henry's produce by the Countess's horses. The fact that during Henry's tenure of office half an oxgang of Keyingham land was transferred to a Peter of Rise suggests that Henry was able to keep an eye open on behalf of his relatives for land coming on to the market.

Henry's accounts show that he was responsible for collecting all the rents from the manor: the tenants' rents, the rent of the mill and the rent of a fishery at Long Bridge which was presumably on the Keyingham Fleet. He also collected the fees due when holdings changed hands, as well as the fines exacted at the manor court. The demesne pastures were let out at certain times of the year and Henry collected these rents. It was his job to collect the money from the sale of demesne produce. By far the largest amount was £95 for the sale of wheat and oats. This compares with nearly £128 collected by Henry Snell, the stock-keeper that year, from the sale of wool and sheepskins from the Countess's flocks at Keyingham and Little Humber. The reeve also sold off a few cattle, pigs and chickens, which brought in nearly £8. For the sale of hay and reeds from the dike he received a few shillings. Henry the reeve also records receiving nearly £1 from Henry the stock-keeper for the carcasses, skins and intestines of eight pigs, the lard from which was used to concoct a mixture for treating sheep-scab. In turn the stock-keeper in his account records his outlay on the lard, together with the tar, the other ingredient in the mixture. The reeve expended 18 pence (7.5p) on the wages of the man employed to skin the eight pigs.

Henry of Rise's expenses were many and varied. A new plough, a new harrow and a new cart had to be made that year. Other carts had to be repaired. Thirty-two yokes were bought for the oxen that drew the ploughs. A saddle and two collars were bought for the horses. There was the outlay on hiring men for ploughing, for mowing and stacking hay, and for reaping, binding, stacking, threshing, winnowing and sacking corn. Food and wages for a ploughman cost a halfpenny (about 0.2p) a day. At a time when the country's population was rising at a much faster rate than food production there was a surplus of workers and a shortage of food. Hence wages were low and food prices high, and the ploughman may have preferred receiving food rather than cash. The food part of his wages consisted of about 32 bushels of corn in the year, enough to feed four adults. The right to the corn may have been something the demesne labourers had to fight to retain, for it probably represented a loss to Isabella. In 1265 at Burton Agnes, in the north of the East Riding, where labour services were still owed, it was estimated that the ploughing by each villein was worth fourpence a year to the lord when no food was given, but with food it was worth nothing 'because it costs as much as it is worth'.

Repairs to fences and farm buildings were a constant source of expenditure on the demesne. What had to be kept a special eye on in the marshlands were the sea-banks and drains. In Henry of Rise's year of office well over a thousand yards of the bank facing the Humber were repaired, and 600 yards of ditches were scoured and widened.

As well as having to keep an account of his finances the reeve also had to account for all the seed and livestock on the demesne, down to the last chicken. Most of the seed stock was grain, and in 1289 this was predominantly wheat and oats, most of which was sold. Some was used as wages, however, and oats were used to feed the cattle and horses, including the stud at Burstwick. Less than three acres of barley were sown that year, and ten acres of beans. The beans were chiefly used to fatten pigs to produce the lard supplied to the stock-keeper. Except for sheep, which were the stock-keeper's responsibility, there were few of the Countess's animals on the demesne, although when the pastures were rented out there were plenty of other people's animals to be seen. Most of the Countess's animals (other than sheep) were draught beasts. There does not seem to have been much of a dairy herd for instance, although Henry accounted for £1 received for renting out eight cows for milking. At the end of Henry's term of office the livestock consisted of 39 oxen and a bull, 14 cows, four heifers, one bullock, three steers, four two-year olds and 15 calves. There were seven carthorses, one pig, eight swans, one capon, and four geese. He had sold off 20 chickens during the year and now had none left.

Details of Henry's corn account may make interesting reading for the modern farmer. For example, 279 bushels of wheat were sown on 115½ acres of land and 1,238 bushels were harvested. This works out at a yield of 10.7 bushels per acre and a 4.44-fold yield on the seed. (The average for the Keyingham demesne for the years 1263-91 was 4.6.) Today, Martin and Graham Jackson, who farm a part of what were Keyingham's demesne lands, sow wheat at the rate of 3.5 to 4.5 bushels per acre and harvest something like 90 bushels per acre, which can rise to close on 180 bushels in a very good year. Their yields are thus about 20- to 40-fold on the seed sown. Fluctuations in yield were greater than this in the Middle Ages, and the farmer lived on a knife edge: if his yields were halved by bad weather then, for every bushel of wheat sown, he might harvest just over two, and one of these had to be retained for seed for the following year. A generation after Henry of Rise left office a series of bad summers were to bring poor harvests and with them starvation and death.

The stock-keeper's duties were just as onerous as those of the reeve. His chief receipts, as already mentioned, were from the sale of wool and sheepskins, but the production of butter and cheeses from sheep's milk was also a thriving business. In the year ending Michaelmas 1289, stock-keeper Henry Snell received nearly £11 from the sale of 20 stone (125 kilograms) of butter and about 250 cheeses each weighing approximately nine kilograms. When the flocks had been at their peak numbers in the 1260s annual output had approached 240 kilograms of butter and 3,300 kilograms of cheese. The labour costs of production were small. In 1289 the dairymaid was paid 2s (10p) wages for the year, and the 18 women milking the ewes received a total of 6s. Repairing the churns and buying cloth for the cheeses cost just over 6s.

There was also outlay on shepherds' wages and repairing sheds and folds. The welfare of the sheep cost 17s for 382 gallons of milk for rearing the lambs and £6 on large quantities of tar and lard (of which Henry the reeve was not his only supplier) for treating the scab. Despite this expenditure 682 sheep and lambs perished during the year. However, through purchase and the birth of lambs Henry Snell's stock increased from 3,894 to 4,352 sheep and lambs, all told. The scab, or murrain as it was then known, first came into Holderness in 1279 and Isabella's flocks, which had numbered about 9,000, were virtually wiped out. The fleeces of the sheep that didn't succumb were worthless. After the first terrible effects, the disease became endemic and the flocks slowly recovered in numbers. Henry Snell's accounts probably indicate part of that recovery.

One of Henry Snell's expenses was on entertaining merchants for three days in Keyingham when they came to choose the wool and oversee its packing into huge 26-stone sacks. Countess Isabella's chief customers for wool about that time were the Riccardi of Lucca: Keyingham's visitors were probably Italian and the sacks destined for Italy via Hedon, the port founded by the Albemarles expressly for the purpose of exporting the surplus produce of their estates.

Henry of Rise and Henry Snell were not trained for their jobs and, in addition, had their own lands to run. As they began to near the end of their term of office they may have had a feeling of relief, especially if they had collected all their debts and the demesne yields had been good. There were, however, hurdles yet to be cleared: their accounts had to be audited. Henry of Rise's accounts show the outlay on the visits, for the purpose of audit, of Sir John of St Helens and William of Radstone when they travelled from Isabella's estates in Northamptonshire to Holderness. They stayed five days, went to Isabella's estate at Harewood and then returned to Holderness for nine days. Besides £4.4s.9d (£4.24) taken out of his account, Henry's stock was also reduced by a considerable quantity of oats for the visitors' horses, and one heifer, two pigs and 11 geese for feeding the visitors themselves.

The accounts were drawn up by a scribe using the information that the reeve and stock-keeper gave him. They were then scrutinised by the auditors who would question each item such as wage-bills, the numbers of workers hired, and prices paid and received for stock. The reeve or stock-keeper might disagree with the auditors on some points, but eventually a final set of figures was decided on, and whether the men about to leave office were in arrears or not. If in arrears they may spend years chasing up their debtors or end up paying out of their own pockets. If they had done a good job it may be that the Countess, through her sheriff, would require them to serve another year in office. They were not free men, and they may have found it difficult to refuse.

6 - The Disaster Years.

As mentioned in the previous chapter, the open-field system was a communal system that put restraints on any variations in agricultural practice. For example, on the demesne lands, where there were no restrictions, the reeve was able to arrange, probably on the directions of Countess Isabella's sheriff, the sowing of a few acres of beans for pig fattening. This would hardly have been possible on the open fields. Firstly, the growing of beans would have been at the expense of the vital corn crop, which the small farmer could ill afford. Secondly, the timing of bean sowing and harvesting is different from that of corn, and the opening of the arable fields to pasture was based on the corn-growing timetable. No villein or cottager was going to give up any rights to pasturage for the sake of someone else's beans. The best any enterprising farmer could do was to grow some beans in the close around his house.

In another way the open-field system was inhibiting. Isabella's stock-keeper spent a large amount of money on treating the sheep scab with lard and tar. Even if a villein farmer could afford to treat the few sheep he had, they were mixing in the open pastures with untreated sheep and running the risk of re-infection. However, the open-field system, and the unfree tenure that mostly accompanied it, did not completely stifle private enterprise. In 1289, during Henry of Rise's time as reeve, demesne land was let out at different times of the year for pasturage. In the same way in the 1280s lands at Saltaugh Grange were being let by the monks of Meaux Abbey. Henry's accounts show the receipt of nearly £5 for the pasturing of 86 oxen and steers and nearly 680 sheep on the demesne during the winter of 1288-9. It is not impossible that one or two of the more progressive villein tenants in Keyingham, if they had the cash to afford it, were amongst those taking advantage of the extra grazing.

Concomitant with the pressure on land everywhere in a time of rising population was an ever-increasing pressure on manorial lords to lease their lands to smaller farmers. The latter years of the 13th century were the peak for the farming of the demesne by the lords themselves. It was at this time that Countess Isabella was using Keyingham Marsh to produce corn and wool for an eager market. Thereafter there was a gradually increasing tendency for demesne lands to be rented out. This tendency was possibly accelerated in Keyingham after the death of Countess Isabella and the dying out of the de Fortibus line, when the Holderness estate reverted to the king. Over the next two and a half centuries the Crown granted the estate to a series of royal relatives and favourites. Keyingham came to have such distinguished lords and ladies of the manor as the Duke of Gloucester, the Earl of Rutland, the Duke of Clarence, the Countess of Cornwall, Queen Isabel and Princess Isabel, mother and daughter respectively of Edward III, and Queen Anne, wife of Richard II. None of these would have had the organisational set-up in Holderness that the de Fortibus family had had and, prompted by economic circumstances, it became preferable to collect rents rather than to arrange the cultivation of the estates. Over the generations, more and more of the demesne was rented out and by the second half of the 15th century at the latest, all the demesne land in Keyingham was being let.

As the 14th century opened, the farmers of Keyingham were probably just about keeping their heads above water. Harvests were reasonable and the scourge of sheep scab had passed its peak. One or two farmers, besides cultivating their own strips and grazing their allotted amounts of meadow and pasture, may have been able to rear extra stock on rented demesne land. The indications are, however, that there were few farmers of any wealth in Keyingham. In 1297 Edward I imposed a tax of one ninth on movable property in order to continue the war against Scotland. People with goods worth less than nine shillings (45p) were excused paying, so that the minimum tax collected from any one person was a shilling. In Keyingham only 12 people were called on to pay. (At that point in time, the holder of the manor was the king, so no tax was exacted for the movable property on the demesne.)

Of those taxed in Keyingham, Peter Rocelin, Richard Neubond and Nicholas Francis paid the minimum of a shilling (5p). The two with the highest value in goods were Peter and Henry of Rise. They paid, in terms of modern pence, 10.5p and 8p respectively. Unfortunately, the record of the detailed evaluation of each person's goods has been lost for the East Riding, but in the West Riding, where the record has survived, a man paying 5p in tax, whose goods were worth a fraction over 45p, possessed one ox worth 25p, 16 bushels of oats worth 10p, five bushels of barley worth 6.25p and a cartload of hay worth 4.2p. A Keyingham man paying the same tax would probably have had wheat instead of oats and would have had some sheep, which were worth about 3p each on average.

The tax returns suggest that the farmers of Keyingham were somewhat worse off than their neighbours. The dozen payers in Keyingham averaged a payment of 6.6p each. In Burstwick, which was also in the hands of the king at that time, ten payers averaged 7.5p each. Fifteen payers at Halsham averaged 9p, and 17 payers at Ryehill and Camerton averaged 11.75p. At Ottringham, which included the hamlet of Ottringham Marsh established on the silt-lands, 31 taxpayers averaged a payment of 12.9p a head. Whereas in Keyingham only Peter of Rise paid 10p, in Ottringham 18 people paid 10p or more, with Beatrice of the Marsh paying almost 48p. There was no one with the equivalent wealth in Keyingham.

If the farmers and cottagers of Keyingham were just managing to struggle along at the start of the 14th century when harvests were reasonable, they were in for untold hardships when the harvests began to fail. The century was only 14 years old when the first of a series of natural disasters hit the country. A wet summer in 1314 led to a bad harvest. The following year was even wetter and wheat prices more than quadrupled. Up to 1321 there were more crop failures accompanied by a fatal epidemic amongst cattle. Many acres were left untilled because of the shortage of draught beasts. Thousands of people died from under-nourishment and lack of resistance to disease. Only after 1322 did harvests begin to improve.

When this first crisis of the century ended, there was a much smaller population to be fed or to do the work. Consequently grain prices fell to less than what they had been in Countess Isabella's time and wages rose. The profit margins of demesne farming declined, another factor that encouraged the renting out of demesne land but at lower rents than were obtainable at the beginning of the century. These movements in prices and wages became hugely magnified following the Black Death, the worst natural disaster, up to that time, to befall western Europe.

The Black Death began tracking its way across the Mediterranean and Europe in 1347. Its arrival was awaited with dread in England. It came into Dorset in August 1348 and spread north-eastwards. In the summer of the following year it arrived in Holderness. At Meaux Abbey, 40 of the 50 monks and lay-brothers died. Fifteen of the 30-or-so parsons in Holderness perished. There are no such precise figures for the lay population, but it has been estimated that this first visitation of the bubonic plague killed one third of the population of the country. Before the end of the century there were three more visitations in the north of England - in 1361, 1369 and 1379. It is thought that at the end of the century the country's population was about half that at the beginning, falling from something like 5 million to 2.5 million, not much higher than at the time of the Domesday survey. In 1438, when a slow recovery in population was being made, Keyingham had 48 houses compared with what would have been the 31 houses of the 30 villeins and the one priest recorded in the Domesday Book.

The 14th-century story of starvation and plague applies to all the country, indeed to most of western Europe. But for Keyingham and other low-lying lands there was added misery. In the middle of the 13th century a slow rise in sea level along the east coast began. In 1256 the Humber flooded up the River Hull as far as the low grounds in Cottingham. Great tracts of reclaimed land along the Humber were inundated. The disaster is recorded in the Meaux Abbey chronicle:

'... the Humber, exceeding its limits, submerged the greatest part of Holderness and caused the greatest destruction. We lost our men and oxen at Orwithfleet; and many of our lands at Saltaugh and Myton were entirely washed into the Humber. Wherefore those our lands remained almost sterile and produced us scarcely any fruit.'

This setback was overcome, but the rise of the sea was inexorable and throughout the 14th century the situation worsened.

'It came to pass that our lands at Tharlesthorpe, Orwithfleet and Saltaugh gradually decreased so that the Humber entirely took away from us the land of Orwithfleet, consumed the grange at Tharlesthorpe and caused us completely to remove all the buildings of the grange of Saltaugh, that they might be built further away from the said inundations.'

Saltaugh Grange was moved to the east of its old site. Tharlesthorpe and Orwithfleet, which lay to the south of Patrington, were lost forever. Sunk Island, which began to grow up towards the end of the 17th century, probably covers the site of Tharlesthorpe. At an inquiry held at Hedon in 1401 into the loss of the abbey's lands it was established that 120 acres of meadowland and $142^1/_2$ acres of pasture, of a total annual value of over £50, had been lost at Saltaugh. There were also reductions in the value of the demesne lands in Keyingham: in 1438 the annual income from the demesne was £52, including the receipts from renting out meadowland and pasture; in 1260 the income from the demesne had been £84. At least part of the reduction was attributed to the flooding of the meadowland.

From the latter years of the 13th century the Crown began to show concern about the floods along the Humber and at frequent intervals appointed commissioners to view the banks and organise their repair. In the 14th century the Crown's concerns came to include the Holderness drainage system, which became less and less efficient as the water level at the mouths of the main fleets rose. At an inquiry held at Skipsea in the north of Holderness in 1367, the whole system was reviewed and orders for scouring the drains were drawn up. Keyingham Fleet, which, like the present drain, stretches all the way back to the North Sea coast at Tunstall was to be widened and deepened. At its upper end at Tunstall it was to be six foot wide and three foot deep. These dimensions became greater on passing down the fleet, and at Keyingham the width required was 24 foot and the depth eight foot.

Whether the required scouring was carried out or not is a matter for conjecture. Clearing a flooded river bed with only spade labour must have been a daunting task even at the best of times. When the population had just been struck by two devastating epidemics, with two more to come, the task may have proved impossible. It may have been that, had the labour force been at the level it was at the start of the century, the Humber banks could have been kept in a better state of containment, and the worst of the flooding avoided. As it was, the century ended with Keyingham's productive marshlands sadly reduced, the carrs rarely fit for pasture, and the population halved. In the 14th century Nature had shown her darker side.

7 - The Church

The entry for Keyingham in the Domesday Book tells us that there was a church and a priest in the village in 1086. Their presence is recorded simply because they were a financial asset to the lord of the manor. (The monetary value was to be a thread that ran through almost the entire history of Keyingham's church.) The church had probably been built at the turn of the millennium by the lord, encouraged by the law that required the local inhabitants to give one tenth (a tithe) of their produce to the church. The need to distinguish which people paid their tithes to which church led to the establishment of parish boundaries. In the case of Keyingham the church unit of the parish happened to be the same as the manorial unit, but it was not always the case. In neighbouring Ottringham, for example, the parish extended over more than one manor.

The lord founding the church also set up a priest, allotting him glebe land by which to support himself. The priest received offerings such as burial fees from the parishioners as well as tithes, but some of the church profits may have gone to the lord. It was the right of the lord and his successors to appoint the priest. In return for the favour the priest paid the lord an annual sum (a pension). The lord of the manor thus benefited in two ways from having a church on his manor - he received the pension from the priest and some proportion of the profits of the church.

The first church at Keyingham was probably built of wood for, although there were plenty of large glacial rocks amongst the boulder clay of Holderness, they were not suitable for use as the important cornerstones of a building or for forming archways, doorways and windows. When the Normans had finished devoting their energy and wealth to building castles, cathedrals and abbeys in the years following the Conquest, they turned their attentions to the village churches, and early in the 12th century Keyingham church was rebuilt. Dressed stone, probably brought from the Wolds area, was used for the structurally important parts of the building. For the remainder, rubble stone from the Wolds and rocks taken from the gravel deposits on the west of Keyingham were used. Some of the typically thick Norman walls of this church still remain on the north side of the chancel and at the west end of the nave. Also in the north wall of the chancel can be seen vestiges of a round-headed Norman window.

This Norman church, although by far the most prominent building in the village, was quite a simple affair, the most impressive feature being the height of the nave (the part occupied by the congregation). The only other section of the building was the chancel from where the priest conducted worship. The building was roofed with thatch or wooden shingles. Consequently the roof was steeply pitched to allow the rapid run-off of rain. The original pitch of the roof can be seen in the plate line on the east side of the tower. The interior of the church presented a very gloomy appearance with only small narrow unglazed windows, set high up in the walls so that the draughts passed over the heads of the congregation.

Probably about the time the church was being rebuilt, Stephen, the lord of Keyingham manor, indulged in an act of piety, perhaps in atonement for his sins on the battle field (early in the century he had made a bid for the English crown). The feeling of the times was that the houses of God should belong to the people of God, and lay owners of churches were encouraged to grant them to religious institutions. Like most Norman lords at that time Stephen had lands and interests on both sides of the Channel. As well as being Lord of Holderness he was Count of Albemarle in Normandy, and in 1115 it was to the priory at Albemarle (elevated to the status of abbey in 1130) that he granted Keyingham church along with the tithes of the parish. At the same time he granted Albemarle 14 other Holderness churches in villages as far apart as North Frodingham, Mappleton, Easington and Wawne. The abbot of Albemarle was now the patron of these Holderness churches; that is, he had the right to appoint the priests there. Not only was Keyingham's priest now appointed by a French abbot, but also its tithes were going overseas to support a foreign abbey. It was in order to administer its Holderness

possessions and transfer produce to France that the abbey established a cell, Burstall Priory, on the Humber shore to the south of Skeffling.

The people of Keyingham had no say in the disposition of their place of worship or in who their priest might be. They did, however, come to have responsibility for the church building. By the 13th century, when lay lords no longer had a direct financial interest in the church, it had become the custom for the priest to be responsible for the repair and maintenance of the chancel, whilst the parishioners were responsible for the good care of the remainder of the church building. How much they could afford to devote to this task depended on the size and wealth of the community. In the 13th century Keyingham was expanding both in terms of population and of cultivable land. The people felt prosperous enough to extend their part

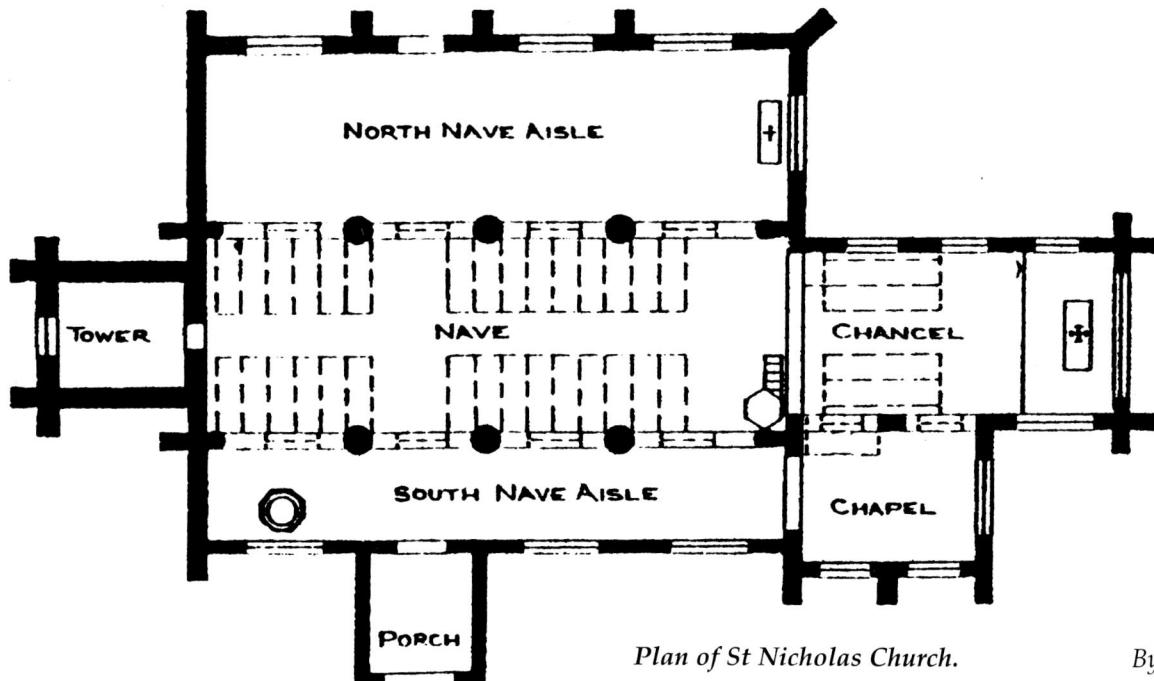

Plan of St Nicholas Church.   *By K Morris*

of the church to accommodate not only the larger congregations but also the greater ceremonial that was entering church ritual.

The first extension to the church was made by expanding the nave northwards. This was the preferred direction as it caused fewer disturbances to graves, the shadowy north side of the church not being a popular place for burial. Usually, only suicides and babies dying unbaptized were buried there. So as to cause the minimum disturbance to the church services the extension (the north aisle) was built on to the side of the church, with the steep pitch of the nave roof continuing over the roof of the aisle. Only then was the aisle connected to the nave by piercing the old nave wall and inserting the arches and columns that we see today. At the same time the walls of the nave were reduced in thickness in accord with the new style of lighter construction and also in order to subject the pillars to less weight. The original thickness of the wall can be gauged from the remains of wall left standing behind the lectern. The job was not a very expert affair; the columns are not in line and the pattern of the carving in the capitals varies somewhat between pillars. The style of this carving suggests that the north aisle was added in the period 1200 to 1220.

Later in the century the south aisle was added (despite the graves). The pattern of the capitals of the pillars was kept the same as that on the north although that particular style had gone out of fashion by the time the south aisle was built. The match was not perfect, however, the columns on the south being wider than those on the north. The marks left by the steeply sloping roof of this aisle can still be seen above the door to the vestry and outside, on the west wall of the vestry. Doorways were inserted in both the north and south aisles to facilitate processions which passed along one aisle

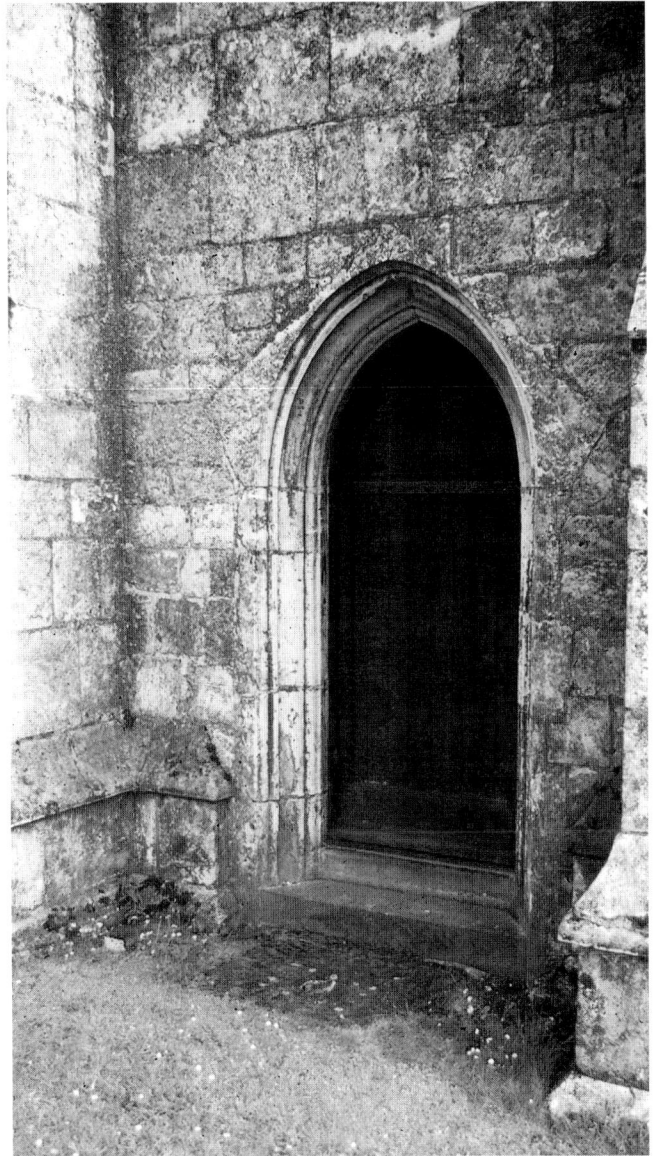

North door of St Nicholas Church, July 1994. Note the marks above the door, signs of a former porch. The outer step is a disused millstone.

41

South porch of St Nicholas Church, circa 1940. In the mid 1960s the double inner doors were found to be in a serious state of decay and were replaced by a single set of doors.
Courtesy of Mrs G Cook

and out of the door, round the churchyard or even the village, and back in the other door and along the aisle. If anything, this extended church was even darker inside than was its predecessor. The eaves of the aisles were much lower than the eaves of the original nave so the windows were lower down, although just as small. The windows now had pointed heads, however, in keeping with the new style of the 13th century.

At the turn of the century the tower was added in order to support a bell. Glass was becoming more easily available and the windows in the tower were made larger than those in the aisles. They now had two lights, giving the tracery of the windows a simple Y pattern. (The windows in the top stage of the tower have since had the dividing mullions removed.) The fact that a window was also built on the east side of the tower looking into the church suggests that the second stage of the tower was used as a room to accommodate the sexton. It was his duty to care for and guard the church and from his room he could overlook the whole interior to ensure there were no intruders. The people of the Middle Ages were not above stealing from churches, and there were security measures. The sexton could bar the church door from the inside and the font was fitted with a hinged lid and hasp and staple to prevent people taking holy water for magical purposes. The repair marks where the hinge and staple once were can be seen in the rim of the font. The sexton had his own entry to his vantage point through a small doorway, now blocked, on the north side of the tower.

The alterations so far made to the church had been at the expense of the parishioners. The money had come from bequests, from the proceeds of church ales (forerunners of our modern garden parties and coffee mornings, but less inhibited) and possibly from rates imposed on the inhabitants if sufficient money was not forthcoming by other means. It was now the turn of the priest to carry out modifications to his part of the church - the chancel.

By the end of the 13th century great changes had occurred in the ritual that took place in the chancel, particularly in the Eucharist. In Anglo-Saxon times this had been a service in which the congregation participated, sharing with the priest in the bread and wine taken at an altar situated in the chancel but close to the archway into the nave. In this way it commemorated the Last Supper. But by the 13th century it had taken on a more sacrificial nature, emphasising Christ's giving up his life on the cross. The altar, of stone, was now at the very east end of the chancel, and the congregation had become mere onlookers on a scene where the priest, with his back to the people and as an intermediary between them and God, acted out the sacrifice of the Mass. The people took communion only once a year, at Easter, receiving only the consecrated bread and not the wine. Services were in Latin, a language that the ordinary villager could not understand, and great store was set on each action and gesture of the priest during the conduct of the service. More symbolism was introduced into the great services of the Church's calendar. At Christmas the Nativity might be acted out before the altar by the priest and assisting clergy. On Good Fridays the altar cross, wrapped in a napkin, and the consecrated bread, representing the body of Christ, were placed in a specially carved receptacle of wood or stone (the Easter sepulchre), which was watched over through the Easter period. On Easter Sunday the cross and bread were laid on the altar together with the napkin to represent Christ's discarded grave clothes. Again, the priest and assistants acted out a scene, this time of the women coming to the tomb and being met by the angel. For the carrying out of these new rituals and to accommodate the extra clergy greater space was needed in the chancel. Consequently, early in the 14th century, the chancel at Keyingham was enlarged by making it longer and wider.

The work was carried out by Philip Ingleberd. He was instituted as rector in 1306. The fact that he, as well as the priests that came before and after him, was dignified with the title of rector shows that he was entitled to the full profits of Keyingham church. There had thus been an alteration to the terms of Count Stephen's grant to Albemarle, the abbey apparently relinquishing the tithes of the parish to the priest. In fact, there had been considerable ecclesiastical wheeling and dealing in the 15 churches of Stephen's grant. Most of those in North and Mid Holderness had come to be in the hands of official Church bodies relating to the diocese of York, whilst the eight in South Holderness, closest to Burstall Priory, were still held by Albemarle. Of the eight, Albemarle took the major profits of six, whereas at Keyingham and Easington the abbey had only the patronage. At Keyingham and Easington matters were slightly more complicated because the Lords of Holderness had the right to nominate the priest whom the abbey appointed as rector. Thus there were three parties with vested interests in Keyingham church: the rector, who received all the profits from the church (worth over £17 a year in 1291), the abbey, which received an annual pension from the rector (13s.4d, or 0.67p, in 1291), and the Lord of Holderness, who could always reward some favourite by nominating him or a relative as rector.

Philip Ingleberd came of a Beverley family. He was a distinguished scholar and quite wealthy. He was educated at University College, Oxford, and, in addition to holding the rectory of Keyingham, held considerable lands in his own right in Molescroft (just to the north of Beverley), Keyingham and Paull. In 1323 he founded a chapel at Molescroft to save the people there the trouble of travelling to their mother church of Beverley Minster to worship.

Besides extending the chancel at Keyingham, Philip Ingleberd probably also founded the chantry chapel on the south of the chancel. At its east end the chapel had its own altar where a priest, financed by an endowment, would be employed to say mass daily, usually for the soul of the founder. The chapel may have been erected on the side of the old chancel first. Its external walls are built entirely of dressed stone with two arches opening into the chancel, but during construction these may have been built against the south wall of the chancel. The work on the chancel was then begun. The old south wall was taken down, revealing the arches to the chapel, and the chancel was lengthened by continuing the wall east in line with the arches. On the north the old thick Norman wall was retained and continued east at the same thickness. Norman windows were replaced by more modern ones with Y tracery, similar to that in the windows of the tower. In the extension work, stone, far inferior to that of the chapel, was used. Much of it was re-used stone. It would seem that even the rubble that came from taking down the wall where the arches to the chapel now stood was used in the extension. This is evident in the smaller stones, broken down partly during demolition, to be seen in the extended part of the chancel, beyond the altar rail. The crudity of this work was hidden by plaster until very recently. The changes to the chancel were completed by building a fine east window and replacing what would have been a narrow round-headed Norman arch to the nave with a very wide pointed arch.

The chancel was now longer, and wider by the width of the wall removed from the south side. Widening the chancel only in a southward direction has meant that the central axis of the chancel is not now in line with the central axis of the nave. The new chancel of Philip Ingleberd was more in keeping with the form of worship at the time. A piscina - a shallow bowl draining to the outside of the church - where the priest washed his hands before consecrating the bread and wine, was set in the south wall near the altar. A set of three seats, enclosed in a pointed arch, was also built into the south wall of the chancel just to the west of the piscina. Here the priest and assisting clergy sat when the scriptures were being read out during the service. In order to emphasise the sanctity of the chancel, and also the distinction of clergy from congregation, a wooden screen was built across the chancel arch. Through this the people could see and hear what was going on in the chancel but had no part in the events. The screen was surmounted by a figure of Christ on the cross, flanked by figures of Mary and St John the Evangelist. A central door in the screen allowed communicants to enter the chancel on the one occasion in the year when they took communion. Otherwise the door was kept locked. The priest had no need to pass through the congregation to enter the chancel because a priest's door was inserted in the north wall of the chancel. Through this he would enter the chancel, don the vestments laid out for him by the parish clerk, conduct the service and leave by the way he had come. The priest's door, which has an old lintel used upside down for its lintel, is now blocked with brick. The reason that both the priest's door to the chancel and the sexton's door to the tower are on the north side is probably that this is the side where the rectory house was. It was here that the rector or his curate lived, together with any other assistant clergy, which included the sexton, who was in minor orders.

Philip Ingleberd died in 1325. Before his death, he had granted his three acres of Keyingham lands and 70-odd acres of Paull lands to support two scholars from the Beverley area at University College. It was probably at Oxford that he spent most of his time (for the first five years of his rectorship of Keyingham he had permission from the Archbishop to study at Oxford) and he may never have resided in Keyingham. Hopefully, for the spiritual welfare of the village, he provided them with a curate in his absence. Philip did, however, choose to be buried in his church, and his last resting-place was in the chantry chapel that he had built. His tomb may well have been in one of the archways looking into the chancel. There is a similarly placed tomb of a former rector in Hornsea church.

Philip's work was the last to be done on the church for a century. But events were taking place elsewhere which greatly affected the fortunes of his successors. Meaux Abbey's port of Wyke at the mouth of the River Hull, from where the abbey exported its wool (including that from Saltaugh), was flourishing. Others began to use the facilities and a town grew up. By the 1280s it had risen to be the third port in the kingdom with regard to the export of wool, England's chief export commodity at that time. At the beginning of the next decade, when war with Scotland impended, Edward I was in need of a suitable port from which to ship arms and supplies north, and in 1292 he began negotiations with the monks for possession of the town of Wyke. By 1293 the transfer was complete and the king granted the abbey lands and property in return for Wyke, which now became the King's Town upon Hull, or Kingston upon Hull as it is called today. One property that had recently come outright into the king's hands was Holderness following the death of Isabella de Fortibus without heirs. Part of that property was the right to nominate the rectors of Keyingham and Easington. This right formed part of the deal with Meaux. It was, of course, of very little monetary value to Meaux as it was still Albemarle Abbey that made the final appointment and received the pension from the rector appointed. For some reason the Crown continued to exercise the right of appointment (it was Edward I who nominated Philip Ingleberd, for example) until Meaux finally received confirmation of the grant in 1337. In that year war with France broke out, and Edward III seized the properties of all alien religious houses in England on the grounds that the proceeds of English lands and churches were being transferred to France. Edward's confirmation not only granted Meaux the right to nominate, but also the right to appoint, the rector, so Meaux now received the pensions from the Easington and Keyingham rectors.

This was not the end of the story, however. By the time the grant of the two churches was confirmed Meaux was considering itself to be in dire financial straits. Due to the rise in sea level the abbey was losing lands all along the Humber foreshore from Saltaugh to Spurn, lands worth, according to the abbey, £250 a year. The abbot, therefore, sought to extract more profits from the churches of Easington and Keyingham. It proved a lengthy and costly exercise. Firstly, the abbot, Hugh of Leven, felt that he needed to demonstrate his right to appoint the rectors at the two churches. To do this he had to induce the incumbents then in possession to give up their livings. This was eventually achieved by 1343, by which time the two rectors had been pressed to resign the livings. They were compensated for the term of their lives with lands, properties and annuities worth well over £150 a year between them, enough to keep them in extreme good comfort. In order to finance this part of the operation the abbot had to borrow £220 from Sir Robert Hilton, lord of Swine and Winestead. The displaced rector of Keyingham, John of Botheby, became rector of Bainton in the north of the Riding. In his will of 1382 he left £2 to the church of St Nicholas at Keyingham, the first mention in the records of the church's dedication.

Now that there were vacancies at the two churches the abbot demonstrated the abbey's right to the patronage by appointing the rectors. The next move in the proceedings then took place. When Edward III had granted the abbey the right to appoint the rectors, he also gave them licence to appropriate the two churches. Hugh of Leven applied to the Archbishop of York for such appropriations, on the grounds of the dwindling income of the abbey. Permission was granted, for Easington church in 1347, and for Keyingham church in 1349, the year Hugh of Leven succumbed to the Black Death. The new deal meant that the abbey now took all the profits of Keyingham church, the abbey now being, in effect, the rector of the church. To see to the spiritual needs of the parish they appointed a vicar (meaning 'supplying the place of another' i.e. the rector) on a fixed salary.

Appropriation of churches by religious houses was a long-established practice and it was not unknown for the houses to pay stand-in priests, with no security of tenure, mere pittances for salaries whilst taking for themselves considerable profits in tithes, rents from glebe lands and other church offerings. In order to prevent this abuse the bishops had begun to insist on properly instituted vicars with the local bishop deciding what the vicar should receive as fair remuneration. For Keyingham the Archbishop of York ordered that the vicar should receive an annual payment of £12 from the abbey, and that the abbey should build him a vicarage house. The abbey was also to pay for all repairs and rebuilding in the chancel of the church. On his part the vicar was to find the bread and wine and provide the candles on the main altar. The Archbishop was recompensed for his trouble by annual payments, totalling £2, from the abbey to the Archbishop and the Dean and Chapter of York.

This was not entirely the end of the negotiations. In 1361, when peace with France was restored, Meaux came to a financial agreement with Albemarle Abbey, in order to confirm the transfer of the patronage of Keyingham church to Meaux. Later still, in 1375, Meaux had to raise the sum of £200 to pay the costs of the court at Rome in obtaining the pope's confirmation of all the dealings that had taken place with regard to the churches of Keyingham and Easington.

So ended the long negotiations regarding the rights in Keyingham's church. Meaux Abbey now had a dual interest in the village - Saltaugh Grange and the parish church. The church was no longer served by a rector but by a vicar, a situation which existed until the parish was united in one benefice with Halsham and Ottringham in the 1980s. The vicarage house built by Meaux probably stood at the north end of the green at the junction of Station Road and Waldby Garth Road. It was there that the vicar's house was in 1685. The old rectory house, to the north of the church, was used as the headquarters by the monks for the running of the glebe land.

The first vicar appointed to Keyingham by

The Garth, February 1999. *View from the south. The vicar's house stood at the north end of this site from the middle of the 14th century until the middle of the 18th century. The large house at the far end of the Garth is Wray House.* *Photo: J A Mcleod*

Meaux Abbey was William Maupas. In 1374 the abbey found it necessary to bring him to book for not providing the lights at the main altar, as required by the terms of his ordination. He eventually agreed to provide four tapers, but no more, in the chancel, as had been done by the rectors who had gone before him.

Because Keyingham church belonged to Meaux Abbey it features in an account of the abbey's fortunes written soon after 1400 by a retired abbot, Thomas Burton. It is he who tells us of an event at Keyingham in 1396, at a time when he was bursar of the monastery. On the night of June 24 the village was hit by a terrible storm and the church was struck by lightning and caught fire. In a vivid account Burton tells of the great damage to stonework, the splitting of beams and the collapse of one side of the tower. The fire destroyed the beams and tiles of the nave roof (the tiles may have been wooden shingles although the manufacture of tiles from clay had existed in England for almost a century). Despite the havoc, certain parts of the church were untouched, particularly those built by Philip Ingleberd. Philip's tomb had remained undamaged even though a great squared stone had been completely knocked out of an adjoining wall. There were other miraculous happenings. The villagers, roused from their beds, had placed ladders against the church and were trying to put out the fire on the roof with beaters and buckets of water. One of the ladders, carrying 13 men forming a bucket chain, collapsed yet no serious injuries were sustained. And from the tomb of Philip Ingleberd there oozed sweet-scented oil. All present then and there prayed to Philip for deliverance from the storm. Their prayers were answered. Later, other miracles occurred at the tomb which became a shrine: the local cult of St Philip had begun. A spring with curative properties, St Philip's Well, in a field to the west of the village, was dedicated to his name. Near by, at the side of a track leading across the fields to the church, St Philip's cross was set up. The sites of both are marked on Ordnance Survey maps of the early part of the 20th century. In 1841 it was recorded that the village girls were in the habit of dropping pins or coins into the well to obtain good luck. The well dried up, as did a number of other springs around the village, when improved drainage lowered the water table. The cross was removed to the grounds of Ebor House in the middle of the 19th century. The base still exists. The final dedication to St Philip came in the 20th century, when a Keyingham street was named after him.

Another storm was to bring Keyingham briefly into the national spotlight. In March 1471 the deposed Edward IV set sail from the Netherlands with 2,000 men in a small fleet of ships. His intention was to regain the crown from Henry VI. Sailing north along the English coast they encountered 'great storms, winds and tempests', as an old chronicle tells us, and were driven into the Humber. Edward himself landed at Spurn, but others of his ships were scattered along the shore as far west as Paull. The little army managed to regroup in the region of Kilnsea and set out to march to Hull. But 'there rose again him all the country of Holderness, whose captain was a priest and parson called John Westerdale'. John Westerdale was the vicar of Keyingham, and he was said to have put himself at the head of six or seven thousand men and confronted Edward at Keyingham High Bridge. Greatly outnumbered Edward decided on negotiation and convinced the militant parson and his followers that he had come not to claim the crown of England but the Duchy of York, which was his by right. He was allowed to pass to Hull, now a walled town, where he was refused entry and so had to continue his march to York. From there he marched south, gathering supporters as he went, until at Barnet he met and defeated the Lancastrians, less than a month after his confrontation with Westerdale. Edward once more ascended the throne, and John Westerdale and Keyingham slipped quietly from the national scene.

After the great storm of 1396 Keyingham's church must have looked a sorry sight. The nave was roofless and the tower had partially collapsed. Fallen stones were scattered everywhere. Moreover, what was left of the church was distinctly old-fashioned. The windows were small and the church had been very dark inside before the heavens were revealed through charred roof timbers. It was not at all in keeping with an age of large windows and light interiors, so brilliantly exemplified in the new church, just being completed at Patrington five miles away.

After repairing the roof the people devoted the 15th century to rebuilding the tower and providing the church with larger windows. It was probably during this phase of building that a spire was added to the tower, thus emulating the efforts at Patrington and Ottringham. All three spires came to be landmarks for sailors in the Humber. The north aisle was made wider, but instead of continuing the slope of the nave roof, as had been done when the aisle was first added, the whole roof of the aisle was given a much shallower pitch. This enabled lead to be used for the covering material. (When used on a steep roof, lead tends to 'creep' under its own weight, eventually letting in the water.) Now that the aisle walls were higher, much larger windows could be inserted. These windows date from the beginning of the 15th century. Later in the century the south aisle was raised and large, more modern, square-headed windows were inserted. Similar square-headed windows were placed in St Philip's chantry chapel. Meaux Abbey, as rectors of the church, took it upon themselves to cast more light on the altar by inserting a large square-headed window in the south wall of the chancel. This cut into the arch covering the priests' seats and this was filled in with brick and rubble. Finally, towards the end of the century more light was admitted to the chancel and to the centre of the nave by replacing the steep-pitched roofs with clerestories (clear stories). For both the nave and chancel clerestories, brick, probably made locally, was used. The windows were square headed and the now shallow roofs were covered with lead.

These additions and modifications of the 15th century represented the last changes made during the Middle Ages in the outline of Keyingham's church. There was to be no other change until the spire was removed in 1969. From 1500 onwards the efforts of the parishioners were to be devoted not only to maintaining the church in good repair but also to modifying the interior in order to keep pace with the change in worshipping practice. In the middle of the 16th century the pace of change was to be particularly rapid.

South aisle, early 1970s. *The aisle was added towards the end of the 13th century. The original steep slope of the roof is indicated by the plate line above the vestry door. As can be seen, the outer wall would have been much lower than it is now. It would have contained narrow pointed-headed windows. In the 15th century the wall was heightened and much larger square headed windows were inserted in order to admit more light into the church.*

North side of the chancel, January 1993. *The building work of eight centuries. The lower part of the wall was built of rubble in the 12th century and contained narrow, Norman round-headed windows, the remains of the jamb of one being visible as a vertical line of dressed stones approximately midway between the existing lower windows. On the left of the jamb, decorated with greenery for the Christmas services, is the pediment of the 17th-century Angell monument. The Norman windows were replaced with the two Y-tracery windows probably at the end of the 13th century, and the small priest's doorway between the two windows was probably inserted at this time. Note that the left half of the lintel is a re-used lintel inserted upside down. The doorway was blocked in the 16th century. In the 15th century the height of the chancel was increased in order to insert more windows and let in more light. This construction was in brick, which, like the lower part of the wall was plastered over. The whole of this work was revealed during restoration work in the 20th century, following which the upper part of the wall was re-plastered.*

51

The 16th century was one in which there were great changes in religion, economic developments and social relationships. Even as the century opened, the Middle Ages, as later historians called them, were coming to an end and the Modern Age had begun. Many of the changes were gradual as peoples and institutions adapted to the quicker tempo of commerce and the more rapid spread of ideas through the new medium of the printed word. The one change that came upon the ordinary Englishman with perhaps confusing speed was the change in religion.

At the beginning of the century scholars were re-examining the early versions of the Scriptures and concluding that there had been many accretions to Christian doctrine since the time of Christ and the Apostles. The result of most of the additions had been to emphasise the importance of the priesthood. The intercessory role of the priest between the people and God during the mass, the hearing of confessions in private, the recital of daily masses for the souls of the dead, the elaboration of church ceremonial, the sale of pardons and the encouragement of pilgrimages to, and worship at, shrines (of which St Philip's at Keyingham was one) were all foreign to the Scriptures and led to an arrogant clergy and a superstitious people. As a result of the arguments the Protestant Church began to arise, mostly in the northern countries of Europe, which one by one broke away from the rule of the Pope.

England did not immediately follow suit. Henry VIII, who was conservative in his religion, in fact earned the title 'Defender of the Faith' from the Pope for his writings against the theses of Martin Luther. Henry, however, did eventually break with Rome, not for religious reasons but for political ones. When Henry wished to nullify his marriage to the ageing Catherine of Aragon in the hope that a new wife might provide him with a male heir the Pope refused his sanction. After long delay Henry gained his way by appointing himself Supreme Head of the Church in England and putting the matter of the annulment in the hands of Thomas Cranmer, Archbishop of Canterbury.

The final declaration of Henry's new power came at the very beginning of 1535. As head of the Church he was entitled to dues which had previously gone to Rome. Henry was desperately in need of the money, primarily for the nation's defence, and the Church seemed a promising source. It was estimated that the religious institutions of the country owned one third of the land. Locally, for example, in the parishes of Patrington, Ottringham and Keyingham, which contained about three and a half thousand acres each, the Archbishop of York held the whole of Patrington except for 150 acres held by the rector; Meaux Abbey held over 600 acres in Ottringham and the 450 acres of Saltaugh Grange as well as the 60 acres or so of the Keyingham rectory; and Thornton Abbey, Lincolnshire, and Bridlington Priory each held about 120 acres in Ottringham. The priory also owned the church at Ottringham.

At the end of January 1535, Henry ordered commissioners to find the net annual income of all churches and monastic establishments with the intention of imposing a 10% tax. The returns, drawn together in the *Valor Ecclesiasticus,* were ready in the September.

The income and outlay for the benefice of Keyingham were included with Meaux Abbey's return. In Keyingham the monks' glebe consisted of four oxgangs of land (about 60-80 acres) and ten other properties and parcels of land which altogether brought them £6.59 a year in rents. The tithes of the villagers were worth over £27 in an average year. This sum included a small amount received in oblations, no doubt some of them collected at the shrine of St Philip. In all, Meaux Abbey grossed about £33.50 a year from Keyingham's church.

The outlay included £12 for the vicar's salary, and sums totalling £2 to the Archbishop and the Dean and Chapter of York, both being the same figures as agreed at the time of the appropriation in the 1350s. Other outgoings came to £4.75, so that the total outlay was £18.75, and Meaux's net income from Keyingham church was about £14.75.

From Saltaugh the monks netted £10 a year. Meaux's income from all its lands and properties, nearly all in the East Riding, totalled £298. The abbey therefore ended up paying £29.80 to the King each year until the monasteries were dissolved. The Crown continued to take the tax from churches until 1704 when Queen Anne granted it to a fund known as Queen Anne's Bounty for augmenting the stipends of the poorer clergy.

The valuation carried out in 1535 no doubt passed over the heads of the inhabitants of Keyingham. The commissioners probably never came to the village except on their way to interviewing the rectors of Winestead and Patrington; all the information they needed about St Nicholas Church could be gathered from Meaux Abbey. As long as the monks continued to collect only the same dues as in the past the people of Keyingham probably remained unconcerned. In the middle of 1535, however, Henry's powers were brought home to them. It was then that it was ordered that parish priests were to declare in their churches Henry's position as Supreme Head of the English Church. They were also to erase any mention of the Pope from the various prayer books used by the priests in the ordering of the services. Although there had long been an undercurrent of anti-papal and anti-clerical feeling amongst the population, the thought that Henry had control of his subjects, body *and* soul, caused alarm amongst some thinking men. If there were any such thinkers in Keyingham they kept their thoughts to themselves, for there is no record of any dissent. At Winestead, however, it was a different matter. There, at church service on Midsummer Day, the priest, Christopher Michell, told his congregation that the Pope should be recognised as Head of the Church despite Henry's injunction. The authorities were swift to act. Four of the local gentry, including Sir Christopher Hildyard, lord of the manor of Winestead, were sent to examine Michell and his service books. Michell did not deny what he had said and soon found himself in the Archbishop of York's gaol at Beverley. Examination of his service books showed that he had not erased the Pope's name 'but had covered it with bits of paper fixed with wax, so that any man could take them off'. Not only was the Archbishop notified of the offence but so also was Thomas Cromwell, Henry VIII's right-hand man. News of Michell's misdemeanour and imprisonment must have buzzed round the district, reminding folk of authority's powers and checking any thoughts of protest.

Having considerably augmented the Crown's income from the 10% tax on the churches and monasteries Cromwell and his master were still not satisfied. The capital wealth of the monasteries attracted them. In many minds the monasteries had outlived their usefulness. They were now merely wealthy establishments with handfuls of occupants with no true vocation. The universities had replaced them as centres of learning, and printing had supplanted their role as copiers of manuscripts. Cromwell thought he needed little excuse to seize their wealth. Before the *Valor Ecclesiasticus* had been completed Cromwell had sent another set of commissioners into the country to inquire again into the income of the monasteries but also into the conduct and behaviour of their inmates. The blatant object of these new commissioners was to discredit the monks and nuns and belittle the monastic way of life. A scathing report was issued in February 1536. Very few monasteries escaped criticism, but Cromwell decided to proceed carefully. In the March an Act was passed for the Suppression of the Lesser Monasteries, namely all religious houses with fewer than 12 inmates or whose income was less than £200 a year, on the grounds that it was they that housed dissolute and idle nuns and monks. Such inmates would benefit from a transfer to the 'great and honourable monasteries' where religion was 'right well kept and observed'. This differentiation between the great and small religious houses helped ease the bill through the upper house, containing, as it did, many abbots of the great monasteries.

The Act was not accepted so quietly in the country, however, particularly in the conservative North. Here, the actual deed of evicting the monks and nuns from the smaller monasteries brought to a head the grievances of many classes of society. The northern barons resented rule from London. The middle and upper classes were discontent with a new tax about to be imposed on their wealth. Village priests were upset because a stricter discipline was being inflicted on them at the instigation of Thomas Cromwell. Inflation, unheard of in the Middle Ages, was just beginning to be felt owing to the production of more silver

for the coinage. Prices were rising. The emptying and despoiling of the smaller religious houses brought a number of unemployed and discontented monks on to the scene as well as a loss of alms to the poor. It proved to be the last straw for many.

The first insurrection began at Louth in Lincolnshire on Sunday, 1 October 1536, and spread through the county in the following days. By the middle of the week news of the Lincolnshire Rising, as it became known, had reached Beverley, and on the following Sunday a vast crowd was assembling on the Westwood. In the days ensuing people were summoned by beacon and church bell to gathering places in the countryside. The men of Holderness, in response to the alarms, assembled at Sutton Ings (in the region where Ings Road, Hull, now is). There they chose their captains. The men of North Holderness chose William Barker, those of Mid Holderness chose Richard Tennant, and the men of South Holderness chose William Ombler. He was probably from Ryhill, where 20 years later the family is recorded as having property. On the Thursday morning when armed and mounted men from the Beverley, Cottingham and Hessle areas were gathered at Hunsley beacon news was brought to them that all Holderness as far as the seaside was in arms. The Holderness men had captured a number of gentry, including Sir Christopher Hildyard of Winestead. Others of the gentry had fled to the safety of Hull's walls.

The policy of the rebels was to force the captured gentry on oath to act as their leaders. As the gentry had their own grievances this may not have been too difficult. Robert Aske, a lawyer, of Aughton in the far west of the Riding was such a man. He had been captured by the Lincolnshire rebels as he set off from home for London for the start of the law term. He had taken the oath of the rebels and returned to the East Riding to become the leader of the new uprising.

Another gentleman forced into leadership, this time by the Holderness insurgents, was Sir Christopher Hildyard, and two days after his capture he was at Bishop Burton consulting with the leaders of the Beverley men on how to lay siege to Hull, whose mayor and aldermen had refused the rebels any support. Later that day 300 men of Holderness mustered on the Westwood under their three captains. On Sunday, October 15, Hull was surrounded by the men of Cottingham, Beverley, Holderness and Hullshire (a district that extended west of Hull to beyond Willerby, Swanland and North Ferriby). Two-hundred Holderness men under Barker and Tennant covered the Holderness side of the River Hull (at that time the town of Hull occupied only the west bank of the river), whilst Ombler, with the remaining Holderness men, and Hildyard, now in charge of the Hullshire contingent, lay on the west of the town close to the Humber.

Meanwhile, Aske had taken his men to capture York, which quickly yielded. Following his success he sent reinforcements to the rebels outside Hull and on October 19 the mayor and aldermen gave up the town. The successful rebels then garrisoned the town with 200 Holderness men under the command of Sir Robert Constable of Flamborough.

By the time of Hull's capture the Lincolnshire Rising had collapsed, but the Yorkshire movement, under Aske's leadership, gathered pace. Known as the Pilgrimage of Grace, because of some of the religious demands of the rebels, it spread to all the northern counties of England. Pontefract castle, held for the king by Lord Thomas Darcy, was captured. Thirty-thousand rebels then marched on Doncaster to confront a royal army of a mere 8,000 under Lord Norfolk. Norfolk entered into prolonged negotiations, knowing the difficulties of provisioning 30,000 men and how rebels so often soon felt the call of home. He promised to listen to the Pilgrims' demands and spent weeks in communication with his sovereign in London. But to Aske's credit he maintained his army and at the beginning of December Norfolk accepted a list of proposals to be put to the king. The list was long and shows the multifarious grievances of the Northerners. Besides the religious demands there were secular demands. On the religious side, the pilgrims wanted the Pope to be reinstated as spiritual head of the English Church, the dissolved monasteries to be restored, and Protestant teachings to be suppressed. On the secular side, they wanted a parliament to be held in the North and recent taxes to be repealed. Princess Mary, daughter of Catherine of Aragon, and made illegitimate by the nullification of the marriage, should be made legitimate. (At that point in time the infant Elizabeth, daughter of Anne Boleyn, was heir to the throne and her upbringing was likely to be more Protestant than Mary's.) Thomas Cromwell, seen as the instigator of all the evils emanating from the king and parliament, should be dismissed. In all, there were 24 demands, some of them relevant to only a small part of the northern counties. One important demand was a pardon for all the rebels.

The king's reply came. Pardon was to be granted to all the rebels (but only after Norfolk had persuaded the king not to execute the ringleaders). There would be a parliament at York, and the monasteries would stand until that parliament had met. Aske persuaded his followers to accept these offers and on December 8 the Pilgrims dispersed. Hull was restored to its mayor and aldermen and the men of Holderness retired to their homes. Except for their captains they remain mostly anonymous and we do not know if there were any Keyingham names amongst them. At that time the Lordship of Holderness was in the king's hands and Keyingham was a royal manor. It might be thought this would inspire some loyalty to the king but it would seem not. Burstwick and Preston were also royal manors and we know that Burstwick people took the oath of the rebels. It was administered to them by Marmaduke Thomson, vicar of Preston. It is also known that Preston men took part in the rising and in a second rising the following January, when certain people thought they saw flaws in the king's pardon to the Pilgrims. This second group of rebels decided to seize Scarborough and Hull, two well defended ports whose capture would seriously hinder the deployment of royal troops in the North. Involved in the plot to capture Hull was William Nicholson of Preston who promised to bring in 40 to 100 followers. The plan was for Nicholson's party and others to infiltrate the town, unite with sympathisers, and take command of Hull. The plot went sadly awry. Nicholson had the date wrong and was the sole member of his party in the town when the other conspirators made their move. They were easily captured. The plot to capture Scarborough also failed.

Although we are not certain that anyone from Keyingham joined the rebellions of 1536 and '37, we can be sure that during the four months of unrest the village buzzed with news of events at Hull and beyond. Also filtering through would be the prevalent rumours, deliberately circulated by the rebels to foment the uprising: there were to be new taxes imposed by the king - a tax on every plough, a tax on every beast, a tax on births, marriages and deaths; the silver and gold communion vessels of the churches were to be confiscated by the king and replaced by vessels of brass or tin; parish churches were to be merged. There was probably no foundation in these rumours, although in 1539, after the clamour of rebellion had died down, Cromwell did introduce the recording of baptisms, marriages and burials by all parish churches (it was to be over 150 years, however, before any parliament dare tax the events). The parish registers resulting from Cromwell's action are a boon to family historian and for some parishes date back to the year of their inception in 1539. Keyingham has no such boast, however. The earliest record surviving is of the burials in 1604 and the registers are only intermittent from that year up to 1659.

The January rising, despite valiant efforts by Aske to discourage it, gave Henry the excuse to go back on his promises and pardon to the Pilgrims. The leaders of the second insurgency were executed and those involved in the Pilgrimage were brought to trial. As a result, Lord Thomas Darcy, considered by Henry to have yielded up Pontefract castle too easily, was executed. Aske, the leader of the Pilgrims, was taken from London to York and on a market day, when witnesses were most numerous, hanged alive in chains. Six days previously, on July 6, 1537, the same fate had befallen Sir Robert Constable, the man who had held Hull for the Pilgrims. He met his fate, also on a market day, at Hull, the scene of his crime. If any Keyingham farmer or his wife had decided to sell their butter or eggs in the town that day and taken the tortuous journey via Hedon, Preston, Bilton and Holderness Road (there was no direct route from Hedon to Hull in those days), then crossed the River Hull by ferry (there was no bridge) and gone to Hull's Beverley Gate, they would have witnessed Constable's suspension in chains. When Henry VIII visited the town in 1541, Constable's bones still hung above the gate, a grim warning to anyone with rebellion in mind. In all, well over 200 people were executed for their part in the northern risings of 1536 and '37. In Holderness, men, including Christopher Hildyard, William Ombler and William Nicholson, were no doubt quietly thankful that only the chief leaders were punished.

As a result of Henry's visit to Hull new fortifications were built at Drypool on the east bank of the Hull. Although the new defences were part of a national scheme of improvement, Henry was no doubt influenced in the siting of the fortifications by the ease with which the Holderness Pilgrims had gained control of the mouth of the Hull from the east bank. To link the town with the Drypool defences, the first North Bridge was built, replacing the old ferry by which people from Holderness had previously entered the town. Visits by Keyingham folk to Hull's market were now a littler easier.

Amongst those executed following the Pilgrimage of Grace were the heads of some religious houses that had lent support to the rebels. The houses were closed and their properties confiscated by the king. Amongst the miscreants was William Wood, prior of Bridlington. Following his execution, the domestic quarters of the priory inmates were demolished (although the priory continued as a parish church) and all the lands and property of the priory went to the king. Thus Ottringham church and about 120 acres of Ottringham lands became royal property. Having discovered that monasteries could be dissolved and their properties confiscated other than by Act of Parliament, Henry and Cromwell began a systematic attack on the greater religious houses. By the occasional hanging of a recalcitrant abbot and the granting of pensions to the inmates of compliant houses all religious houses had been dissolved by 1540. Meaux Abbey surrendered in December 1539. The abbot, Richard Stopes, received a pension of £40 a year for life. The remaining 24 monks received pensions of between five and six pounds. Saltaugh Grange and Keyingham's church with its property passed to the king.

Most of the value of Keyingham church lay in the villagers' tithes. These consisted of fleeces and corn taken to the rectory tithe barn, lambs and haycocks in the fields, or money, in the case of the tithe on such things as calves and foals. Converting payments in kind in Keyingham into silver in the king's coffers in London was a tedious and loss-making process. There were at that time probably few people that wished to buy or rent the right to take the tithes: there were more profitable pickings to be had from the confiscated properties of the monasteries.

A solution to the king's problem with tithes did exist, however. The Archbishop of York held many manors, the profits of which were in cash. In 1545 the archbishop was the newly promoted and very compliant Robert Holgate. He had been the superior of Watton Priory, near Driffield, at its dissolution and had received for his pension the profits formerly accruing to the priory - a clear £360 per year. Henry now made him an offer that he probably felt he could not refuse - churches for manors. The logic could not be denied: churches to an ecclesiastic, manors to someone of a more secular bent. A great number of churches and tithes were transferred to the archbishop who, in return, granted approximately 90 manors, of considerable greater value, to the king. Thus Keyingham church came to belong to the archbishop, and Patrington, a manor of the archbishops of York since the time of King Canute, became a royal manor.

Henry VIII died in 1547. Although he had

replaced the Pope as the head of the Church in England and dissolved the monasteries he remained essentially conservative in religious outlook. One of his few concessions to the new thinking was to order a chained copy of the Bible in English to be set up in every parish church. For any literate person in Keyingham it was available to be consulted. Otherwise, despite all the turmoil in the English Church, worship continued as it had for centuries and the people of Keyingham resorted to the comforting mystery of the Latin mass to ease their journey through an often-hostile life.

Despite his own religious outlook Henry had entrusted the education of Edward, his son by his third wife Jane Seymour, to Protestant teachers. When, at the age of nine, he came to the throne as Edward VI he was surrounded by Protestant advisers, including Archbishop Cranmer of Canterbury, who was coming more and more to the Protestant view. By Acts of Parliament and royal injunctions worship was ordered to take on a more Protestant complexion. Superstitious paintings and images were to be removed from churches. Altars of stone, indicative of priestly sacrifice, were to be replaced by wooden tables. Masses for the dead and worship of the Virgin Mary and other saints were to be discontinued. There were to be no more private confessions to priests. The celibacy of the clergy - a matter that had drawn another sharp dividing line between the priesthood and the laity - was no longer insisted on: priests could marry. Cranmer had already married a German Protestant during the reign of Henry. Archbishop Holgate of York, who, as a one-time member of a religious institution, had taken a vow of celibacy, now showed that he was a good Protestant by, at the age of 68, taking to wife the 24-year-old Barbara Wentworth.

One of Edward's earliest acts concerning the Church was prompted by financial matters. Inflation in Europe was continuing, exacerbated by the influx of large amounts of gold and silver from the New World. The Crown's income derived mainly from old, fixed, dues and, despite all Henry's confiscations, the exchequer was short of money. In the year of Edward's accession Parliament passed an Act suppressing the chantries. This followed naturally from the banning of masses for the dead but it was the endowments supporting the chantries that prompted Edward and his advisers in their action. The endowments went to the Crown. Although Philip Ingleberd built a chantry chapel at Keyingham church in the early 14th century and left lands in Paull to support a chaplain, there is no record of Edward's commissioners discovering any such endowment. It may be that Philip left the endowment for only a short term, sufficient for mass to be said for a fixed term of years and not in perpetuity. Consequently, there were no lands relating to Philip's chapel for Edward's commissioners to confiscate. There were, however, two small endowments to be collected from Keyingham. Rents worth 11s.8d (58p) a year, from properties belonging to Elizabeth Tuney and the Blyth family, were being paid to support an obit. Whereas a chantry was an endowment to maintain a priest to say mass daily, an obit was for a mass said annually, usually on the anniversary of the death of the benefactor. It is probable that the obit financed by the Tuney and Blyth rents was recited at the altar in Philip Ingleberd's former chantry chapel. The annual duty was no doubt carried out by the vicar, supplementing his stipend of £12, which, due to inflation was coming to be worth less and less each year.

Edward VI extracted yet another ransom from

the Church. In 1552 an inventory of Church goods was carried out and all the more valuable items were taken by the exchequer. Consequently Keyingham would have had to give up its silver-gilt chalice and the priest's costly vestments, especially the one of blue velvet embroidered with flowers of gold.

During Edward's reign two new prayer books were published. Both were in English and both the work of Thomas Cranmer. The first English prayer book of 1549 was, in 1552, replaced by the second, which was far more Protestant in emphasis. No longer were the saints to be commemorated. The services of baptism, marriage and burial came to be wholly within the church building. No more were evil spirits exorcised from the child outside the door of the church before baptism at the font, or the promises and vows of marriage taken in the church porch before the couple moved to the altar. The first part of the burial service was not conducted over the body at the lych (meaning 'corpse') gate before the party entered the church. There were no prayers for the dead, even in the burial service. The priestly function of the clergy was played down. Priests were now referred to as ministers and their wearing of special vestments during what was now called communion instead of mass was stopped. At communion the people received the wine as well as the bread. The communion changed from being a sacrificial service to one of commemoration. Thus, the opening words spoken by the celebrant when he offered the bread became, 'Take and eat this in remembrance that Christ died for thee...' rather than, 'This is my body which is given for thee...'. In the Latin service the first words of the latter phrase were, *'Hoc est corpus meum'*, which Protestants had mockingly corrupted to 'hocus-pocus'.

How well the second English prayer book was received in Holderness or how far its requirements were followed is not known. From the few records available we know that the Yorkshire clergy, despite any religious conservatism, had soon followed the government directives of Edward's time. However, the 1552 prayer book had been in use for little more than six months when Edward died and the Catholic Mary Tudor came to the throne. By 1554 things returned to their old order. The new prayer books were destroyed, the English Bible was removed from the churches, and churchwardens were laying out money for the purchase of Latin books, the erection of stone altars and the buying of vestments for the priest. Married priests were removed from their benefices, although, after suitable acts of contrition and agreeing not to live with their former partners, they were allowed to take up another benefice. Robert Towers replaced William Norwin as priest at Keyingham, although it is not expressly stated that it was because Norwin was married. Robert Holgate, after making abject excuses for his marriage, was deprived of his archbishopric and retired quietly to London. Other Protestant bishops were not so lucky. Cranmer was burnt at the stake in 1555 after England's reconciliation with Rome.

The one thing that Mary was unable to do was restore the monasteries; too many members of her parliament had benefited from the sale of monastic property for that to happen. Consequently, Saltaugh remained in lay hands and St Nicholas Church remained with the Archbishops of York. Keyingham's parishioners were no doubt quietly happy that they could return to the old way of worship but, like the rest of the country, alarmed at Mary's marriage to the Prince Philip of Spain in 1554 and the terrible persecution of Protestants. The concern did not last long, for in 1558 Mary died. At the age of 25, Elizabeth I ascended the throne with what she considered to be the task of reconciling religious groups of widely different views. It was an era when the concept of religious tolerance was unknown: religion and state had to be of one mind. Elizabeth, in an attempt to please all parties, chose the *Via media* - the middle way. The breach with Rome was reopened, however, and Elizabeth became Supreme Governor of the Church of England (rather than Supreme Head, as Henry had declared himself). Priests were once again allowed to marry. For the litany the more Protestant prayer book of 1552 was adopted with some concessions to Catholic practices. Thus, kneeling at communion and during prayers was encouraged, and ministers were required to wear the special vestments during communion. At other parts of the service and during other services a simple surplice was to be worn. The communion took on both a sacrificial and a commemorative nature, so that at the administration of the bread the words, 'This is my body which is given for thee, take and eat in remembrance that Christ died for thee,' were used. The words of the old service and those of the 1552 prayer book were thus joined together, a nice illustration of the taking of the 'middle way' by Elizabeth and her advisers.

Over a period of 12 years and under four different monarchs there had been four different forms of the official religion. The Church's most important service had changed from the mass, conducted by a priest at a stone altar with his back to the congregation, to a communion, taken by the minister and all the people round a table, kept in the chancel but brought towards the nave for the service. In the new order of things there was a strong emphasis on the sermon and the expounding of the Scriptures.

In order to ensure that all parishes fell in with the latest royal requirements, the Queen issued a set of injunctions to the clergy and laity. They covered all aspects of church practice, both religious and practical in nature, and formed the basis of inquiry when the bishops subsequently conducted visitations of their dioceses. The visitation conducted by the Archbishop Thomas Young of York in 1567 indicates that the York diocesan authorities had been very lax in implementing the royal injunctions during the eight years since they were issued. Holderness, in particular, had been slow to adapt.

Visitations were held at a prearranged date and place. The parson and churchwardens from the Holderness deanery usually reported to Holy Trinity Church, Hull, where they would be confronted with a whole range of questions. In 1567 Archbishop Young was particularly concerned to ensure that the new practices were being adhered to. He wanted to know if all signs of superstition in the church had been removed and whether a pulpit had been set up from where the minister could deliver his sermon. He enquired whether the parson was giving a sermon at least four times a year, as required by the queen's injunctions, and whether on other occasions the parson was reading a passage from the Book of Homilies, a collection of sermons compiled by learned clerics. The churchwardens had to see that the Book of Homilies was provided as well as the correct prayer book and a Bible in English. None of the old Latin service books was to be retained. On the more general side there were questions about the state of repair of the church, whether the parish registers were properly kept, whether a poor man's box (properly locked) was kept and whether the parson and his parishioners lived decent, moral lives.

To all these questions the Keyingham

representatives were able to give satisfactory answers. At Ottringham there were some minor misdemeanours - the churchwardens were failing to collect the fines, imposed by Elizabeth's government, on those who failed to attend church each Sunday and the parish register was not properly kept. In the more remote corners of Holderness, matters were more serious. At Welwick, for instance, there was still a carved image of St John, pictures and paintings on the walls, a priest's cope with images on it, and many other relics of the past. At Skeffling a stone altar was still in position and a holy-water stoup remained. The stoup, in which the people dipped their fingers and blessed themselves as they entered the church, is still in existence at Skeffling. Halsham, too, had retained its altar and stoup. At Owthorne the vicar 'omitteth his sermons, useth the Communion for the dead and seeth not a sufficient Bible provided'.

One can imagine that parishioners, in an area where Church officials rarely strayed, were reluctant to remove altars and other church furnishings that had already been destroyed or hidden away once and then hastily restored when Mary came to the throne. At Halsham and Welwick, however, the slowness to change may have been due to the influence of Catholic gentry families like the Constables of Halsham and the Wrights and Thorpes of Welwick (the Wright family were later to provide two of the Gunpowder-Plot conspirators). These families remained staunchly Catholic, despite persecution and heavy fines through the centuries. In Keyingham Catholics were few in number. In 1604, when the vicar and churchwardens had to present the names of the Catholics living in their parish, only Margery Dickenson was reported at Keyingham. In 1676, out of 100 communicants (that is practically everyone over the age of 14) in the village, there were six Roman Catholics, and in 1706 the number was down to one.

Following the findings of the 1567 visitation, orders were given for their rectification, and the churchwardens of offending parishes had to certify that they had done such things as destroying stone altars, removing paintings and supplying an English Bible. By the time of Archbishop Edmund Grindal's visitation in 1575, matters regarding religion seem to have been pretty well put to right. Skeffling, in fact, could report, 'All is well'. Elsewhere there were reports of lack of sermons or defective Bibles, but outward signs of the old religion appear to have been removed. But there were complaints of a more mundane nature. The Keyingham churchwardens reported that the chancel had fallen into decay and tactfully pointed out that as patron the archbishop was responsible for repairing it. Sixteen years previously at a visitation by Crown officials the churchwardens had reported the poor state of the chancel. The ruinous condition of church chancels was a common complaint at that time, especially from the parishioners of those churches that had passed to the Crown and then on to others after the dissolution of the monasteries.

By the end of the century there was a whole generation that had never known the old Latin service, and the uniformity of worship desired by the government was probably as well observed as it was likely to be in Holderness. At the visitation of 1596 only a handful of people in the deanery were reported as persisting in the Catholic religion and not attending the parish church. There were signs, however, that there were people walking on the other side of 'the middle way'. At Easington the vicar, Mr Johns, was showing strong leanings towards Puritanism, the more extreme wing of the

Protestant faith. He did not wear a surplice when conducting services and he did not sign babies with the sign of the cross in baptism. In Keyingham there were no such extremists although a certain Constance Thomson was reported for not attending church and not taking communion at Easter. One can imagine her as being a stubborn old lady refusing to change her ways even after nearly 40 years of the Elizabethan prayer book. There were other things amiss, too, in Keyingham. There were two 'incontinent' persons, and the archbishop was still neglecting the repair of the chancel:

'The chancell is in decay and so haithe bene manie yeres paste it is to be repayred by the L. Arch. of Yorke his Grace it haithe bene manie tymes heretofore presented in severall Visitacions withoute anie reformacione. The decayes yerelie increase and oneles the same be spedelie repayred it will fall to the grounde and so require greate chargies to be builded upp again which may be saved by lookinge to it in tyme. Thay humblie desire soom order for the survey and amendemente thereof.'

'Incontinence', in the language of Elizabeth I's time, meant having a relationship (in the language of Elizabeth II's time) outside of marriage. The couple in Keyingham would be called upon by the Church authorities to rectify the situation, if it was legally possible, and perform a penance in church before their fellow parishioners. These penances were usually very humiliating, such as standing up in church dressed in only a shift, reciting ones sins and expressing contrition before the congregation. The local Church authorities then notified the Archbishop's court that the penance had been performed. Unfortunately for the inquisitive local historian the record of such notification in the case of the two from Keyingham no longer exists.

Regarding the repair of the chancel, we can only assume that the archbishop eventually did something, as the chancel is still standing today.

- o -

The inflation that caused so many problems for Henry VIII and Edward VI continued through Elizabeth's reign and into the next century. Elizabeth dealt with the problem by exercising extreme parsimony, indulging in no wars or costly adventures abroad. Henry and Edward dealt with it by their confiscation of Church property. They also debased the currency. By withdrawing all the silver coinage and reissuing it alloyed with base metal they were able to take off the surplus silver for the exchequer. They may have temporarily solved their own financial problems but, since the intrinsic value of the coinage was lowered, they aggravated the effects of inflation felt by their subjects. Prices and wages rose. The great landlords had to try and raise their rents in order to maintain their standard of living. It was not always easy, because villein and cottager tenants had established certain rights by long custom. In fact, they were now referred to as customary tenants. They were also known as copyholders because the title to their lands was a copy, taken from the manor court roll, of the record of the transfer of the lands to them. Most of the tenants' lands in Keyingham were copyhold, corresponding to the lands that were held by villein and cottager tenure in the Middle Ages. The lands that had been held by military tenure in the Middle Ages were now described as freehold..

At the beginning of the period of inflation Keyingham was in the hands of the Crown, which appears to have been singularly lax in increasing its rents to keep pace with rising prices. By the time the Lordship of Holderness had been granted to Henry Neville, Earl of Westmorland, in 1558, who then sold it on to his son-in-law Sir John Constable of Halsham in 1560, the tenants of Keyingham appear to have established a right to fixed rents. Consequently, the copyholders of Keyingham were paying the same rents for their lands at the end of the 16th century as they had in the Middle Ages, when money had more than three times the value it had in 1600. These rents persisted through to the 20th century, by which time they barely covered the cost of collection. Of course, the Constables and their descendants still had the demesne lands in Keyingham. These they could farm themselves, and get realistic returns, or they could rent them out for fixed terms, increasing the rent at each change.

Thus it was possible for the small farmer in Keyingham to do quite well for himself from the middle of the 16th century onwards. His rent was low and if he could produce more food than his family required the prices at the market for the surplus were good. If he could manage to purchase any more land he could prosper. As we shall see there were a number of enterprising Keyingham farmers in the 16th and 17th centuries who managed to expand their holdings and become quite well-to-do.

The Keyingham men not benefiting from the century of inflation beginning about 1530 were the labourers and the parson. For the labourers, wages rarely kept pace with the price of goods, although at least in Keyingham most cottagers had the right to pasture one or two animals and a few geese on the common pastures. Keyingham's parson was on a fixed stipend of £12. He did not even receive a portion of the tithes (as many vicars did) whose value would have at least kept pace with the cost of living. The benefice was not eagerly sought after.

Besides the alarms of inflation there were alarms of a more immediate nature during the reign of Elizabeth. In the early 1580s there were real possibilities of invasion by foreign powers from the Netherlands, France or Spain. Defensive measures were taken, and the warning system and local military forces were reviewed. The warning system consisted of a series of beacons passing any warnings of attack from the coast inland. There was no beacon at Keyingham as there was to be during the Napoleonic wars; warning of any invading craft sailing up the Humber was passed from Welwick beacon to the beacon at Patrington and thence to Boreas Hill in Paull and another beacon in Paull and on to Marfleet and then to Tranby on the west of Hull.

The local forces were raised by muster, all the able-bodied men between the ages of 16 and 60 being liable to serve. The men had to be provided with armour and weapons at the village's expense although men of above a certain wealth also had to provide weapons and armour in proportion to their wealth. In 1584 Keyingham could raise 40 able-bodied men. For comparison, Ottringham raised 80 men and Patrington 63. These men were assessed for their ability to handle different weapons, the sturdier men being called on to be pike- and billmen, and the more dextrous to be musket men or archers. Keyingham's 40 men were made up of nine pikemen, 14 billmen, seven musket men, five archers and five labourers. The task of the labourers was to dig any ditches and other works needed to impede the advance of enemy landing parties. The village's weaponry and armour consisted of five muskets, one bill, six helmets, a protective leather jacket and pikes and armour for four pikemen. Pikes were spears, 12 to 15-foot long with a 12-inch, or longer, iron head. Bills were similar, but with a kind of axe-blade incorporated into the head. Even though not all the men were selected for training, Keyingham seems to have been a bit short on weapons. There was only one bill to go round and there were no bows and arrows for the archers. There was a similar situation in other villages. Historians consider it fortunate for England that the Spanish Armada was unable to land its army of crack troops in 1588.

There was only one man in Keyingham rich enough to provide weapons on his own account, Richard Awchon supplying one of the sets of equipment for a pikeman. This was about the minimum that a private person could be assessed for and indicates that he held land in his own right worth about £5 a year.

As part of the preparations for defence a survey and map of the seacoast from Scarborough to Hull was made in about the year 1580. Amongst other things notes were made of where invading ships could land. At Withernsea, for instance, there were 'two small creekes for landing of fysher bootes wherein small shippes at spryng tyde may also enter and do annoyaunce'. It was also remarked that there were two breaches in the sea wall at Saltaugh. These were Crown lands 'And therefore the said breaches ought to be made and amended at hyr Highnes Coste expences and charges, or ellse the countrey and hir Maiesties Landes there wilbe drowned'. It was probably the state of flooding at Saltaugh that prevented the Crown from selling off this particular piece of property confiscated at the Dissolution. The best the Crown could do was lease it out. In the 1580s it was being leased to Richard Awchon, as already noted, the only man in Keyingham of sufficient wealth to supply weapons and armour towards the national defence. Awchon would appear to be one of those farmers able to benefit from the rising cost of commodities and take on extra land. He was also leasing Bridlington Priory's former lands in Ottringham. The annual rent he paid to the Crown for Saltaugh was £13.6s.8d. This was low, consideration being taken of the fact that the sea walls, ditches and buildings were in such a poor state of repair that, according to the information of the inhabitants, £200 or more would be required to put matters right. One of the conditions of the lease was that Awchon undertook all repairs over the 30-year term of the lease.

Beginning in the middle of the 16th century the men of Keyingham came to have more and more public responsibilities. Since the Middle Ages they had had certain duties as tenants of the manor. They might have to serve as jurors at the Burstwick manor court, suffering fines for non-attendance. They might be called on to act as constables, aletasters, or inspectors of bread or carcasses, all of which duties were unpaid. Also, as parishioners, they would have to take their turn at serving as one of the two churchwardens, with all the responsibilities hinted at in the visitation returns mentioned above. From 1555 their duties as parishioners began to expand, as the Tudors came to use the parish more and more as a unit for civil administration.

It was in 1555 that a law was passed making the parish responsible for the roads within its boundaries. The roads of those times were in the main mere tracks, passable in summer by horseback and on foot but usually difficult to traverse with wheeled vehicles or in the winter months. They had not prevented travel in the Middle Ages (witness the great pilgrimages; the journeying of monks and lay brothers between their monasteries and their granges; the de Fortibus officials travelling between estates stretching from Holderness to Cumberland and down to Devon and the Isle of Wight; and the officers of the Archbishop conducting their visitations) but they had restricted it. As commerce began to expand in Tudor times it became more necessary to facilitate overland transport. The 1555 statute required the parishioners to give four days a year free labour towards the repair of the roads and to annually elect two honest persons to organise and oversee the work. In 1563 a second Act increased the labour to six days, each working day to be of eight hours.

The men chosen to oversee the work were usually referred to as the surveyors of highways. Their unenviable task was to organise their neighbours in carrying out road repairs on six days of the year. The poor man gave his labour. Richer men, depending on the amount of property they had in the parish, might provide a horse or a horse and cart to help carry out the work. In the course of time statute labour, as it was known, became commuted to a rate. It was then the surveyors' duty to collect the rate and expend it properly on the repair of the roads. The office of surveyor continued until 1894 when parish councils came into being.

Statute labour was notoriously inefficient. William Harrison, writing in the time of Elizabeth I, commented that '...the rich do so cancel their portions and the poor so loiter in their labours that of all the six, scarcely two good days' work are performed.' One can imagine a Keyingham farmer being quite happy to tip a load of gravel into the potholes outside the gate leading to his stackyard but when it came to repairing the roads leading out of the village it might be a different matter.

Holderness roads were well known for their impassability in the wet season and even foot passengers foundered. In the March of 1615 a certain Marmaduke Stutt of South Frodingham was found drowned in Winestead Lane, and eight years later, also in March, George Tummond, a Patrington butcher, 'coming from an Alehouse in Ottringham' was found at dawn in Winestead bottoms. He died a few hours later. The road going west from Keyingham towards the bridge over the drain passes over a long stretch of carr-land. The road in fact was a causeway, as can still be seen today. (Higher up the drain the road crossing from Halsham to Burstwick is called Causeway Ings Road.) For the parishioners of Keyingham there would have been a difficult choice - maintain the causeway at a height making for safe and comfortable travel or leave it low enough for the winter flood waters to run off their pastures to the north. The parish could be fined or have an extra rate imposed if their roads were thought to be bad. As one of the local Justices was usually a member of the Hildyard family with property interests in Winestead and Hull, it may be that Keyingham erred on the side of caution and maintained a passable causeway.

Another duty that came to be thrust on the parish in the Tudor period was the care of the poor. In the middle of the 16th century an attempt to deal with the problem of poverty had begun with the government calling on the parsons to urge their congregations to put more in the poor box. When this proved insufficient Elizabeth's government in 1598 passed an Act for the Relief of the Poor, which was renewed in 1601 and remained in force until 1834. Under the Act the parish came to be responsible for the care of the poor within its boundaries. The office of overseer of the poor was created. The average-sized parish usually had two overseers, 'substantial householders', who were elected annually. It was their job to collect the rate decided on by the parishioners and use it to maintain orphans, the disabled and the out-of-work. To cater for the last group the overseers were required to provide work by laying in a stock of materials, such as wool, to be worked up into finished products. Like the surveyors of highways the overseers were unpaid.

Thus by the end of the 16th century the public duties of the parishioner of anything like reasonable standing had been extended. There had always been duties of such kind but now a man could be expected to serve the community as manor juror, constable, alefiner, churchwarden, surveyor of highways or overseer of the poor. All were duties served annually but in a small village they could come round pretty frequently.

9 - Civil War and Revolution

When the 17th century opened, Keyingham's long-established system of local government by the manor court, meeting at three-weekly intervals at Burstwick, was still continuing. The aletasters were kept just as busy in the 17th century as they had been since the manorial records began in the 14th century, with regular breaches of the assizes of ale and bread. In 1656 Margaret Ingleby was fined 3d (1.25p) for breaking the assize of bread, that is selling loaves below the required weight. At the Michaelmas courts of 1651 and 1652 a total of seven men were fined for selling poor-quality ale. Edward Dishworth and Anthony Cornwall were fined at both these courts and also at the Easter court in between. It may be that, as these men were brewing regularly and yet only being fined the same small amount at the six-monthly court, the penalty was more in the way of a licence fee than a fine.

In the 17th century, in addition to the manorial officers of constables, aletasters and pennygraves mentioned in Chapter 5, the homage was also choosing a pinder and two bylawmen. It was the pinder's duty to round up any stray livestock and keep it in the village pinfold until a fine had been paid for its release. It was not unknown for people to try and 'rescue' their animals from the pinfold. In 1658 Elizabeth Verity was fined 12d for her swine and geese trespassing in the West Field and the Ings. She compounded the offence by committing a fold breach and was fined a further 3s.4d (17p). The pinfold was at one time situated at the west end of Waldby Garth Road, then known as Pinfold Lane.

It was the duty of the bylawmen to report to the homage any infringements of the village laws ('by' is a Scandinavian word for village) passed at the manor court. The offenders were then brought to the court and fined. The various village officers could themselves be fined for neglect of duty. In 1651, for example, John Gooseman and John Bird were each fined for not carrying out their bylawmen duties correctly. Perhaps the mantle of office did not sit comfortably on their shoulders: when not in office they themselves were sometimes guilty of infringing the law, John Gooseman, for instance being fined in 1652 for allowing his pigs into the West Field at the wrong time of the season.

The bylaws were designed to ensure good husbandry of the land, and that neighbours did not steal a march on each other. In an area where drainage was so important the bylaws were particularly concerned with keeping the ditches clear. There will be further reference to this later in this chapter. Other bylaws were passed to protect crops. In 1658 it was ordered 'that noe inhabitant turne their horse loose in barley seed time in pain [penalty] of every defalt - 2s (10p)'. Infringements of the laws regarding the trespassing of animals were numerous. At the court held on the 4 August 1652, 18 villagers were fined amounts up to a shilling for allowing their geese and pigs into the arable fields outside the stipulated times of the year. Elizabeth Verity was not alone in her misdemeanour.

In addition to their ancient manorial duties and responsibilities, the people of Keyingham had the duties imposed on them as parishioners by the Tudors. At the start of the 17th century they had had 50 years to get used to maintaining the roads within their boundaries. Now they were having to accustom themselves to the running of the Poor Law in their parish. As the overseer of the poor was a parish officer he was elected at the same time as the other parish officers - the churchwardens and the surveyors of highways. The election took place in church at Easter. When the constables came to have duties connected with the Poor Law they, too, in time came to be elected at the parish meeting rather than at the manor court. Some of the parish duties were onerous and time-consuming, especially the overseer's, and they were often carried out by rotation rather than election. Because the overseers were handling public money - collecting the poor-rate and disbursing relief - they had to produce a set of accounts at the end of their year of office. Unfortunately, no accounts of the overseers of the poor for Keyingham have survived but we do have one indication of their activity in the early 17th century. It occurs in the parish register, which records the apprenticing of Keyingham's poor children in the year 1616:

'A list of all the poore children dwelling in the parish of Keyingham in the year of our lord god 1616 putte apprentice by the consente of the minister churchwardens and the overseers of the same towne for the time being the xxviiith day of April 1616. And till evrye man childe shall accomplishe the full age of xxiiii years and evrye woman childe to accomplishe the full age of xxi years and then to surcease'

The names of ten boys and three girls then follow, with the names of those to whom they were to be apprenticed. Adam Shields, for instance, was to go to William Halliday, and Barbara Hearon was to go to John Taylor. The apprenticing of poor children, up to the ages of 24 for boys and 21 for girls, was a requirement of the Poor Law. However, in the case of Keyingham the children were not being apprenticed to a true trade - they were being taken on as farm servants. Thirteen apprenticeships in one year is a large number for a village the size of Keyingham. These were the early years of the Poor Law and it may be that the local Justice of the Peace had had to remind the inhabitants of their duties, and the large number of apprenticeships was due to a backlog. On the other hand, it may be that 1616 was a year when some fatal disease left a large number of orphans to be taken care of by the parish. This cannot be confirmed because the burial register is defective for the early part of the century. The farmers who took on these 'apprentices' were just the same men who carried out the many parochial and manor-court duties. They perhaps provide a good example of communal responsibility, although we shall never know how they treated their charges.

Church worship in Keyingham probably quietly followed the Middle Way required by authority. Any wall paintings in the church would have been whitewashed over long ago and all images removed. Because the emphasis was now on preaching there would be a pulpit for the preacher. A plan of the church interior drawn just before the restoration work of the 1880s shows that the pulpit was in the same position as it is today. Fixed into the wall within reach of the preacher there is still an hourglass stand. It is said to date from the time of Elizabeth I. It contained the hourglass, which the preacher turned over at the beginning of his sermon. He was expected to continue preaching until the sand ran out. The present glass in the stand belonged to Mr W Richardson, who illustrated it in the book *A History of Withernsea*, which he wrote with G T J Miles in the early years of the present century. On the death of Mr Richardson in the 1920s, his widow gave the glass to Keyingham church.

Because sermons could occupy such a long time, congregations were no longer expected to stand through the service as they did in the Middle Ages. They began to provide themselves with box-pews - benches in compartments with high sides to cut out the draughts. The first pews were probably built in the middle of the nave. Two of the aisle pillars, one on the north and one on the south, were cut away to take the backs of pews. When the pews were replaced with the present ones during the Victorian restoration work the recesses were repaired with new stone. The repair marks indicate how high the backs of the old pews were, bearing in mind also that the floor level was raised in Victorian times. During the early years of the 17th century more box-pews were built in the aisles at the expense of the families who used them. Pews were bought, sold or bequeathed as people died or left the parish. In 1775, for example, a pew, four and a half foot by three foot, was assigned to Thomas Jackson, yeoman of Keyingham, 'for the use of himself and his family to sit kneel pray and hear divine Service and Sermons in so long as he shall continue to be a parishioner and inhabitant of the said parish and duly Frequent the said church'. The pew was adjoined on the south by the 'pew where Matthew Kemp usually sits', on the west by the 'pew where Mary Wintringham, widow, now sits' and on the east by the churching pew. This last was the pew where a new mother would sit for the Service of Thanksgiving of Women after Childbirth.

In the early 17th century the chantry chapel built by Philip Ingleberd was probably used as a vestry, where the minister donned his vestments before celebrating communion. However, after the Civil War, when services were of a more Puritan nature and vestments were abolished, the vestry took on a new use. The Easter meeting for the election of parish officers took place in church, and it was probably in order to have a more comfortable meeting place that the vestry was blocked off from the rest of the church and a fireplace installed. Because the vestry was also used as a schoolroom a new doorway to the outside was inserted in the east wall. Pupils, and parishioners attending the Easter, or Vestry meeting, as it was also called, now had to enter the vestry directly from the outside, helping to preserve the sanctity of the church. The vestry, with its long association with St Philip Ingleberd, found favour as a place of burial, despite Protestant views on saints. An entry in the register tells us that Robert Jellison, son of Robert Jellison the minister, was buried in the school-house called St Philip's Aisle in 1713. Other members of the Jellison family, including the minister, were also buried there. One wonders how the pupils reacted each time they found the floor of their classroom newly disturbed. Because of such burials churches always had their peculiar odour. Piles of surplus excavated soil stood around so that graves could be topped up as the earth subsided.

For most of the 17th century spiritual life in Keyingham would seem to have been at a low ebb, with rarely a minister to take the Sunday services. The benefice was certainly vacant in 1632, '33 and '34 when assessments for the 10% annual tax to the Crown were carried out. In 1632 Preston was the only other vacant benefice in Holderness, and in the other two years Keyingham was the only one vacant. There is in fact no record of a vicar being instituted at St Nicholas in the 17th century, and the church probably relied on ministers coming from other parishes. Robert Jellison, for example, was vicar of Burton Pidsea from 1692 until his death in 1717, when he chose to be buried at

Keyingham. In the first quarter of the century Alexander Barden and Thomas Verity each acted as minister at Keyingham when they were also serving as the minister at Ottringham. In 1662, Thomas Elliot served as minister at Keyingham whilst he was rector of Hilston, ten miles away on the Holderness coast. It would have been difficult for him to provide a Sunday service at both places in the winter months.

The vestry, 1978. A modern altar has been placed in the position of the stone altar of Philip Ingleberd's time, and a modern statuette has been placed on the bracket that would have supported a figure of a saint in the Middle Ages. The medieval piscina, visible in the south wall to the right of the bracket, was blocked in after the Reformation, not to be revealed until restoration work in the 19th century. Following the Reformation all entry to the chapel from the church was blocked off, and the chapel became a schoolroom and the meeting place for the annual Vestry. There is a small doorway to the left of the altar this was inserted to allow entry directly from outside without having to pass through the church. The doorway was blocked in the 19th century.

The problem at Keyingham was the extremely low stipend afforded to a vicar there, despite the fact that he was the archbishop's appointee. The stipend, which had been fixed in the middle of the 14th century, was worth less and less owing to inflation. For example, by 1641 the rectorial estate, that is the glebe land and tithes, of Keyingham had come to be worth nearly £200 a year to the archbishop, compared with the £33.50 going to Meaux Abbey in 1535. Out of both amounts £12 was paid to the vicar. It was not until about 1670 that the Archbishop raised the stipend to £20.

The Middle Way of worship required by the king and the archbishops in the early part of the 17th century did not go far enough towards Protestantism to suit the Puritan element in the country. This, and the differences between a monarch, who believed in the Divine Right of Kings, and a parliament that wanted more constitutional government, eventually led to the outbreak of the Civil War in 1642, with Royalists on one side and Parliamentarians on the other. In the early months of 1642, before the opening of hostilities proper in the August, Parliament had taken control of the walled town of Hull, where Charles I had previously laid up an arsenal. Parliament appointed Sir John Hotham, of Scorborough, near Beverley, as governor of the town, and it was he who, on a famous occasion, refused Charles entry to Hull in the April. Consequently, Charles gathered troops together and laid siege to the town in the July. As one of the defensive measures Hotham ordered the cutting of the banks of the Humber and the River Hull. The surrounding countryside was flooded, greatly hampering the movement of the besieging Royalists but also ruining the crops within a four-mile radius of Hull, including those in Holderness. Any inclinations which the people of Holderness might have had towards Parliament were dispelled, especially as Hotham had also rounded up the sheep and cattle from around Hull to feed his garrison and unlawfully taken men from the village militia to defend the town. In Hull, for its part, any Royalists sympathies quickly evaporated when the Royalists bombarded the town for a fortnight before lifting the siege. In the East Riding the Civil War became mainly a difference between the conservative elements of the countryside and the radical elements in Hull.

With a large part of his arsenal tied up at Hull the king needed to look elsewhere for arms and ammunition. Almost as soon as Parliament put Hotham in charge at Hull, Charles had sent his queen, Henrietta Maria, to Holland with the crown jewels in order to purchase munitions. At the end of June sufficient had been obtained to be sent back to England on a small ship, the Providence. However, the Providence was intercepted by the Parliamentary ship, the Mayflower, and chased up the River Humber towards Hull. Fortunately for the Royalists there were men aboard the Providence who knew the Humber well, and off Paull they turned the ship about and sailed along a channel between Cherry Cobb Sands and the Humber shore. Today, Cherry Cobb Sands is an extensive piece of fertile land attached to the mainland but in 1642 the sands were off shore and visible only at low tide. The channel was too shallow for the Mayflower to follow, and the Providence was able to enter the mouth of the Keyingham Fleet and there unload her cargo of 'six pieces of ordnance' which were escorted by the local militia to Beverley, the Royalist headquarters during the siege of Hull. On July 6, in the early days of the siege, the king journeyed from York to Beverley to view the guns from Holland. It was probably at Beverley that he received a petition signed by about three hundred of the Holderness gentry and other inhabitants complaining of Hotham's actions. The signatories included Robert and Christopher Hildyard of Winestead and Francis Cobbe of Ottringham.

In the following year a much more serious siege of Hull took place. It opened on 2 September and it did not end until the Royalists withdrew on 12 October. Holderness men were part of the Royalist forces - an entry in the Patrington parish register for November 12 records the baptism of Thomas Dunn, son of the widow of Thomas Dunn, killed before Hull on 1 October.

Oliver Cromwell's victory at Naseby in June 1645 virtually brought the Civil War to an end. All the Parliamentarians had to do now was to pay their army and their allies, the Scots. One solution was to fine their defeated enemies. The wealthier Royalists were assessed for the value of their real estate and movable goods and fined two years' income from the former and one-tenth the value of the latter. The great majority of the gentry in the southern half of Holderness were Royalists and were fined, including three of the Hildyards from Winestead, Christopher Hildyard of Routh, Sir Francis Cobbe of Ottringham, two of the Holmes of Paull, William Rand of Preston, William Richardson of Ganstead and John Angell of Saltaugh Grange. Saltaugh had come into the hands of Robert Angell, John's father, in the earlier part of the century. Robert and his brother William were London merchants, one a grocer and one a fishmonger, who appear to have acquired property in South Holderness by finding flaws in the existing claimant's title, especially to former monastic property or to property subject to erosion and deposition by the sea. Thus the Angells had gained Meaux Abbey's former grange of Saltaugh, Bridlington Priory's former lands in Ottringham

and the ever-fluctuating Spurn Point. It was William's grandson, Justinian, who built the first lighthouse of modern times at Spurn.

John Angell, fined because 'he was in arms against the Parliament', had succeeded to Saltaugh, which was valued in 1646 at £213 a year, of which the odd £13 was the rent to the Crown. His fine, at two years' value, was therefore £400 as he had no movable property. Angell pleaded extenuating circumstances in an effort to have the fine reduced: he was in debt to the tune of £300, and the annual cost of maintaining the Humber banks at Saltaugh 'amount to at the lowest 50£ sometimes 80£ and sometimes 100£ as the water is more or less, but I never knew it less then 50£'. His pleas were in vain and the full fine was imposed. The following year he died at the age of 28 and was buried in the chancel of St Nicholas Church. His resting-place is marked with an inscribed stone. His only sister, Anne, also had a wall monument erected to his memory. It was on the north wall of the chancel, but in recent years it was found to be in danger of collapsing and was removed to the north aisle where it now stands. The plinth of the memorial is still in its original position.

Anne Angell married Rev John Townson and the couple came to hold Saltaugh jointly. In 1685 Townson settled the estate on a charitable organisation, the Corporation of the Sons of the Clergy, with whom it remained until the 20th century. The Townsons and their descendants continued to farm Saltaugh for some years after its transfer to the Corporation.

With a Puritan parliament victors in the war they were now able to impose their preferred form of church worship. The Book of Common Prayer was abolished (Parliamentary soldiers burnt those from Hull's Holy Trinity Church in the market place) and the Directory of Public Worship took its place. Under this it was an offence to kneel to receive communion, use any kind of symbolism in religious ceremonies, such as the sign of the cross in baptism or the ring in marriage, or to bury a body using any kind of religious ceremony. It was against the law to observe the great festivals of the Church; Christmas Day was a day of national fasting. A few years later, in 1653, the performance of the marriage ceremony was taken out of the hands of the ministers and entrusted to the local Justices of the Peace. Couples now had to take themselves off to the abode of the magistrate, carrying with them a certificate stating that the banns had been read in church on three separate Sundays without any objections. Keyingham's parish register records that on December 7, 1653, Matthew Ward and Anne Dyne and William Adam and Margaret Fetherstone were married before Robert Overton, Justice of the Peace. He lived at Easington.

During the turbulent times of the Civil War and the years of the Commonwealth following the execution of Charles I in 1649, many new Christian sects arose. One such sect was the Society of Friends, or the Quakers, as they were more commonly known. The founder of the movement was George Fox, who began his mission in earnest in 1651. That year he came into the north of Holderness at Ulrome, making converts. He travelled south to Patrington, thence into the tip of Holderness, before returning to Patrington and then proceeding to Hull. As a result of his missionising and that of his lieutenants, Quaker congregations, or meetings as they were called, were established in the area. One such meeting was the East End Meeting, which had members in villages extending from Ottringham to Kilnsea and north to Withernsea. Another meeting was the Paull Meeting, which had members in Ryhill and Keyingham.

The Quakers were violently persecuted during the early years of their formation. They were mistrusted by parliament, both during the Commonwealth and after the Restoration. Even Cromwell, who was tolerant of most Protestant denominations and sects, was averse to the Quakers, especially as they preached pacifism to his soldiers. The parsons hated them because they refused to pay the normal dues of parishioners to the church. The magistracy, on the whole, disliked them for their apparent familiarity - because they believed all men were equal they would not remove their hats in the presence of a magistrate and addressed him in the familiar terms of 'thou' and 'thee' instead of 'you'. When brought before the courts the Quakers refused to take the oath before giving evidence, as it was against their belief - people should be relied on to tell the truth at all times, not only when they were on oath. Again, this raised the ire of the magistrates. The Quakers therefore usually received little sympathy from the bench when they were brought before the courts for offences against the State or the Church. Many Holderness Quakers were sent to the prison at York Castle, and some died there.

Because of the persecution it was a brave man or woman who stayed true to the Quaker faith in those early days, and their numbers were comparatively few. However, what they lacked in numbers they made up for in the volume and detail of their records. They meticulously recorded the minutes of their meetings, the births, marriages and deaths of their members and the persecution (or sufferings, as they called them) that they underwent. Consequently we know the names of practically every member of the movement in Holderness. There were rarely more than two or three Quakers and their families living in Keyingham. We know that John Bird was sued in 1654 by the parish clerk, Thomas Jewet, for not paying his parish entitlement towards the clerk's wages. He was sued again for the same offence in 1660, this time by Henry Whelpdale. On the first occasion the sum demanded was 8d (3.3p), and a horse worth £3 was taken from him to pay the debt. The second time a horse worth £2 was taken, 'and nothing returned'. In 1669 Daniel Hardy of Withernsea married Anne Bell of Paull 'in the dwelling house of Peter Drew in Keningham'. The following year Ralph Tennison of Keyingham married Mary Campon at Ralph Tennison's house. Ralph Tennison, however, must have had doubts about the legality of a Quaker wedding (and the consequent threat to the inheritance of any children of the marriage) for in the previous year the couple had married in church. The Quakers had great contempt for the Anglican Church and church buildings (which they referred to as 'steeple houses') and Peter Drew and Andrew Adams were called on to admonish Ralph for his misdemeanour. The outcome was that Tennison sent a letter of self-condemnation to the Holderness monthly meeting, acknowledging 'my Transgression in going to a preist to take a wife & I am condemned for it in my own conscience ...'.

The Quaker registers record the births, marriages and deaths of a few Keyingham people during the 17th century but by 1743, when the vicar of St Nicholas was required to state if there was a meeting house or any dissenters in the village, his reply was 'No'. There is no mention in the Quaker records of a meeting house in Keyingham but tradition has it that an old barn still standing on the south side of Waldby Garth Road was used for such a purpose.

When John Angell claimed he was having to spend large sums on the repairs of the Humber bank at Saltaugh, he was probably exaggerating. Well before he was making his plea the process of erosion along the Humber shore seems to have come to a halt and the long slow cycle of silting and deposition was once more beginning. Down river from Saltaugh, a six-acre island emerged by the 1660s, on the site of the lost lands of Tharlesthorpe. Today these 'sunk lands', or Sunk Island, occupy an area of over 7,000 acres. At Saltaugh itself 20 acres of new growth had been added to the estate by 1716. Although this silting eventually produced new and fertile lands, it caused problems for the farmers of Keyingham. The water from the ditches and dikes draining their lands now had to take a longer and longer route through accumulating silts to the Humber. Throughout the 17th century Keyingham's representatives at the Burstwick manor court were systematically setting out which section of the drainage system was to be thoroughly scoured by the inhabitants. For example, at the Easter court in 1652 it was 'Ordered by the homage that the dike betwixt langbrigge lane end and the west carre be sufficiently slowed [sloughed] and groundscoured before 20 May in paine of every cord undone xiid [i.e. 12 old pence or a shilling]'. This was one of four lengthy stretches of dike that were ordered to be scoured that year. It was not until the 18th century, when the Keyingham Level Drainage Board was formed, that the problems presented by the formation of new siltlands began to be overcome.

John Angell was paying an annual rent to the Crown of just over £13 for Saltaugh Grange, virtually the same rent as Richard Awchon was paying in the 1580s. Angell cleared £200 a year from Saltaugh. We do not know what Awchon's returns were, but in 1535 Meaux Abbey netted £10 from the grange. Comment has already been made in the previous chapter regarding the tardiness of the Crown in raising rents in a period of inflation and how it was possible for a Keyingham farmer to take advantage of low rents established by custom during the Crown's possession of the manor. The 17th-century manor court rolls show old-established farming families, such as the Tennisons, Hallidays, Hutchinsons and Goosemans, building up their holding to 50-100 acres, and becoming moderately wealthy. Some, such as the Goosemans and Hallidays moved from the husbandman class to the yeoman class, suggesting that they also had freehold property (the transfer of which is not recorded in the manor rolls) as well as copyhold property in Keyingham. Members of the Tennison and Hutchinson families became wealthy enough by the 18th century to be designated 'gentlemen'. The story of the Goosemans provides a nice example of small farmers improving their holding and expanding their farming interests.

On the evidence of wills at the York registry, the Goosemans, like the Hutchinsons and Tennisons, were living in Keyingham from at least as early as the beginning of Elizabeth's reign. In the 17th century we find the Goosemans performing all the usual manorial and parochial duties. A John Gooseman was one of those farmers who, in 1616, took on one of the poor children of the village as a farm servant. In the years around the middle of the century a John Gooseman frequently served as one of the Keyingham homage at the Burstwick manor court and also acted as bylawman and pennygrave. The parish register, deficient though it is for that period, shows him to have been churchwarden in 1629 (the churchwardens along with the minister were required to sign each page of the parish register). Gooseman, no doubt, would have served the other parochial duties of surveyor of highways and overseer of the poor many times in his career. When he died in 1654 he held about 70 acres of land copyhold. Most of this land was, of course, distributed as portions and strips throughout the meadows, carrs and the two arable fields. Two years before his death he was busy consolidating some strips into a compact block of land. In half a dozen transactions with William Halliday, William Tennison, Matthew Hutchinson and others he received nine strips totalling five acres, all on the 'South Hill'. In exchange he gave strips in various other parts of the two arable fields. It was easier to work a group of strips all together, but it seems to have been Gooseman's intention to enclose the block, probably to use it for pasture instead of arable at a time when meat prices were attractive. Gooseman appears to have carried out his intention for at his death some of his lands were described as 'intacks', that is land 'taken in' from the common fields. Later, the Gooseman intacks were described as being on the South Hill with buildings on them (the site is now occupied by Manor Garth). To compensate the rest of the community for the loss of common pasture when the rest of South Hill lay fallow, Gooseman may have had to pay an annual fine, or open the gates of his enclosure to others' livestock at the time of common pasturing.

John Gooseman's farming interests were not confined to his copyhold lands. In 1653 he was leasing the rectorial estate at a rent in excess of £200 a year, which gives some indication of his wealth. Thus he was cultivating the glebe land, which totalled more than his own copyhold, and collecting the tithes of his fellow villagers. The fact that he was prepared to collect the tithes and hopefully profit from their sale suggests contact with the markets. In the same way that the Goosemans were taking on more than their copyhold lands, so were the Hutchinsons. In the parish registers they are frequently described as 'of the Marsh'. As mentioned in Chapter 5, Keyingham Marsh was the demesne lands of the manor, which, by the 17th century, the Constables were leasing out for fixed terms. Thus, the Hutchinsons, besides having copyhold lands at the ancient fixed rents, were also in a position to pay the current, realistic, rent being asked for one of the farms into which the Marsh had been divided. The will of a descendant of John Gooseman, another John Gooseman who died in 1710, shows that he, too, had land in the Marsh in addition to his copyhold lands. We can see in all this the change from the medieval family-run farm of 20-30 acres, providing enough for the family's wants, to a larger, more business-like establishment, catering for the markets and needing the employment of hired labour.

The Puritan regime, during which the first John Gooseman happened to die, could not survive for long in England - the ordinary Englishman prefers feasting to fasting at Christmas. In 1660, the exiled son of Charles I was restored to the throne as Charles II. With his restoration came the restoration of the old form of worship, which followed the Book of Common Prayer. Although there had previously been a custom, dating from the time of Henry VIII, to display the royal coat of arms in churches it now became more common as a sign of loyalty to the restored monarchy. In Keyingham's church the coat of arms, painted on a board, was placed above the chancel arch. It was flanked on either side with boards on which were painted the Ten Commandments. At Ottringham

these features still exist, although they have been removed to the back of the church.

- o -

Two years after Charles II came to the throne parliament discovered that, in order to run the country, even in peacetime, it needed money over and above that derived from the usual revenues. Supplementary taxation was therefore imposed. One of the new taxes was Hearth Money. Under the Hearth Tax an annual due of 2s (10p) was collected for every hearth in a house. It was to be collected in two instalments by the constable of the township. The tax was payable by the occupier, not the landlord. Occupants could be excused on the grounds of poverty, that is those who were already excused from paying the church rate and the poor rate or whose house was worth less than £1 per year. The constable's return was sent to the Quarter Sessions. Fortunately for the local historian, many of these returns survive, so we know the name of each occupier in a village and how many hearths he or she had. The tax was abolished in 1689, to be eventually replaced by the Land Tax and the Window Tax.

In 1672 Keyingham's constable recorded that there were 72 houses in the village. By comparison there were 118 houses at Patrington, 24 at Winestead, 82 at Ottringham village and 18 in the hamlet of Ottringham Marsh. The occupants of 13 of Keyingham's houses were excused payment of the tax on the grounds of poverty. On the face of it, it might appear that Keyingham had 72 families, but five of the houses, with only one or two hearths, are recorded as being in the occupation of Lord Dunbar. This was the then title of the Constables, Lords of Holderness, who by this time had moved their seat from Halsham to Burton

Constable. It is probable that the five houses were empty, and the constable had entered the landlord's name on his list. Keyingham's population at that time was probably less than 70 families.

The perhaps striking thing about the return is the indication of the simplicity of the houses. In Keyingham 49 had only one fireplace, that is, a single source of cooking and heating. The two most elaborate houses, with five hearths each, belonged to William Hutchinson and a Mr Wilkinson. (At Winestead Henry Hildyard paid tax on 17 hearths, and Lord Dunbar had 40 hearths at Burton Constable.) In Keyingham thriving farmers like the Hallidays and Tennisons had no more than three hearths, and the Goosemans had only two. It was probably a two-hearth house that John Gooseman the elder occupied when he died in 1710. The inventory of his household goods, taken for the purpose of proving his will, showed them to be in four ground-floor rooms and two upper rooms. By comparing with the cottages displayed at Ryedale folk museum in the North Riding, John Gooseman's kitchen would have contained one fireplace with its back to the fireplace in 'ye house' or main living room. The 'house', with its table, a form and seven chairs was where everyone, including the farm servants, ate. The other two ground floor rooms probably led off the 'house' at the end remote from the fireplace, and would be unheated. One was a bedroom-cum-sitting room with one bed, a table and five chairs. The other contained three beds and a linen chest. The upper chambers were probably dormers immediately beneath the thatch and reached by a ladder. They contained 'One Bed & Bedding, Corn & other Implements'.

If John Gooseman's house was simple, that of the vicar was even simpler. 'A Terrier of the proffitts belonging to the Viccar of Kainingham' in 1685 shows that in addition to his miserable stipend of £20 from the archbishop he had a vicarage consisting of 'three low rooms', namely a kitchen, a bedroom-cum-sitting room and a back room. Small wonder that there were no ministers prepared to take on the living as their sole source of income. The vicarage did, however, have a little stable, which would have proved convenient for those ministers riding over from other parishes to take services at Keyingham. The vicarage and its grounds occupied part of the green, now known as the Garth, at the junction of Station Road and Waldby Garth Road. A house like the vicarage was a fairly impermanent affair, and it took on a new form in the 18th century. In 1764 it consisted of only two rooms, separated by a passage that ran from the front of the house to the back. The house was about 40 foot long and 14 foot wide and was built of wood, mud and thatch. In 1743 the minister was John Pearson. He lived in Keyingham, although he also served at Burton Pidsea. He described the vicarage as 'only a Poor mud Cottage & therefore I live at another house in this Town'. This may have been the house now called the Old Vicarage, dateable to this period, in Station Road. By 1777 the vicarage on the green no longer existed.

The simplicity of the house and belongings of a 17th century villager are emphasised by the full inventory of John Gooseman's movable goods, which included, besides his furniture and personal possessions, all his livestock, agricultural equipment, corn, etc. Their total value was £207. This was somewhere at the lower end of the scale of wealth of a yeoman, which is what John Gooseman described himself as in his will, but he was wealthier than most other folk in Keyingham. Despite this, none of his possessions can be described as luxury goods. Even a gentleman like

The Old Vicarage, June 1992. Dating from the mid-18th century it may have been the house used by John Pearson in 1743 in preference to the vicarage of mud, wood and thatch that stood on the site of the present-day Garth.

John Townson of Saltaugh, who died in 1693 and whose goods totalled £1683 in value, could boast only a chest of drawers, a looking glass and a clock above the usual run of household furniture. There is no mention of silverware or the like. Townson's house was two-storied and probably timber-framed - the present Saltaugh Grange was found to have some timber framing when alterations were made in the middle of the 20th century. In 1693 its best bedroom was upstairs, as was the servants' bedroom. Townson was not living in Keyingham when the Hearth Tax return was made in 1672, so we do not know how many fireplaces his house had.

At the other end of the social scale - those families with only one hearth, and especially those excused paying the Hearth Tax - people must have lived in houses of the starkest simplicity, smaller even than the vicarage. There are no surviving probate inventories for Keyingham labourers of this period, but one for John Brown of Welwick, 'labouring man', who died in 1690, shows his worldly goods to be valued at well below £5. No separate rooms are mentioned in the inventory, so he may well have lived in a one-roomed house. There is another side to the coin, however. John Brown's most valuable possessions were his seven sheep and four lambs, valued at just under £2. Many of Keyingham's cottagers must have been in a similar position of having livestock which they could pasture on the common lands, so making them partially independent of wages as a labourer. A little over a century later this independence was to be taken from them.

It is interesting to reflect on what was the fuel being burned in the hearths rendering revenue to the government. In Keyingham it was rarely, if ever, coal. No fuel is mentioned in the inventories of either John Gooseman or John Townson, although the omission may have been an oversight by the valuers. John Brown had 'one hundred of whins' - a cartload of gorse. Gorse was frequently used as fuel in Holderness - the overseers of the poor at Withernsea in the 18th century often accounted for a hundred of whins delivered to one of their charges. In Keyingham, gorse may well have been allowed to grow in the carrs, and an area in the Ings known within living memory as Whincups may have been a copse set aside specially as a source of fuel. Whinhill in Ottringham may have served a similar purpose.

The probate inventory of Robert Greenshaw of Patrington, who died in 1680, listed together 'Whinns Turves and Helmwood'. A helm was a temporary wooden structure that provided a raised platform on which to store crops and under which farm implements could be stored or cattle could shelter. Robert Greenshaw's helmwood was either timber for making a helm or disused timber from an old helm to be used for the fire. The turves, or peat, were certainly for the fire. In Keyingham, turves could be obtained from the Marsh on payment of 'smoke penny' to the lord of the manor. Turves could also be dug from the carrs, but as the drainage of the carr land gradually improved this source must have dwindled. Today there are no signs of peatiness along Keyingham's former carr lands, unlike there are in the aptly named Turf Carr to the east of Wawne. In Keyingham's East Field there was an area known as Great Torker. The name was probably a corruption of 'Turf Carr'. It lay on the fringe of a mere, now dwindled in size to a pond. The mere was on the boundary between Keyingham and Ottringham and was referred to as 'Keyingham Field Mere' in Ottringham's records. From earliest times it must have served as a watering place for the livestock of both communities. With the passage of time, the word 'Torker' has been further corrupted, and fields on both sides of the boundary are today called 'Turkey Bottoms', 'bottoms' meaning low-lying land. In Ottringham a nearby field on higher ground has in the last generation become referred to as 'Turkey Tops'!

There were few trees in Keyingham from which to obtain fuel and the gradual depletion of the turf supply must have presented a problem to the people of Keyingham and of South Holderness generally. The need to set aside some land for the growth of whins would also have hindered agricultural production. It was probably not until the second half of the 18th century, when Patrington Haven came to be redeveloped and Newcastle coal could be brought in by water, that fuel supplies improved in this area. Even then, the cost of transport from Patrington Haven added about 30% to the price - the Withernsea overseers paid 6d for the carriage of a 20d bag of coal for delivery to Widow Simpson.

80

- o -

Charles II died in 1685. He was succeeded by his brother James II, who was openly Roman Catholic. However, he was accepted, especially as he successfully quelled the Monmouth Rebellion soon after his accession. But when he began to install Catholics into positions of authority, against the provisions of the 1673 Test Act, the country became alarmed. James's Protestant daughter Mary and her husband William of Orange were invited to take the crown of England. William sailed from Holland and landed in Devon in November 1688. James's army, commanded mostly by Catholic officers, failed him. At Hull the Catholic governor, Sir Philip Langdale, plotted with other officers to seize the town on James's behalf. But the plan was apprehended and the Protestant officers, with the help of the town's magistrates, arrested the governor and his followers on 4 December, a day commemorated as Town-taking Day for many years after. James fled the country and William and Mary were jointly crowned early in 1689. The Great Rebellion, as it was called, was over and virtually bloodless.

William of Orange was strongly Protestant and one of his first acts as William III was to grant toleration to Protestant dissenting groups. As a consequence the handful of Quakers in Keyingham could now meet legally, as long as it was not behind locked doors and the meeting place had been licensed by a bishop. However, they could still be fined or distrained of goods for refusal to pay church dues. It was to be another century before Catholics were allowed to legally meet together for worship. Meanwhile the majority of Keyingham's worshippers went to the parish church, whenever there happened to be a minister in attendance, and called on him to marry them, baptize their children and bury their dead. There was little religious fervour, in either Keyingham's clergymen or their parishioners. It was not until the coming of Methodism to the village in the 19th century that anything like fervour was to be shown.

Left: The last vestiges of Keyingham's mere, August 1991. View from the north with the spire of Ottringham church just visible on the horizon on the left. The ditch running slightly diagonally across the picture is the boundary between Ottringham and Keyingham. The low-lying land surrounding the mere on both sides of the boundary is known as 'Turkey Bottoms'.

Most of the land that John Gooseman the elder was cultivating in the early years of the 18th century still lay scattered in numerous unfenced strips throughout the East and West Fields, as it had been for centuries. His animals, whose numbers were limited by the by-laws, still grazed alongside the animals of all the other villagers on the common pastures. He still gathered his hay from a patch allotted to him in the Ings. He still planted the crops decided on by the homage. When he sent his produce to market it went by packhorse or lurched out of the village in cart along unmade roads to Patrington or Hedon, or on to Hull if the journey was worthwhile. A century later, when Thomas Owst, another Keyingham farmer, was cultivating his lands they were grouped together in a few decent-sized enclosed fields. In those fields he could grow the crops he chose to grow, or rear the animals he chose to rear. When he sent his produce to market it went along gravelled roads to Patrington Haven or Hedon Haven, where there were well made wharves, and agents eager to buy his corn for shipment to the populace of London or the swelling West Riding towns. In the years between John Gooseman's career and Thomas Owst's there had been revolutions in industry, agriculture and transport.

When John Gooseman died in 1710 he held an oxgang of land. This was less than the holding of his ancestor John Gooseman, mentioned in the previous chapter, because the first John had divided his land between his sons. Owing to the bringing into cultivation of more land by the villagers the oxgang in Keyingham had come to be considerably greater than in the Middle Ages. During the reign of Elizabeth I a 'little new field' called Kirn Croft field was brought under the plough. For the purposes of managing the crop rotation, Kirncroft was included with the West Field. Kirncroft derived its name from a nearby plot of land, 'Crynokcroft', which had been given to the monks of Meaux Abbey by Henry Pethy about the year 1200. Pethy's name still survives in the name of a field, Petty Lands, part of the Saltaugh estate and adjacent to what was Kirncroft. In the 18th century a Keyingham oxgang consisted of ten acres of arable in the West Field and Kirncroft, ten acres of arable in the East Field, four acres of meadow in the Ings, and the equivalent, in terms of pasturage of livestock, of nine and a half acres in the West and East Carrs, the Saltmarsh and the fallow field. In all, therefore, an oxgang of land in Keyingham was equivalent to $33\frac{1}{2}$ acres. We do not know how many separate strips and plots John Gooseman's oxgang was divided into, but we do know the composition of the four and a quarter oxgangs of glebe land belonging to the Archbishop. Towards the end of the 18th century the glebe consisted of a 24-acre block of land and 28 strips in the East Field (total 51 acres); 61 strips totalling 49 acres in the West Field and Kirncroft; and 11 pieces of meadow, totalling $12\frac{1}{2}$ acres, in the Ings. The strips of arable ranged in size from a quarter of an acre to two and a half acres, and the pieces of meadow from half an acre to four acres. John Gooseman's lands would have been divided in a similar way. The tracks needed for him and his fellow villagers to move their ploughs and plough teams from one strip to another meant that a lot of land was wasted, as did the need to reserve some land for the growth of whins for fuel.

As the demand for food for the growing towns became greater, particularly after the middle of the

18th century when the Industrial Revolution got under way, it became increasingly profitable for the farmer to produce for the market. There was a need for greater efficiency in farming. One solution was to do away with the old open-field system and grant each farmer his land in compact enclosed blocks so that he could grow the crops and rear the animals that produced the best returns. He could also, by a system of crop rotation, grow produce every year instead of having his lands lie fallow one year in every two as they did in most open fields in Holderness.

Enclosure of the open fields began in Holderness before the middle of the 18th century, but it only proceeded village by village, as the majority of the owners (in terms of the amount of land held) demanded it. It usually required an Act of Parliament for the lands in a village to be enclosed, because people's old customary rights were being infringed. Some villages, however, managed to be enclosed without the cost of going to Parliament. Winestead's lands were gradually divided into separate fields by agreement amongst the owners between the early 17th century and the late 18th century. Catwick, in 1732, was the first village in Holderness to be enclosed by Act of Parliament but the great majority of Holderness villages were enclosed either in the period 1760-80 or in the period 1793-1815. In the first period the West Riding textile towns, and consequently Hull as a cloth-exporting port, were growing fast. Moreover, during this period England had wars with France and America and the import of food was difficult. In the years 1793-1815, England was at war with France and, again, the country had to rely on its own crops. Ottringham and Patrington were both enclosed in the earlier period; Keyingham had to wait until the war with Napoleon.

Around the time that Ottringham and Patrington were enclosed (in 1760 and 1768, respectively) improvements in transport began to be made in the area. In 1745 the ancient route from Hull to Hedon via Bilton and Preston was turnpiked, that is, the maintenance of the road was taken out of the hands of the surveyors of highways of those villages through which the road passed and put into the hands of a turnpike trust. The trust charged tolls on the traffic passing along the road and used the income to keep the road properly surfaced. Although the Hull-Hedon turnpike did not extend into South Holderness, it did improve the journey to Hull somewhat and its importance to the area can be judged by the fact that the list of trustees included Sir Robert Hildyard of Winestead and Henry Maister, lord of the manor of Patrington, whose country house was in Winestead and town house in Hull's High Street.

Sir Robert Hildyard was the prime mover in the turnpiking, in 1761, of the road from Hedon to Patrington and on to Patrington Haven. Henry Maister also contributed £50 towards the costs of obtaining the necessary Act of Parliament. Improving the haven at Patrington by scouring was part of the scheme. A few years later, in 1774, the Hedon Haven Improvement Act was passed. The Keyingham farmer could now cart his corn along a gravelled road to either Patrington Haven, paying his toll at the Winestead bar (close to the present Winestead Drain) or Hedon Haven, paying at the Keyingham bar on the east side of the Keyingham Drain. From the havens the corn was shipped to London or the West Riding. By the end of the century the havens were in contact, through England's extensive canal and navigation system, with places like Halifax, Barnsley and Birmingham. Many products could therefore be

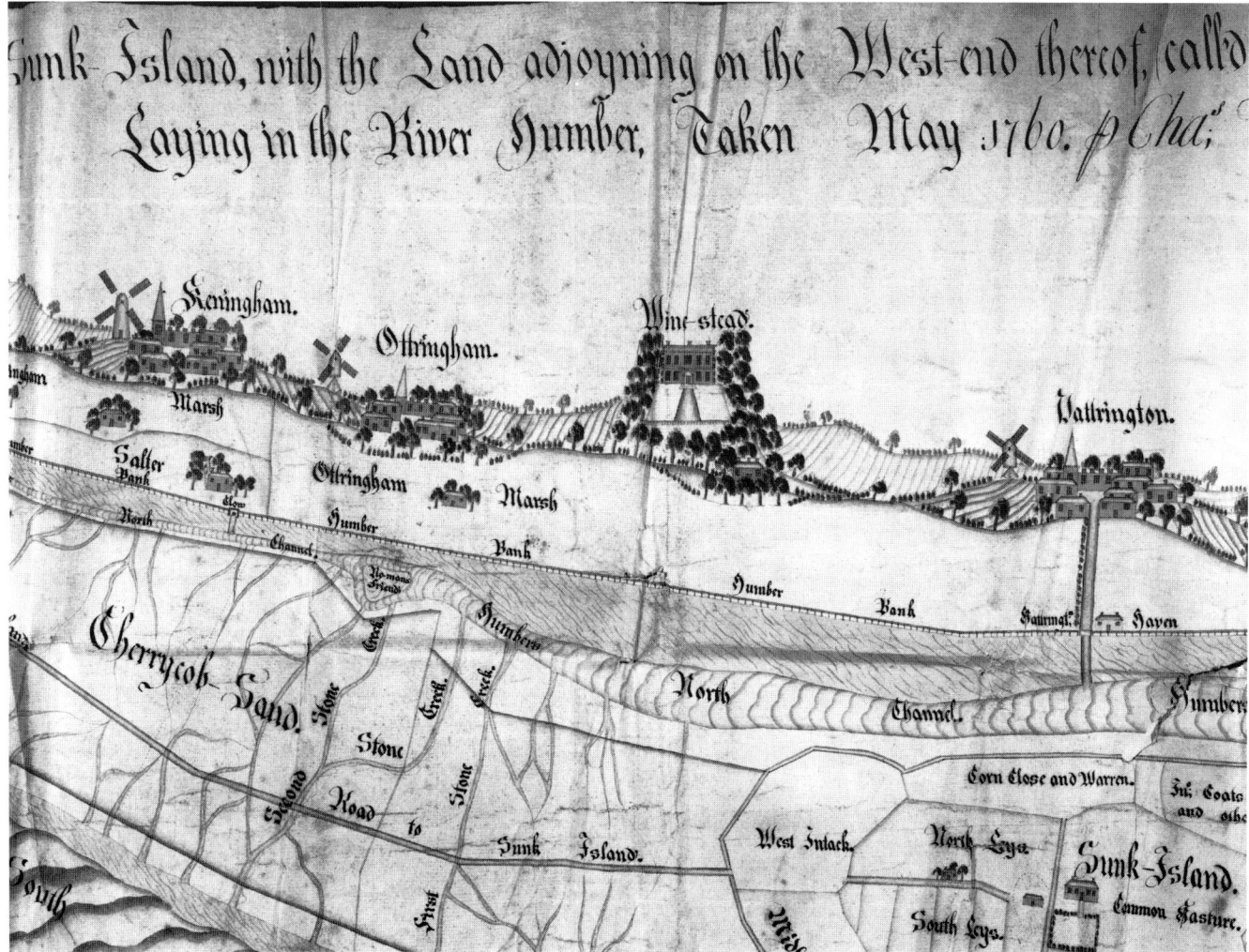

Section of Charles Tate's plan of Sunk Island, 1760. The plan shows part of Sunk Island and Cherry Cobb Sands. To the west of the section shown, Cherry Cobb Sands joins the mainland. The North Channel, containing the tiny mud bank known as No Man's Friend, is fed by the waters of the Keyingham Fleet, which is also to the west of this section. Water also enters the channel from Kirncroft Drain by way of the clow at Saltaugh. To the north the church spires and windmills of Keyingham, Ottringham and Patrington are depicted, as is Red Hall at Winestead. The four villages are all represented as having the ridge and furrow of the open-field system. South of Keyingham is marked Keyingham Marsh and Saltaugh Bank. Patrington Haven is still connected to the Humber.

By courtesy of the University of Hull, Brynmor Jones Library (ref: DRA/531).

brought easily into Holderness. If he had wished, the farmer after delivering his corn to the haven could have picked up coal, or lime for fertiliser. The havens thus provided more than one benefit to Holderness farming: they were an outlet for its produce and a means of bringing in cheap fertiliser. Even the fact that coal could be brought in meant that scrub land, reserved as a source of whins for fuel, could now be brought into agricultural production.

By an Act of 1773 milestones had to be erected along turnpikes, indicating the distance to the next large town. Those on the Hedon-Patrington Haven turnpike show the miles to Hull and to Patrington. Because the route to Hull was via Preston and Bilton the distance was about three miles longer than the present route along Hedon Road, which was not opened until 1833. The 13th milestone from Hull was in Keyingham. That stone has disappeared but quite a few others remain. One still stands about a hundred yards west of Keyingham Drain, opposite Bridge Bungalows. During the last war the markings on them had to be removed or the milestones hidden to prevent giving assistance to enemy invaders. The milestone between Keyingham and Ottringham was buried by the roadside, and was only resurrected when the footpath was being improved in 1997. It has been restored to its original position.

Before Keyingham came to be enclosed further improvements of benefit to agriculture were being made. Silting and reclamation were continuing along the Humber foreshore. By 1770 Cherry Cobb Sands were joined to the mainland. Keyingham's southern boundary was now no longer the Humber but an extended Keyingham Fleet, with the Sands, in the parish of Paull, on the other side. Keyingham's lands were not now threatened by the direct action of the Humber waves. There were, however, other problems. With the fleet having to wind a longer distance to the river, the drainage in the carrs along the fleet became impaired, and they became more subject to flooding. Up to this point the overseeing of the drainage of Holderness had been the responsibility of the Commissioners of Sewers. They ensured, through juries and the bylawmen, that watercourses were kept adequately scoured. But their efforts were insufficient to deal with the problems caused by reclamation, and in 1772 an Act of Parliament was obtained, taking the valley of the Keyingham Fleet (the Keyingham Level) out of the jurisdiction of the Court of Sewers and putting it into the hands of the Keyingham Drainage Authority, created by the Act. The Authority acted by moving the clow, at the old mouth of the fleet, further downstream to the eastern end of Cherry Cobb. The clow was a pair of gates across the fleet designed to allow the outflow of water but to prevent the ingress of the Humber at high tides. Within the new clow, called No Man's Friend Clow, the fleet was deepened and widened. The effect was a considerable improvement in conditions in the Keyingham Level.

The improvement did not last long. The fertility of the Humber silts encouraged further reclamation and by 1800 the western end of Sunk Island was joined to Cherry Cobb Sands. The Keyingham Fleet now had to continue its tortuous way along the north of Sunk Island (which was no longer an island) and past the mouth of Patrington Haven. Its draining ability was severely reduced. The solution was to cut a new drain across Cherry Cobb Sands direct to the Humber. This measure was carried out under an Act of Parliament obtained in 1802 and the drain to Stone Creek was dug. Those with a vested interest in Patrington

Haven had to be compensated for the loss of Keyingham Fleet's scouring action at the mouth of the haven. At the same time as the drain was being extended the upper reaches of the fleet were deepened and straightened, and the whole waterway became known as Keyingham Drain rather Keyingham Fleet. Above Keyingham Bridge the boundaries between the parishes were adjusted to the new course of the drain, but below the bridge the old meandering boundary between Keyingham and Ryhill was retained so that, as depicted on the Ordnance Survey map, part of Keyingham is on the west of the drain and part of Ryhill is on the east.

In the early stages of discussion about the cut to Stone Creek consideration was given to the idea of making the drain navigable and in 1800 the *Hull Advertiser* was referring to the proposed 'Keyingham Canal'. Canals were still the best answer to the transport of bulky goods. It was in 1801, for example, that the Act for the building of the three-mile Leven Canal in Holderness was being obtained. However, navigation interests usually conflict with drainage interests, one requiring the maintenance of a high water level and the other a low, and at a meeting at the Cross Keys in Lowgate, Hull, it was decided 'that the drain from Stone Creek to Roos Bridge ...should not be made navigable'.

At the end of 1801 the time seemed ripe for enclosing the open fields of Keyingham. There was the prospect of improved drainage in the carrs and, although there was a temporary armistice in the war with France, farmers were getting good prices for their corn. In the neighbouring parishes of Ottringham, Winestead and Patrington the benefits of enclosure could be seen. Even nearer home was Keyingham Marsh. This, the lord of the manor's demesne land, had been divided into separate farms, with enclosed fields, and leased out since the 15th century. These farms could be run far more efficiently despite the fact that the rents were much higher than for the unenclosed copyhold lands. At least one long-established Keyingham farming family, the Hutchinsons, had given up their copyhold lands and were farming solely in the Marsh. Towards the end of the 18th century John and William Hutchinson between them were leasing nearly half of the 1,200 acres of the Marsh.

With the benefits of enclosure obvious (at least, to the large land-holders), a meeting of the proprietors of unenclosed lands in Keyingham was called for 18 December 1801 at the Cross Keys in Hull in order 'to consider on the propriety of an Application to Parliament for an enclosure of open fields and pastures'. The Bill was also to include a measure for the commutation of the tithes of Keyingham. Although this appears to have been the first meeting of the proprietors, the sounding of their opinion regarding enclosure had been going on for some time. As early as 1793, William Iveson, a Hedon lawyer acting on behalf of the interested parties, had written to Henrietta, Baroness of Bath, asking her views on an intending enclosure. Her view was important because she was the Archbishop's lessee of the rectorial estate in Keyingham and, as such, held a large proportion of the land. The rectorial estate consisted of the four and a quarter oxgangs of glebe together with the tithes of Keyingham. Under the Bill the tithes were to be commuted to an amount of land, and the commutation was weighted very much in the tithe-owner's favour. In return for giving up the right to one-tenth of the produce, the baroness was to receive land equivalent to one fifth of the arable, one seventh of the meadows and one eighth of the pasture. When the final award was made she, in fact, received 358 acres for the glebe and the tithes of the open fields out of a total of about 1,400 acres allotted. As the rule adopted by Parliament in passing Enclosure Acts was that four parts in five of the *property* should be consenting, it must have come as a blow to Iveson and his clients when the baroness, in answer to Iveson's letter, replied, 'I am by no means an advocate for Inclosures and would not chuse to Promote the one You mention'. This no doubt caused Iveson some head-scratching. But his keen legal brain was equal to the task and he pointed out that the interest of the Archbishop must be coequal with that of Lady Bath, and the Archbishop had consented to the enclosure. This reduced the strength of the lady's objection by a half. There were no other significant dissenting parties and the Act received approval in July 1802.

Under the Act three commissioners were appointed to oversee the fair division of the lands in Keyingham. The men chosen were Thomas Wilson of Haverfield House (between Patrington and Welwick), John Hall of Scorborough, near Leconfield, and Robert Stickney of Ryhill Manor. The surveyor was Thomas Barrow of Welton. All but Wilson had wide experience in the making of enclosure awards.

Meetings between the commissioners and the landholders usually took place 'at the house of Richard Rooss, Innholder, in Keyingham'. The inn was in Main Street opposite the end of Church Lane. The first meeting was on 19 July 1802 when the commissioners swore (or affirmed in the case of Robert Stickney, who was a Quaker) to carry out their 'commission according to equity and good conscience'. Notices of meetings were posted on the church door and in the blacksmith's shop, besides being advertised in the *York Courant*, the *Hull Advertiser* and the *Hull Packet*. At the meetings the commissioners received the claims of the proprietors, listened to any objections and announced their proposals for action, such as what new roads they planned to lay out, as they proceeded with the enclosure. Claims had to be supported by the title to the lands in question. In the case of copyholders their titles were the copies, taken from the manor court record, of the entry relating to their receipt of the property.

The commissioners found that, in all, there were 41 oxgangs of land in Keyingham. Four and a quarter were the glebe. Another four and a quarter were freehold (these were the lands that had originally been held by knight service in the Middle Ages). The remaining oxgangs were copyhold. There were also some cottagers with rights of common. The make-up of the copyholders had changed considerably since the time of John Gooseman at the beginning of the 18th century. In his day they had been mostly, like himself, Keyingham men with no more than two oxgangs of land and many of them with only a fraction of an oxgang. On the eve of enclosure the major portion of the copyhold (about 21 oxgangs) as well as most of the freehold was in the hands of people from outside the village, many of them investors from the town. James Mander of Derby had four oxgangs of copyhold and three oxgangs of freehold. William Williamson, of the great Hull shipping firm of Williamsons, had four and a half oxgangs. Robert Carlile Broadley, a leading Hull banker, had over seven oxgangs (his bank, in fact, was appointed to hold the money collected to finance the enclosure).

It was not new for Hull merchants to invest in Holderness lands. The low rents that prevailed on manors like Keyingham had long attracted such investors. As early as 1556 Thomas Dalton, merchant and alderman of Hull, and who had

KEYINGHAM   AD 1805

To Burstwick

KEYINGHAM DRAIN

East Carr Road

Burstwick Foot Road

East Field Road

Ottringham Public Foot Road

pond

Gravel Pit Road

N

OTTRINGHAM

Marsh Cottage

Marsh House

Keyingham Grange

The Marsh

Pettylands

To hamlet of Ottringham Marsh

Cherry Cobb

Saltaugh Grange

SHORE LINE

River Humber

represented the borough in Parliament, was bequeathing his freehold lands in Keyingham to his youngest son Edward. Thomas Dalton, besides his property in Hull and the outlying villages of Drypool, Sculcoates and Sutton, also had lands in Patrington, another manor where the rents remained at their medieval level. Patrington continued to attract the attention of Hull merchants and shipowners in the 17th century, with prominent names like Lister, Ripley, Chambers and Barnard featuring amongst the largest landholders there. In the 17th century few, if any, Hull men ventured to buy Keyingham lands. It may be that in such times of political and religious uncertainty, becoming the tenant of the Catholic Lord of Holderness was not considered a safe investment. In the more settled times of the 18th century, however, the Scotts and the Williamsons, both of Hull, began to build up their holdings in Keyingham. It was in 1796 that Robert Carlile Broadley moved in and purchased the Scott property.

Keyingham in the year 1805. The parish is shown divided into its three main sections. To the north are the newly enclosed lands mostly of the of the copyhold tenants. In the southwest corner are the demesne lands of the Constables, lords of the manor. These lands have long been divided into farms - Marsh Cottage, Marsh House, The Marsh and Keyingham Grange - and leased to farmers. In the southeast corner is Saltaugh Grange, belonging to the Corporation of the Sons of the Clergy and in 1805 tenanted by Edward Ombler. Map by I Lanham

Broadley was a man of immense wealth, with large acreages of land throughout the East Riding. (The family soon came to be the sixth largest landowners in the riding with nearly 15,000 acres.) Broadley inherited some of his lands, but he was also active in buying lands especially, as at Keyingham, in unenclosed villages during the agricultural boom. He would then, with other leading landowners, seek enclosure and often while the process was under way buy out some of the smaller owners for whom enclosure was not going to be profitable. The reason that some of Keyingham's small farmers had sold out in the earlier part of the century, despite the low rents, was probably that they could not afford the capital investment required to take advantage of the expanding market for their produce. They continued to farm the lands as tenants of the new men and paid higher rents, but they did not have to maintain farm buildings or invest in new equipment.

Keyingham's enclosure commissioners estimated that at $33^{1}/_{2}$ acres per oxgang the 41 oxgangs due for enclosure contained approximately 1,350 acres. They also estimated that there were about 130 acres of 'ancient enclosed lands'. These were the plots adjoining the cottages but also included 'intacks' taken in over the centuries from the common fields in the same way that John Gooseman had taken in some strips of arable on South Hill in the 17th century. Following an actual survey of the lands it was found that the open fields in fact contained 1,418 acres and the old enclosures 168 acres. The reason the commissioners were interested in the old enclosures was that the tithes from them were also to be commuted to an amount of land. In this case Lady Bath, in return for giving up her right to a tenth of the produce, was to receive an area in the newly allotted fields equivalent to one seventh of the old enclosures. Other lands not subject to the commissioners' interest were the 1,200 acres of demesne land in Keyingham Marsh and the 445 acres of Saltaugh Grange belonging to the Corporation of the Sons of the Clergy.

Before allotting any lands the commissioners made it their first task to redefine old roads and lay out new ones to facilitate the movement of owners to and from the new enclosures they would be receiving. The most important road they dealt with was the turnpike passing from the gate at Keyingham High Bridge to the gate at the boundary with Ottringham. Previous to enclosure this was a gravelled track, thirty foot wide at the most, crossing the open fields. It was now marked out by a fence and ditch on either side and was fifty foot wide, although the width of the gravelled section was still a matter for the turnpike trustees to decide. Other roads marked out by fences and ditches (where they were not already defined by the boundaries with old enclosures) were Marsh Lane, Saltaugh Road and Ings Lane, all forty foot wide. These were only marked out as far as the point where they entered Keyingham Marsh. New roads, thirty foot wide, laid out by the commissioners included Eastfield Road, East Carr Road and the eastern end of Waldby Garth Road. All the roads were far wider than necessary for the traffic passing along them, but the thinking was that if a section became deeply rutted and impassable then carts and wagons could create a new track a little to one side. The width of these 'enclosure' roads accounts for the wide verges we have on some of our country roads and lanes today. No further new roads were to be laid out in Keyingham until the 1960s.

To ensure that the roads were kept in a reasonable state of repair the commissioners set aside a four-acre plot on a shallow gravelly mound to the south of the turnpike road 'to be used as a Quarry or Gravel Pit for repairs to the Highways in Keyingham'. A road, leading to the gravel pit was marked out. It was originally called Gravel Pit Road but is now known as Boyes Lane. The pit was not the first site for the removal of gravel in Keyingham: there was a site known as High Gravel Pits at the top of Marsh Lane.

As well as setting out the roads the commissioners also set out three public footpaths across the fields, and it is gratifying to note that all three are still in existence today. Four new drains and watercourses were also cut at the commissioners' direction: agriculture in Keyingham was to be improved in more than one way.

Having decided on the positions of the roads, footpaths, watercourses and gravel pit the commissioners next allotted the lands to the various proprietors. The claims of Lady Bath, elevated to Countess Bath since the passing of Keyingham's Enclosure Act, were dealt with first. She received a total of 386 acres in lieu of glebe lands and the tithes of the open fields and the old enclosures. With 31 acres of old enclosure in addition, she was by far the largest landholder in Keyingham, Robert Carlile Broadley being the next with 192 acres of new enclosures and 12 of old. Besides receiving a good deal more than one tenth of the land in compensation for forgoing a tenth of the produce, the countess also received the extra concession of having the fencing and ditching of her new lands done at the expense of the other proprietors. Such was considered to be the burden of tithes that the proprietors were willing to acquiesce to these conditions, conditions that had been dictated by the powerful Church interest in Parliament.

Others receiving large allotments, besides R C Broadley, were James Mander (183 acres), Thomas Owst (138 acres) and William Williamson (117 acres). Owst was the only Keyingham man to receive a large allotment at the enclosure. He lived at North End Farm. The family originated from Halsham and had begun buying land in Keyingham in the 1760s. Two proprietors, both from outside Keyingham, received allotments of about 70 acres. The remaining allotments were all of less than 50 acres. Because the commissioners were working on the drawing board and making their allotments with scrupulous accuracy the new fields and plots had perfectly straight boundaries. They can thus still be distinguished from old enclosures, which in the main had irregular boundaries that followed natural features such as banks or waterways.

North End Farm, April 1999. *Thomas Owst, the largest local landowner at the enclosure of Keyingham, was living here in 1805, although the house has been extensively modified since then. The evidence is that Owst was a keen planter of trees, and the trees shown may date from his time.*

ENCLOSURE AWARD 1805

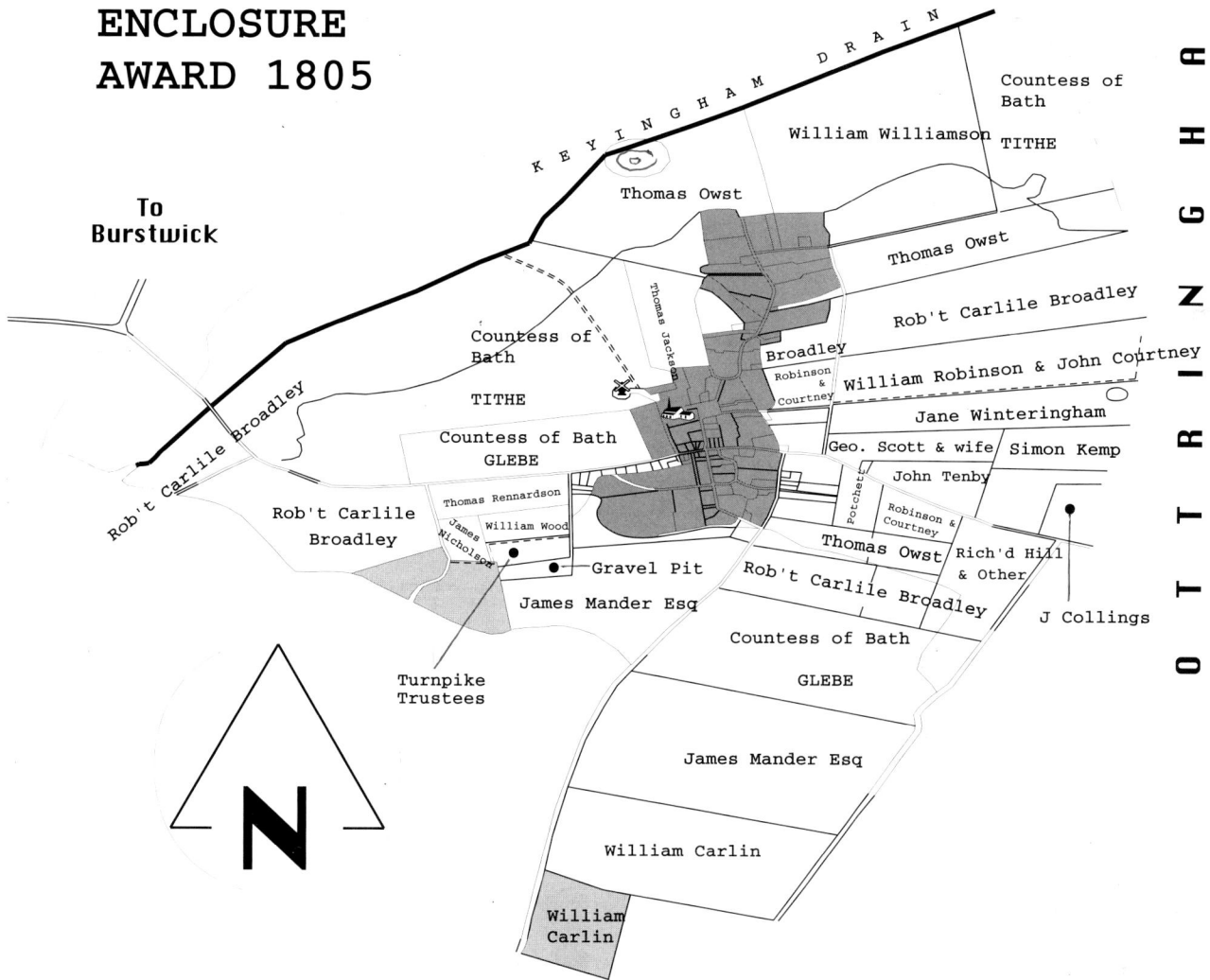

To Burstwick

KEYINGHAM DRAIN

Countess of Bath

TITHE

William Williamson

Thomas Owst

Thomas Owst

Rob't Carlile Broadley

Thomas Jackson

Countess of Bath

TITHE

Broadley

Robinson & Courtney

William Robinson & John Courtney

Countess of Bath

GLEBE

Jane Winteringham

Geo. Scott & wife

Simon Kemp

John Tenby

Thomas Rennardson

William Wood

Rob't Carlile Broadley

James Nicholson

Robinson & Courtney

Potchets

Rich'd Hill & Other

Gravel Pit

Thomas Owst

James Mander Esq

Rob't Carlile Broadley

J Collings

Rob't Carlile Broadley

Turnpike Trustees

Countess of Bath

GLEBE

James Mander Esq

William Carlin

William Carlin

N

OTTRINGHAM

The enclosure of Keyingham's common fields, 1805. The new, enclosed, fields awarded by the commissioners are shown. Most of the large awards belong to outsiders using the land as an investment. The largest holder is the Countess of Bath, the lessee of the rectorial estate. Differentiation of the lands she received in lieu of tithes and in lieu of glebe has been made. The lands of Thomas Owst, the largest Keyingham holder, have mostly been laid out close to his farmhouse at North End. Thomas Jackson was allotted 20 acres of land close to his farmhouse, the present Wray House. Note how fields cut across the old boundaries between the carrs and the former East Field and West Field (compare with the maps in Chapter 2). Some of the smaller awards are laid out along the south side of the road to Hull. The trustees of the Hedon-Patrington Haven Turnpike have been awarded a plot in a gravelly area next to the parish gravel pit. The old enclosed lands, shown shaded, have increased in area since 1300, owing to the consolidation of strips mentioned in Chapter 9. The straightening of the Keyingham Fleet to give Keyingham Drain has taken place. Map by I Lanham

In most cases the commissioners placed the new allotments next to a proprietor's old enclosure where his or her cottage or farmhouse was already sited, so making it easier to manage the new lands. Thus, Thomas Jackson received his 20-acre plot adjacent to his farmstead, which was on the site of the present Wray House. Most of Thomas Owst's new fields were next to North End Farm. Joseph Meek, the miller, received a quarter of an acre next to his mill. The major portion of the Countess of Bath's allotment stretched from the rectory farm on the north side of the church (where Ebor Manor now is) westwards to Keyingham Drain. However, like many of the outsiders with large holdings, she also received lands in the remoter parts of the parish and detached from any of the old enclosures. Some of James Mander's lands were a long way down Saltaugh Road. Others, whose only interest in the land was as an investment, had their allotments placed on the edge of the parish

by the commissioners. The Unitarian Church in Bowlalley Lane, Hull, had been endowed with Keyingham lands, and the trustees (Richard Hill and others) had their allotment placed at the corner of the Ottringham Road and Dam Lane. In other ways the commissioners showed common sense and co-operation with the proprietors. The trustees of the turnpike bought lands in Keyingham shortly before the enclosure act. They received six acres of gravelly land to the north of the gravel pit awarded to the parish. Their intention when buying had obviously been to obtain a source of material for repairs to the turnpike. Both gravel pits down Boyes Lane were used as rubbish tips in the 20th century and are now filled in.

Because it was outsiders who received the lands at the extreme edge of the parish they did not go to the trouble of building farmhouses on them. Their tenants had to farm the lands from the centre of the village. This was unlike the situation at Ottringham, where five new farmhouses, remote from the village, came into being after the enclosure. The farmhouses in Keyingham Marsh were all provided by the Constables well before the enclosure of the rest of the parish. White House Farm, down Saltaugh Road, stands on an old enclosed field and may have been built before the enclosure. Thus, Keyingham was mostly farmed from ancient farmhouses standing in the centre of the village. Some of the old enclosed land bought by R C Broadley included the farmstead later occupied by Mount Airey and its farm buildings in Chapel Lane and Ings Lane. It was from here that Broadley's tenant ran the Broadley estate in Keyingham. It is only in the last two years of the 20th century that Mount Airey has ceased as a working farm and what was the Broadley estate fragmented and sold off. Most, but not all, of the other farmsteads in the village have disappeared.

The effect of the inroads made by the tithe compensation on a person's holding can be judged by the fact that the 20 acres of land received by Thomas Jackson was in lieu of the oxgang of land he had held before enclosure. As already mentioned, an oxgang in Keyingham had amounted to about $33\frac{1}{2}$ acres. Only a small part of the decrease was due to the land taken by the commissioners for new roads, drains etc.

Besides those people receiving allotments in return for their open-field lands there were those who received land in lieu of the rights of common appertaining to their cottages. The land amounted to about a quarter of an acre for each cottage. Where possible the commissioners placed the new plot close to the cottage. Thus, Hannah Ruddiforth had a cottage on the site of what is now Bryn Ferra, the former smithy at the corner of School Lane, and received a quarter-acre plot in Saltaugh Road opposite the end of School Lane. However, because many of the cottages were in the centre of the village and surrounded by old enclosures, their associated plots had to be sited at a distance. Ten cottagers, living in the centre of the village, received small plots on the south of Hull Road in a row stretching from the corner of Boyes Lane up to Hill Top. The one at the corner of Boyes Lane was awarded to John Gibson, whose cottage, consisting of three low rooms, was on the site of the present Blue Bell Inn. In the year that the enclosure award was finalised Gibson borrowed money from John Newmarch, a Hull liquor merchant, to rebuild his cottage, which was then referred to as the public house 'known by the sign of the Blue Bell'. By the time the enclosure award was made Gibson was referred to as 'innkeeper', whereas earlier, in the parish register, he had been referred to as 'labourer'. He probably had some experience of keeping a public house, however, as his father-in-law, John Ellotson, was a publican, the first man referred to as such in Keyingham's parish register. Gibson, in changing his calling, was no doubt hoping to take advantage of the influx of labourers required to carry out the work connected with the enclosure. Gibson, or one of his successors, seems to have taken further advantage of the increase in population and the rising traffic through the village by obtaining a licence for the house built on the plot at the corner of Boyes Lane. This beer-house was known as the Spotted Cow and survived to the end of the 19th century. The first public house on the site of the Ship appears to have been opened in 1816. It was then known as the Gate and was run by farmer Thomas Lotan and his wife Jane. Later, in 1834, it was advertised for sale by Robert Elletson as the Dog and Bull Inn, along with $1\frac{1}{2}$ acres 'well stocked with choice fruit trees'. Robert Elletson is recorded in the parish register as being a gardener, a reminder that inn keeping was rarely such a flourishing trade as to be a man's sole occupation. It was in 1840 that the Ship Inn is recorded as having the name it has today. It is worthy of note that although Keyingham's housing was mainly stretched out along the north-south spine extending from North End Farm to the bottom of Ings Lane, all its inns and its beershop - The Spotted Cow, the house of Richard Rooss, The Blue Bell and The Ship - have been located on the east-west street along which the traveller passed.

More than three years after the commissioners first met, the enclosure award was finally made and published at Hedon. The date was 12 December 1805. It was proclaimed in Keyingham's church by the minister, John Tickell, the following Sunday. Its contents were now law. The allotments, roads, ditches etc. had been defined on paper by the commissioners early in the proceedings - the apparent delay in making the final award was simply that its requirements had to be carried out whilst crops were being grown and harvested. The usual procedure was to start marking out the new allotments in the open field that happened to be lying fallow. The new proprietors then got busy digging the ditches and erecting post-and-rail fences round their properties. They could then get on with farming their new lands. Marking-out and fencing then proceeded on the rest of the lands. In some cases work amongst standing crops could not be avoided. The new owner taking over crops already growing on the former strips had then to pay due compensation. Nearly £260 changed hands in this way.

There was a lot more money to be paid out. The total cost of enclosure was high and it was shared out amongst the proprietors in proportion to their allotments. Only the Countess of Bath was exempt. Commissioners' and surveyor's expenses were usually a guinea (£1.05) each per day. The charge for Mr White's 'attendance at the Houses of Parliament overseeing the passage of the Enclosure Bill' in the session of 1802 was £226. White was probably a Member of Parliament, but does not seem to have been a local representative. The cost of ditching and fencing along the new roads, the cost of digging the new drains and the cost of enclosing Lady Bath's lands were all added to the general bill, which in total amounted to £2,283. Fifty-two proprietors shared the costs. They ranged from the £379 paid by R C Broadley to the 13s (65p) paid by Joseph Meek for the quarter acre next to his mill. For his 20 acres Thomas Jackson's share of the bill was £50. For the oak posts and rails he erected round his own lands he paid a further £20. In order to pay the bills he mortgaged his land for £96.

The enclosure may not have been the greatest change there had been in Keyingham's landscape but it was certainly the most rapid. The deforestation and reclamation of the Middle Ages had been more dramatic but had taken generations to accomplish. The change from a landscape of open fields, meadows and pastures to closed fields bounded by straight fences and ditches took place within less than four years. At the end of the process the outlying fields must have looked very much as they do today - very large, with a monotony of long straight boundaries. It was not to last long. The biggest fields were too large for the methods of agricultural management of the time. A four-crop rotation was often used with one of the courses being a period of a few years when pasture, or leys, was laid down for grazing. A large field would therefore be sub-divided into four by hedges to prevent animals from straying. The original post-and-rail fencing of the enclosure was also in time replaced by hedges. New supplies of drinking water had to be provided for livestock. In the past, when cattle and sheep roamed half the parish they had access to the Keyingham Fleet on the west or Keyingham Field Mere on the east. Now animals had to be provided with ponds sealed with puddled clay. Until the introduction of troughs served by piped water, there were many of these small ponds about, acting as a refuge for newts and tiddlers and a haunt for small boys armed with jam jars and fishing nets. Under modern agricultural practice larger fields are preferred by the farmer. Consequently, the sub-dividing boundaries have been removed and most fields have resumed the size allotted at the enclosure. The ponds have now been filled in, and, at the time of writing, the troughs, too, have disappeared because of a decline in outdoor animal husbandry in Holderness.

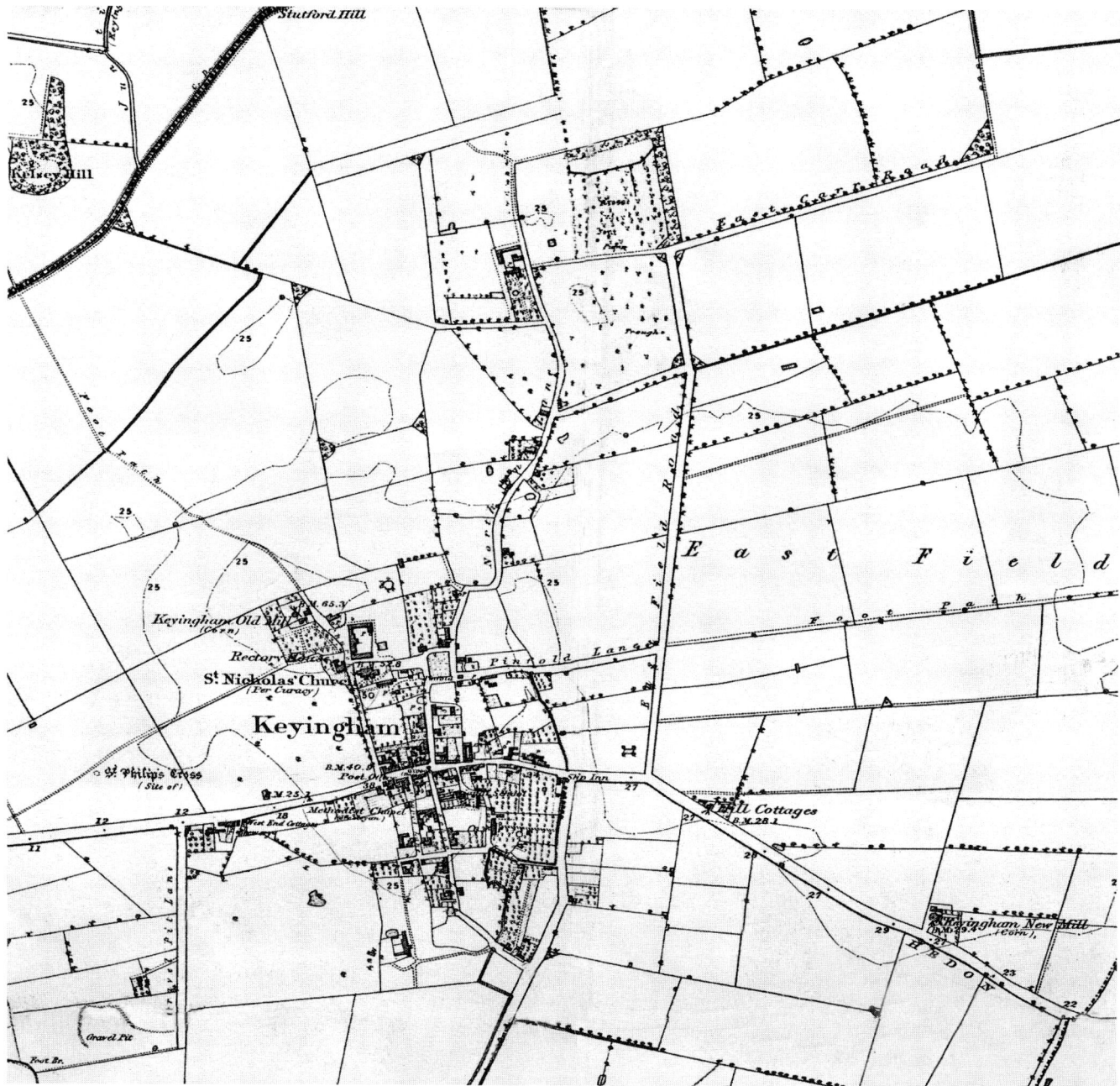

Stutford Hill

Incy Hill

East Garth Road

Keyingham Old Mill
(Corn)

Rectory House

St Nicholas' Church
(Per Curacy)

Keyingham

St Philips Cross
(Site of)

Post Office

Methodist Chapel

West End Cottages

East Field

Foot Path

Pinfold Lane

Ship Inn

Hull Cottages
B.M.28.1

Keyingham New Mill
(Corn)

HEDON

Gravel Pit

Foot Br.

Pit Lane

Another change in the Keyingham landscape that occurred soon after the enclosure and which has since been mostly reversed was the introduction of more trees. The scarcity of trees in Keyingham has already been referred to and it was a matter of general concern to agricultural commentators at the beginning of the 19th century. In his *Agricultural Survey of the East Riding of Yorkshire* written in 1812, Henry Strickland bemoaned the lack of trees in the Riding. He recommended that they should be planted along the new hedgerows of the enclosures to provide 'shelter to livestock, an ornament to the neighbourhood, and a source of profit [as timber] to the landlord'. Some farmers objected to planting trees in hedgerows as they destroyed the quickthorn of the hedge. In that case, Strickland argued, trees could be planted, at trifling expense and little loss of land, at the corners of fields, which were difficult to till anyway. If planting was done at all four corners of every field a considerable amount of timber could be grown with little sacrifice of land. Moreover, livestock would obtain shelter, whichever quarter the wind was in. It seems that some of the Keyingham landowners followed his advice. The first six-inch

Ordnance Survey map, 1855. This section was surveyed in 1851 and some members of the survey team were staying in Keyingham on the day of the census that year. The tree-planting activity that had taken place around North End Farm can be noticed. In the well-wooded field (later known as Crawshaw) north of the junction of Eastfield Road and East Carr Road are marked a cross, a font and a pump. The site of St Philip's cross to the west of the village is also marked. Note how some of the larger fields awarded at the Enclosure of 1805 have been sub-divided.

Hull Central Library, Local Studies

Ordnance Survey map of Keyingham, surveyed in 1851, shows trees in both the hedgerows and the corners of the fields, especially on the north of the village. The Owst family seem to have been particularly keen planters and, in addition to planting trees around their fields, they set aside a whole field for the growing of timber. This field, at the northernmost end of Eastfield Road, was known as Crawshaw and was a popular spot for villagers to take a Sunday stroll. The timber was not taken until the 1930s and the field is now back to arable, presenting an appearance that cannot be much different from that immediately after the enclosure.

The last of the male line of the Owsts was Thomas Joseph, a keen collector of old stonework, which he set up in Crawshaw. One of the pieces was the bowl of an ancient font, which had been used as a horse trough. Its position is marked on the Ordnance Survey map already referred to. It was later identified as having come from Winestead and, as such, must have been the font in which Andrew Marvell, the poet, was baptised in 1621. It was later restored to Winestead church. It must be one of the few fonts to have been marked on a map. Also set up in Crawshaw were two crosses, one of which was taken from Ottringham. The other cross was brought from Lincoln in 1837. It was quite new and had been carved in 1821 to the design of Lincoln architect, E J Willson, who was related to Owst's son-in-law, Edward Oldfield. Oldfield succeeded to the Owst estate and when he died the cross was removed to the north side of St Nicholas Church, where it still stands as a memorial to the Oldfield family. The Owsts are commemorated in the name of a modern road in the village.

One result of enclosure was the loss of the common grazing that had been available on the

97

open fields. However, a new form of common grazing became available, provided one could pay for it. Because the new roads had been made very wide there was plenty of grass on the verges. This was auctioned, lane by lane, twice a year, usually at the Blue Bell, for mowing or grazing. For example, Edward Oldfield paid £4 for the herbage of East Carr Road, near his farm, from June to December 1873. The money went to the account of the Surveyor of Highways, who used it to help keep the village roads in repair. The last time the lanes were let was in 1951 when G W Beadle paid 12s.6d (62.5 p) for the herbage in Dam Lane.

The enclosure of the open fields brought great advantages to the country and to the large go-ahead farmers. The poor, perhaps, did not fare so well. Besides Lady Bath, there had been only one objector to the proposal that an enclosure bill for Keyingham should be put to Parliament. However, only those with land were canvassed; those with merely cottage rights had no say. Before the enclosure of Keyingham the cottager had the right to pasture animals, perhaps a pig and a few geese, on the open fields, so that he was not entirely dependent on a wage. After the enclosure he had about a quarter-acre of land that may have been at some distance from his home. Many cottagers sold up and became completely dependent on a wage. Initially, such wage earners fared quite well. The enclosure award required much work to be done. New drains and ditches had to be dug. The new roads had to be laid out. Every new field had to be fenced, and the majority had to have ditches round their boundaries. Owners of large fields wanted them sub-dividing. In addition, the straightening and deepening of Keyingham Drain was being continued south of High Bridge. There was plenty of work, not only for Keyingham men but also for others. Keyingham's population went up from 399 at the census of 1801 to 550 in 1811, an increase mainly due to new labouring families coming into the village. For a few short years Keyingham was a boom village.

Trees planted on Thomas Owst's lands in the early 19th century, August 1994. View from the south of one of Thomas Owst's old enclosed fields. The hedge borders the northern end of Eastfield Road. The tree in the hedgerow was probably an accidental seeding, but the clump of trees beyond it was planted deliberately to provide shelter for cattle, and the 1855 Ordnance Survey map shows the clump as well as a trough in the field to water cattle. To the right of the tree in the hedgerow can be discerned a tree that forms part of a clump at the corner of the adjacent field.

11 - The Ups and Downs of an Agricultural Community

In 1811 the enumerator conducting the census at Keyingham counted 105 families in the village. Of these he reckoned that 85 were connected with agriculture and the remainder with trades or crafts. As some of these crafts included smithying, making wheels for farm vehicles, saddlery and milling, it will be seen how closely Keyingham's fortunes were tied to agriculture. If farming prospered so did Keyingham; if farming declined the whole village felt the effect.

When the 19th century opened the country was at war with France, a war that was fought at sea and on the Continent. Only for brief periods was there a threat of the conflict reaching these shores. At the close of the 18th century, there had been the possibility of a French invasion. The Holderness coast was considered to be open to attack, and preparations were made to deal with any such emergency. Instructions were set out for burning corn stacks, driving cattle inland and conveying women, children, invalids and the elderly to safety beyond the River Hull. The coast was watched and a system of beacons was established to send warning of invasion inland. The system was more elaborate than the one set up in Elizabeth I's time; between Patrington and Paull there were two further beacons, one at Ottringham and one at Keyingham. The one at Keyingham was probably near the site of the house called Beacon Hill opposite the end of Church Lane. The invasion scare subsided when the Treaty of Amiens was signed in 1802 and the beacons were soon in disrepair. The treaty lasted a little over a year. In May 1803 war broke out again and Napoleon was making overt signs of preparing to invade England. A certain Major Popham was promptly instructed to make an estimate of the expense of repairing and putting in order the 21 beacons in the East Riding. His estimate of the total cost was £89. Keyingham's beacon was in an average state of neglect. It needed £4.2s spending on it in order to replace the post, fill the barrels with tar, and repair and thatch the watchmen's hut. The smoke ball, torch, flag and flag ropes were all 'good' and needed nothing spending on them. Although Napoleon's invasion plan quickly fizzled out the beacons were kept in a state of readiness until the end of the war. In 1807 they were refined when it was ordered that close to the door of each hut a post was to be firmly driven into the ground, with its top at eye level. There were to be grooves across the top pointing to the nearest beacon 'for resting the spy glass so that the eye may not be deceived at night'. Previously the spyglass had been aligned from the beacon post or through a tube set in the wall of the watchmen's hut. However, in the former case the post was liable to shake in high winds owing to the two tar barrels fastened on the arms at its summit, and in the latter case the turf walls had a tendency to give way 'so the Tubes in the Huts were much out of direction'.

Although the French army never reached the shores of England the war had a great effect on the countryside and the people. Napoleon's blockade of imports meant that, in the main, England's farmers alone had to feed the country, a factor that encouraged more efficient farming. Hence the enclosure of Keyingham's open fields in 1805 described in the previous chapter. It was in 1795, during the war, that the Holderness Agricultural Society was formed. Meetings were held at the Sun Inn, Hedon, on Monday nights nearest to the full moon, when visibility was better for travelling. Go-ahead farmers from all over South and Mid

Holderness belonged. Keyingham members included Thomas Owst, John Hutchinson and John Champney, the latter two both farming in the Marsh. The society discussed such things as crop rotation, animal and plant diseases, the varieties of corn and whether putting more meat in the diet of a farm labourer got more work out of him. The society, which was in existence for the whole of the 19th century, also promoted the improving of animal breeds by awarding prizes for the best animals exhibited. In 1814 John Champney won five guineas for the best bull.

The wartime boom in English farming ended with Napoleon's defeat at Waterloo in 1815. This is well illustrated by events in Keyingham. Table 1 shows Keyingham's population figures at each census taken during the 19th century.

Table 1. Keyingham's population, 1801-1901

Year	1801	1811	1821	1831	1841	1851
Pop.	399	550	639	636	728	746

Year	1861	1871	1881	1891	1901
Pop.	639	620	635	587	549

The first census of Great Britain was carried out in 1801. Since then a census has been taken every ten years, except in 1941, when there was a war on. The results of the 19th-century censuses showed the population of the country as a whole to be expanding at a high rate. For example, between 1801 and 1851 it approximately doubled from 9m to 18m. The rapid rise was due to factors such as a lowering of the age at which people married, thus leading to larger families, but particularly to a reduction in mortality rates, especially amongst children. The parish registers of Keyingham indicate that in the period 1751-1800, 48% of the 129 children born to permanently residing families died by the age of five; in the period 1801-1830 the

figure was down to 15% for the 46 children born to permanently residing families (in the second period, Keyingham's population was much more mobile and there were fewer families of long-term residence).

Between 1801 and 1811 Keyingham's population went up from 399 to 550, an increase of 37.8%, far greater than the 14.6% recorded for the whole of England in the same decade. Keyingham was expanding faster than what may be considered the natural rate because people were moving into the village. They were being attracted by the work needed following the enclosure of the open fields, when much extra labour was required to dig the ditches, make the fences and set out the roads stipulated by the enclosure commissioners. At the same time the Keyingham Drain was being improved by making a new five-mile cut between Keyingham Bridge and Stone Creek, thus necessitating more labour centred on Keyingham. The demand for extra labour would seem to have continued throughout the next decade, with Keyingham's population increasing to 639 by 1821. However, from the parish registers it appears that most of the increase had occurred by 1815, and that thereafter there was a shortage of employment. It is from 1815 onwards that there are a number of labourers who are recorded only once in the parish register - at the baptism of one of their children. At that time one child in a family was truly a rarity, so most of these labourers must have resided in Keyingham for only a year or two. Men and their families were coming into the village seeking work but, now that the war was over and the boom in agriculture was waning, they were having to move on and look for work elsewhere. In the 1820s any increase in Keyingham's population due to reduced mortality and increased birth rate was counteracted by migration from the village, and in

1831 the population was no higher than ten years previously.

Table 2. The number of families and houses in Keyingham at each census taken in the 19th century

Year	1801	1811	1821	1831	1841
Families	89	105	141	135	150
Occ. houses	80	98	132	132	150
Empty houses		1	0	12	1

Year	1851	1861	1871	1881	1891
Families	155	150	151	142	136*
Occ. houses	155	150	149	142	136
Empty houses	6	9	17	14	19

*The figure for 1891 includes two families who were described as temporarily absent.

The influx of people into the village caused pressure on housing and in the early decades of the century there were more families than there were houses for them to live in (Table 2). There would have been a number of families lodging with others. Gradually more houses were built, filling in spaces on plots where only one dwelling had stood before. Thus the terrace of two houses and a shop adjacent to the Blue Bell are on a plot that was occupied in 1769 by only William Cookman's cottage and shoemaker's shop. By 1841 there were three cottages on the site with two farm workers and a pauper woman living in them. It may have been about this time that more substantial houses of brick and tile rather than of mud and thatch came to grace the Keyingham scene. In 1813 a new house was built for the miller on Mill Hill. Skeckling farmhouse, brick-built and standing on the north side of Main Street until recent times, bore a stone with the year 1816 inscribed on it, and it is possible that some of the older cottages in Keyingham date to this period of expansion. Many have since been extended and altered, with the alterations and original shell covered by rendering. The first mention of a brick maker - William Jackson - in Keyingham occurs in the parish register in 1839, although a bricklayer, William Sutton, was mentioned as early as 1715. The 1855 Ordnance Survey map of Keyingham shows a brick and tile works near Sands Bridge in Keyingham Marsh where the clay pit is still visible.

When the decline in farming began after 1815, farm workers' wages went down, and the practice, which had begun at the end of the 18th century, of making up their wages out of the parish poor-rate intensified. It was something that the farmers took advantage of. For example, in 1832 George Bryan and George Andrew, two Keyingham farm workers, received money from the overseers of the poor 'for broken weather'. In other words, their employer had laid them off temporarily because the weather was too bad to do any farm work and sent them to the parish officers for relief. In the winter of 1833 the Keyingham select vestry, a committee selected to deal with relief of the poor, agreed that all unemployed labourers should be sent out to the farmers and do a day's work for every £50 of the farmer's rateable value. At that time the large farms in the Marsh were rated at between £100 and £700, and in the village Thomas Joseph Owst's farm of about 140 acres was rated at £87. The farmers were to pay the labourers one shilling per day. In addition the parish was to pay them three shillings a week and give them half a stone of flour (over three kilos) a week for each member of their families. This looks like an attempt by the vestry to extract some work from those seeking benefit, but it meant that the farmer was getting the work at a very low price, the normal wage in 1833 being about two shillings a day. There were other drawbacks to the scheme. The labourer had no incentive to do his work properly because he received his wage and his allowances from the parish no matter how badly he worked; married men with families received more in allowances than single men for the same work; and through the rates the wage bill of the large farmer was supplemented by householders, shopkeepers and the smaller farmers. Worst of all, it made the farm worker dependent on the charity of the parish.

Because of such defects in the Poor Law the cost of maintaining the poor in England and Wales rose from £2m in the early 1780s to nearly £8m in 1818. In rural areas the increase was much greater (in the towns economic factors caused more realistic wages to be paid). We cannot calculate the increase for Keyingham because the account books of the overseers of the poor have not survived, but at Withernsea, which was then a village of fewer than 100 people, the poor-bill went up from less than £11 per year in the early 1780s to £134 in 1818. There were similar increases in other Holderness villages.

The national poor-bill declined slightly after 1818 but was still a cause for concern to the Government, and in 1832 a Royal Commission was set up to investigate the matter. One source of the trouble, the Commission decided, was that decisions about the poor were entirely in the hands of the overseers backed by the vestries. 'In every respect,' went their report, published in 1834, 'the vestries form the most irresponsible bodies ever entrusted with the performance of public duties or the distribution of public money. They render no account; no record of the names of those present is needed, or of their speeches or their votes. Each vestryman who is an employer of labour is interested in keeping down wages; if he owns a cottage he tries to get the rent paid by the parish; if he owns a shop he tries to get allowances for his

customers or debtors; if he is in humble circumstances, his own friends or relatives may be among the applicants'. These objections applied to open vestries, which consisted, following the Vestries Act of 1818, of all the ratepayers in the parish. It seems that the people of Keyingham had tried to overcome the objections to an open vestry by adopting the provisions of an Act of 1819 and electing a standing committee, known as a select vestry, to deal with matters concerning the poor. Under the Act the committee consisted of the minister, the churchwardens, the overseers and other householders chosen by election. The parish could also appoint an assistant overseer, with a salary paid out of the poor-rate, to help the annually elected overseers of the poor. To discourage the granting of long-term benefits the committee had to meet every 14 days or oftener to listen to applications for relief and the decisions had to be set down in writing. Records of the meeting of Keyingham's committee survive from May 1832 in the vestry minute book. They show that the committee met every Friday to interview applicants and make the necessary provisions for their relief. Two of the committee's decisions have been quoted above and indicate that they were perhaps guilty of some of the accusations levelled against open vestries by the Commission but other entries show them to be compassionate on occasions, and at other times prudent when handling public money. When Mrs Allyn applied for relief because her husband, James, was ill and they had four children, the family was granted ten shillings and four pound of mutton, with a pint of porter a day for the ill man. This last provision was easily arranged as the meetings took place in the Blue Bell. For the next few weeks these arrangements were continued until, presumably, James Allyn recovered. Sadly, this was not his last contact with the vestry. Early in 1833 he was applying 'for something towards his child's funeral'. He was granted ten shillings. Fanny Allyn was the second of the couple's children to die in infancy, an occurrence not unusual in those days. Many other examples, recorded in the vestry minute book, indicate a similar true concern for the poor by Keyingham's select vestry.

The vestry, however, does not seem to have been prepared to distribute relief willy-nilly and was particularly reluctant to pay rents on behalf of the poor. When John Bewhill applied for some clothing and his rent to be paid the committee 'refused rent. Agreed to clothing'. Again, when Thomas Lotan, a farmer who owned some cottages, applied for the rent of one of his tenants 'or to see if the Parish would be responsible for the rent in the future' he was refused. (The Poor Law Commission considered it particularly iniquitous that poor people's creditors should apply directly to the overseers for their debts.) Parish overseers often did provide accommodation for the poor, either by paying their rents, boarding them with someone or actually building a house for them. In 1805 the parishioners had decided there was a need for a poorhouse in Keyingham, but the only land that the parish owned was the gravel pit, used as a source of material for mending the roads. They therefore sought possession of some wasteland. On the south side of the parson's glebe at the junction of what is now Station Road and Waldby Garth Road was a small piece of waste ground belonging to the lord of the manor. The vestry therefore wrote to Mr Constable begging 'to submit to his consideration, in consequence of the increase of the Poor and the want of Tenements for them', the erection of a poorhouse on the waste ground. Permission was granted and the poorhouse was built.

In its report of 1834 the Royal Commission made many recommendations, which were embodied in the Poor Law Amendment Act of the same year. By this Act, known as the New Poor Law, control of administration was taken out of the hands of parish officers and put into the hands of a central government body. The unit of administration was no longer the parish but the union, made up of a group of neighbouring parishes. Locally, Patrington was made the centre of a union, covering 27 parishes in an area from Paull and Burstwick to Spurn and Hilston. The union workhouse was built at Patrington. In order to receive any assistance the able-bodied unemployed had to enter the workhouse, where conditions were deliberately made worse than those of the lowest-paid labourers outside. The intention, expressly stated in the Act, was to discourage the able-bodied poor from applying for relief.

Unions were administered by boards of guardians. Each parish in the union was represented by at least one guardian elected by the ratepayers who had from one to six votes depending on the values of their properties and whether they were tenants or owners. The guardians themselves, who gave up their time freely, had to have a property qualification. The election of guardians was a small step on the way to local democracy. They were elected annually but could serve any number of successive terms. George Cole Francis of Saltaugh Grange, whose monument stands in Keyingham churchyard, represented Keyingham on the Board in 1848 and '49 and in every year from 1857 to 1865.

According to the New Poor Law the workhouse was for the able-bodied unemployed, who were to receive assistance only on the condition that they entered the house and did work, such as stone breaking, in return for their keep. Widows, orphans, the disabled and the insane were to be treated more leniently and could receive relief at home or in appropriate surroundings. In practice this rarely happened and workhouses were used indiscriminately as workhouse, poorhouse, old-folk's home, orphanage and asylum. On census day in 1851 two orphan brothers from Keyingham, George and Solomon Richardson, aged 11 and eight, shared Patrington workhouse with 14 other orphans, 25 men and women of employable age, eight people aged 70 or over, and nine unmarried mothers and their 17 children. Entries in the Keyingham burial register show that a number of old people from the parish died in 'the Patrington Union', the last being in 1908, just before the State old-age pension was introduced.

Because of the availability of the Patrington workhouse for housing the poor there was no need for Keyingham's poorhouse as free accommodation. In 1859 the central Poor Law authority insisted on the payment of full rent on all parish property. At that time the occupants of the poorhouse were Jacob Hodgson, a horsebreaker, and his wife Dinah. They continued to live there until 1868 when he died. In 1869 the vestry ordered its demolition. Dinah was then in her mid-fifties, so could presumably provide for herself. One imagines that very little effort would be needed to knock down the poorhouse. The ground on which it stood appears to have been absorbed into the glebe which stood to the north of it. Together they form the present-day Garth.

Centralisation of Poor Law administration did not terminate the position of the parish overseers of the poor. They were still needed to collect the poor-rate in order to contribute to the maintenance of the poor by the Union. They could also grant relief in emergency, and the apprenticing of poor children was still their responsibility. In 1859 the parish paid for the apprenticeship of Kirkwood Harper, a cripple boy with only one leg. He was bound to Richard Wright, a shoemaker. However, within two months it was found that Kirkwood could not continue in shoemaking and so was apprenticed to a tailor, Henry Coupland, for five and a half years at a cost of £10 to the parish. Henry Coupland was to supply him with a suit of clothes and at the discretion of the overseers was to allow him to work at the harvest for one month each year. In 1863 the parish paid for a new artificial leg for Kirkwood.

An assiduous overseer might make valiant attempts to keep down the poor-rate. In 1862, George Kendall, Keyingham's overseer and also the schoolmaster, three times attended the court at Grantham to prove that a child maintained by the Keyingham poor-rate was the responsibility of the grandfather, who lived near Grantham. The child had been brought from Hull by its mother to Keyingham for a change of air after suffering from a fever. From Keyingham the mother eloped to Africa with her lover, leaving the child to be supported by the rates. The whereabouts of the mother's husband were unknown. At the third hearing of the court, Kendall managed to obtain 1s.6d (7.5p) a week from the grandfather, after saying he would produce the mother from Africa rather than be beaten. Luckily for the Keyingham ratepayers he did not have to, but he had already spent nearly £9, excluding court fees, in pursuing the case.

The severity of the New Poor Law, although at the cost of considerable individual hardship in the short run, succeeded in checking the demoralisation and pauperisation of the working class. The harshness of conditions in the workhouse discouraged applications for assistance, and the degrading conditions brought shame on those who had to end their days there. Working men began to insure against temporary setbacks and also to ensure themselves a decent burial rather than a pauper's funeral. To this end the Keyingham Friendly Funeral Society was formed in 1842 with the object of assisting 'each other in paying the last tribute of respect to the remains of any of its Members, or his or her lawful Wife, or Husband'. There were to be 204 members and membership, which cost a shilling, was limited to healthy 16-60 year olds. On the death of a member a shilling was collected from each of the surviving members. From the collection one shilling each was paid to the president and the two stewards, and the remainder, approximately £10 - a goodly amount - went to pay for the funeral. The deceased person's membership might be taken over by his or her spouse, provided they were in good health, or by another applicant. The president was the village schoolmaster, John Escreet, and one of the stewards was farm worker Thomas Braimbridge. The other steward, William Ancock, probably came from outside the village - with an intended membership of 204 there had to be outsiders. We do not know how long the society lasted, but the last record we have is of Jane Bonfrey, a Keyingham dressmaker, being admitted as member in early 1843. The Keyingham society may have suffered from competition for, the day after it formulated its rules, the first entry was made in Ottringham's Funeral Club book. Its rules were similar to Keyingham's and its membership certainly approached 200, drawing on villages from all over South Holderness. In 1842 there were 18 members from Keyingham, made up of farm workers or their wives, a gardener, a carrier, a cartman, a brewer, two tailors and a farmer's wife. Entries of membership in the Ottringham book continued up to 1869.

For those who wished to provide for the journey through life as well as for its end there were the friendly societies, which gave sickness as well as funeral benefits. Friendly societies were in existence, especially in the towns, well before the passing of the Poor Law Amendment Act. The Amicable Society, for instance, was formed in Patrington in 1792, and a number of Keyingham working men belonged to it, but it was after 1834 that many more friendly societies came into being. In 1839 both the Independent Order of Oddfellows of the Manchester Unity and the Ancient Order of Foresters Friendly Society opened branches in Keyingham. In January of that year at the Blue Bell the Aeneas lodge of the Oddfellows was ceremoniously opened with a membership of about 40. The membership had increased to 60 by 1845 and stayed at around that figure until the 1880s. The last record of its existence occurs in 1900 when the membership was 33. In its latter years the lodge met in what is now the Church Room but was then known as the People's Institute and occasionally as the Oddfellows' Hall. Within living memory the motto 'Silence, Order, Obedience' remained painted on the wall opposite the door.

Court Friendship of the Ancient Order of Foresters was begun in June 1839 by four local men who had been initiated into a Hull court of the society. The membership was then 32 with prominent among them Thomas Lotan, mentioned earlier, and Robert Ellotson, a Keyingham gardener. By 1858 the membership was 233 and it climbed steadily into the 400s by the 1870s, making it one of the largest branches of the order in the country. In its early days the court met at the Blue Bell but in 1856, with the rapid expansion in membership, the decision was taken to build the court's own meeting place. The following year the present Foresters Hall was completed at a cost of £600. On the ground floor were two cottages to let and so provide further income to the court, and on the first floor was the meeting hall, capable of holding 300 people. Also on the first floor was a small committee room at the entrance to the main hall. This was where one of the officers sat to ask for the password before entry was permitted to general meetings.

Keyingham Foresters recruited members from all over South Holderness. The great majority were farm workers, many of whom joined in their early 20s. However, because of the mobility of farm workers (in their early years of employment they usually changed their place of work annually at the Martinmas hirings) they rarely became officers of the court. These posts were usually filled by tradesmen and craftsmen, men with more static occupations. Of the Keyingham men who occupied such posts in the last quarter of the century we know of Robert Wreathall, druggist, Henry Clark, grocer and draper, James Tarbotton, tailor and shopkeeper, and Richard Westmorland, shoemaker. Some of the wealthier local farmers, who saw in the friendly societies a way of encouraging self-help, became honorary members of Court Friendship, among them Matthew and William Carlin of the Marsh, E T Oldfield of North End Farm, and G C Francis who, it will be remembered was one of the guardians on the board of the Patrington Union. The promotion of friendly societies by the boards of guardians was something encouraged by the central Poor Law authorities.

The Foresters Hall, at the corner of Beck Lane and Main Street, June 1992. Built in 1857 at a cost of £600. The main hall, lit by the three large windows, is on the first floor. Below are two cottages. The annexe, nearest the camera, contains the entrance and stairway to the hall. Above the door are the arms of the Keyingham Court. The blocked window of the annexe covers the stairway and is there to give symmetry to the east side of the building. The tiny forecourt had iron railings set in the wall but they were taken for the war effort in World War II.

The Foresters' annual feast day was one of the highlights of the village calendar. It usually took place in Whit week. All members living locally had to attend or pay a fine. Headed by a brass band and men carrying a huge banner (which is now with Hull Museums) the Foresters would first process to a place of worship - Anglican or Methodist. In 1843 it was the Keyingham Primitive Methodist chapel, in 1849 it was Keyingham church and in 1851 it was Burstwick church. The parade then marched to the clubroom for the feast. There might then be a further procession and the day ended at the clubroom with speeches, toasts, music by the band, and singing. The flavour of the occasion is no better captured than in an account appearing in the *Hull Advertiser* in May 1862 and quoted by David Neave in *Feasts, Fellowship and Financial Aid* in the Hedon Local History Series.

'The twenty-third anniversary of Court Friendship of the Ancient Order of Foresters, held at Keyingham was commemorated on Wednesday last, on which occasion the members assembled at Burstwick, where a procession was formed, and displaying their magnificent flags and banner, and accompanied by the Patrington brass band, proceeded to Burstwick Grange, the pleasant farmstead of the late Abraham Leonard, Esq., who had been an honorary member of this court. Here the procession halted, and received refreshment. Being now prepared for further progress, the procession wended its way to Ridgmont, the beautiful retreat of William Stickney, Esq., and here also the procession met with the same hearty welcome, partaking of similar cheer, and which they enjoyed as Englishmen only can do. The procession then took a circuitous route, and returned to Burstwick, where after being comfortably seated in the parish church, full service was observed. The Rev. Brother [i.e. of the Foresters] F. B. King, M.A., the worthy vicar, presided at the harmonium during the service after which he preached a very appropriate sermon taking as his text the cxxxiii Psalm, 'Behold how good and how pleasant it is for brethren to dwell together in unity'. After leaving the sacred edifice, the procession moved to the vicarage house, where on the beautiful lawn, they displayed their flags and banners, the members forming in semi-circular position, and presenting on the whole, a most animating spectacle. After the band played the National Anthem the procession proceeded to Keyingham, where dinner being prepared for them in the Foresters' Hall, and having sharpish appetites from their long walk and the bracing air of the morning they displayed pretty considerable enjoyment in disposing of the same. Dinner being concluded the procession once more formed, and paraded the village. On their return, the members, attended by a number of ladies and gentlemen, again met in their spacious hall. It was announced that Brother Backwell (of Hull) would give a lecture on 'Robin Hood' but being rather unwell, he requested Brother John Howe (of Hull) to read it for him. The meeting passed off most convivially; the speaking, singing, and the lively strains emanating ever and anon from the talented brass band, being thus diversified, rendered the whole one of the most charming gatherings ever held in this prosperous and thriving neighbourhood.'

In 1847 Keyingham had provided the brass band when the Foresters marched to Ottringham for the service then back to Blue Bell for a 'sumptuous repast' provided by the landlady, Mrs Wreathall, but after that year there is no mention of a Keyingham band and in the 30 years from 1860 the Keyingham Foresters called on the services of bands, not only from Patrington, Paull and Thorngumbald, but as far afield as Sutton, Cottingham, Hull and Grimsby.

The entire village participated in feast days, and stalls and amusements were set up in the streets, and presumably it was amongst these that the Keyingham Foresters paraded in 1861. It was towards the end of the 19th century that the drunkenness and brawling associated with friendly society feast days began to be looked on askance, and it may have been the presence of a strong Primitive Methodist element on the Keyingham Foresters committee, coupled with the temperance movement growing in all denominations, that brought in the more sober tea party as the form of annual celebration. However, the villagers continued to have their stalls and amusements, which continued as Keyingham Fair in every Whit week until the start of the First World War.

Court Friendship, Keyingham, survives today, with membership approaching a hundred. The Foresters Hall is no longer suitable for meetings, however, and the annual gathering takes place in the Church Room.

- o -

The stringency of the New Poor Law checked the pauperisation that had been engulfing the village working man and woman. As indicated by the founding of funeral clubs and friendly societies, people began to shift for themselves. Many emigrated to seek new lives overseas. Between 1853 and 1860 over 450,000 people left England, amongst them Job Elletson, a Keyingham gardener in his early twenties. He went to America and did well for himself. Sixty years later his widow came to Keyingham to make a generous bequest towards the restoration of the church.

The years following the passing of the New Poor Law happened to be a period of industrial expansion, when towns, railways and public works were being developed. It provided the opportunity for country people to move to the towns where plenty of work was to be had. Between 1841 and 1851 the population of South Holderness went up by less than 6% whilst Hull's population increased by nearly 23%. The national increase was 13%. Keyingham's 19th-century population reached its peak in 1851 when there were 746 people in the parish on census day. However, on this occasion and at the census ten years previously, the numbers in Keyingham were increased by the presence of visitors. In 1841 the enumerator - John Escreet, the schoolmaster - stated in his return that there was a temporary increase of 12 people owing to 'an influx of Labourers employed in cleansing the Keyingham Drain'. In 1851 an Ordnance Survey team was in the village. With the surveyors, labourers, soldiers (the Ordnance Survey was still a department of the Army) and their families they numbered 18. The occupation of one of their members, 11-year-old chain boy John Garvey from Ireland, reminds us of how the measuring was done at the time. The outcome of their labours was the six-inch-to-the-mile Ordnance Survey map of 1855. The team's lodging money would have provided a welcome boost to some family budgets. Moses Walker, a farm worker, and his wife, were no doubt pleased with the rents handed over by three members of the survey who stayed with them and their six children in what would have been a not very spacious abode.

From 1851 to the end of the century Keyingham's population declined (Table 1) despite natural factors predisposing to expansion (between 1851 and 1901 the national population almost doubled). Whereas in the early part of the century there had occasionally been empty houses standing in Keyingham because they had been replaced by better ones, in the second half of the century there were empty houses standing because there were insufficient families to occupy them (Table 2). Gradually people were being drawn away from the village. This movement began at a time when, in fact, British agriculture was making a recovery in response to the demands of the country's growing population and from the middle of the century entered a period of what was known as high farming. It was a period characterised by improvements in technology in farming, particularly in the use of machinery, fertilisers and under-soil drainage. In Keyingham the brick and tile works in the Marsh was probably making tiles for drainage as well as bricks for building - in the early days of under-soil drainage flat tiles, rather than drain pipes, were laid A-fashion along the bottom of the drainage trench. One of the biggest users of the bricks produced was probably the Constable family as they improved the farm buildings of their tenants in the Marsh.

Machinery was coming to be more and more used in farming. By 1841 James Brooks, a Hull man, had set up in Keyingham as a machine maker and wheelwright, and in 1851 there was an engineer of machines from Leicester staying at the Blue Bell. In 1871 three men described themselves as machine owners. Two of them were Keyingham-born, in their early twenties, and no doubt men of enterprise who would be contracting with farmers to thresh corn. These machines may have been stream driven, the first such machine having been introduced into Yorkshire soon after the middle of the century. Only the threshing operation was driven by steam - the machine had to be drawn by horses to the threshing site. Before the introduction of steam the power for the threshing operation was provided by three horses walking in a circle and pulling on a capstan device connected to the machine. By 1881 there were five people in Keyingham whose occupations were linked to threshing machines, including two who stressed that their machines were stream-driven. By the end of the century, machines such as the horse-drawn reaper, the horse hoe and horse rake as well as the steam threshing machine and steam plough (first mentioned as being in Holderness in 1862) were all available to the farmer and all reducing the need for manpower.

It was during this heyday of British farming that the railway came to Keyingham. The time was ripe for a new transport system in South Holderness, since one of the main outlets for the farmers' produce - Patrington Haven - was silting up as Sunk Island grew in extent. The chief promoter of the scheme was a leading Hull businessman, Anthony Bannister, with strong support from local landowners such as Sir Thomas Aston Clifford Constable of Burton Constable and lord of Keyingham manor, J G B T Hildyard of Winestead and T J Owst of Keyingham. The prospectus, issued in 1852, pointed out how the farmer would, through the railway, be able to send his produce to the best market and obtain coal, lime and manure more cheaply. The gravel deposits in the district could be more profitably exploited and, with the line terminating at the coast, it would bring visitors from Hull and the West Riding to the seaside. It was also stressed that many landowners were prepared to sell land on the proposed route at reasonable prices. One might assume that T J Owst was one such landowner as a large part of the eventual line in Keyingham passed over his lands.

The Act for the railway was obtained in July 1853 and Bannister cut the first sod at Kelsey Hill just beyond the Keyingham Drain, in the parish of Burstwick. From Kelsey Hill gravel was extracted as ballast for the line which was laid westwards to its terminus near Victoria Dock and eastwards to the terminus at Withernsea. The new rails themselves provided the means of transporting the ballast to where the work was proceeding. The line wound to take in the market towns of Hedon and Patrington and to serve as many villages as possible in between. Thus it passed halfway between Burstwick and Ryhill (renamed Ryehill by the railway company) and halfway between Halsham and Ottringham. Keyingham, cut off by the drain from any contacts to the north, had a station all to itself and conveniently near (in the days before walking went out of fashion) to the centre of the village. The creation of the posts of station master and railway porter brought new job opportunities to the village, as did the exploitation of the gravel pits for building developments going on in Hull, particularly Alexandra Dock and the Hull and Barnsley Railway later in the century. However, the gravel deposits at Ken Hill, referred to as Cain Hill in early documents, and on Mill Hill

were not exploited until the 20th century.

The proximity of Hull and the competition for labour kept farm workers' wages comparatively high in the countryside around - not as high as in the town itself but higher than in purely rural areas such as Lincolnshire and Norfolk. Consequently, the East Riding attracted many workers from further south. Many came to Keyingham, travelling easily, no doubt, on the country's rail network. The census returns indicate that over twenty labourers and a few craftsmen from Lincolnshire and Norfolk settled with their families in the village. In addition to these there was a more transient population of Norfolk and Lincolnshire men amongst the farm servants living in Keyingham. They were hired on a yearly basis at the Martinmas hirings and passed on elsewhere without settling in Keyingham. Some of those who did settle, such as the Westmorland and Howes families, came to have quite an influence on the development of the village and its institutions.

Martinmas hirings occurred in the week beginning 23 November, when farm servants were hired for the year. The hirings took place in the chief market towns, Hull and Beverley being the largest centres in the East Riding. In Holderness many men and women were hired in the Hedon and Patrington market places. A few hirings even occurred at Keyingham cross. In the early 1860s, when an average each year of 500 men and 100 women found employment at the Hedon hirings and 180 men and 116 women at Patrington, 15 men and ten women were being hired at Keyingham. Martinmas week was the sole week's holiday in the year for the farm worker. It was then that farm servants received their year's wages. If employer and employee had been happy with the previous year the farm servant might stay on. Otherwise, he or she went to one of the hirings. There the farmers were on the lookout for good workers. If they saw someone they thought suitable they would interview him, wages would be discussed and, if the man was agreeable, he would be taken on for the ensuing year. The bargain was sealed with the payment of a 'fest', a few shillings, more or less, depending on the position - wagoner, third hand, least lad, etc. - obtained. The fest was the only money the hand received until the following Martinmas, unless the farmer advanced him something during the year. The hands lived-in on the farm. Girls were hired to cook and clean, chiefly for the hands, and it was often the farmer's wife who had the say in their hiring.

In the early part of the century farm servants lived with the farmer, but later it became more usual for them to live with the foreman and his family in a house built close to the farmhouse. At Saltaugh Grange in 1841, for instance, there were nine male farm servants and three female farm servants living-in with the farmer Richard Fowler and his wife and their eight children. In 1861 six farm workers and a dairymaid lived-in with G C Francis and his wife and five children. There was also a domestic staff of two maids, a nursemaid and a governess. Later in that decade houses for the farm hands were built at Saltaugh, so that in 1891 we find three male farm servants and one female servant lodged at the hind's house with the foreman and his wife and two children, whilst one farm servant was living at the shepherd's house with the shepherd and his family. At the Grange itself there were no hands living-in. George C Francis, now a widower in his seventies, lived there with a grown-up son and daughter and a cook, housemaid and kitchen maid. There was also a groom and his family living in the groom's house. The same sort of thing happened at most of the other large farms in the Marsh and in the village. In the 1840s and '50s ten farm servants lived-in at Ebor House, from where the 436-acre rectorial estate was farmed; at the end of the century there was only a domestic servant in Richard Mook's household at Ebor House. Two farm servants were lodged at the nearby foreman's cottage (today called the Dower House). Richard Mook probably did not have to engage too many workers as he had two grown-up sons. One farm where the hands continued to live-in was Keyingham Grange. There, in 1891, lived the farmer, 21-year-old Isaac Beal, with two grown-up sisters and four farm servants. He had succeeded to the tenancy of the farm after the death of his father. His widowed mother and seven other younger sisters lived in the village at the Old Vicarage in Station Road. Isaac's sisters were the cause of his downfall in farming for, under the terms of his father's will they were each to receive a sum of money from the estate on reaching their majority. Such was the state of farming at the turn of the century that it broke him. As the younger sisters came of age Isaac Beal was forced to give up the farm and became landlord of the White Horse at Ottringham.

Farm workers' wages in the East Riding may have been higher than in some southern counties, but this did not prevent discontent on occasions. In early 1872, when there was unrest amongst farm workers in many parts of the country because of rising food prices, a meeting was called at Patrington. There the workers decided to ask their employers for three shillings a day for regular work, giving them a weekly wage of 18 shillings (90p). Higher daily rates were to be asked for occasional work or threshing. They also asked for their hours to be reduced to 65.5 per week, with Saturday work finishing at 5 p.m. They were to put these requests to their masters and report back the following week. In most cases the men came back with favourable responses. John Clayton, who worked for Benjamin Dunn of Ebor House, reported that all the farmers in his village, with one exception, had agreed to give three shillings a day to men in their regular employ. It was the exceptions and the fact that there was no yielding on the hours of work that caused the meeting to resolve 'that a labourers' union or club be formed for the purpose of assisting in carrying forward the movement for an advance in the rate of wages and shorter hours of labour'. The enrolment fee was to be a shilling and the weekly subscription three pence. Several workers joined on the spot. A month later, in the April, the farm workers met at Hedon for the purposes of forming a club to help those thrown out of work and to assist those wishing to emigrate. The attraction of emigration can be judged from the columns of the *Eastern Counties Herald*, which in the same year that it was reporting the events at Patrington and Hedon was reporting that labourers in New Zealand were receiving 7s.6d a day and were asking for 10s in order to run a horse and buggy. There is no further record of unionisation by South Holderness farm workers in the 1870s, which might suggest that at least some of their demands had been met. However, there were no concessions on their hours of work and farm workers continued to work until 6 p.m. on Saturdays. There was a reduction in the early years of the next century, but it was not until 1919 that farm workers received Saturday afternoons off, a benefit their town cousins had been receiving since the 1870s.

Farm workers' wages remained virtually the same up to the end of the century, but their buying power became greater with the import of cheaper food from abroad. This may have been another reason for quietude amongst farm workers.

However, the success of the London dock strike of 1889 encouraged a resurgence of interest in trade unionism, and in 1890 200,000 unskilled workers joined a trade union. In that year the National Union of Gas Workers and General Workers held a recruiting campaign amongst farm workers in Holderness. The organising secretary visited Preston, Thorngumbald, Keyingham, Ottringham, Patrington and Easington and enrolled new members from amongst 'our brothers of the plough'. A branch of about 100 members was formed at Patrington. At Keyingham, officers were elected from the farm workers and a delegate to the newly formed district council was appointed. However, unionisation amongst farm workers gradually fizzled out. The National Agricultural Labourers' Union, which had been formed during the unrest of the early '70s and reached a membership of over 86,000 in 1874, declined thereafter except for a brief resurgence in 1891. It was dissolved in 1896. The fact that the membership was dispersed thinly over the countryside with numerous employers made agricultural unions difficult to organise. Furthermore, the drift to the towns made the farm worker more valuable to the farmer so that the need for industrial action was not needed. A fitting epitaph to the agricultural trade union movement of the 19th century is perhaps provided by the following extract from the *Hull News*, 1 February 1902:

'Keyingham. About three years ago a branch of the Agricultural Union [which one is not stated] was formed in the village with a fanfare of trumpets. The second and last meeting of the branch was held on Wednesday night in the Parish Council Chamber. Mr. Thomas Eyre relinquished the office of honorary secretary and treasurer and the meeting, presided by Mr. H. A. L. Francis, decided to give the funds in hand, which amounted to something like £2.6s, to the poor, in the shape of coals.'

The fact that the chief offices were held by a miller and one of the leading farmers in the district speaks volumes for the lack of militancy amongst Holderness farm workers.

- o -

The golden age of British farming came to an end in the middle of the 1870s, but for cattle farmers there was a setback before then, which is recorded in the Keyingham lane-letting account.

'The Cattle Plague, or Rinderpest, broke out in this country in Sept. 1865. The deaths have kept increasing until for the week ending Feb. 24th they amount to 13,011. February 23rd the Cattle Plague broke out in this Parish on the North end Farm belonging to and occupied by Mr. E. T. Oldfield. An Act of Parliament entitled "The Cattle Disease Prevention Act" was published Feb. 15th 1866 ordering the slaughter of all animals infected with the plague and compensation from the County Rate to the extent of half the value of the cattle so ordered to be slaughtered.'

This was the first time the disease came into this country. To stem its spread all cattle markets were closed, not to reopen for another two years when the disease had been temporarily conquered (Hedon's fortnightly cattle market never reopened). In Keyingham the letting of the lanes for grazing was brought to a halt for the time being. Instead they were let for mowing only, with the consequence that the income went down from over £31 in 1865 to under £11 in 1866.

The real blow to British farming, however, came a few years later as improvements in technology and transport made foreign imports cheaper. From America came grain grown on newly won prairie lands, harvested by the most advanced machinery, and transported rapidly by rail and steamship to these shores. From Argentine came beef and, from New Zealand, lamb and butter carried in refrigerated ships. Similarly, butter was brought from Denmark. Between 1874 and 1895 imports of wheat doubled; imports of butter doubled in value although the price was falling; and meat imports rose from £13m to £47m. The result was a severe depression in British agriculture and the continuing exodus of farm workers to the towns. As far as can be estimated from the census returns, the number of men working in agriculture in Keyingham declined from 155 in 1851 to 94 in 1891. These figures include market gardeners, machine owners and grooms working on farms, but do not include jobbing gardeners, grooms employed by someone other than a farmer, or general labourers as opposed to agricultural labourers.

The records of the Keyingham Foresters indicate where the men of the village and the surrounding area were moving to. Of the 472 members, the majority of them farm workers, who joined the society in the years 1858-69, 129 had moved to Hull by 1875, but still continued their membership. Others moved to the factory areas or coalfields of the West Riding, Lancashire, Northumberland or Durham. William Middleton, who joined the Foresters in 1866, moved from Keyingham to Low Spennymoor in Durham in 1870. His address in 1880, from where he was sending his dues, was Castle Eden Colliery.

Despite the exodus Keyingham was still a predominantly agricultural village at the start of the last decade of the century. The 94 men employed in agriculture in 1891 formed 60% of the working male population. And, notwithstanding the advent of steam power into agriculture, most of the work in the field was done by horses or human hand. The steam plough, a device drawn on a drag line set up between two engines on either side of the field, was provided by contractors and was more a feature of the following century. Even in the domain where steam was used - the stack yard at threshing time - the threshing machine required a team of nine or ten men, three provided by the contractor and the rest by the farmer, from his permanent work force if he was a large farmer, or otherwise using casual labour. The casual labour might well be itinerant Irishmen. At the 1881 census there were six Irish workers described as 'sleeping in barns' in the village.

Besides the 94 men directly connected with farming in 1891 there were others in Keyingham whose occupations were closely tied to agriculture. They included three blacksmiths, two wheelwrights, a veterinary surgeon, two saddlers and an apprentice saddler. Two windmills were operating. Other tradesmen and craftsmen in the village made it almost self-sufficient, with six tailors, five shoemakers, a joiner, a bricklayer, a plumber, ten dressmakers, four grocers, a spirit merchant and a brewer.

The make-up of Keyingham's population may not have been too dissimilar from that at the beginning of the century but there had been great changes in the village during that time, especially in farming. At the beginning of the century the corn was cut by scythe or sickle; at the end of the century reaping was done by horse-drawn machine. At the beginning of the century corn was threshed by flail; at the end it was threshed by steam. Many other operations done by hand at the beginning of the century were now done by machine, horse-driven or steam-driven.

There was also a great change in the appearance of the village during the course of the century. Although there was probably an air of dereliction about the place with 19 houses standing empty and probably neglected in 1891, the great majority of houses were now of brick and pantile rather than mud and thatch - a thatched cottage was something to be remarked upon. Some of the better buildings, such as the new vicarage on Ottringham Road, or the Board School in Saltaugh Road, or the Foresters Hall, were roofed with slate brought by rail from Welsh quarries. There was not now quite so much overcrowding as previously. In 1811, when workers were flooding into the village, there had been an average of 5.6 people living in each house. At the end of the century the figure was 4.4. (From a limited survey conducted by Matthew Rees in 1998 for his geography course work, today's figure is 2.6.) The make-up of households, especially those of craftsmen and tradesmen, at the end of the century was much different from that in the earlier years. In the same way that few farmers now had their workers living-in with them, the craftsmen of the village rarely had their men boarding with them. In the 1840s a typical master craftsman had his journeyman (someone who had learned his trade but who was not master of his own business) and his apprentices living in his household. For example, in 1841 John Coupland, a tailor, had a journeyman tailor and two apprentices living-in with himself, wife and four of his children. One of his sons was a third apprentice, and a daughter was a staymaker (a craft soon to end with the substitution of steel for whalebone in the making of the stays used in corsets). Another girl staymaker also lodged with the family. At the same census Joseph Marling, a wheelwright, had his two journeymen and an apprentice living with him and his wife and child. The family also had a maidservant and there was a lodger. At the end of the century it was different. In 1891 William Roydhouse, wheelwright, had only his own family of wife and eight children in his household. Thomas Guy, one of Marling's former apprentices who succeeded to Marling's workshop in Main Street, also had none of his workmen living-in. He, too, had eight children. A child born later to the family was Clive, who followed in his father's footsteps as a wheelwright and joiner. Both father and son left memorable carving work in the parish church. Clive's son John continued at the workshop until 1978.

Even though households were becoming more confined to family members, they were crowded by today's standards. Large families, such as the Roydhouses and Guys, were common. Often grandchildren or grandparents lived with the family. Houses were not so spacious as today's. Of the 136 occupied houses in Keyingham in 1891, 48 had only four rooms, 19 had three rooms, seven had two rooms and one had only one room. Even in the smaller houses large families were accommodated. On the south side of Main Street today is a smallish cottage. In 1891 it was two cottages, one of which contained four rooms and housed widower William Bulleyment and six of his children. In another four-roomed semi-detached cottage in Station Road lived William and Mary Jackson and five young children. A married daughter and granddaughter were also living with them. The cottage, on the west side of Station Road and immediately to the south of Northfield, is occupied today but, needless to say, by a good deal fewer than nine people. Seven members of the Blyth family lived in a three-roomed cottage in a row of four that stood to the east of the present Wray House. The heads of all these families were farm workers and, as was the case for most of the poorer families at that time, there were no children in the house above the age of fifteen. They had left home, usually to work as farm hands or domestic servants.

Besides the change in the appearance of the housing and the make-up of the households during the century, Keyingham was becoming a healthier place to live in owing to legislation on sanitation, a fuller account of which is given in Chapter 13. The result was that although the village was shrinking because of the changes in agriculture, the people were living longer and more children were surviving to adulthood. The future of the great majority of the children was not to lie in the countryside, however, but in the towns and cities.

- o -

The year 1887 was the golden jubilee of Queen Victoria's reign. Not only was it a time when there was a great feeling of loyalty to the queen, it was a time when the British could look back on 50 years of unprecedented advance by a single nation. Although there was a depression in agriculture due to foreign competition, it was not yet realised that there was increasing competition in the industrial field. The feeling of intense patriotism and pride in success was reflected in the jubilee celebrations. There were festivals in every corner of the land. The National Anthem seems to have been sung on every possible occasion, including at the meeting in the Foresters Hall to arrange what form Keyingham's celebrations should take.

On the great day, 21 June 1887, the village's celebrations began with George Cole Francis presenting medals to all the children. In the afternoon there was a church service - ending with the National Anthem. From the church the villagers processed to the celebratory meals, for adults at the Foresters Hall, and for children at the school. It was perhaps the first time in the history of the village that people of every class and walk of life sat down in equality together. In all, about 600 people feasted, the old and the infirm having their food taken to them in their homes. Sports on one of Mr Tindall's fields followed and the day ended for most people with one more singing of the National Anthem and cheers for the queen and all the organisers. However, 'some of the more lively spirits adjourned to a room, where a dance was inaugurated and kept up until twelve o' clock'.

In 1897 Queen Victoria's diamond jubilee was celebrated. The people's feelings for their sovereign were as strong as ever, but the country's self-confidence was ebbing, with the strong industrial competition from America and Germany becoming apparent and having its effect on the nation's economy. Celebrations were not so whole-hearted and go unrecorded for Keyingham, although we do know that a meeting of the inhabitants was convened to consider what should be done to celebrate the day. It was not until the next century that we again have records of how Keyingham celebrated royal events.

The Church of England, fully restored along with the monarchy in 1660, continued along the middle road of Christian worship established by Elizabeth I. With the advantage it had over the Nonconformist and Roman Catholic denominations, whose members were excluded from the universities and from public offices such as serving in Parliament or on town corporations, it became in the 18th century a complacent institution with little or no religious fervour. Many rural livings were poorly paid, so that in order to have a reasonable income ministers had to serve more than one parish, or install a curate at a very low salary whilst they themselves served a richer benefice. Mention has already been made in Chapter 9 of how John Pearson was minister at both Keyingham and Burton Pidsea in the first half of the 18th century. In the second half of the century the vicars of Paull took on the cure of Keyingham. The Archbishop of York was the patron of both livings and paid £93 per annum to the benefice of Paull and £20 per annum to the benefice of Keyingham. Joseph Dawson was instituted to both livings in 1763. John Bennett succeeded to both livings in 1788, and Lamplugh Hird to both in 1793. Hird was a prebendary at York Minster, and probably rarely visited Holderness. In 1764 Joseph Dawson was living at Thorngumbald. He was conducting weekly services at Paull, services every third Sunday at Thorngumbald, which was in the parish of Paull, and services at Keyingham on alternate Sundays, usually in the afternoon. Later, he began to employ a curate at Keyingham, and Rev John Tickell, who ran a school at Hedon, was frequently in attendance at St Nicholas Church. He had time between teaching and preaching to compile a history of Hull, which was published in 1798.

Dawson's income of £20 from Keyingham was supplemented by the surplice fees, paid to the vicar for marriages, burials and the churching of women after childbirth. In 1764 the fees were one shilling (5p) for a churching, 2s.6d (12.5p) for a marriage, 1s.8d for a burial in the churchyard, 3s.4d for a burial in the church, 10s for a burial in the chancel, and £1 for a burial within the sanctuary rails. For burials there were also fees to be paid to the parish clerk, who had to organise the digging of the grave and the re-paving the floor in the case of burials within the building. Keyingham folk were not the only ones buried in the church or churchyard. Sunk Island had grown up outside any parish and had no parish church. Its people came to Keyingham for baptisms, weddings and burials. In the middle of the century the journey from Sunk Island would have been partly by boat, with the cortege probably coming along Keyingham Fleet as far as the bridge at Hull Road. Later, as the west end of Sunk Island became joined to the mainland, a bridge was built over the fleet at Saltaugh. It was known as Ombler's Bridge after the family who were tenants at Saltaugh Grange.

With absentee parsons and ill-paid curates, church matters, both general and spiritual were sadly neglected. This is well illustrated by the state of Keyingham's parish register for the four-year period beginning when Joseph Dawson was instituted to the benefice. It looks as though he left the register to be filled in by John Nixon, the parish clerk. The handwriting is very poor, the minimum of information is given, abbreviations, such as 'd' for daughter, are used and there are fewer entries than in other years. All this was noted by Thomas

Watson, who, already curate of Bilton, became curate of Keyingham in 1798. He saw that attempts had been made to cover up errors by changing the years in which some baptisms took place, but on the testimony of the families in the village, he knew the entries were wrong. He was so appalled by the state of that particular volume of the register, which began in 1754, that he carefully copied out the whole of it:

> 'The original Register Book of the Parish of Kayingham from the year 1754 to the present, having been in some instances negligently kept, and the ink fading, the same (while it is yet legible) is here faithfully transcribed by my hand.   Tho. Watson, Minr. 1799.'

There are thus two copies of Keyingham's parish register for this period. Thomas Watson remained as curate of Keyingham until at least 1817 and as curate of Bilton until his death in 1824. Up to 1819 John Tickell, now well into his 70s, also occasionally travelled from Hedon to officiate at services at St Nicholas. By this time the stipend of Keyingham's vicar (but not necessarily the curate) had been increased. In 1704 the tax that had been taken from churches from the time of Henry VIII (see Chapter 8) was transferred to a fund known as Queen Anne's Bounty and used to supplement the incomes of churches worth less than £10 a year. In 1788 this was extended to livings worth less than £35, so Keyingham became eligible for a grant, and in 1795, 1811 and 1812 the benefice received sums of £200 from the fund. With the money, six acres of land in Cowden and five acres of land in Burstwick were bought and the rents from the lands were used to augment the vicar's stipend. In 1821 a grant of £1,200 was received from Parliament and this was invested in 18 acres of land in Thorngumbald. In 1830 the living, with the archbishop's £20, the surplice fees and the rents, was worth about £92 a year. In real terms it was still worth less than the £12 the archbishop had insisted that Meaux Abbey pay the vicar in 1349. For comparison, in 1830, the living at Ottringham was worth about £83 and that at Patrington about £628 a year. At the other end of the ecclesiastical ladder, the Archbishop of York had an income of tens of thousands of pounds, some of it coming from the 416 acres of the rectorial estate in Keyingham and the tithes of Keyingham Marsh. The great differences in the apportioning of the Church's wealth attracted much criticism. In a satirical commentary, *The Churches of Holderness not Destroyed but Anatomized, to Demonstrate the Unhealthy State of their Antiquated Constitution*, written in 1837, the author 'Geoffrey de Sawtry, Abbot' estimated that the archbishop gained about £1,000 from his lands and tithes in Keyingham, out of which he paid the parson £20. However, the archbishop had made up for it by granting the vicar the perpetual curacy of Burton Pidsea (worth £42 p.a.). 'Thus did his Grace create an UNNECESSARY plurality - but his curate was better paid, and his Lordship's funds in no wise diminished - this was a cunning stroke of worldly policy, worthy of apostolical vultures and not the only one I shall have to record in the course of these investigations.' De Sawtry's investigations did, indeed, reveal many other shortcomings on the part of the archbishop. In 1830 Sunk Island was made a separate parish. There was already a chapel there, built in 1802, and it was now created a parish church. However, it was some time before the archbishop got round to consecrating the church (it should be remembered that the post of Bishop of Hull had not yet been created). Eventually, the opportunity arose: 'In 1833, the Archbishop's new farm-house, at Kayingham, being complete, and fit for his Lordship's inspection, his grace took the opportunity of consecrating the church of Sunk Island on the same day, and afterwards held a confirmation at Hedon, which was considered a great accommodation, as the children from the eastern part of Holderness were spared a journey of eight miles further to Hull, so that some of them had only to travel sixteen miles to Hedon and back in the same day; and it will long be remembered in the annals of Holderness, that the spiritual wants of so many parishes coincided so happily with the temporal convenience of his Grace.' The new farmhouse referred to by de Sawtry was Ebor House, from which the rectorial estate was farmed by the tenant.

In 1833 a review of the archbishop's financial interests in Keyingham describes the lands and tithes belonging to the archbishop and mentions the stipend of £20 to be paid to the incumbent. It also mentions the incumbent's duties, which were 'until lately, prayers and a Sermon once a month' but now, because of the augmentation from Queen Anne's Bounty and the government, these duties were once a week.

The lack of spiritual leadership by the established Church during the 18th and early-19th century produced a reaction. It was in 1738 that John Wesley, an ordained Anglican priest, felt his 'heart strangely warmed' and that the salvation of a man's soul could be achieved through repentance and the full acceptance of Christ's teachings. For the remaining 53 years of his life he travelled the length and breadth of the country, proclaiming his message. It was a long time since this sort of doctrine had been preached in the Anglican Church. The type of message that would have been delivered in the all too infrequent sermons at Keyingham would have been about morals and the performance of good works and, for the poor, the acceptance of one's lot in life and respect for one's betters. Wesley's message struck home with the masses. In his days at Oxford, long before his conversion, Wesley had belonged to a religious club, whose members, because of the methodical way they organised their lives and worship, became known as Methodists. The name was attached to the new movement.

Because Wesley was frequently refused permission to preach in the churches as he travelled the country, he began to hold outdoor meetings, but always outside service times. He also began to use the services of local preachers, men and women not ordained to the priesthood, to carry his message. As the Methodist movement spread, groups, or societies, were formed, which met in houses for bible-study and to pray and sing hymns. They built their own meetinghouses, or chapels, where the society gathered, usually on Sunday evenings, after Anglican church services were over, as Wesley did not want to draw worshippers away from the Church - above all, he wanted the Methodist movement to stay within the established Church.

Wesley took his message chiefly to the towns, which during the Industrial Revolution were expanding rapidly and whose religious needs were largely ignored by the established Church. He visited Hull and Beverley and the market towns of the Wolds many times. He never came into Holderness, and his opinion of the farming community seems to have been low. Of farmers he once wrote, 'Their life is extremely dull, and it is usually unhappy, too. Of all the people in the kingdom they are the most discontented, seldom satisfied either with God or man.' Farm labourers were worse. They were grossly stupid, with no understanding of this life or the next. They were on the same level as a heathen or a Turk. The Reverend John Benson, a Methodist stationed in Hull in the 1780s, feared, 'we are not to expect any great good to be done in Holderness, the country being thinly inhabited and the people wretchedly poor'. Small wonder, perhaps, that Methodism was slow in penetrating Holderness. It seems to have been in the north of Holderness that organised Methodism first appeared, chapels being built at North Frodingham, Beeford and Skipsea by 1800, probably owing to the influence of Driffield where Wesley had preached and where a chapel was built in 1777. Then in the period 1805-10 about half a dozen places in South Holderness were registered as places of worship for the Methodists. Among them was Keyingham.

The former Wesleyan chapel, Waldby Garth Road, July 1999. *Built in about 1806 and closed as a place of worship when a new chapel was built in Chapel Lane in 1848. It was later used by the Keyingham Level Drainage Board as a storage shed and housed the boat used in keeping Keyingham Drain clear.*

By this time Wesley had died and Methodism, despite his wishes, had split from the Anglican Church and become a separate denomination. The Methodists had their own organising body and their preachers could administer the sacraments if there was no Anglican priest to do so. Not all Methodists were in agreement with the change. In 1791, the year of Wesley's death, when the possibilities of change were being discussed, Hull Methodists circulated a letter, the *Signal Gun from Hull*, to Methodists throughout the country, saying if there was a split Methodism would 'dwindle away into a dry, dull, separate party'. The prophecy proved untrue. Methodism became a separate, strong, denomination and by 1817 had its own ministers with full authority to administer the sacraments. In 1818 these ministers were authorised to use the title 'Reverend', and in 1836 it was decided that such ministers should be set apart from the laity by the laying-on of hands.

It was on 27 September 1806 that Jeremiah Matcham, yeoman of Keyingham, sold a building, apparently already in use as a Methodist chapel, to a group of 13 trustees. The trustees included Jeremiah himself and one other Keyingham man, William Hancock, a shoemaker. Eight of the trustees, craftsmen and small farmers, were from neighbouring places, from Hedon to Hollym and Sunk Island. The remaining three were from Hull, one being Thomas Thompson, merchant, banker, local preacher and in 1807 the first Methodist to enter the House of Commons. He was also a signatory to the *Signal Gun from Hull* so one might expect that as the richest and most influential of the trustees he would insist on the Keyingham Methodists staying as much as possible within the fold of the Anglican Church. As at that time there was worship only once a month at St Nicholas Church it would not be too difficult for the Methodists to avoid a clash of services. On 20 May 1807 the chapel was registered as a place of worship.

The chapel was on the south side of Waldby Garth Road on the site of what tradition says was a Quaker meeting house, although tradition may have confused Quaker with Methodist. Jeremiah Matcham's building was 13 yards long from east to west and 11 yards wide from north to south, which doesn't quite tally with the dimensions of the present barn on the site. The barn, however, does have remains of interior plastering, which suggests a grander use than simply as a farm building. It may be that the original building was demolished soon after purchase by the Methodists and a new chapel erected in its place.

John Wesley died less than two years after the start of the French Revolution. The violence of the mobs and their success in overthrowing the French aristocracy made the British Government wary of large gatherings in this country. The Wesleyan leadership, not wishing their movement to be seen as in any way revolutionary, began to frown on the great outdoor Methodist meetings that had been the hallmark of Wesley's day. They preferred recruitment to be by consolidation and chapel building. Methodism became respectable and the leadership decidedly Tory, opposed to anything revolutionary in politics, religion or social life. But there were some that yearned for the old way of things. In the early years of the 19th century outdoor, revivalist, meetings began in the Midlands and northwest England. In May 1807 Hugh Bourne and William Clowes, both Methodist local preachers, organised a camp meeting at Mow Cop on the border between Cheshire and Staffordshire. There were prayers, hymn singing and rousing sermons. Thousands attended and the meeting lasted all day. More camp meetings were arranged, despite a ban imposed by Conference, the Methodist ruling body. Bourne and Clowes were expelled from the movement, and in 1812 they and their followers formed a breakaway group at Tunstall in Staffordshire. They named themselves Primitive Methodists, as they sought to follow the early, primitive, form of Methodism. After a slow start, the movement spread rapidly, especially among the poorer classes.

In 1818 some sympathisers in Hull asked Tunstall to send them a missioner. The first one who came failed, so William Clowes, the movement's most charismatic preacher, was sent. He arrived in Hull in January 1819. He was no stranger to the town, for he had come from the Midlands to work there as a potter 15 years earlier. Then, he had been a dissolute young man, drinking, gambling and fighting. It was during the war with Napoleon, and one night he was almost captured by one of the notorious press gangs that roamed the streets seeking men for the Navy. He escaped and returned to Tunstall. Soon after, he was converted to Methodism, became a local preacher, and then helped to found Primitive Methodism. In Hull in 1819 he preached and converted many. Within nine months of his arrival Mill Street Chapel, built to seat 790 worshippers, was opened. Hull became the head of a circuit, extending from Spurn to Carlisle, the most prominent of the four early circuits of the movement.

The former Primitive Methodist chapel, Main Street, June 1992. Built in about 1823 in house form so that if it failed as a chapel it could be sold off as a dwelling. It was, in fact, sold off as two cottages after the building of a new chapel in Ings Lane in 1846. In 1891 one of the cottages housed a widower, William Bulleyment, and his six children. The building has since been converted to a single cottage and the mock Tudor effect added.

Appealing as it did to the poor, Primitive Methodism spread quickly through the farm-working community in Holderness. In 1819, whilst at Hull, Clowes conducted a successful campaign in the area, preaching in barns, farmhouses and the open air. We do not know what words Clowes preached on these occasions, but we have an indication of his style 25 years later, when he was a national figure and preached at the Hull District camp meeting, which in 1844 was held at Driffield. Thousands flocked to the town from 30 miles around to hear the great man. He addressed them in the market place, urging the 'saints to set themselves in battle array against the powers of hell'. He shouted, 'God will scatter the hosts of hell from Dan even to Beersheba. The glory is coming; the power from on high is descending; the fire is burning. Don't you feel it?' 'Yes. Glory!' shouted

the people. 'Don't put it out! Don't put it out! Sinners! The light is flashing on your minds; the fire is beginning to burn on your hearts. Don't put it out; don't put it out; don't put it out!' 'Amen,' shouted the crowd. Rousing words, which converted many, who, if they went to church, would have been used to some far less inspiring sermons.

Part of the Primitive Methodist chapel in Ings Lane, viewed from the west, April 1989. The tops of the round-headed windows of the building of 1846 can be seen above the modern kitchen extension. The 1846 chapel became the schoolroom when the new chapel adjoining it on the north was built in 1909.

In the year following the establishment of Primitive Methodism in Hull the first Conference of the movement was held in the town. On Conference Sunday three great camp meetings took place in the region. One of them was at Keyingham. A year later, in 1821, Clowes was again in Holderness. He recorded in his journal, 'At Keyingham, in the open air, I delivered the Word to a quiet multitude. The work increased. A small chapel was erected.' The chapel was registered for worship on 22 August 1821 by Edward Hutton, an agricultural labourer. This building may have proved unsuitable, or too small, for in May 1823 a new chapel was registered by George Willingham, blacksmith. It stood on the south side of Main Street and was built in house-form, so that if the project failed it could be sold off as a dwelling. The project did not fail, but when a larger chapel was later built on another site the meetinghouse was converted to two cottages and sold off. It has since been converted to a single cottage and received extensive modification.

Perhaps because of the history of its founding, Keyingham became the head of a branch of the Hull Primitive Methodist Circuit. The branch covered 15 villages from Preston to Easington and as far north as Hatfield near Hornsea. Later, when the branch became a circuit, Patrington was made the centre. In 1846 the Primitive Methodists in Keyingham considered themselves in a sound enough position to build a new chapel on the site of the present building in Ings Lane. The plot for the building, 11 yards square, was bought for £16.12s.9d, the money being provided by the general Primitive Methodist fund. The six trustees included two Keyingham men - Richard Hudson, wheelwright, and John Coupland, tailor. The other trustees - two labourers, a gardener and a boot maker - were from Burton Pidsea and Burstwick. The cost of the building was £200 of which £140 was still owing when the building had been completed. By 1879 the debt was down to £40. Although the chapel has since been extensively modified, the original round-headed windows can still be seen on the west side of the present building. Inside the building is a stone plaque bearing the words, 'Primitive Methodist Chapel, 1846'.

Not to be outdone by the Primitives the Wesleyan Methodists built a new chapel in 1848. It was on the west side of what has ever since been known as Chapel Lane. The building survived until the 1950s. The old Wesleyan chapel in Waldby Garth Road was sold off and was later used as a storage shed by the Keyingham Level Drainage Board.

The attendance at the two chapels and at the parish church can be judged from the religious census of England and Wales conducted on Sunday, 30 March 1851. On that day a return was made of the attendance at morning, afternoon and evening services at every place of worship. Although there was accommodation for three separate denominations in Keyingham it seems as though provision was made for the inhabitants, if they so wished, to attend more than one place of worship each Sunday. For example, St Nicholas had one service each Sunday, in the mornings and afternoons alternately, and the Primitives had a service in the afternoons and mornings alternately so as not to coincide with the Anglican services. The Primitives also had an evening service. The Wesleyans had services on Sunday afternoons and evenings but for some reason not explained had only an evening service on the day of the census. On that day there were 45 people in the congregation at the Primitive Methodists in the morning. At St Nicholas 190 people attended in the afternoon and there were 59 children in the Sunday school. As yet, neither the Primitives nor

the Wesleyans had a Sunday school. In the evening there were 114 in the Primitive's and 78 in the Wesleyan's congregations. In 1851 Keyingham's total population was 746, about 510 of them being aged 14 and over. As there was a possibility that some people attended both church and chapel on a Sunday it is not easy to fully interpret the figures, although it can be said from the evening attendance figures that, of the two Methodist congregations, the Primitives were the stronger. This was generally true of the rest of Holderness, but not for the country as a whole, attendance at Wesleyan chapels throughout the country being greater than at Primitive chapels on the day of the census. It is interesting to reflect that in an era noted in retrospect for church attendance, only about half the adult population of England and Wales went to a place of worship on the day of the religious census. For Keyingham it can be said that a goodly proportion of those aged 14 and over did not go to church that Sunday.

At the time of the census both the Wesleyans and the Primitives in Keyingham were providing local preachers to their respective circuits. For the Wesleyans there were Robert Sykes, a master shoemaker with three men in his employment, Ralph Burnell Clough, grocer, draper and the village postmaster, and a man called Sargeant, who may have been John Sargeant, an agricultural labourer. Local preachers with the Primitive Methodists were Francis Ford, a market gardener, Edward Hudson, a young wheelwright and son of one of the chapel trustees, and John Longhorn, a shoemaker.

- o -

In 1819 Rev Joshua Smyth, a well-educated man from the south of England, arrived in Holderness at the age of 27 to act as curate to Rev Jonathan Dixon of Burton Pidsea. He also acted as curate at Keyingham and in 1821 was instituted as minister there. He probably needed a good deal of encouragement to take on what was a fairly poor living. Although the stipend of £20 from the archbishop had been augmented with the rents from the lands bought with grants from Queen Anne's Bounty, the living was worth well under £100 a year. Only when it was augmented with a government grant in 1821 did the value of the living approach £100. Consequently, the archbishop followed the practice of his predecessors and, when Jonathan Dixon died in 1832, offered Smyth another living, that at Burton Pidsea, worth, as 'Geoffrey de Sawtry' said, £42. Even with the extra living, Smyth's income seems to have proved insufficient, especially with the arrival of children to him and his wife Hannah. His second child was born in 1828, and in 1829 he was advertising in the *Hull Advertiser* that he wished to take boarding pupils:

> 'Rev. J. Smyth, Keyingham begs respectfully to inform his Friends, that he wishes to take Six PUPILS, under Twelve years of age, to instruct in the elementary principles of the Classics, and general knowledge; the utmost attention will be paid to their morals, as well as improvement in Literature.'

The terms were £30 a year, including board and lodgings (washing two guineas extra), which, if the advertisement had been a total success, would have more than doubled his income. We do not know if Smyth received any pupils or where his house was where he intended to board them, but do know he received further encouragement to stay at Keyingham when he was provided with a new parsonage. In 1832 a house was bought from Matthew Wreathall and altered with £200 from Queen Anne's Bounty and £200 from the archbishop. The house, now called Ellesmere House, stands on the north side of Main Street, although the bow windows have been removed since Smyth's time.

At that time the village school, whose targets were considerably below the elementary principles of the classics, was held in the church vestry, which was bricked off from the rest of the church. Here those parents interested in their children's education would send them to be taught by the parish clerk or some other literate person in the village who wanted to make a living from the few pence a week paid by the parents. In the previous century, schooling in Keyingham seems to have been a spasmodic occurrence, no doubt depending on whether there were enough pupils to make it worthwhile for someone to run a school. When asked in the archbishop's visitation articles in 1743 whether there was a public or charity school in the village, Rev John Pearson replied that there was no such school, 'but, my Lord, we have a poor woman yt. Teaches a few children'. In reply to the same question in 1764, Joseph Dawson answered, 'the parishioners generally Mantain a Master who instructs their children & servants in Reading, Writing & Accounts and care is taken to teach them the Church Catechism'. Such a teacher as this would have had to have a licence to teach from the archbishop in order to ensure that the principles of the established Church were being taught. At the beginning of the 19th century a school in Keyingham probably became a more permanent institution when the teacher's income was put on a slighter sounder footing by two bequests for education. In 1802 Edward Ombler of Saltaugh Grange left the interest from £200 to teach 'so many poor children of Keyingham as the proceeds will permit' and in 1811 Edward Marritt, a schoolteacher and native of Keyingham, left for the same purpose the proceeds from £255. There is a wall plaque in memory of Edward Ombler in the parish church and both benefactors are commemorated in village street names. At the present day, both bequests are invested in land in Keyingham and are run by the Marritt-Ombler trust for the benefit of Keyingham children.

With the certainty of some income from the two bequests, schooling in the village seems to have become more regular, and in 1818 there were about 40 pupils at the school in the vestry. In 1827 it was suggested at the annual vestry meeting that another venue for the school should be found. It may be that, now that there were two Methodist chapels in the village, there were those who wanted their children's schooling to be without undue influence from the Anglicans. On the other hand, there may have been those who thought that a group of noisy children was an inappropriate adjunct to a church. Whatever the reason, Joshua Smyth offered to build a new school at his own expense provided he could have the school furniture from the church, no doubt thinking it would be useful for his own private educational venture. Nothing, however, came of this suggestion, and it was not until 1835 that a new school was built.

If the Methodists had wanted a school without any Anglican influence, they were to be disappointed. There was at that time no national system of elementary education and it was left to the religious bodies to take the lead. In the early years of the century, there had been formed the British and Foreign School Society, sponsored by Nonconformists, and the National Society for the Education of the Poor in the Principles of the

The old National School in Ings Lane, October 1978. Built in 1835 at a cost of £96, it was closed as a school in 1875 when the new Board School was opened. It later served as People's Institute, Reading Room, Oddfellows Hall, Council Chamber and finally as the Church Room.

Photo: Mrs F K Charlton

Established Church, backed by the Anglicans. It was the latter, usually referred to as the National Society, which had the greater, in fact the only, influence in Holderness (the British and Foreign Society had more influence in the towns, where Nonconformity was often stronger). Consequently, it was from the National Society that Keyingham's school received help in building.

The new school was built in Ings Lane (it is now the Church Room) at a cost of £96, of which £25 came from the National Society, and £35 from the parliamentary grant begun in 1833 to assist local enterprise in the building of schools. Keyingham was the first school in Holderness to receive aid from the grant. The rest of the money was raised by contributions from the villagers and the local farmers - a tribute to their interest in education. Considering the low outlay on the new school, the builders managed to incorporate a certain degree of grandeur. The single room, which had the luxury of a fireplace, was designed to accommodate 70 children. It was lofty and lit by five lancet windows in the Gothic style. The diamond panes of the windows, however, instead of being leaded, were constructed in cast iron more suited to the industrial era in which they were made. On the front of the building, carved in stone, were the arms of the archbishop who, as patron of St Nicholas Church, had given the land, part of the glebe, on which the school was built. The stone, carved with the crossed keys of St Peter, and presented by T J Owst of North End Farm, now resides in a Keyingham garden. The school was run by trustees who, amongst other things decided the master's salary.

Despite the Ombler and Marritt legacies the new school often had difficulties in making ends meet. In 1844 the legacies produced £18 and the children's weekly pence £28, which together were insufficient to meet the teacher's salary of £50. The following year there was a drop in attendance - so that the total income was only £42 - and a drop in the teacher's salary to £42. Moreover, a further £18 was spent on books, repairs, coal and candles. The difference had to be made up by appeals to the generosity of the local population. The following year the school received a grant from the government of over £2 for books and maps and £15 for a pupil teacher. This was in 1846, the first year the government gave grants towards teacher training.

The award of parliamentary grants to schools led to the establishment of an inspectorate in 1840, and in order to receive a grant a school had to admit Her Majesty's inspector. The first inspector in this area was Rev F W Watkins, and in 1845 he reported of Keyingham school: 'Arithmetic is the only subject that is efficiently taught here. No improvement since last year; the master has other occupations than his school.' The master was John Escreet whose other occupations in the 1840s included parish clerk (a church duty for which he received £5.5s a year), tax assessor for the parish, surveyor of highways and assistant overseer of the poor. The assistant overseer received a salary and helped the annually elected overseers as well as carrying out a number of other parochial duties. At the Easter vestry meeting of 1847 it was resolved that he be paid £15 a year plus expenses for assisting the parish officers. His handwriting is found everywhere in Keyingham's parish records, and in 1841 it was he who completed the census return for the village. It would seem that Escreet took heed of Watkins' criticisms for when the inspector visited the school in 1847 he reported the school to be 'in tolerable order, and making fair progress, more in arithmetic and writing than in Scripture and the Catechism. The master is quick and has some experience in teaching'. There were then 26 scholars at the school. Despite the school having been built for only 12 years, Watkins reported that much repair was needed to the floor. Two years before the vestry meeting had agreed to have half the floor flagged (it was probably only an earthen floor up to then) out of the income received for letting the herbage at the side of the lanes, and it was not until 1851 that they could afford to have the other half flagged. Escreet was the only teacher in 1847 (despite the grant for a pupil teacher in 1846) but the following year his 15-year-old son, William, joined him as pupil teacher. In 1850 Escreet gave up teaching in order to farm the 260-acre North End Farm, and the teaching post was advertised in the *Hull Advertiser*. The position was taken by George Kendall, a West Riding man, who had to undertake to complete young William Escreet's teacher training. Kendall remained as master until 1875 and took on the parochial duties formerly held by Escreet. How these could take him away from his obligations at the school is shown by his visits to the court at Grantham in 1862, already related in Chapter 11.

The school, being a National Society school, came under the aegis of the Church of England and probably had regular visits from the parson, who may have helped with religious instruction. As there was no difference in doctrine, only a difference in organisation, between the Anglican and Methodist Churches, probably the only grumbles to come from Methodist parents centred on the possibility that the day school could be a recruiting ground for the Anglican Sunday school. At the religious census of 1851 there had been no Wesleyan or Primitive Sunday schools in the village and it was not until 1860 that the Primitives established their first Sunday school with about two dozen scholars and 15 teachers. By 1862 there were over 50 scholars and 19 teachers, men and women. By this time there was probably a Sunday school at the Wesleyan chapel, which had been provided with a schoolroom at its rebuilding in 1848. Meanwhile, St Nicholas Sunday school seems to have suffered a setback. In 1841 Joshua Smyth became ill and retired to Woodbridge in Suffolk for the next 12 years. In the visitation return for 1864 he claimed that when he left there had been 100 scholars at the Sunday school, but now (in 1864) there was no Sunday school. As mentioned above the attendance at the school on the day of the religious census was 59. The Sunday school was not re-established until the coming of a new vicar in 1873, and in 1877 there were about 20 Sunday school scholars compared with 60 at the Wesleyan chapel and 70 at the Primitive Methodist chapel.

During Smyth's illness a succession of eight different curates served both Keyingham and Burton Pidsea, only one of them, Jackson Porter (1842-48) serving for longer than a year. As many of them were only in deacon's orders they could not administer communion. It may be the lack of religious leadership that led to apathy amongst the parishioners and the demise of the Sunday school. It would seem that when Keyingham did get a curate of ability the parishioners appreciated it. Joseph Charles Edwards, MA, was the last but one of the curates (but only the second to have a degree) before Smyth returned from Suffolk in 1854. Shortly before leaving, Edwards presented a collection of 300 books towards forming a library for the village, and on his departure in June 1853 Edwards was himself presented with a silver salver and cup, two silver candlesticks and some money. The cup was inscribed: 'This Cup With Other Plates and a Purse of Gold are Presented to the Revd. J. C. Edwards M.A. by his attached

Parishioners as a token of their admiration of his talents as a preacher and faithfulness and diligence as a Christian Paster [sic]. Keyingham 9th June 1853. Henry Carlin, Churchwarden.' Unfortunately, during his stay at Keyingham, Edwards got into debt (not too difficult, one imagines, on a curate's salary) and had to borrow money from George Meadley, a Keyingham butcher, soon to be the founder of a prominent farming family on Sunk Island. Edwards could not repay his debt before he left the parish and so gave Meadley the silver instead. Part of the silver is still with the family.

It was during Edwards' curacy that Keyingham church obtained its first organ. Before that time accompaniment to hymn singing was provided by musicians, who sat in the gallery at the west end of the church. The only indication of the type of instrument played is from the church accounts, which show an expenditure of 11 shillings on fiddle strings in 1848. There was also probably a choir, for in 1820 the Ottringham churchwardens paid six shillings to the 'Keyingham singers'. The new organ, built by Forster & Andrews, was opened on Whit Sunday 1852, and the following day a tea party was held in a tent set up near the church in order to raise funds to pay for the organ. It was a fine-looking instrument with the visible pipes being gilded. After its installation, the repair of fiddle strings no longer featured in the churchwardens' accounts, although they began paying a guinea a year to Forster & Andrews for organ tuning.

When Joshua Smyth returned to Keyingham in 1854 he was coming back to a village whose population was about to decline. In the remaining 19 years of his incumbency the village's population went down from 746 to 620. By 1891 the figure was 587. The decline was reflected in the attendance at both church and chapel. In 1864 Smyth returned the congregation as 50 in the morning and 150 in the afternoon, '& in the afternoon increasing'. In 1868 the numbers were 60 in the morning and '100 in the afternoon and increasing' - an indication of human optimism and of how wary the historian has to be of subjective answers. In 1877 Jeremiah Sharp Thomlinson, vicar from 1873, gave the average congregation to be 'about 70. Increasing but fluctuating'. In 1884 he returned a figure of 50 'at present rather on the increase, the Wesleyans having recently discontinued their morning services'. There was now no afternoon service, except 'in the depth of winter' when the evening service was switched to the afternoons. There was a similar story of decline from the Primitives. The average congregation was returned as 150 each year between 1855 and 1861. In 1867 it was 110.

The Anglican ministers tried to give reasons for the smallness of their congregations. In 1864 Smyth said it was due 'Partly to the taste for Methodism - & the apathy of the lower orders & partly - to the want of more energy in the Minister from ill health'. In 1868 he pointed out 'we have Methodist and Ranter [Primitive Methodist] chapels and the attendants I imagine form one third of the parish - the church a third - and the other third can be made nothing of from distance or apathy'. Later his successor, Thomlinson, attributed the hindrance of his parochial work to 'the prevalence of dissent which has long existed and which my predecessor who was vicar for over 50 years helped to foster by himself attending the Wesleyan services'. Thomlinson perhaps gave a truer reason for the smaller congregations in 1884 when he said, 'the young persons after leaving my Sunday School, have all left the village, Hull absorbing the most'.

By this time the control of weekday schooling in Keyingham had passed out of the hands of the Church. In 1870 an Act was passed whereby if a voluntary educational body, such as the National Society, failed to provide adequate school accommodation in a particular area then a school had to be set up that could be partly funded from the rates. Such a school was run by a board of managers elected by the ratepayers. In these new board schools, as they were called, religious instruction, if given at all, was to be undenominational. Locally, both Burstwick and Hedon took advantage of the Act and elected school boards in 1872. It may be thought that Keyingham, with its strong Methodist element, would have been quick to follow suit and demand a school uninfluenced by Anglican teachings. There certainly seems to have been a need for more accommodation. In the 1871 census of Keyingham, of the 120 children aged from four years to 12 years, 71 were described as 'scholars'. In addition, there were 'scholars' under the age of four (one was aged two) and over the age of 12 (it must be borne in mind that at the same time there were 13-year-old girls and boys who were in employment as house servants and farm workers). All told, there were 82 children described as 'scholars' and, even if their attendance at school may not have been regular, their numbers indicate that many villagers set some store by education in the days when there was no compulsory attendance and schooling cost money. Most of the scholars were the children of farmers or tradesmen, but half a dozen farm workers were also sending their children to school, as were two unmarried mothers. Some of the poorer children would have had their school pence paid out of the Marritt-Ombler Trust. The youngest children would have gone to an infant school in the village, run by

widow Liza Kirkby and her 17-year-old daughter, but the remainder would have attended the National Society school, where George Kendall was the schoolmaster assisted by his wife Jane. The school supposedly had accommodation for 70 children, but any one who stands in the Church Room and imagines it filled with 70 children, divided into two classes, with space taken up by the master's desk and a blackboard and perhaps some chairs for the children, will realise there would have been a bit of a squeeze. There is no doubt there was need for extra school accommodation in Keyingham in 1871, and if the National Society could not provide it, then a board school was the solution. But a board school meant an addition to rates, and Keyingham seems to have been reluctant to implement the Act. In such a case the government Education Department had the power to enforce the election of a school board, and Keyingham has the dubious distinction of being the first village in the East Riding to have a compulsorily elected board.

A meeting of ratepayers to nominate the board was held on 18 November 1872. The five chosen were William and Matthew Carlin, George Cole Francis and Frederick Dunn, all substantial farmers, and Joseph Tong, a master tailor. The following year the board was chosen by election, as required by the Education Act, and Dunn and Tong were replaced by Henry Clark, grocer and draper and a leading Wesleyan Methodist, and William Usher, grocer, postman and a local preacher for the Primitive Methodists. Under the Act the board was elected every three years. The board also replaced the vicar and churchwardens as trustees of the Marritt-Ombler charity.

The board's first task was to provide a larger school. Land in Saltaugh Road was purchased for £100 and a competition was opened for architects to submit plans for a new school - a cheap method, prevalent at the time, of finding the best design. Of six entries, the design of Robert Clamp of Hull was chosen, the plan consisting of an infants' classroom, a classroom for older children, the master's house and a meeting room for the school board. Building began in 1874, and in September that year a memorial stone was laid below the window of the board room in a typical Victorian ceremony after the members of the board, the building contractors and the architect had walked from the old school in Ings Lane. William Carlin, chairman of the board, was presented with 'a silver and elegantly chased trowel with an appropriate inscription' and a mallet with which to lay the stone. When the stone had been declared well and truly laid there were half a dozen speeches and several rounds of cheering. The company then departed, the building workmen to 'a substantial repast, provided for them at a neighbouring inn by the liberality of the Chairman'.

In October the following year the school was opened with similar ceremony. The new school had a turret to house the school bell and there was also a clock that chimed 'the hours so as to be heard in all parts of the village'. The clock was presented by William Carlin and G C Francis. The total cost of the site and the building with internal fittings was £1,700. A new master, Thomas Anthony who had previously taught at Holmpton, was employed at a salary of £100 a year. George Kendall continued his connection with the school by being clerk to the school board at a salary of £10.

Robert Clamp's plan of the board school and master's house, 1874. The school has two classrooms, labelled 'Mixed School' and 'Infants' School' and the school was often referred to in the plural. The school board held its fortnightly evening meetings in the board room.

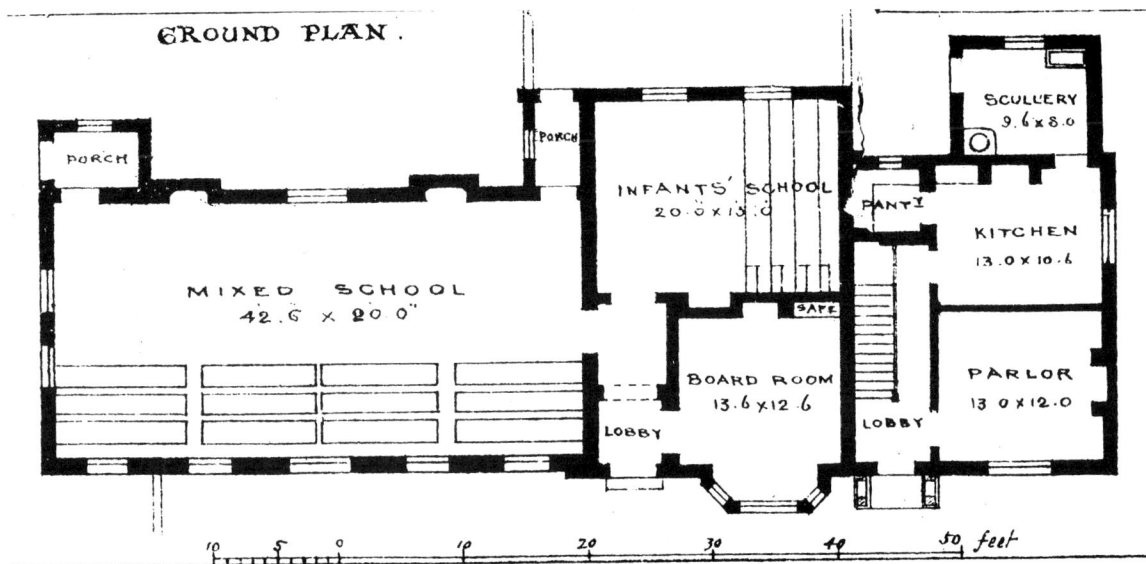

GROUND PLAN.

PORCH

PORCH

INFANTS' SCHOOL
20.0 x 13.0

SCULLERY
9.6 x 8.0

PANTY

KITCHEN
13.0 x 10.6

MIXED SCHOOL
42.6 x 20.0"

SAFE

BOARD ROOM
13.6 x 12.6

PARLOR
13.0 x 12.0

LOBBY

LOBBY

10   5   0   10   20   30   40   50 feet

New uses were soon found for the old school. In 1877 Jeremiah Thomlinson had complained of the need for a suitable building in the village as a counter attraction to the public houses. The building could serve as a reading room, a lecture hall and meeting place. The suggestion seems to have been taken up and very soon the old school became the People's Institute, serving as a reading room and a meeting place for, amongst others, the local lodge of the Oddfellows, the annual vestry and later the parish council. When the parish council moved its meeting place to the board school the room was sold in 1906 to the York Diocesan Trustees for use as a church room, which is its use today.

The new board school was immediately used to its capacity, the *average* attendance in the first three months being 103 in a building designed to accommodate 105, and the board decided that no more children from outlying districts were to be admitted for the time being. In 1877 there were 136 children on the books, in addition to the 16 small children being taught at Eliza Kirkby's dame school. As the village population began to decline in the latter years of the century, so did the number of children at school. In 1887 there were 108 children on the board school's books with an average attendance of 83, and in 1892, the year after school fees were abolished, the average attendance was 90.

The board had decided the fees before the school opened. For the under-sevens they were 2d a week, for the seven-to-nine-year-olds they were 3d and for those over nine they were 4d. Children were to be admitted to the infants' school at the age of three. The fees were to be paid each Monday morning in advance. In the first three months of the school's existence the school pennies amounted to over £16. Under the 1870 Act school boards could pay the fees of the children of poor parents, and the Keyingham board made reductions, especially for large families. In 1876, for example, it was agreed that John Brown 'pay 6d a week for his five children for the next six months'. The Marritt-Ombler charity, of which the board had become the trustees, was used towards reducing fees. The Act also enabled school boards to frame by-laws making school attendance compulsory, and early in 1876 the board appointed George Kendall as school attendance officer at a salary of £5.5s a year. He was also paid a guinea to make a census of all the children in the village under the age of 13. His duties were to visit the school each Monday morning after the school pence had been collected, note any absentees and then see the parents. If he saw any children of school age about the village during school hours, he was to report them. With schooling costing money and the opportunity for the older children to find occasional work on the farms, absenteeism was quite frequent, and the board often had to threaten parents with being summoned before the courts. The threat was occasionally resorted to and in 1877 Richard Rudd was fined one shilling at the magistrate's court for not sending his son to Keyingham school.

In order to reduce absenteeism the school holidays were carefully chosen to coincide with the occasions when the children might be tempted to stay away from school. Thus, holidays were given during Whit week and the following week to allow children to attend Sunday school feasts and excursions. In 1876 the school was closed for harvest holidays from 18 August to 2 October, and the attendance officer was to grant leave of absence to children wishing to work in the week preceding 18 August.

A high attendance was important for the school as the size of the government grant depended on the average attendance. In 1887, when the average attendance was 83 (77% of the number on the books) the grant was £61.8s.7d. The remaining money to make up the running costs of the school and the teachers' and other officers' salaries would have to come from the children's school pence, the Marritt-Ombler Charity and a rate imposed on the parish.

The Methodists in the village may have been pleased when Keyingham's school became nondenominational. They would certainly have been pleased when church rates were abolished by an Act of 1868. Up to that year the fabric of the parish church had been maintained by a rate imposed, along with the poor-rate and the highway rate, on all the ratepayers in the parish, whatever their denomination. In Keyingham the church rate was also used for expenses other than maintaining the building - payment of the clerk's wages and the cost of tuning the organ, for example. In 1869, the last year of church rates, Methodists like Ralph Burnell Clough, Henry Clark, Francis Ford, Robert Sykes and William Usher, were contributing to the running of the Anglican church at a time when their own chapels were still owing money on their buildings. True, their contributions were not great. Their rateable values were only five to six pounds (the large farmers were rated at £250 to £650) and the rate never exceeded 2d (1p) in the pound in the 1860s, but the payment must have still rankled.

With the total rateable value of the whole parish well exceeding £4,000, a 2d rate brought the church about £36 a year. After 1869 the parish church had to seek income from other sources. Initially, most of the Anglican ratepayers gave donations roughly in proportion to the rate they formerly paid, but gradually there began to be more offertories taken at the church services. In 1870 half a dozen offertories were taken in the course of the year, often after special sermons. In 1880 over a dozen offertories were collected, and in 1892 offertories were taken every week. In the 1870s harvest thanksgiving services began to replace the more secular harvest homes of old times and in a farming community the collection at harvest festival was always the largest one of the year. In 1892, for instance, when collections were usually in the range of three to four shillings (at one service during the year it was only 3d), over £2.12s (£2.60) was taken at the harvest festival. With the abolition of church rates the parish church was now on a par with the chapels and like them had to raise its money in a variety of ways besides from the offertories, and the proceeds of such things as concerts, teas and bazaars begin to feature in the church accounts from the 1870s onward. The problem was (and still is) that the Anglicans had a larger, older and less comfortable building to maintain.

- o -

Joshuah Smyth resigned the vicarage of Keyingham in 1873 at the age of 81 and went to live in the south of the country. He died at Colchester in 1878. His place as vicar of Keyingham was taken by Jeremiah Thomlinson. By this time the rectory, held by the Archbishops of York since the time of Henry VIII, had been vested in the Ecclesiastical Commissioners. This meant that they held the rectorial estate, the proceeds of which were now devoted to the benefit of the Church nationally, and it was they who had a new house built for the vicar in 1879. It was designed by Robert Clamp, the architect for the board school. It was a typical Victorian vicarage with three main rooms, kitchen, scullery, pantry and store room on the ground floor, four bedrooms and a nursery on the first floor and two servants' rooms in the attic reached by a back stair. In the grounds of the vicarage was a stable block consisting of coach house, stable and cow house, with harness room above. Mrs Horrox, wife of the last vicar to live in the house, described how the kitchen wing, which was paved with old brick tiles and in her time overshadowed by a huge lime tree, was dark and damp. Outside the door from the scullery was a two-hole earth closet, intended for the staff. On the first floor were a bathroom and water closet, both on the original plans of the house and intended for the family. Up to 1950, water was obtained from two pumps in the back kitchen and pumped by hand to a large tank in the roof to supply the facilities on the first floor. Hot water for the bath had to be boiled in a copper in the scullery and carried upstairs. On census day 1881 the household consisted of Mr Thomlinson, his wife and four children, a governess and two maids. The eldest son was absent from home that day and a sixth child was yet to be born.

In the half-century between the institutions of Rev J Smyth and Rev J Thomlinson to the benefice of Keyingham there had been great changes in Anglican worship. These changes had begun at Oxford in the 1830s when a number of dons began to re-assess Anglicanism. Although Elizabeth I had adopted the 'Middle Way' of worship for the Church of England the English had always considered themselves to be a Protestant nation. As such it had rather stood by during the 18th century and let more nonconforming denominations come to the fore. The leaders of the Oxford Movement, as it became known, wanted the established Church to re-assert itself, not by becoming more avowedly Protestant, but by being proud of its Catholic origins. If the established Church was following the Middle Way it was just as much Catholic as it was Protestant. There should be more dignity and ceremonial in worship, and emphasis should be placed on the sanctity of the altar. Over a generation the ideas of the Oxford Movement spread. Any new churches built were built in imitation of the medieval Gothic style. Great reverence was attached to the altar, the floor of the chancel being raised in many churches to make the altar the chief focal point of the church. The practice of having a cross and candles on the altar was re-introduced. Some ministers preferred to be called 'priest' and began to wear more elaborate vestments. Robed choirs, singing in the chancel, replaced the old singers stationed in the gallery at the west end of the church. Incense began to be used in some churches. The taking of communion more frequently was recommended. Slowly these ideas entered Holderness, to a greater measure in some churches than in others. All Saints Halsham, under the influence of the Shipton family as both patrons and rectors, became noticeably 'high church' with the burning of incense and the setting up of an altar to the Virgin Mary. In Keyingham the changes were not so drastic. In 1862 candlesticks were bought for the altar. In 1864, when Joshua Smyth was also vicar of Burton Pidsea, communion was taken four times a year at St Nicholas. In 1868, when Smyth had given up Burton Pidsea, communion was taken six times a year. Under Jeremiah Thomlinson communion was offered every month as well as at the chief Christian festivals.

For this emphasis on the communion and the importance of the altar, Keyingham's church furnishings were ill fitted. In 1884 the interior of the church was still laid out to accommodate the old form of service with its emphasis on the sermon. The box pews in the nave faced every direction but towards the altar, and box pews cluttered up half the chancel and the approach to the altar. The singers and the organ occupied the gallery at the west end of the church. The upper tracery of the east window was blocked up, so that the altar was but dimly illuminated. Above all the church was in a poor state of repair. 'What impedes your ministry and the welfare of the Church around?' enquired the archbishop in 1884. 'The discomfort of the building through not being rainproof & the miserable arrangement & character of the pews,' replied Thomlinson. Twenty years before, Joshua Smyth had reported the church as greatly out of repair and in need of a new roof.

In 1885 a programme of restoration was at last begun. As rectors of the church the Ecclesiastical Commissioners were responsible for the repair of the chancel. Mr Thomlinson managed to prevail upon them to repair the chancel if he would deal with the nave and vestry, and it was in the chancel that the first restoration work began. The box pews were replaced by the present choir stalls, the upper tracery of the east window and the roof were restored and the two archways into the vestry were re-opened. The work on the chancel was completed in 1885, the date being cast on the rainwater heads for the benefit of all those interested in the history of the church.

St : Nicholas · Chvrch · Keyingham Proposed · Restoration · of · Nave ·

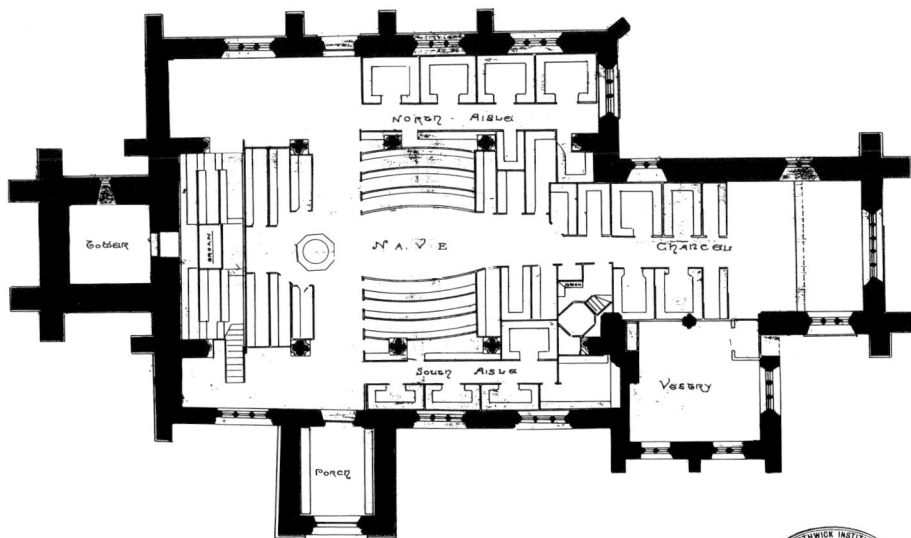

Plan · as · at · present ·

Plan of St Nicholas Church shortly before restoration began in 1885. The plan was drawn by the architects, Smith & Brodrick of Hull. Note the box pews crowding the nave and the chancel, the gallery and organ approached by stairs at the west end of the nave and the desk below the pulpit for the parish clerk. From here the clerk led the responses. The vestry is boarded off from the chancel and is entered by a door and lobby in the northeast corner. Reproduced from the original in the Borthwick Institute, University of York (Faculty 1886/11)

135

The remaining work on the church was carried out partly at the expense of the parishioners, although the Ecclesiastical Commissioners made a grant. The vestry was dealt with first, so that, together with the chancel, it could provide a place of worship whilst the nave underwent repair. Besides the necessary repairs to the roof, the archway between the vestry and the south aisle was unblocked and the doorway, which had formerly given admittance from the churchyard, was blocked. The fireplace, which had been introduced when the vestry was converted from a chantry chapel, was removed. During the restoration the piscina in the south wall was uncovered. The work was completed in 1886 as indicated by the date on the rainwater head.

The major work of restoring the nave was finished in 1888. Externally, the repairs consisted of replacing with dressed stone any patching-up with brick that had been done by past generations of churchwardens. The roof was entirely replaced with the fine beams and rafters that exist today. Internally, the colour wash of three centuries was carefully removed from the walls by brushing with a strong solution of soda. (One of the last applications of colour to the church was in 1870 when John Harbron had received £15 for 'painting and colouring the church'.) All the old box pews were removed and replaced with the present benches. The window opening into the nave from the tower was unblocked. The west gallery with its organ was taken down, the organ being transferred to its present position between the chancel and the vestry. The font was moved to its present position and provided with stone steps. Whilst the flooring was being replaced a new heating apparatus was installed. Previous to this there had been heating in the church, just over £5 being expended on a stove in 1848. This may have replaced the fireplace in the vestry, and an old print of St Nicholas Church shows the stove pipe emerging from the southeast corner. Money was spent on coals and there are references in the accounts to chimneys being swept. The new heating apparatus of 1888 consisted of a horizontal furnace placed in a $4^1/_2$-foot-deep pit in the central aisle at the back of the church. The hot gases from the furnace passed along a horizontal flue under a floor grill along the aisle towards the chancel steps. From there the flue passed under a grill to the north aisle and out of the building. On cold Sundays, well before the service began, Joseph Marling the sexton, or his deputy, would have had to descend the pit by ladder, start the fire and have the furnace well stoked to last through the service. The warmest place in church would have been near the grill over the furnace, which may account for the custom that still persists of the majority of the congregation being at the back of the church. The furnace may have been a good idea in theory but perhaps not in practice because on 1 February 1902 the *Hull News* was reporting that, 'The work of fixing two large stoves in the parish church has been completed, and this place of worship should be very much more comfortable next Sunday.' The stoves were placed at the east end of the north and south aisles. The furnace, grills and flue pipe of the old system still lie beneath the floor along with the sexton's ladder and some early-20th-century pieces of coke.

By 1888 the cost of the restoration project had reached £1,500 and there was still much work to be done. Already, some of the specifications of the architects, Smith & Brodrick of Hull, had had to be abandoned. For instance, the pulpit was made wholly of wood instead of the lower part being 'in the best Caen stone' and the steps of hard York stone. In August 1888 the vicar wrote to the Ecclesiastical Commissioners pointing out repairs were still needed to the steeple and both aisles were in poor condition. The roof of the south aisle was having to be propped up 'which sadly spoils the effect of the Nave restoration'. A further £300 was needed in addition to what was already in hand or promised. He had exhausted all local sources and was having to depend on outside help. Casting round for ways of extracting further grants, he referred to the strong connection that had once existed between Keyingham and Sunk Island, saying how Keyingham had virtually been the mother church of Sunk Island until it was created a separate parish in 1830. If the Ecclesiastical Commissioners could not give a grant on these grounds could they advise him 'whether, if a petition to her Majesty were got up, there might be a likelihood of Her Majesty assisting us'. Thomlinson's hopes in this direction were pinned on the fact that Sunk Island was Crown land. As Sunk Island now had its own rather fine parish church, built only ten years before mostly at the Crown's expense, one can only think that Thomlinson's suggestion was the act of a desperate fund-raiser. As it was, little more money was forthcoming, so that only the south aisle was restored, the work being completed in 1893. In 1894 £116 was still owing to the builders, and two bazaars were held in the vicarage grounds in order to help raise the money. Although the money was eventually found, there was no let-up in the need for fund-raising. In 1905 the church porch, which was in a serious condition, was restored and in the same year an organ fund was begun in order to repair the organ. It was not until Mr Thomlinson had left the benefice and only through the generosity of a private benefactor that the north aisle was restored in 1914, and it was not until 1930 that the spire was repaired.

Thomlinson's difficulty hinged on the fact that probably less than a third of the villagers attended the parish church. Although they were mostly from the farming community and the richest section of the village, farming at that time was going through a long period of depression. Furthermore the village population was declining as farm workers moved to the towns in search of work. With farming in such a bad way, the whole village economy suffered, and there was little money for charitable purposes. At the same time rural churches all over the country - Halsham, Patrington and Winestead, to mention but three local ones - had undertaken similar ambitious restoration schemes, and there was a limit to the amount of grants that could be obtained from such bodies as the Ecclesiastical Commissioners or the Church Building Society. The limited extent of the restoration to Keyingham's church in the last two decades of the 19th century tells a tale of the decline in farming and the beginning of the gradual decay in rural communities.

13 - Local Government

At the beginning of the 19th century the manor court at Burstwick had died out as a unit of local administration in Keyingham, other than as a means of transferring copyhold property. On each transaction a fee went to the lord of the manor, a custom that did not end until the Law of Property Act of 1925. Many owners of older houses in Keyingham will note that their property deeds include copies, taken from the manor court roll, of the early transfers, although in later years the transactions are occurring, not in the manor court, but in a solicitor's office. In the margin of each document is entered the fee paid to the Constables of Burton Constable.

The chief unit of local administration, which since the 16th century had run side by side with the manor court, was the parish vestry. The vestries, under the direction of the justices of the peace, were in fact almost the sole administrators of public affairs in rural areas, central government being responsible only for the defence of the realm, public order and the protection of property. The care of the poor, the maintenance of law and order, the upkeep of the roads and the administration of common property, as well as the upkeep of the parish church, all fell on the vestries. The common property under the care of Keyingham's vestry was the poorhouse, referred to in Chapter 11, the pinfold and, after the enclosure, the gravel pit and the herbage at the sides of the lanes. Until the creation of the post of assistant overseer following an Act of Parliament in 1819 all the officers of the vestry were unpaid. The justices, overseeing the work of the vestries, were men of some property and local standing, and were also unpaid.

At the annual vestry meeting, held each Easter, the churchwardens, overseers of the poor, surveyors of highways and constables were chosen. The choice of surveyors and overseers had to be approved by the justices of the peace, and after 1842 the justices chose the constables from a list of the able-bodied men of the parish rated at £4 or over for the poor-rate or county rate. For Keyingham the lists for the years 1842 to 1845 survive. The accounts of the outgoing officers were examined by the annual vestry and after acceptance were sent to the justices of the peace for final approval. The justices also had to approve the highway rate and poor-rate decided on for the forthcoming year by the vestry. Usually, one vestry meeting a year was considered sufficient, unless something of pressing importance to the parish needed to be dealt with. Most of Keyingham's meetings, especially during the first half of the 19th century, seem to have been held at the Blue Bell, and the minutes usually end with the resolution, 'That one pound be allowed by the Parish for this day's dinner'.

Other matters dealt with by the vestry meeting were connected with administering the parish property. The herbage at the sides of the different roads and lanes was let off to the highest bidders, as was the gravel pit when its source of material for repairing the roads had been exhausted. A herdsman was appointed to tend the animals grazing in the lanes and in 1847 he was paid eight shillings a week out of the highway rate. His hours were from 6.30 a.m. to 6 p.m. and any cattle turned out after that time had to be tended by the owner. In the 1840s horned cows had to have their horns covered. The vestry also appointed a pinder and decided his pay. His job was to impound stray animals and keep them in the village pinfold until the owner, or the village herdsman if the fault were his, had paid a fine. In 1847 George Willingham was the pinder and was to 'have 4d per head for impounding any horse, ass, sheep or other cattle'. In 1853 the pinfold was moved from its position at the west end of Waldby Garth Road to just south of where the board school was later built in Saltaugh Road. In 1875 when the school was built the surveyors of highways were asked by the school board to remove the pinfold.

Stemming from a law passed in the time of Elizabeth I, parishes were responsible for the extermination of vermin. Sparrows were particularly destructive of both growing and stored corn and in 1849 the Keyingham vestry resolved that 'James Brooks [a wheelwright] buy the sparrows: that he pay one penny for 12 eggs, for 6 young sparrows or 2 old ones'. One can imagine boys bird-nesting and using various devices to capture sparrows and present them or their eggs at the wheelwright's shop. The practice of killing sparrows did not end until 1886, when the vestry resolved, 'Sparrows be not bought for the future'. Another creature considered verminous was the mole and the parish employed a mole catcher, whose wage was increased from £2 to £3 a year in 1863.

As the 19th century progressed the business of the vestry came to have a more modern aspect. In November 1853, when the building of the railway through the village was in progress, the vestry unanimously agreed that the railway station should be at the crossing of the line with Eastfield Road and not, as the directors of the railway had planned, on the crossing at North End Road. The motives of the meeting are not clear. Those calling the meeting may have had vested interests along North End Road - there were at that time no buildings in Eastfield Road. As later parish councils were to discover, the railway directors paid little heed to public opinion and the station was built in North End Road, later called Station Road. The vestry exacted some measure of revenge on completion of the railway when they assessed the station at £40 for the highway rate and the line at £246 per mile through the parish.

Keyingham's vestry was not an elected body - at the beginning of the 19th century it consisted simply of all the resident ratepayers. Non-resident ratepayers were not included. This is indicated in a document, already mentioned in Chapter 11, when the parish requested the lord of the manor to grant land on which to build a poorhouse. The wording begins, 'We, the *occupiers* of lands in the Parish of Keyingham...'. Thus, non-resident owners of lands, usually the highest ratepayers, had no say in how the rates were spent. This was corrected in 1818 when the Vestries Act gave participation in the vestry to all inhabitants contributing to the poor-rate, including non-resident ratepayers, and the petition to the railway directors mentioned above began, 'We, the *owners* and occupiers of lands in the Parish of Keyingham in vestry assembled...'. The 1818 Act also gave plural voting to the members of the vestry, so that those rated at less than £200 had one vote, those rated at £200-400 had two votes and those rated above £400 had three votes. Property *owners* had up to six votes depending on the value of their property. Thus any decision-making in vestry was strongly weighted in favour of the better-off, and the government of the parish was for all practical purposes in the hands of the wealthier farmers. Their rule was reinforced by the fact that it was overseen by the justices of the peace, men with a property qualification who were nominated to their post, not elected.

During the course of the 19th century there were two trends in local administration: central government began to have a larger and larger controlling influence, and there was an increasing emphasis on the election of representatives to serve the local community. The right to choose representatives of any kind belonged to very few Keyingham folk. Before the parliamentary reforms of 1832, the only men in the country, as opposed to the boroughs, eligible to vote were freeholders with property worth £2 a year or more. As mentioned in Chapter 10 there was very little freehold land in Keyingham and most of that belonged to a non-resident. At parliamentary elections there was probably no one wending his way from Keyingham to York to cast his vote for the county's representatives. After the passing of the Reform Bill in 1832 the vote in the country was extended to the £10 copyholder and certain leaseholders. As mentioned in earlier chapters, copyhold rents in Keyingham had remained at their medieval level (the Constables' steward was collecting the same £1.6s.8d for the rent of the mill as collected by Keyingham's reeve in 1289) and there were in fact no £10 copyholders in Keyingham in 1832. A rent of about £5 was paid on the Broadley estate, the largest lay estate awarded at the enclosure in 1805. The only Keyingham people to whom the 1832 Act would have brought the vote were the large leasehold tenants in the Marsh. In 1867 the vote in the country was extended to the owners of property worth £5 a year, but it was not until 1884 that all male householders were given the vote, thus bringing the agricultural labourer into the electorate for the first time.

The right to vote in elections of a local nature had come a little earlier to some Keyingham folk. The Poor Law Amendment Act, mentioned in Chapter 11, which brought the care of the poor more under the direction of central government, also made the unit of administration the union rather than the parish. Keyingham became part of the Patrington Union. Each parish was represented on the union board by a guardian, who was elected by the ratepayers and property owners with the same plurality of voting as applied to the ratepayers meeting in vestry. This gave voting rights to about 70 people in Keyingham - farmers, shopkeepers and tradesmen. The person renting a cottage and not paying rates, but the one perhaps most likely to have dealings with the board of guardians, did not have a vote. The guardians themselves, who were unpaid, had to have a property qualification and came from the upper echelons of the farming community. George Cole Francis, Keyingham's highest ratepayer, of Saltaugh Grange, represented the village many times on the board of the Patrington Union.

The election of guardians came to have added significance following the passing of the Public Health Act of 1872, when the poor law unions in those areas where no local board of health had been set up were constituted rural sanitary authorities. In 1872 the Patrington Board of Guardians chose a nine-member rural sanitary committee from amongst its ranks and soon after appointed a clerk, a medical officer of health and an inspector of nuisances. This last post was awarded to Robert Frost, an Ottringham builder and contractor, at a salary of £50 a year plus expenses. Although Frost was not expected to give full-time service, he seems to have been a tireless worker on behalf of the authority and was still in the post (at the same salary) in the latter years of the century. The salaries of the different officers and the running expenses of the authority were paid out of a rate levied on the whole union, but any work carried out was paid for by the parish or the individual concerned. The rate imposed by the sanitary authority amounted to only one halfpenny in the pound. The new authority was very much under the control of the Local Government Board in London, and the clerk was continually writing to the central authority for approval for the committee's actions.

To assist the sanitary authority in its dealings with the parishes under its control, parochial committees were appointed. Keyingham's first committee consisted of three farmers, George Marshall, Frederick Dunn and E T Oldfield. At their first meeting with Robert Frost in January 1874 it was resolved to replace some of the public drains and open sewers with nine-inch pipes, over 200 yards in all. It was left to the parochial committee to arrange the work, but when they had failed to do anything within three months the sanitary authority took on the task and put the work out to tender. With commendable speed the job was completed by May 1874, at a cost of £70 to the parish rate. The replacement of Keyingham's open drains and sewers by pipes taking the waste to ditches on the periphery of the village was a piecemeal process that continued into the 20th century.

The cost of works like these was something that the ratepayers balked at, and the Local Government Board had to remind the sanitary authority that it was they who had to ensure that the parishes were provided with proper sewers and that they were not relieved of the responsibility by resolutions passed at meetings of ratepayers.

Improvements required on private property had to be paid for by the owner. Privies had to be moved a proper distance from living accommodation and had to be provided with ash bins or, alternatively, settling pits. In 1893 the owner of the Ship Inn was called upon to fit the urinal with a trough and pipes to convey the 'water' into the drain in Saltaugh Road. Robert Frost in 1874 reported that several houses of which E T Oldfield was the landlord were in a very unsanitary condition through bad drainage. Two years later the fault had not been rectified and the magistrate was asked to summons Oldfield to answer the complaint. No doubt in a fit of pique, Oldfield refused to serve any further on the parochial committee. The extent of Robert Frost's energies can be judged from the fact that he was constantly dealing with cases like this in all 27 parishes of the union, including the growing seaside town of Withernsea.

With the passing of the Local Government Act in 1894 the rural sanitary authorities became the rural district councils, so that the Patrington sanitary authority became the Patrington Rural District Council. The RDC was chosen directly by the electorate and not from amongst the guardians. There was now no plurality of voting - every parochial elector had one vote.

The principle of equal voting rights had already arrived in Keyingham with the creation of the board school. The board was chosen every three years by the ratepayers, who each had five votes, as there were five members to be chosen. The ballot was secret, as required by the Education Act of 1870. It proved such a good idea that it was adopted for parliamentary elections in 1872. Before then, the vote for MPs was open and the voting lists were published. It needs little imagination to appreciate the bribery and corruption that flourished, which, locally, led to the disfranchisement of the borough of Beverley in 1870.

As the democratic principle grew in both parliamentary elections and the choosing of local bodies, it became generally accepted that rule at the county level by nominated justices of the peace was an anachronism. Although the justices served the community well, it was felt that unelected men should not be taking important decisions affecting the community or setting the county rate. Moreover, the justices' duties had increased greatly with the increasing legislation of the second half of the 19th century, and there were fewer men with enough spare time to fulfil the duties. At the same time it was believed that central government was now exercising too much power over local affairs, as no doubt the clerk to the Patrington Union felt as he laboriously penned letters to Whitehall with queries regarding sanitation or the Poor Law. The outcome of these various objections was the passing of the Local Government Act of 1888, which took almost all the duties, except the judicial ones, out of the hands of the justices and gave them to county councils elected by the ratepayers. In the case of Yorkshire, each riding had a county council. For the election of members of the East Riding County Council, the riding was divided into 47 divisions each electing one councillor. The Keyingham division consisted of Burstwick, Keyingham, Ottringham, Paull, Ryhill and Camerton, and Thorngumbald. Elections were held every three years. The first councillor elected by the Keyingham division was the indefatigable public servant George Cole Francis. Following his death in 1894 his place was taken by his son, Herbert Francis.

One responsibility immediately taken on by the county councils was the maintenance of main roads. These were the former turnpike roads, which one by one had been dis-turnpiked owing to the lack of returns to the share-holders caused by competition from the railways. The Hedon-Patrington turnpike was wound up in 1874, the Hedon-Preston-Hull in 1878 and the Hull-Hedon

direct in 1881. Tradition died hard, however, and the main road through Keyingham was referred to in the lane-letting book as 'the Turnpike' as late as 1932. The effect of winding up a turnpike was that the parishes became once more responsible for the whole maintenance of trunk roads within their boundaries, and England's trunk-road system came to be in a very bad way. The burden on the parishes was ameliorated when an Act of 1878 allowed the justices in Quarter Sessions to grant half the cost of maintenance out of the county rate, and the parishes were relieved of the whole burden when the county councils came into being.

Besides the main roads, the East Riding County Council had the responsibility of dealing with a whole range of matters previously dealt with by the JPs. They included policing, weights and measures, protection of wild birds, contagious diseases in animals, and parish allotments, to mention just a few. Diseases in animals were dealt with by the cattle plague committee, of which Herbert Francis was a member in 1895. In the first quarter of that year the committee, through its veterinary and police inspectors, dealt with many cases of swine fever, sheep scab and anthrax, although none occurred nearer to Keyingham than Sunk Island.

The ERCC also had a technical instruction committee that provided classes on practical matters in the villages. For men there were classes and lectures on bee keeping, poultry keeping, dairy work and carpentry, and for women there were classes in cooking, laundry and dressmaking. In the summer of 1894 a ten-day course on dairy work held at Keyingham had an average attendance of 18 pupils and 34 'spectators'. The instructor was Miss Joseph. Later that year 25 women attended Miss Margrate's dressmaking class. Most of the women in the class were the wives of tradesmen but four were the wives of farmers and seven were the wives of labourers. That winter a lecture on 'Health' organised at Keyingham by the technical instruction committee attracted an audience of 58.

Despite the extension of the democratic principle to the election of the member for parliament, the members of the school board and the representative on the county council, Keyingham's vestry was still plutocratic in nature. Although all ratepayers could attend the meetings, the voice of the wealthier members was the strongest because of the system of plural voting. There was another problem in that the vestry, as its name implied, was strongly connected with the Anglican Church. The churchwardens were chosen at the annual vestry along with the civil officers. The chairman of the meeting was nearly always the minister of the church, and up to 1869 the vestry decided the church rate. One imagines there would have been some resentment amongst the Methodists, who on the whole came from the ranks of the lower ratepayers and so had reduced voting power. One wonders what the Methodists' views were when the vestry approved expenditure on the church Sunday school, or agreed, as it did in 1855, that the 'Parish bears the expense of erecting a pew in the chancel for the Clergyman'. What did the Methodists think in 1891 when the vestry accepted the vicar's proposal that Mr James Tarbotton perform the duties of clerk, sexton and church cleaner at a yearly salary of £10 out of the parish rate?

If the Methodists did object to rule with a strong Anglican slant, it does not seem that they took the opportunity to contest it in the three-yearly election of the school board in which all ratepayers had an equal vote. As mentioned in the previous chapter the first school board elected in 1873 included a Wesleyan Methodist and a Primitive Methodist. The other three members were substantial farmers, two of whom - George Cole Francis and William Carlin - served as churchwardens at different times. Thereafter a contest for the election of a school board did not take place for many years. Three years after the initial election of the board 90 ratepayers signed a memorandum expressing 'themselves satisfied with the manner in which the present board had carried out its duties' and requesting them to allow themselves to be put forward for a second term of office. There were no other candidates and the board was re-elected without a contest. It was not until 1891 that there was a contest for the election of a school board, although there had been co-options as well as changes in the candidates put forward every three years as members retired or died. What prompted the contest is not clear although we might discern two possible adversaries on the retiring board - Richard Westmorland and Rev Jeremiah Thomlinson.

Richard Westmorland, a Primitive Methodist local preacher, had come on to the board in 1888, replacing another Primitive Methodist, William Usher. Westmorland was a shoemaker and a leading member of the Foresters, with its strong working-class membership. On occasions he seems to have been at odds with the rest of the board. In 1888 he had suggested reducing the schoolmaster's salary and in 1889 he proposed a reduction in school fees. In neither case did he receive support from the other members. Both proposals suggest he was the poor man's champion, because reducing the master's salary could have led to a reduction in fees, although it could also have led to a reduction in the rates. Westmorland's later actions, recounted in the next chapter, show that he definitely considered the established Church to be over privileged, and he may well have raised the hackles of Thomlinson on occasions.

Thomlinson had become vicar of Keyingham in 1873 and had been co-opted on to the board in 1881. By the 1890s he seems to have had his fill of Methodist local preachers. At the archbishop's visitation in 1894, in answer to the question, 'Is there anything which specially hinders your parochial work?' Thomlinson replied, 'The prevalence of dissent..... Local preachers and agitators poison the minds of the labouring classes by false statements, and exciting their hopes in the share of the spoils should the Church be disestablished and disendowed.' One cannot help but think that it was Primitive Methodist preachers in particular he was referring to, because historically in Keyingham there seems to have been more of an affinity between the Anglicans and the Wesleyans than there was between the two Methodist groups. Twenty years earlier, the vicar, Rev Joshua Smyth had been known to attend Wesleyan services. In 1894, at the election of the first chairman of the parish council, it was a Wesleyan who proposed an Anglican, and in 1900 parish councillor John Gibson, a Wesleyan, defended the payment at the parish expense of the cost of consecrating part of the new cemetery, purely for the benefit of the Anglicans. On the other hand, the schoolmaster whose salary Westmorland suggested should be reduced was Thomas Anthony, a Wesleyan local preacher. Moreover, the Wesleyans tended to be of the middle class and more akin to the Anglicans, whereas the Primitive Methodists were mostly made up of small tradesmen and working-class people. There was also a political element to the differences between the Primitive Methodists and the Anglicans, particularly the clergy. The latter were almost all openly Conservative. In 1886 when there was a move to open a local branch of the Primrose League, a kind of women's Conservative support group, there was backing from the parsons of Roos, Patrington, Withernsea and Halsham, and the wives of three of them went on to the council of the new branch. On the other hand, Primitive Methodist ministers supported the Liberals. In 1903 a bazaar, held at the Foresters Hall to raise money towards Keyingham Primitive Methodist funds, was opened by the Liberal candidate for Holderness. He took the opportunity to make an election speech and received support from Rev T Vaughan, minister of the Patrington Primitive Methodist circuit, as well as from Richard Westmorland's son, George.

In the 1891 contest for the positions on the Keyingham school board there were eight candidates for the five positions. The retiring members, who all sought re-election, were Thomlinson, Westmorland, Henry Clark, a Wesleyan local preacher who had been on the board since its formation, Joseph Tong, master tailor and on the board since 1880, and William Snaith, a farmer at Keyingham Grange. The other candidates were Richard Mook, churchwarden and farmer at Ebor House, Robert Tarbotton, blacksmith, and Thomas Eyre, miller. From Keyingham's 134 households the turnout for the election was about 120 electors, each able to cast five votes, with the liberty to distribute them amongst the candidates or give them all to one. The system had its drawbacks including the fact that someone who was the second favourite for different parties could come top of the poll. The outcome was the re-election of the old board with the exception that Thomlinson was replaced by Richard Mook. Thus, the denominational make-up of the board remained the same. The election proved the popularity of Henry Clark, who polled 161 votes. Richard Westmorland received 127 votes and no one else got more than 84. Thomas Eyre received five votes and may have cast all his for himself. Three years later, in 1894, there was no contest for the places on the board, and Rev Jeremiah Thomlinson replaced William Snaith. In 1894, however, there were what may have been considered more important contests to be fought, when the first parish council was elected.

The Liberals had long wanted to reform parish government in order to give the ordinary working man a say in the running of his community, and a Parish Council Bill was introduced in 1892. All rural parishes were to hold a parish meeting, which would elect a parish council, providing the parish had a population of at least 300. Councils would have the powers, amongst other things, to provide baths, washhouses and libraries and to hire land for allotments. To finance these projects they could borrow money - with the consent of the Local Government Board at Whitehall - and spend the product of a three-penny rate. Although this was considered by many as far too democratic a proposal, the Bill was passed and the Local Government Act of 1894 arrived on the statute book.

Keyingham's first parish meeting for the election of the parish council was held in the school on the evening of 4 December 1894. Jeremiah Thomlinson, who was not a candidate, was elected as chairman of the meeting, before voting for the members of the council took place. Voting was open to all those on the parliamentary register of electors, that is men aged 21 and over, and owners or occupiers of rateable property. The latter group meant that certain women - those owning property or paying rates in their own right - had the vote. Owners living beyond three miles from the village were not eligible to vote. Those women with the right to vote also had the right to stand for the council, but all Keyingham's 19 candidates were men. There were 11 positions on the council (the number was decided by the ERCC for each parish) and each elector had 11 votes, each of which had to be given to a different candidate. After due procedure the council was elected. In all 697 votes were cast, indicating a turnout of 65 or so voters. After this initial election, which was by show of hands, it was possible for any member of the meeting to demand a properly conducted ballot of the ratepayers, but this did not happen at Keyingham because eight of the candidates withdrew, including two who had been elected at the first poll. The council members came from a wide spectrum of society as their backgrounds indicate:

Locking Charlton, aged 58, chemist, grocer and draper. Living outside the parish at Kelsey Hill, but a ratepayer by virtue of his shop in the village. Churchwarden.

William Dobson, aged 56, agricultural labourer. Primitive Methodist.

Isaac Denton Dunn, aged 39, farmer at Marsh House. Churchwarden.

John Gibson, aged 57, carrier. Wesleyan local preacher.

George Haith, aged 26, farm foreman at Ebor House Farm.

W H Hodgson, farmer at North End Farm.

Enoch Howes, aged 54, agricultural labourer.

Walter Coupland Kirkwood, aged 27, butcher. Churchwarden in 1899 and 1900.

Richard Mook, aged 55, farmer, of Ebor House. Churchwarden 1886-9.

James Tarbotton, aged 38, tailor, shopkeeper, parish clerk and sexton.

Robert Tarbotton, aged 40, blacksmith.

At the election of some parish councils there are indications of strong inter-denominational and political rivalry. At Patrington, for instance, the rector and Richard Marshall JP, son of the lord of the manor, stood as candidates for the 13-strong council. Both failed at the preliminary show of hands and a council with a strong Primitive Methodist make-up was elected. A ballot was called for and a fortnight later both the rector and Marshall, as well as other Anglicans, were elected and the council had an almost equal balance of the two denominations. Things seem to have been different at Keyingham where the apparent flare-up of inter-denominational rivalry that occurred at the school board election in 1891 did not persist. At the top of the poll for the council was Richard Mook with 62 votes, showing that nearly every one of the 65 or so electors gave him a vote. It was he who was chosen as chairman of the council, on the proposal of John Gibson, when the 11 members met a fortnight later. Locking Charlton was elected vice chairman. One of the men withdrawing his candidature following the poll at the parish meeting, despite the fact that he was joint ninth in the poll, was Richard Westmorland. The withdrawals made way for Isaac Dunn and W H Hodgson, two farmers. It would be interesting to know what machinations, if any, occurred during the meeting. If religious and political differences *were* set aside it seems that the electorate chose, on the whole, older, well-respected members of the community with some experience of managing affairs, because besides those like the current and past churchwardens, there were men who had served on the parochial committee, and others who helped run the Foresters or the Wesleyan and Primitive Methodist chapels.

The old vestry, whose civil responsibilities had now been taken over by the parish council, continued to have a role in church affairs. Today, the vestry, which consists of all baptised parishioners of 18 years or over, not belonging to any rival religious organisation, is eligible to vote in the election of churchwardens that takes place each year. The vestry also has the right to express its views on applications for alterations and additions to the church building. Otherwise, the running of the parish church is in the hands of the parochial church council, created by an Act of 1919.

The parish council did not inherit all the vestry's old civil responsibilities. The maintenance of the parish roads was taken out of their hands by the same Act of 1894 that created the parish councils. Parish constables were no longer chosen, as there was a full-time police force under the control of the ERCC and, ultimately, the Home Office. One of the East Riding constabulary was stationed at Keyingham, although his 'beat' covered villages outside Keyingham. One of the old vestry duties remaining was care of parish property, so that the parish council was overseeing the lease of the gravel pit, the twice-a-year letting of the lanes and the administration of the Marritt-Ombler lands.

Of the possible new responsibilities that a parish council could take on was the provision of a library. It was for this reason that at the annual parish meeting held in the Wesleyan schoolroom in March 1895 the council was presented with a library of 400 books by Rev Edward Wright, a Methodist minister, born in Keyingham in 1811. He told the meeting 'he had travelled considerably during his lifetime and he had always had a warm corner in his heart for his native village - (cheers).

He would be glad to donate his books to the village now that there was a council and a proper body to look after them. The library should become the property of the parish for the use of the inhabitants - (loud cheers)'. The books were no doubt kept in what is now the Church Room, which had recently been converted to a reading room, as well as a meeting chamber for the council. A responsibility that the council took over from the ERCC was that of providing allotments, principally for farm workers. The council allotments are dealt with in the next chapter, as is also the provision of a cemetery by the parish council.

It would seem that as the limited powers of the parish council became evident the interest in the election of councillors waned. At the election of the 11 councillors in 1904 only 215 votes were cast, indicating that only 20 people voted, compared with over 60 voting at the first election. Jeremiah Thomlinson and Richard Westmorland were both on the council before 1900, possibly because of a sense of duty and lack of interest by others. Councillors were no doubt feeling that they were able to give only small pinpricks to higher authorities, and pinpricks that were generally ignored. Despite the possibility of women being on parish councils from the beginning, it was not until the late 1950s that Keyingham had its first women councillors, when Mrs Gladys Cook, grand daughter of Richard Westmorland, and Mrs Elsie Pashby both gained seats. Elsie's husband, Wilfred, also served on the Holderness RDC as well as on the ERCC.

The 1894 Local Government Act that created the parish councils also created the rural district councils, which took on the duties of the former rural sanitary authorities. The Patrington RDC was made up of members elected from the different parishes in the union and replaced the rural sanitary committee that had been chosen from the guardians. Richard Westmorland came to serve on the Patrington RDC in the 20th century and was still a member of the council in 1922 at the age of 75. The Poor Law duties of the guardians continued although the guardians no longer had to have a property qualification. The electorate for both the RDC and the guardians was the same as for the parish councils, and the same class of women were eligible as candidates. It was well into the 20th century, however, before there is any record of women coming to sit on any of the local governing bodies.

In addition to matters concerned with the sanitation of the district, Patrington RDC had charge of the roads, except the main roads, which, as mentioned above, were in the care of the ERCC. Under the 1894 Act the parish surveyors of highways were abolished and replaced by a single RDC surveyor. In March 1895 the Patrington RDC appointed William Henry Snaith at a salary of £100 a year. With the ending of the repair of the roads by the parishes their road-mending equipment was no longer needed and it was sold off by the RDC. Keyingham had three barrows, two digs, three rakes, one spade, three scrapers and a horse-drawn scraper - total secondhand value, £7. The scrapers were instruments used to take off the surface layer of old stones before laying the new.

William Snaith's first task was to go round the district and assess the condition of the roads. In Keyingham the two miles of main road were 'bad', suggesting that the ERCC had been failing in its duties. Main Street was 'good'; Marsh Road, East Carr Road and New Road (Eastfield Road) were 'passable'; Station Road and Saltaugh Road were 'moderate'; and Dam Lane was 'bad'. This last road had been a bone of contention between

Keyingham and Ottringham for over 20 years. The road forms the boundary between the two parishes. The problem was that it was within the parish of Keyingham but led only to two farms in Ottringham. The Keyingham ratepayers were paying for an amenity that benefited Ottringham people. In 1873 the Keyingham vestry resolved that the surveyors of highways discontinue the repairs to Dam Lane. Keyingham wanted the road transferring to Ottringham or alternatively the houses it served transferred to Keyingham. The dispute dragged on until 1892 when the ERCC, after a meeting with all parties at the Keyingham school, decided to leave matters as they were.

William Snaith estimated that 420 tons of stone were required to repair the roads in Keyingham. At Ottringham 230 tons were needed, at Winestead 180, and at Patrington 170. For the whole of the Patrington District a total of 4,640 tons was required. Most of the material was whinstone brought in through Stone Creek from the West Riding. Before the use of the steamroller the stones were laid on the road in a large chequer-board pattern, with only the right-hand side of the road being laid with stone for a stretch and then the left-hand side, alternately. To have laid new stone on the full width of the road would have caused too much of a drag on horses and carts, and if all one side was done then the drivers would have avoided the newly laid side, and the rolling action of their cartwheels, necessary to complete the job, would not have occurred. Cyclists had an interesting time zigzagging down the middle of the road to avoid loose stones. After a suitable passage of time when the new stone had been well rolled in by the traffic, the remainder of the road was treated.

- o -

By 1894 the three-tier system of elected local government bodies - the parish council, the rural district council and the county council - had been created. There came to be some changes. In 1935 Patrington RDC was merged with Skirlaugh RDC to form Holderness RDC, which in 1974 became the Holderness District of the newly formed county of Humberside, but the three-tier system endured until 1996. In that year the two-tier system was introduced. Humberside was replaced by the East Riding of Yorkshire Council as the local government body at the top of the pyramid, with no intervening body between them and the parish councils. Hence, of the all the elected local government bodies, the parish councils have the longest continuous history. Keyingham Parish Council continues today, with 13 members elected every three years.

The 20th Century

The 20th century was one in which greater technological advances than ever before took place. Excluding the reign of Edward VIII, which lasted less than 11 months, it encompassed the reigns of four English monarchs from Edward VII to our present queen, Elizabeth II. Each reign has had its own characteristics that are reflected in the history of Keyingham. Edward VII's reign was a period of peace in which scientific and engineering invention portended events in the coming century. It was in Edward's reign that Marconi sent the first wireless message across the Atlantic and that the first manned flight in a heavier-than-air machine took place. It was also the reign in which the telephone first came to Keyingham. In the reign of George V there was a world war and later a world recession. During the reign of George VI there was a second world war succeeded by years of austerity. The names on Keyingham's war memorial bear testimony to the contribution and sacrifice of Keyingham folk during both wars. The near half century of Elizabeth's reign has been characterised by gradually increasing prosperity and huge and rapid developments in science and technology. For many Keyingham people the beginning of the reign is remembered by their first viewing of television pictures as they watched the coronation of the new queen. Less than 20 years later they were watching pictures of men on the moon. In the village today is a recently erected telecommunications mast, part of a link in a chain by which someone with a mobile phone standing in the middle of a field in Keyingham can communicate instantly with any place in the world.

The reigns of our monarchs make convenient periods in which to divide the last one hundred years of our story. By doing this we have sought to capture the different moods and outlooks of times not too long gone but which are already fading from memory. The dividing lines between the periods have not always been strictly adhered to, however, and some themes and topics that stretch across the whole century have been dealt with within a single period in order to present a coherent story. Particular topics may be found by reference to the index.

'The Ploughboys'. There was plenty of homemade entertainment at the turn of the century, and it was the custom for groups of ploughboys to travel around the local countryside at Easter time entertaining in the villages and collecting money to supplement their low wages. This group came from farms in the Owstwick area. The photograph, taken in the 1890s, was lent by 'Ces' Gardner and shows his grandfather, John Ford (extreme left) and his great uncle William (extreme right). The second ploughboy was called Crawforth and the one with the whiskers is Stickney Hoe.
Courtesy of Ces Gardner

On 30 January 1901 Keyingham Parish Council sent a message of sympathy to King Edward VII on the death of his mother Queen Victoria. It was recorded in the council minutes:

'Before commencing our business a very sad duty takes precedence viz. to propose a resolution of our deep sympathy with the King, Edward VIIth, on the great loss His Majesty and the nation has sustained by the death of the late Queen, and to offer His Majesty our congratulations on his accession to the throne. I beg to move that we, the Parish Council, as representing the inhabitants of Keyingham desire most humbly and respectfully to tender to His Royal Majesty King Edward VIIth and to all the members of the Royal Family our most sincere and heartfelt sympathy in the sad bereavement that has fallen upon them by the death of Her Most Gracious Majesty Queen Victoria and to express our deep sense of the great loss which has been sustained by the nation by the demise of our late beloved Sovereign. We further beg to offer your Majesty the King our most respectful homage and congratulations on your accession to the throne and to express a fervent hope and prayer that every blessing may attend your Majesty throughout a long, happy and prosperous reign'.

The coronation of Edward VII took place the year after this letter was written and was celebrated as a public holiday. In Keyingham the parish council, after long discussion, voted that ten pounds, a considerable slice of the budget, be given towards the village celebrations. Saint Nicholas Church expended 18s.8d (93p) on 32 coronation souvenirs for the Sunday-school children, and the rest of the village all contributed something to make it a day to remember. Many, often after a long day's work, were busy until midnight festooning the streets with flags and flowers. On the day itself there was an athletic competition in one of the farmer's meadows and a free tea in the Foresters Hall. Mrs Susannah Westmorland made 1,000 curd cheese cakes and Mrs Edith Woodhouse 1,000 ground-rice cheesecakes for the feast. Susannah Westmorland recalled, 'It certainly was a great tea with plenty of home-fed beef and ham. The day was enjoyed by all.'

So began another reign and another century. The decline in Keyingham's population that had begun in the middle of the 19th century at last began to slow. There was a slight drop from 587 inhabitants in 1891 to 549 in 1901. The next census in 1911 saw a decline of only two, indicating that the exodus had slowed to a rate that just balanced the natural rise in population and the arrival of any newcomers.

Most of the village's houses still stood around Main Street and the old core of the village, although towards the end of the previous century a few houses had been built in Saltaugh Road and along Hull Road and Station Road. Working-class houses were usually semi-detached cottages or short terraces of houses, such as those in Extoby Row, which ran from Ings Lane to Beck Lane. These homes often provided shelter for large families - nine children and over were not unusual, although the older children had usually left home before the later ones were born. Jim Garsides described one of the smaller cottages, which stood in a row of four next to Wray House in Station Road. Jim was born in the cottage in 1919. The living room opened directly on to the street. Building bricks were laid on the packed-earth floor and were always damp. The ceiling had wooden beams from which food and tools were hung, together with an oil lamp that had to be taken down each day to be filled with paraffin and have the glass chimney cleaned with newspaper. The only other downstairs room was an extension at the back, made of wooden framing covered with corrugated iron. It contained an enamel wash bowl on a stand. In one corner was a cupboard - the larder. The rest of the extension was the wash house. It was a cold place to go for a wash with cold water. There was one room upstairs, approached by a twisting stairway, closed off by a door at the bottom. The bedroom was really an attic. Its sloping roof almost touched the floor and the bottom of the window was level with the floor. The room was furnished with two beds and a sea chest. The house was demolished in the 1930s.

Village centre, before the development in the 1960s. *Aerial view looking south over the crossroads of Main Street, Station Road and Ings Lane. Beck Lane winds southwards from the centre of the picture. The row of cottages in the top right of the picture was Extoby Row in front of which an alleyway ran from Ings Lane to Beck Lane. The Church Room, in Ings Lane is to the north of Extoby Row, and the Foresters Hall in Main Street is on the right of the junction with Beck Lane.* Courtesy of Miss Phyllis Middleton

The water supply for most houses came from wells, up to 20-foot deep, dug in the garden. The water was drawn by means of a hand pump. In some cases a cistern, separate from the well and with its own pump, was dug to collect roof water, which was soft and more suitable for washing and bathing. The plan for the vicarage built on Ottringham Road in 1879 shows that the water from six down pipes from the roof was directed into a cistern near the back door and close to the scullery where the washing was done. Digging and lining wells and cisterns was a costly business, and families from the poorer houses had to use the village pump situated on Hull Road a little to the west of the house, Beacon Hill. Mains water, from Hull, was not brought into Keyingham until 1932.

Movement around the village on foot was becoming easier as roadside paths began to be laid in the most-used areas. In 1904 cobblestone footpaths were laid along Main Street and Station Road, no doubt using cobbles from the locality. There were no kerbs to the paths and, in fact, in 1897 the parish council had turned down an offer of £15 by T O Gibson towards kerbing and channelling Main Street in commemoration of Victoria's diamond jubilee. One of the first buildings to have flagstones laid in front of it was the Blue Bell, where the landlord, James Sonley, was said to be fed-up with his customers falling over the cobblestones - more usually, on their way out.

Communication with the outside world also improved. Keyingham already had a post office and had had one since the middle of the previous century. Then it had been run by draper and local Wesleyan Methodist preacher Ralph Clough and was situated to the west of the site of the present war memorial. Letters, brought on horse-back, had arrived at 10 a.m. and been despatched at 3.20 p.m.

In 1905 the post office was on the same site and was run by James Tarbotton, tea dealer, grocer and tailor, the diversity of whose occupations conjures up a wonderful image of the inside of an Edwardian village shop. He, too, had religious affinities, serving the parish church as sexton, bell-ringer and church cleaner. Letters were now brought by rail and arrived at 6.40 a.m. and were despatched at 6.20 p.m. There was also a Sunday delivery and collection. The hours of work for the postmaster were long, although conditions improved slightly in 1909 when hours of post office business were reduced to a half-day on Sundays and Bank holidays.

To send messages by telegram the people of Keyingham had to go to the post and telegraph office at Ottringham, where the postmaster or his assistant would have been skilled in Morse code. Another method of long-distance communication was available, however, and in 1904, after a petition from some of Keyingham's residents, the clerk to the parish council wrote to the National Telephone Company asking their terms for laying a line out to the village. The NTC, which was operating the telephone system in Hull, replied that it could not establish an exchange at Keyingham as it was outside its area of operation. Individual residents could, if they wished, have a line run out from the Hedon exchange, but that would be very costly. Keyingham thus did not become part of the NTC's set-up in Hull, which was soon to be taken over by the Hull Corporation and survived until 1999 as the only municipally owned telephone system in the country.

Having failed in their approach to the NTC the parish council approached the GPO and in 1908 signed an agreement guaranteeing a return of £6 a year from the service. It is from that year that telegraph poles or, as they were correctly called in

the parish council minutes, telephone poles begin to feature on photographs of Keyingham. The service consisted of a call office at James Tarbotton's shop, from where the caller could communicate with Hull, Patrington or Withernsea. Columnist 'Paul Pry', writing in the *Hull Times* in 1913, considered the price of a call 'somewhat excessive' so that the acquisition was not used as much as it might have been. This is confirmed by the fact that the parish council was having to make up the guaranteed £6 with one or two pounds a year. It was not until 1915 that the Postmaster General informed the council that the revenue from the 'Telephone Call Office at Keyingham' was sufficient to cover the amount guaranteed by the council. The Great War had begun and perhaps the presence of soldiers in the village meant that there were some officers who were in the privileged position of being able to telephone their families. Meanwhile, in 1913, the council had had the temerity to ask the PMG if they could be included in the Hull area when the NTC transferred to Hull Corporation. As the GPO was trying at the time to institute a government monopoly of the country's telephone systems, the council was hardly likely to receive a favourable reply. The GPO's virtual monopoly of the telephone system no longer exists, and in 1999 the Hull company, as Kingston Communications, extended its line, by underground cable, to the village, and many residents have changed over from British Telecom, the successor to the GPO operation. The parish council's hopes in 1904 of being linked to the Hull system were thus realised.

The village may have had its telephone but it was without gas, electricity or piped water, all established amenities of the towns. Medical attention was available only to those who could afford to pay for it or, paradoxically, to the very poor, who had it paid for by the Patrington Union through the poor-rate. There was none of the labour-saving devices of today in homes or on the farms. There were no streetlights, although a lamp hung at the gate leading to the railway station, and Main Street was illuminated at night by the lamps in the windows of the half-a-dozen shops between Church Lane and a few yards beyond Beck Lane. It was in 1910 that the *Hull News* reported that Keyingham's 'trades people have unanimously decided to close at eight; after which the village is in darkness'.

For everyday living the village was virtually self-sufficient and most of the inhabitants contributed directly to the village economy in some way. *Kelly's Directory* of 1905 (see extract) lists the commercial interests in Keyingham. The farming and market gardening interest is evident. Serving the farmers were blacksmiths, wheelwrights, saddlers and joiners. Taking some of their produce were two millers, a brewer and a butcher. Milk, butter, curd and eggs from the farms and particularly the cow keeper were available to anyone who cared to buy. Farmers in England were continuing to adjust to the setbacks that had begun in the 1870s and were shifting from cereal growing towards more livestock rearing, which required the employment of fewer men. In 1905 Herbert Francis of Saltaugh is listed as grazier as well as farmer. Only thirteen years previously his father, farming the same lands, was listed as farmer only. Similarly, Isaac Beal of Marsh Farm is listed as farmer and grazier in the 1905 directory, but only as farmer in the directory of 1892. Fresh milk was one of the few commodities that could not be imported from abroad, and in both directories there were Keyingham people listed as cowkeepers - family concerns that needed no outside labour.

Extract from the Keyingham section of *Kelly's Directory* of 1905

Henry Beadle, shopkeeper
Isaac Beal, farmer and grazier
Sarah Beal, farmer
Henry Bosman, Ship Inn
Henry Brown, carrier
Francis Calvert, blacksmith
Edward Cautley, farmer
Elizabeth Clark, shopkeeper
Maurice Winzar Compton, surgeon
Thomas Stephen Eyre, miller
H A L Francis, farmer and grazier
Robert Garton, surveyor of drainage
John Gibson, carrier
Thomas Guy, wheelwright and joiner
John Henry and William Harrison,
      market gardeners
Joseph Harrison, farmer
William Howes, shoemaker
Ann Jackson, cowkeeper
James Jackson, brewer and farmer
Christopher Moor Johnson, flour dealer
Langdale & Norris, saddlers
Joseph Langdale, farmer
Richard Langdale, farmer
John Langthorpe, plumber and glazier
Robert Meadley, farmer
Richard Mook, farmer
Herbert Smith, plumber
James Sonley, Blue Bell
Robert Meadley Tarbotton, blacksmith
James Tarbotton, grocer, tea dealer and tailor,
      Post Office

Joseph Tong, tailor
John Tuton, farmer
Wreathall Tuton, bricklayer
Robert Walker, shopkeeper and tailor
Herbert Westmorland, butcher
Richard Westmorland, shoemaker and draper
Arthur Williams, farmer
John Woodhouse, grocer and coal merchant

Serving the other needs of the inhabitants in 1905 were tailors, shoemakers, shopkeepers and grocers, just as there had been in the previous century. But there were signs of change. Bulmer's Directory of 1892 listed four tailors and six shoemakers in Keyingham; in 1905 there were only three tailors and two shoemakers and, of these, all but Joseph Tong and William Howes had diversified into other trades. People were finding that cheaper, readymade shoes and clothing could be bought in Hull, and Keyingham was soon to have no tailors and only one shoemaker - Richard Westmorland, operating from his shop in Main Street, opposite the end of Beck Lane.

The livelihood of these folk - farmers, craftsmen and tradesmen - depended, directly or indirectly, on the muscle power of Keyingham's farm horses and farm workers. Horses were still the chief source of power in farming, and nationally there were about 885,000 kept for agricultural use in the Edwardian period. It was generally considered that two horses were required to work a 50-acre farm if it was devoted chiefly to arable. About half of Keyingham's working men were employed in agriculture, and many of them were tied to the farm seven days a week in order to look after the horses. Agricultural labourers normally worked 11 hours a day, six days a week, including Saturday afternoons. For the hired farm hands who lived-in on the farms, Sundays in autumn and winter were not free until the horses, which were stabled at that time of the year, had been fed and bedded down. In the days before the 1914-18 war, wages of farm workers living-in varied between £5 and £20 a year according to age and ability. That was in the days when for a shilling (5p) you could buy a pound of best steak or two dozen eggs or have a shirt made by hand by a woman in the village. The farm hands' wages included board and lodging. Their only recognised holiday was Christmas Day. Martinmas week, beginning about 21 November, when the farm worker could seek employment elsewhere, was an unpaid holiday.

There were a few private residents listed in the 1905 directory. Some of them were better-off village people who had retired, but others were names new to the village and were probably professional and clerical workers who commuted by train to Hull. It was said that you could set your watch by John Russell as he walked from his home at Sunthorp House, School Lane, to the station. He was a newcomer to Keyingham but participated actively in village life and is commemorated by Russell Drive, chiefly for his work as clerk to the parish council.

The railway provided easy travel to Hull and Withernsea and other stations along the line. People travelled not only to shops and markets but also to theatres and music halls. From the village milk could be conveyed quickly to Hull, the farmers bringing their full churns to the station in the morning with empty churns being returned on the afternoon train. Corn, in sacks, and other agricultural produce went to Hull by rail. Cattle and sheep being moved out of the village were driven through the streets to be loaded on to railway wagons, but if stations were not conveniently placed it might be necessary to walk the animals the entire route to their destination.

Arthur Clark, at the age of 11, helped his father walk five bullocks from Wawne to Sunk Island just before the First World War. There was an overnight stop at Keyingham, where the animals were kept in a paddock at the corner of Eastfield Road and Ottringham Road.

Trains brought goods to the villages. Coal was an essential commodity that had to be 'imported', and there is still a yard at the side of the station that was used as a coal yard. People took barrows and handcarts to the yard where coal could be bought for 14s (70p) a ton. The railway also brought jobs to the village, and work with the railway company was much sought after.

Although the railway provided one means of transport of goods into Hull, village carriers were an essential part of the trading chain. Henry Brown and John Gibson were the Keyingham carriers For a fee they would transport goods in horse-drawn carts from the villages to Hull market on Tuesdays and Fridays, setting off very early. The farmers or their wives would bring their produce - eggs, butter, poultry, rabbits - to be taken to the market or the shops in Hull. The carriers would also accept orders for goods to be bought in the town. In Hull they left their carts at stands in Mytongate and stabled their horses at one of the nearby inns, Henry Brown at the Rampant Horse and John Gibson at the Bull and Sun, both in Mytongate. They did the various errands requested of them and picked up return loads before their journey home the same afternoon. Their advertised time of departure was 2 p.m. but it was usually much later than this when they eventually set off. On the way home they would join up with other carriers from villages between Hull and Withernsea and Spurn. There are recollections of this convoy of carts slowly wending its way up Keyingham Hill at eventide although in wintertime it was only their lamps that could be seen. If conditions were bad and a horse with a particularly heavy load found difficulty ascending the hill, then a carrier who had reached the top safely would unhitch his horse and lead it back to give assistance.

- o -

The month in which the parish council sent its message of sympathy to the new king was the sixth anniversary of its first meeting. In that time it had had many problems to deal with and there were many more to come. The most difficult usually concerned drainage and sanitation, and the council spent many hours dealing with them, not only at meetings but also at the sources of the trouble. Most of the toilets in the village were earth closets, which contained a pail, or pan, usually with a layer of ashes placed in it. The closets were draughty places as the door had large gaps at top and bottom and there was another door at the back through which the pan could be removed. The pan had to be regularly emptied, often into a hole dug in the garden, proof of which can still be seen in the old gardens with their fine black soil, fertilised by centuries of ashes and dung, contrasting with the unworkable clay usually encountered in the gardens of the modern estates. For those who had no garden or were too infirm to dig a hole there was the night-soil man who went round with his cart collecting night soil for sale to the local farmers, market gardeners and allotment-holders. Night-soil collection had its inconveniences. The cottages in Extoby Row, for instance, had their privies at the bottom of the gardens, although there was no access to the garden other than through the house. Consequently, the pans had to be carried through the house for emptying. Some houses had shared privies, which could lead to embarrassment. 'Butcher' Westmorland's house in Church Lane shared its privy with The Chestnuts. One dark night the Westmorland's maid went to the privy and found herself sitting on neighbour Mook's knee!

Instead of pans, some of the larger houses had settling pits, which still needed emptying occasionally. The vicarage had a water closet, flushed by water that had to be pumped up to a tank in the roof from a well. The flushings, along with the bath water and the water from the scullery sink went into what the architect delicately termed a manure pit a few yards from the house. In order to clear settling pits the parish council in1898 had authorised the purchase of a sewage cart and ladle. The cart, a small contraption, five-foot long by three-foot wide and two-and-a-half foot deep, was sold off in 1918 for 2s.6d (12.5p).

Privies were usually sited well away from the house and especially from any well or cistern. The jaunt down the garden would be to a retreat hidden by bushes and often surrounded by elderberry (said to discourage flies), honeysuckle, or some other fragrant shrub to mask the smell. A walk in the dark, the way lit only by a hand lantern, could be quite an adventure with many a scare on the way. When the final destination was reached you had to sit on a one- or two-hole wooden seat. In the dark, young sisters often accompanied each other. Evidently the Ship Inn used to provide its customers with a candle in order to make the trip to the 'convenience' less hazardous, which is not surprising when the said accommodation was in a copse close to where Jellison Walk now is.

Allied to the sanitary arrangements was the drainage system, which came in for discussion by the parish council on numerous occasions. In 1902 the parish council 'respectfully desired the adoption of a more methodical manner to the cleaning of the village ditches' by the Patrington Rural District Council. In 1904 a further memo was sent to the RDC calling to their attention 'the lax manner in which the cleansing of the drains and ditches was carried out'. In 1907 the RDC was asked 'to fix sanitary gullies, properly trapped, instead of the present [open] gullies in the main street'. The replacement of open ditches (which amongst other things took the overflow from settling tanks) by underground glazed pipes was a gradual process, taking place over many years, and there were frequent complaints about the obnoxious smells from the drain leading down Saltaugh Road from the Ship Inn. In 1910 the *Hull News* attributed an outbreak of diphtheria, from which a Keyingham child died, to the defective drainage. In the same year Dr Coates, Medical Officer to the Patrington RDC, made an inspection of the village and found a choked-up settling pit that hadn't been cleaned out for about 30 years. He also discovered that sewage removed from other pits was being deposited on the roadside.

A problem that the parish council had inherited from its predecessor, the vestry meeting, was that of the over-crowded graveyard at St Nicholas Church, as the following extract from the *Eastern Morning News*, 11 August 1897, shows:

'It is satisfactory to observe that the time is approaching, when the burial scandal which has continued for so long at the village of Keyingham will be put an end to. Years ago the small churchyard became quite full, but still no steps were taken to provide further accommodation. With all the available space long since occupied, and no fresh ground provided, only one course was open, and that was to heap the dead upon dead. This went on time after time, until it was stated it was no uncommon thing when opening a grave for a fresh interment to disturb the remains of as many as half a dozen, or even more, of the "rude forefathers of the hamlet."'

St Nicholas Church overlooking the area now known as The Garth, circa 1910. *The churchyard was closed for burials at the end of the 19th century. Most of the gravestones were moved to the edge of the churchyard in 1967. Note the more elegant shape of the spire compared with the shape in later photographs taken after the repair of 1931. The row of four cottages (extreme right) was demolished in 1939.*
From the Kathleen Stancer collection

It was in December 1895 that the council had sought to buy land for a new cemetery, and half a dozen possible plots in the village were selected. Four of the sites were in various fields in Eastfield Road, but a fifth was on Cherry Garth, the field on the west side of Church Lane. This caused some consternation to James Jackson, whose brewery was downhill from Cherry Garth, on the opposite side of Hull Road (on the site of the present Rose Cottages). He took his water for brewing from a well on his premises and was afraid of what might find its way into his beer. The Cherry Garth site was rejected. The eventual plot chosen was in Eastfield Road (then known as New Road, as it was only 100 years old, and soon to be known as Cemetery Lane). The nearest well and pump was

160 yards away at the vicarage on Ottringham Road. The half-acre plot cost £100, when other agricultural land was selling at £33 an acre. As the newspaper put it, it was a 'long' price. With draining, fencing, laying out, legal fees and consecration fees the final cost amounted to £250, which was raised by a loan from the Local Government Board. When the cemetery was ready two-thirds of it was consecrated for use by the Anglicans. The remainder was left unconsecrated for nonconformists. The payment of over £10 in consecration fees at the expense of the ratepayers did not go without protest from some of the Methodists on the parish council, particularly Richard Westmorland. The first gravedigger appointed was Mark Goundrill, and the first burial in the new cemetery was of seven-month-old Florrie Goundrill, on 28 December 1898. The cemetery was extended in 1980 and now includes a garden of rest for the ashes of the cremated.

As the church and both chapels were some distance away from the new cemetery the parish council bought a hand bier to convey the dead to their final resting place after the funeral service. The bier, made by local joiner and wheelwright Thomas Guy, might be used by any of the three denominations, and there was some difficulty in storing it when not in use. In 1916 the parish council decided that a shed should be built for it in the cemetery. Perhaps because of the war, it was not until 1923 that the shed was built, Wreathall Tuton's tender for the job being the one accepted. The bier was last used in 1948, at the funeral of Eliza Lowther.

During the first few years of its existence the parish council held its meetings in the old school in Ings Lane. The building, now known as the Church Room, had ceased to function as a school when the board school in Saltaugh Road was opened in 1875. It had then been used as a meeting place for the vestry and was known as the People's Institute. It was also referred to as the Oddfellows' Hall as it was the headquarters of the local lodge of the Oddfellows. When the parish council used it, it was called the Council Chamber. Soon after the start of the 20th century the parish council was finding the hall inconvenient and in 1902 instructed the clerk to 'take the necessary steps to clear the Keyingham Parish Council of the tenancy of the Old Schoolhouse at the earliest opportunity that may be legal'. An inventory of the council's furniture, taken preparatory to moving, listed a dozen chairs, three tables, four wooden forms, one cupboard, one lamp and hanging apparatus, sundry parts of chairs and five spittoons (for the benefit of the tobacco-chewers). In 1903 the council moved its meetings to the board school, which was hired from the East Riding County Council at the rate of 1s.6d (7.5p) per meeting. The old meeting place was then sold to the York Diocesan Trustees for use as the Church Room and it has remained as such ever since.

The East Riding County Council to whom the parish council paid rent for the use of the school had only just become responsible for the school. By an Act of 1902 school boards had been abolished and the ERCC became the local education authority in this area. The county council was required to appoint an education committee with a proportion of co-opted members with experience of education, some of whom were to be women. The former board schools, such as Keyingham, as well as voluntary schools, such as the Patrington Church of England School, came under the general control of the new education authority. The voluntary schools still maintained their buildings and appointed teachers but were now assisted by the rates, as the board schools had always been.

The parish bier. Made by local joiner and wheelwright, Clive Guy, to carry coffins to the cemetery after a funeral service at the church or either of the chapels

This aroused bitter antagonism amongst nonconformists, who balked at the idea of supporting denominational education through the rates. The Passive Resistance Movement was born and consisted of members who refused to pay that part of the rate levied for education. There were two such in Keyingham - Herbert Seymour and Richard Westmorland, both strong Methodists and respected members of the community, who naturally objected to the rates supporting Church of England schools. Westmorland was a former member of the old school board and now a manager of the school. In October 1903 both Westmorland and Seymour were brought before the Withernsea Court for non-payment of rates. They said that on conscientious grounds, they would not pay the part intended for educational purposes. The magistrates, one of whom was Rev Charles Day, vicar of Withernsea, were unbending and ordered the defendants' goods to be distrained to the value of the unpaid rates and court costs. Consequently, the following week, George Miles, the assistant overseer, was at Keyingham to seize six polished oak chairs, an eight-day clock and a watch from Seymour's house for payment of £1.10s.9d (£1.54). From Westmorland, who had paid all but 1s.9d (9p) of his rate and costs, he took a pair of half-boot tops. A week later the goods were put on sale at Charlesworth's auction rooms in Whitefriargate, Hull. There was a large attendance of Passive Resisters, including many local Methodist ministers. Also present was the reporter of the *Hull News*, which had followed the case from its beginning. The sale began amid jeering. Richard Westmorland's son, George, bought the half-boot tops and Seymour's clock (saying, 'Send it to Seymour'). The Reverend Bowell, secretary of the Passive Resistance League, bought Seymour's watch, which Seymour said was of great sentimental value to him. As the full amounts of the fines had now been realised the sale of the chairs did not proceed. The Passive Resisters then adjourned to the nearby post office where a resolution of sympathy for Westmorland and Seymour was passed.

Some days later a similar meeting was held at Keyingham Foresters Hall to again pass a vote of sympathy for the pair, and a vote of censure on the new Education Act. Heated words were spoken. 'The return of the Tory Party,' said Rev T Vaughan, minister of the Patrington Primitive Methodist Circuit, 'was an opportunity for the Church party to institute that wicked and iniquitous Act, and by passing it to put a large majority of children under the doctrine of the Anglican clergy'. Despite the rhetoric and the efforts of the League, the Act stayed in force.

Life and progress in the school, as recorded in the school logbook, appears to have continued very much as before, despite the change in management brought about by the Act of 1902. The logbook is a constant reminder of history, both local and national, as well as giving an insight into the problems confronting staff and pupils in the early years of the century.

> '1900. May 1st - Holiday on account of the relief of Mafeking.
>
> July 4th - Closed all day for the Withernsea Sunday School Treat.
>
> July 5th - Poor attendance this morning, several of the children being too tired to attend school.'

Five days after this epic outing George Laking, took up duties as headmaster, living in the house attached to the school. His task was pretty daunting. He was responsible for the education of over 100 children ranging in age from three to 14. His staff consisted of his wife, Emma, who was the needlework mistress, Mary Jackson, who was a pupil teacher, and two monitresses, one of whom was Lily Middleton. Monitors and monitresses were chosen from older pupils in the school and helped to teach the younger children. If they showed an aptitude for the work they could be taken on as pupil teachers on attaining school-leaving age. It was the headmaster's responsibility to instruct pupil teachers for one hour each day either before school or in the evening. This instruction was checked by a member of the school board or, after 1902, by one of the school managers. Lily Middleton succeeded in becoming a pupil teacher at the age of 14 years and 7 months, and in time gained her teacher's certificate and continued teaching at Keyingham until her retirement in 1951.

Absenteeism from school was always a problem. There were 112 children on the roll and yet the average attendance was only 89. As mentioned above, a Sunday School outing could result in tiredness and consequent absences the next day. Bad weather always caused absences, especially amongst children who had to come from a distance. With no waterproof clothing and no means of drying clothes quickly, a child could spend all day in wet clothes on a rainy day. There were plenty of diversions to keep children away from school. In June 1900, Laking recorded, 'several children still absent getting berries and mushrooms'. Older boys were frequently absent at harvest time, either making straw bands to tie up sheaves of corn or tending pigs turned out on the stubble. The logbook records that in August 1904 both boys and girls were found to be working illegally and were returned to school by the Attendance Officer. Despite the award of silver badges for good attendance it would appear that education took low priority in some homes: 'Parents seem to regard Fridays as anybody's day' lamented Mr Laking after a particularly heavy bout of absenteeism. He tried to interest the parents in their children's education by setting exams every three months and sending the results and reports to the parents. He also improved the

Keyingham school, circa 1910. The school as it was when Mr. Jefferson became head teacher. The bell tower, the ventilator and the chimneys have been removed over the years, as has the wall that divided the boys' playground from the girls'. The iron railings were taken for the war effort in World War II. The clock has the dedication: 'The gift of Wm Carlin and G C Francis 1875'. Bryn Ferra was built on the site of the cottage on the right in 1916.

Courtesy of Ann Braithwaite

syllabus by extending it from the basic three Rs (plus needlework for the girls) to include drawing, geography, elementary science and optional drill. In 1903 dumbbells were provided for the older children and the logbook records details of object lessons, in which the children were, for example, given a flower and asked to make notes on its shape, size and structure, draw pictures and write poems and stories. Mr Laking took the children on nature study trips to places like Kelsey Hill and received favourable comments for his efforts from the government inspector - 'The teaching of practical botany and plant life is a most praiseworthy feature of the school.'

In November 1903 Mr and Mrs Laking moved on, both with glowing tributes from the government inspector. In the same month Robert Jefferson was appointed headmaster with his wife, Elizabeth, as infants' mistress. He was a highly qualified man and in his early days the school was used as an example of good practice to other schools. His stay at Keyingham was not easy and he had to overcome many difficulties including alterations to the school, closures through the illness of pupils, the ill health of himself and his wife, and competition from private schools in the village. Competition from other schools was regarded as a threat, because the government grant depended on numbers as well as the performance of the pupils at the inspector's visit. A small cottage on the Main Street had been used as a dame school in the 1880s, and in the 1891 census return it is recorded that Sarah Freeman kept a Ladies' School, which was on a site between The Chestnuts and the present Humber View in Church Lane. The school was advertised in the *Hull News* as 'the Keyingham School for Young Ladies - Healthy and pleasant locality with home comforts'. In 1906 the logbook records that a new private school had opened in the village - 'in consequence 4 children have been removed from the roll'. This may have been the school started by Agnes Eyre, who would have been 21 at the time. She certainly ran a school in 1920, when a present resident of Keyingham began school there as a girl of five. Agnes Eyre was the miller's daughter and the school was held in the dining room at the Old Mill house in Church Lane. About eight children aged five to seven were taught. There was no system of punishment as 'the children were too little to be naughty, and they dare not be anyway!'. The school closed when Miss Eyre married Wreathall Tuton.

Like his predecessor, Mr Jefferson was forward-looking and tried, within the constraints of the system, to broaden the curriculum being taught. He was keen to introduce football and was also instrumental in introducing violin lessons for several pupils. Teaching methods continued very much as before, however, with the children being given little opportunity for individual development and being left in no doubt as to who was in charge. It was in 1910 that detention, aimed at improving behaviour, was introduced into schools. It was not to exceed 15 minutes after morning school or 30 minutes in the afternoon, an unwritten rule that continued until the 1960s.

Immediately after Jefferson's arrival one of His Majesty's inspectors visited the school. He made the usual sort of comments on the progress of the pupils, stating that he was 'particularly pleased with the infants but wished that the reading throughout the school be less jerky with more attention to phrasing. The two upper standards should do a good deal of private study and be provided with atlases'. He also recommended many improvements to the building and its surrounds. The playground should be asphalted, sloped, drained and a shelter provided. Two powerful [paraffin] lamps should be provided in the main classroom. The classrooms should be enlarged, and extra space made in other ways such as by mounting the blackboards on the walls. The number of pupils at the school was obviously increasing. The school consisted of only one main room and a small classroom for the infants. This classroom had a gallery that took up almost half the room (see plan, Chapter 12). There was another room, the board room, where the old school board had held its monthly meetings but which was kept locked and not used for teaching. The improvements suggested by the inspector were completed in 1905. The board room was converted into a cloakroom, and two wash-bowls were installed. Previous to this the front lobby had been used as a cloakroom but was totally inadequate. A new infants' room was built behind the main

Keyingham school, 1911. *Gladys Cook (nee Westmorland) lent the photograph and remembers some of the children. Olive Jefferson, Grace Walker (Capes) and Doris Webster are holding violins, and the boy musician is Harry Etherington. The picture also includes Dolly Smith, Daisy Thompson, Dolly Gray, Ted Westmorland, George Smith, Stanley Ream, Jim Welbourn, Mary Whatling, Gladys Westmorland (Cook), Connie Ream, Mary Ream, Herbert Smith, Clarrie Gray, Grace Thompson, Topsy Walker, Nancy Smith, Beatie Gray, Brenda Gray and Kitty Smith. The teachers are Mr and Mrs Jefferson* Courtesy of Mrs Gladys Cook

classroom. Compared with the old rooms it was very light and airy, with large windows facing south. The gallery, with its long bench seats, was taken out of the infants' room, and two-seater desks were provided. These arrangements served for the next half-century.

Sanitary arrangements at the school were primitive, the earth closets being described in June 1903 as 'absolutely insanitary'. A Government inspector suggested that a footstool be placed in the infants' toilets, to enable them to reach the object of their intention no doubt! Great concern was shown about the cleanliness of the school. Soon after the building operations of 1905 it was stated that the school had not been scrubbed for over a year. During that time children had suffered with scarlet fever, ringworm, measles, diphtheria and scabies. They say nothing in this world is new: on 8 March 1907 the infants had to spend time out in the playground as asbestos dust, probably produced during the installation of a new stove, was flying about the room causing irritation of the throat and incessant coughing. Despite the stove the school was often very cold. It was recorded in 1910 that throughout January temperatures in the classrooms were mainly below 50 degrees Fahrenheit. In 1911 it was stated that in some of the rooms the temperature was as much as ten degrees below the outside shade temperature.

Despite improvements in health care and the introduction of medical inspections there was much sickness amongst the children, Childhood illnesses often reached epidemic proportions and closure of the school was enforced on several occasions. The school log of 11 November 1908 records 'Attendance decreases daily. Only 29 children present.' It was the start of a measles epidemic and the school was closed for seven weeks until the following January. The diphtheria epidemic of 1910 caused the school to be closed for three weeks. Illnesses, such as bronchitis, diphtheria and whooping cough, were sometimes fatal. Houses frequently had to be fumigated with sulphur, and everything boilable was boiled. Adults tended to suffer from consumption and this ran rife through larger families living in poor conditions. Many of the illnesses could be traced to bad drainage and polluted water, and hence the concern of the parish council over these matters.

The conditions in which people lived meant that diseases spread quickly and doctors had to be versatile people willing to treat a variety of ailments. They were, on the whole, skilful men but lacked the equipment and methods available today. Keyingham was fortunate, considering its size, in having a doctor in the village. This seems to have been the case at least as far back as the middle of the 19th century - a doctor is mentioned in every census return from 1841 to 1891. In 1834 Mr Mackreth, surgeon, was advertising for an apprentice for his practice at Keyingham. At the start of the 20th century his son, Dr John Frederick Mackreth, was living at Ellesmere House in Main Street. He was regarded as something of a quack by the villagers and may have attracted some odium because his 25-year-old son had made their 15-year-old servant girl pregnant. He does not seem to have claimed any qualifications, although he was one of the six Medical Officers serving the Patrington Poor Law Union. He was responsible for part of the West District of the Union and would have attended to sick paupers and granted medical certificates to allow them to receive relief from the guardians. Mackreth died a few months after Queen Victoria and within a year his place as doctor had been taken by Maurice Winzar Compton, a man in his early twenties who was properly medically qualified. Compton also took on public-health duties, acting as Surgeon, Medical Officer and Public Vaccination Officer to part of the West District of Patrington Union. He moved into Mackreth's former house, where Eva Levitt carried out the daily chores as housemaid. He married Mabel Thomlinson, the vicar's daughter. He seems to have been a conscientious and popular doctor, at least one baby that he helped bring into the world being named after him. He died in 1914 of pneumonia, contracted after getting soaking wet in his pony and trap when visiting a sick patient in the Marsh. He left three young children. A reading desk, carved by Thomas Guy, was set up to his memory in St Nicholas Church, where he had served as churchwarden in most years from his arrival in Keyingham to his death. Compton Drive is named after him. After his death there was no resident doctor in Keyingham until after the Great War.

There were others in the village who provided medical assistance, although after the retirement of Locking Charlton in the 1890s there was no chemist. Keyingham always had four or five women in the village who described themselves as nurses, who could be called on to look after the sick, act as midwives and lay out the dead. When Hannah Hewitt was dying of breast cancer at her cottage in Boyes Lane, she was tended by a rota of women, including Susannah Westmorland, and treated with quack remedies prescribed by a Dr Palethorp.

There was little escape from the noise outside if you were ill in the early 1900s but with their usual ingenuity people found an answer to the noise created by iron-shod cartwheels rattling along the road. Straw was used to make a covering over which the wheels travelled. This deadened the sound and brought some relief to those in need of peace and quiet.

Peace and quiet were not features of a normal village during the working day. Besides the sound of cartwheels and horses' hooves, there was the sound of hammers smiting anvils coming from the two blacksmiths in Main Street. In the winter months there was the hum of threshing machines. The creaking of windmill sails contributed to the noise as millstones ground corn into flour. A change took place in 1911 when the sails and gallery of the Old Mill in Church Lane were removed and steam was relied on as the sole source of energy. Previously a steam engine had been used only when there was no wind to turn the sails. The engine was housed away from the mill and was connected to the mill gearing by an external belt and pulley. There was no reduction in noise level.

Church Lane might be expected to have been a busy road, with the mill and Ebor House Farm at its summit, but Susannah Westmorland had vivid memories of the 'rules' governing traffic to the farm. Mr Mook, the farmer at Ebor House, did not allow his employees to use Church Lane for farm transport. All wagons coming from his lands on Hull Road had to go round by the old cross and along Station Road to the farmyard. In fact, very little traffic used Church Lane because it was the way to the church and must be kept tidy. There was to be no straw caught up in tree branches from passing rulleys and as few horse-droppings as possible. The lane was swept weekly by the roadman. One such roadman in his later years was Methodist Herbert Seymour, who was just as assiduous in sweeping the road to church as the roads in the vicinity of the two chapels.

Places of worship provided spiritual guidance for the people but were also places for social gathering on the one rest day of the week. On Sundays, all roads led to one of the three churches in the village - St Nicholas Church, the Primitive Methodist chapel on its present site in Ings Lane or the Wesleyan chapel in Chapel Lane. The Wesleyan chapel is now demolished, although one of the walls survives as a garden wall, detectable by the superior brickwork and the ventilation bricks. On Sunday morning Main Street was alive with people making their way to one or other of the churches. There was no animosity over which road they were taking, and pleasantries were exchanged as people made their way to their places of worship. Recently, Gladys Cook, who was born in the early years of this century, reviewed the 1891 census return for the purposes of this book. Of the 134 families named in the return she could identify just over 70 that had continued in the village into her girlhood. Fifteen of the families were Anglican, 22 were Wesleyan Methodists and 27 were Primitive Methodists. Only one or two did not attend either church or chapel. There was a similar balance of callings - farmers, tradesmen, craftsmen etc. - in the three congregations except that Gladys could not recall any farm workers as being Anglicans.

Eyre's Mill viewed from the east circa 1890. The house on the left was built in 1813 and has since been demolished. The house on the right was built in 1881 just prior to the purchase of the mill by Thomas Stephen Eyre and is still occupied by a member of the Eyre family. At the beginning of the 20th century steam power was used to drive the mill when there was not enough wind. The sails and gallery were removed in about 1911 after a new steam engine and engine house had been added. The steam engine was replaced by an oil engine, which in turn was replaced in 1932 by an electric motor mounted inside the tower. The mill continued working until the early years of World War II when it was producing animal feeds. Painting by unknown artist.

From the Eyra family collection

The vicar of St Nicholas was Rev Jeremiah Sharp Thomlinson, incumbent from 1874 to 1914. His descendants still live locally. We have no exact indication of the numbers attending the Anglican church in the early years of the century, although the fact that there were 32 children in the Sunday school when the coronation souvenirs were handed out and that there were 112 on the day-school role might indicate that something under a third of the population had Anglican affinities. In 1894 Thomlinson had complained at the Archbishop's Visitation of the diminishing offertories, which he attributed to the long agricultural depression and the consequent poverty of the parishioners. He also bemoaned the fact that the rich landowners did not live in the village. 'We have neither Squire nor resident Gentry and two important Farms have Hinds [foremen] to look after them. Could I in any way be helped by the *Owners of the Property here* we should be able to pay a salary to the Organist, increase the Choir, and in many ways make the Church more attractive and have brighter services.' He pointed out who were the large landowners in Keyingham - the Chichester Constable family who owned the whole of Keyingham Marsh, the Ecclesiastical Commissioners who now had the rectorial estate, and the Corporation of the Sons of the Clergy who owned the valuable farm of Saltaugh Grange. Any hopes he may have had of funds from those directions never materialised. However, it does seem that the prosperity of his parishioners or the numbers in his congregation increased, as we learn from the church accounts that the total annual offertory increased steadily from £18.10s in 1904 to £21.12s in 1910. Substantial sums of money were also raised by whist drives and concerts. Sufficient funds were realised to pay an organist a salary. In 1905 Agnes Eyre received £5 for her year's service as organist, and in 1907 Thomas Guy's 15-year-old son, Tom, was receiving £4 a year for playing the organ. Tom (his correct name) was later to give distinguished service in the Royal Engineers in the Great War and after the war served as organist at Patrington church for 40 years. For acting as organblower in 1907 young William Blanchard was paid ten shillings. There was a choir, and Mr Laking, the school head, was choirmaster during his short stay at Keyingham. Surplices were bought for the 22 members of the choir in 1909.

Methodism was very strong in Keyingham and both chapels flourished. In 1907 the Wesleyan chapel was restored and enlarged, and in 1913 'Paul Pry' of the *Hull Times* described it as 'one of the largest in the district and also one of the best attended'. It, too, had its Sunday school with a special room set aside for the children. There are annual references in the day-school log of the closing of the school for the Wesleyans' Sunday school outing. The yearly trip to Withernsea, in which children of all denominations joined, was always a joyful occasion with transport being provided by local farmers. It was a colourful and noisy occasion, as the horses, decorated with ribbons and shining brasses, drew the wagons laden with children and their parents to the seaside.

In the first decade of the century Keyingham Wesleyans usually provided four lay, or local, preachers to the Withernsea circuit, of which Keyingham was part. By the end of Edward's reign most of them were getting on in years - Robert Langdale, saddler, John Gibson, carrier, and Robert Meadley, farmer, were all over 60 and had each served the circuit for at least 20 years. The only younger member was Mr Jefferson, who had joined their ranks soon after coming to take up his post as schoolmaster.

At that time it was the Primitive Methodists who were really flourishing in Keyingham as in most other South Holderness villages. While membership of the Wesleyan circuit, based on Withernsea, was on the decline, that of the Primitives, based on Patrington, was increasing. The Primitive Methodists were actively recruiting in the years before the Great War. A mission band for open-air evangelism was started in 1910 under the leadership of 24-year-old William Seymour, the son of Herbert. He conducted well-attended meetings round the village cross on Sunday evenings. He may have been recruiting for the Christian Endeavour Society in which other chapels in the Patrington circuit were also involved. In 1910 there were 22 members in the Keyingham branch of the society, as high as in the much larger centre of Withernsea and higher than in any other village in the circuit. The secretary of

Keyingham Sunday school outing to Withernsea, circa 1910. The driver is Walt Westmorland. Some names are remembered: Jessie Walker, Kitty Walker, Annie Milner (with a big hat). The smallest girl is Nellie Clark (Lowther) and the two people on the tailgate are Bob and Edie Woodhouse. The Queens Hotel (or Convalescent Home) is in the background.
Courtesy of Mrs Gladys Cook

the Keyingham branch was 21-year-old Harriet Walker who went on to become one of the first women local preachers in the district.

Besides active campaigning there were more subtle ways of bringing people into the Methodist fold. When, after the First World War, the post office had passed into the hands of William Clark, Mrs Clark would light a fire in her baking range in an outhouse on Saturday nights so that the lads coming into the village from the farms on Keyingham Marsh had somewhere warm to go. She was a staunch Methodist and her hospitality, conditional on their promise to attend chapel on Sunday, also helped to keep them out of the pubs. That she had some measure of success is borne out by Gladys Cook's recollection that there were usually a dozen farm lads in chapel on Sunday mornings.

Camp meetings, which dated back to the arrival of Primitive Methodism in Keyingham, continued to be held each year at Whitsuntide. The venue was Keldgarth, a field in Clay Lane. The preachers stood on rulleys to give their sermons. A harmonium was carried into the field to accompany the boisterous singing of the enthusiastic crowds that attended. Just about everybody in the village went to these meetings, although Gladys Cook and Rachel (Peggy) Clark say they were not allowed to go because their mothers considered the meetings too noisy. Ill-educated as some of the preachers were, they gave some rousing sermons, or testimonies, as they were called. The local preachers on these occasions came from all over the Patrington Circuit. Keyingham itself provided a number of local preachers, including the indomitable Richard Westmorland. Local preachers were called on to preach all over the circuit, and Westmorland is said to have walked to Spurn to preach at the afternoon service there. This would have been in the days before the provision of the circuit's horse hire fund, whereby preachers were allowed 1s.6d to hire a horse if the round journey was greater than 12 miles. Later Westmorland's family provided him with a horse and trap to make such journeys easier. Other Keyingham local preachers of that period were Ambrose Bulleyment and Samuel Dobson.

In 1909 a start was made to building a new Primitive Methodist chapel in Keyingham. It was erected to the north of the 1846 building. Ruth Cowan tells of her friend Grace Capes, nee Walker, as a little girl, buying a 'foundation brick' in 1907 - these were sold for a donation of 2s.6d (12.5p) to raise funds for the re-building. Money had already been raised in a variety of ways, including a Grand Martinmas Bazaar in 1906. When the foundation stones were laid on 28 October 1909, an afternoon's holiday was given to the school children. The school log also records that some were away in the morning preparing for the event.

Camp meeting on Keldgarth. *The camp meetings were held every year in Whit week. The preacher is using a horse-rulley as a platform. The presence of soldiers in uniform suggests that the photograph was taken during the First World War.*
From the Vic Lanham collection

The Primitive Methodist chapel circa 1910. *The new chapel was erected in 1909 to the north of the 1846 building, which was converted to the schoolroom. The entrance to the new chapel was from Ings Lane under the tower. The iron fence enclosed Dan Hill where the war memorial was erected in 1921 and the stump of the village cross was placed in 1968.*

Courtesy of Mrs R E Clark

An account of the opening of the new chapel on August bank holiday 1910 tells us that 'The inhabitants of the village rose to the occasion, with flags and bunting being exhibited all over the village. Mr. George Westmorland, Hull, Coal Merchant, brought 100 visitors on his lorries and hundreds came from the surrounding districts. Once inside the people were not slow to express their admiration. The seats are comfortable and the rostrum and the space ample, perhaps rather too much so. An adjournment was made to Foresters Hall and the old reading room [now the Church Room] at which 500 people sat down. The opening of this new chapel was an occasion of great rejoicing marred only by the conscience of those responsible for the building, as a cost of £800 had not been fully met.' This difficulty must have been quickly overcome because in 1911 further money was being raised towards the cost of installing a new organ. When the rebuilding had been completed the chapel had seating for 180 people.

At that time the Wesleyan chapel could seat 160 and the parish church 200.

On completion of the new chapel the old chapel adjoining was used for the Sunday school. The membership of the Sunday school confirms how Primitive Methodism was flourishing at that time. In 1910, when the membership of St Nicholas Sunday school was 17, there were 54 children attending the Primitives' school, which had 12 Sunday school teachers, seven of them women. The average attendance at the half-hour morning school was 40 and at the hour-long afternoon school 49, so that most children were in chapel at least twice on Sundays. Most of them also went to the evening service with their parents. Gladys Cook can well remember an occasion at an evening service when 'the preacher had gone on a bit' and her grandfather, Richard Westmorland, who had some small boys sitting near him in the pew, interrupted and said, 'Now, Brother, don't you think you've gone on long enough, these bairns

171

have had enough.' As well as being a local preacher Westmorland was a Sunday-school worker, as was Herbert Seymour. Wall monuments to both Westmorland and Seymour are to be found in a corridor in the Methodist Church. The one to Richard Westmorland tells us that by the time of his death at the age of 89 he had served 59 years as local preacher. A more evident, present-day tribute to Seymour is the naming of Seymour Road.

Herbert Seymour (1858-1938). A farm worker, he lived in Beck Lane and walked to his work at Sands Farm each day. In 1928, at the age of 70, he and his son cycled to Sunderland in order to visit another son. He was a Primitive Methodist and a Passive Resister during the Education Act controversy of 1903. *Courtesy of Mrs E Pashby*

As evidenced by the coronation celebrations and chapel events people found time and energy and the wherewithal to enjoy themselves despite long hours of work and low wages. People drew greatly on their own resources for entertainment and enjoyment. Singing around the piano was a favourite pastime and these musical evening were often augmented with fiddles, melodeons and mouth organs. Two married daughters of the Howes family, together with their husbands, made up a locally renowned quartet. The local newspapers frequently featured announcements or accounts of dances and other entertainment in the village. A report in the *Hull News* in 1904 tells of the 'popular Keyingham Dance Classes' holding a dance, 'presided over by Mr. Speckley at the piano' on New Year's Eve. Dancing continued until 3 o'clock in the morning. A variety of public performances were given in the school or in Foresters Hall, with the Pom-Poms Concert Party being a popular attraction whenever they appeared.

As families were large and houses small, children spent much of their time playing outside, enjoying the open air and the pleasures the countryside had to offer. Favourite pastimes included marbles, diabolo, whip-and-top, pitch-and-toss, put-and-take and bowling hoops. In winter time people eagerly awaited the freezing over of the water at Kelsey Hill and on the Ings where many villagers would congregate to enjoy themselves skating and sliding. At the bottom of Eastfield Road, beyond the railway track, was the Crawshaw and on fine days people would enjoy the pleasures of this 'parkland', often taking picnics.

The village cross was always a popular meeting place for all age groups. In the day-time the older members of the community exchanged yarns and tales there, and in the evenings it was where the younger members congregated. As the number of vehicles using the streets increased people became concerned about the safety of children who used the roads as playgrounds. Cars speeding along at 20 mph with limited braking capability were considered a danger. Playground provision was discussed by the parish council, and in June 1908 it was resolved 'that seeing that there is no open space in Keyingham suitable as recreation or playgrounds for children, and recognising also the increasing danger to life and limb of children playing in the highways and by-ways of the Parish, due to motor cars, vehicles, horses and other animals passing through the village, We respectfully request the Rural District Council to provide some suitable field within the Parish for the special purpose of affording the children a playground free from the above mentioned danger and its harmful consequence'. It is possibly as a result of this request that in 1911 the Lord Paramount of Holderness, Major Chichester-Constable, granted the area known as Dan Hill, in front of the Methodist chapel, to the parish council for use as a recreation area (before the extension of the Methodist chapel in 1973 the area was slightly larger than it is today). In 1913, a rate of $1^1/4$ d (about 0.5p) in the pound was imposed on the parish to cover the cost of fencing the plot, which was also shrubbed. It was not until the 1930s, however, that active steps were taken to provide Keyingham with a recreation area large enough to accommodate football and cricket pitches.

Keyingham Fair was a lively event eagerly anticipated by the villagers each year. It was held on the Wednesday of Whit week, the last one being held in 1915, the war no doubt hastening its end. The fair was one of the big attractions in

The Crawshaw, circa 1910. A wooded 'pleasance' on North End Farm and a favourite place for a picnic or a Sunday stroll. The trees were felled and sold to a Hull timber firm in the 1930s.
Courtesy of Mrs Gladys Cook

Holderness, with stalls stretching from the vicarage on Ottringham Road to Boyes Lane. In a field opposite the Ship Inn were coconut shies, Aunt Sallies and other amusements for people to enjoy. Gladys Clark (nee Dunn) told of her grandfather Ted Robinson, engineer and wheelwright, who made his own roundabout for the fair. He also made the first penny-farthing bicycle in this area.

Maurice Clark could recall the holding of an annual sports day, incorporating horse and cycle races along with athletic events of all kinds. Not only local people took part but also many competitors from out of the area. There were also impromptu sporting contests. Gladys Cook tells of an event that took place in about 1906. Richard Westmorland, the shoemaker, had a pony called Sausage which he claimed could reach Hedon Road Jail in 25 minutes. This bragging led to butcher Herbert Westmorland putting up his horse Beefsteak against the said pony in a race from Thorngumbald to Keyingham. Beafsteak won by just over five lengths, a result commemorated in verse:

Keyingham village cross. The village children's freedom to use the roads as their playground was soon to end when motor vehicles became more abundant and their speed gave cause for concern. The Blue Bell Inn sign can be seen as well as the shoemaker's shop at the end of the row of cottages. Clark's shop on the right has the door across the corner and displays an advertisement for tea. This photograph was taken before the telegraph poles were erected in the village in 1908.
Courtesy of Ann Braithwaite

The race war fra Thorn to Kenninghum road eand,
Wheear tweeak refrees stood all eager and kean.
Yon 'oss war call 'Beefsteak' which yon refree did admire,
And often wad sing of its afoor cobbler's fire.

T'other war called 'Sausage' and war mair of pony-like breed,
And a chap who buys up pigs ae toon - thowt it would lead.
Soa this race war settled to stop mair argument,
And foaks wad then know the 'oss as best went.

The race war a merry yaw, a reet good start made,
An as they gan up t'hill each tiv his saddle war laid.
The way war led wiv 'Beefsteak' who war better in 'is stride,
And he finished up wiv five lengths, a hand and a little mair beside.

To the north of North End Farm was a field known as Race Course with a track about a quarter of a mile long, which suggests that racing horses was not uncommon in the village. It was at this field that the Holderness Hunt met on occasions.

For those men who wished to spend their free hours in more productive fashion there was the possibility of renting one of the village allotments. The Local Government Act of 1894 gave parish councils the right to compulsorily hire lands for allotments for the use of working men. In 1895 upwards of a score of labourers and others living in the village put in a request to the parish council, asking for allotments. After some discussion it was resolved 'That the land known as the gravel pit be let as from April 6th 1895 by the Council in sixteen lots of a quarter acre each, at a rental of 8s each plot, to such applicants as the Council may determine. The tenant in each case before entering upon his tenancy, to pay, apart from the question of rent, a sum of 1s towards the cost of staking out the ground etc., it being understood that the Council will pay all rates.' A few months later the council received a memo from T O Gibson, rural district councillor, asking that steps might be taken to obtain additional allotments for the parishioners, pointing out that under the Local Government Act the term labouring population meant not only agricultural labourers but all persons who obtained their livelihood by manual labour. The memo was accompanied by 29 written applications for allotments, the total quantity required amounting to 43.5 acres. Considerable discussion ensued as to the legality of some of the applications. Ultimately the clerk was instructed to write to the tenants of desirable land in the parish asking if they could hire to the council portions of the amount of land required. There had been no such difficulty with the gravel pit because it already belonged to the parish, having been granted for road-mending purposes at the Enclosure in 1805. A further five acres of allotment land were obtained in 1896 by renting from the school board the Edward Marritt lands, the rents from which were used to provide education for poor children under the terms of Marritt's bequest in 1811.

The call for allotments has fluctuated greatly over the years. Fortunately, the present tenants do not have to conform to the rule written into the 1904 tenancy agreement whereby allotment holders had to 'lay on 2 tons of good rotten manure or 2 tons of night soil per rood'! (A rood is a quarter of an acre. Today's allotments are only a quarter of a rood in area in extent).

At the present time allotments are falling into disuse but in 1904 they must have been a popular acquisition as the parish council was requested to arrange with the ERCC Technical Instruction Committee a series of lectures on 'allotments and their culture or a kindred subject'. Further lectures on horticulture were requested in 1910. Allotments provided an important means of supplementing food supplies for the hungry mouths of large families. The allotments at the old gravel pit no longer exist and are used as farm land, and part of the Marritt land allotments have been taken to extend the Saltaugh Road playing field.

- o -

In Edwardian Keyingham although men and women worked long hours at their jobs or their chores they still had energy in plenty for their few leisure hours. After a long day's work there was still time for an evening's cricket in the summer or a dance in the winter. Practically everyone seems to have attended church or chapel on their one day off a week. And on any other occasion when the opportunity arose - a coronation celebration, Keyingham Fair, Martinmas week or a Sunday school outing - the event was entered into with gusto by the whole village. It engendered a community spirit that we might envy today.

King George V came to the throne in 1910 on the death of his father, Edward VII. During his reign there were to be many changes in the way Keyingham people lived. The Great War accelerated the development of motor transport and, though horses and steam engines continued to provide the motive power for transport and farm machinery well into the 1940s, by the mid-1930s motorcycles and cars were beginning to be within the means of private individuals, and motor buses were becoming a serious challenge to the railways. On the farms tractors were coming into evidence. Improvements in living standards were effected in the early '30s when piped water and electricity became standard fittings in new houses in the village and welcome additions to older properties. The wireless widened the horizons of the rural community when the BBC started broadcasting in 1922. In the mid-1930s Keyingham's first private telephones were connected. *Kelly's Directory* for 1937 shows that William Arthur Clark, at the Post Office, had Telephone No. 1 and Albert Jackson, of Mount Pleasant, had the highest number listed - No. 46.

- o -

In April 1911 a public meeting was called in Keyingham to consider how best to celebrate the coronation. By order of the king all schools were granted a holiday and, for a week from June 19 to June 26, Keyingham school was closed for the coronation festivities. Unfortunately, neither the school logbook nor the parish council minutes describe what the festivities were. We know there had been a great deal of community involvement in the celebrations for both of Queen Victoria's

jubilees and the coronation of Edward VII, and it is likely that similar arrangements were made for George V's coronation. In the week before the celebrations the coronation committee presented a flagpole to the school and no doubt some event took place round this on coronation day. The records tell us that on Empire Day in subsequent years the flag was hoisted and the children were gathered below it to sing the National Anthem and other patriotic songs. The legacy of Victorian pride in the British Empire was expressed in this way for a long time into the 20th century, and a powerful feeling of patriotism and pride in king and country prevailed. When King George and Queen Mary visited Hull on 26 June 1914 the school children were granted a whole day's holiday. A great number of children were said to be going to see the royal party arrive at Hull's Paragon Station at 12 noon.

- o -

The most calamitous and far-reaching event of the reign was the Great War of 1914-18. The general perception of the war is of the mud and the trenches and the terrible personal sacrifices of the men who answered Lord Kitchener's call, 'Your Country Needs You!' The men and boys of the era, imbued with the patriotic spirit, felt compelled to enlist in the forces. It was not until 1916 that conscription was thought necessary, more as a gesture towards the popular feeling that every fit man should be prepared to fight for his country than for the actual need for more troops at that time. All men between the ages of 18 and 41 were required to sign on. At the archbishop's visitation in 1919 when Keyingham's vicar, Ivor Griffiths, was asked, 'How many of the Parish served with the King's Forces during the War?' the answer he gave was '43'. However, the war memorial records 64 names, which perhaps includes those who enlisted while engaged for only one year's employment on a Keyingham farm. Certainly, Tom Carr, who gave his life in the war and whose name is on the Keyingham memorial, was a member of an Ottringham family and three of his relatives are commemorated on the Ottringham memorial. Some of the families mentioned on Keyingham's memorial still live in the village, although there are few who are old enough to have personal memories of the Great War. There is just a distant memory of one man's childhood sighting of a zeppelin, and being told to 'Come in, and shut the door!' and that of Harry Etherington who wrote of seeing a zeppelin in the searchlights when he was leading in a load of hay.

The first zeppelin raid on Hull was in the middle of 1915. That the raids disrupted life in Keyingham is shown by the entries in the school logbook where the first relevant entry is on 4 April 1916: 'At 9.40 a.m. today only 41 children in school as the warning against zeppelins has been issued on four successive nights'. On 10 April is entered, 'Another zeppelin raid at night'. In the quiet of the countryside the sound of the zeppelin engines could be clearly heard as the pilots, navigating along the Humber on their way to Hull, passed very close to those who lived in Keyingham Marsh. The school log records an 'attempted air raid' as late into the war as 9 August 1918. The raids against civilian targets sparked off the persecution of Germans living in this country. In Hull, mobs ransacked shops belonging to Germans. A German family named Wittman, who were pork butchers in Hull, had lived at The Chestnuts in Keyingham's Main Street, and their

daughter, Julia, had fallen in love with Richard Tarbotton, the postman and son of the postmaster. Three months before the first raid on Hull the couple married. It seems that Julia then helped in the post office but there were those who doubted whether she should be allowed to work in such a sensitive area, although the Wittmans had been in Hull since well before the opening of the century, and Julia herself, as a girl of 17, had been the organist at Keyingham church in 1902. There are also vague recollections of people no longer patronising the Tarbottons' shop.

The air raids prompted blackout precautions. Lamps were not lit on the railway station and the blinds in the carriages were kept drawn, so that passengers had to listen for the porter calling out the name of the station. The parish council had to transfer its meetings to the Foresters Hall because the ERCC declined to provide blinds at the school. At the church £2.13s was expended on 'darkening the Church windows'. The churchwardens also considered it prudent to take out an air raid insurance policy for a premium of £3.7s.

In October 1914 the parish council met to consider the question of a War Relief Fund. They decided to obtain subscription cards and to have weekly collections during the war. Monthly meetings of the collectors were held in the Foresters Hall, and an entry in the parish council minutes for 6 March 1915 tells us that, of the £8.10s collected, £6 was allocated to the Belgian Relief Fund and £2.10s to the ladies' committee, for wool to be knitted into extra garments for the troops. The report ends with the comment, 'The amount which is collected here is most creditable to the village and all concerned.' A month or so later it was arranged for the village to be divided into 11 sectors, each with a collector making weekly house-to-house collections. The average weekly amount was £2.2s and the total collected in the six months to the end of March was £52. The committee also organised concerts and dances and there were collections at places of worship, which altogether raised a further £45. By these various means a grand total of £100 was raised in the six months. In January 1917 a donation was made to the Bread Fund. The War Relief Committee was still making comforts for the troops in 1921, and a War Savings Association formed in 1916 was still active in 1924.

The most dramatic change to occur in Keyingham during the war was the sudden loss of the young working men. The 64 men named on the war memorial came from every walk of life and represented the fittest part of the village work force. Farm workers were amongst the earliest volunteers for the Army and were gladly accepted especially as they were fit and the war was not expected to last long. As the conflict lengthened and the country needed to produce more of its own food, the government short-sightedly did not make agriculture a reserved occupation during conscription. As early as February 1915, just six months into the war, the *Hull & Yorkshire Times* in a feature 'Round Keyingham Cross' referred to 'the old-fashioned custom existent in Holderness of helping a new in-coming farmer to plough his land, but young farmers who are starting this year are not finding much help to be forthcoming, largely on account of the scarcity of labour'. To replace the farm workers who had gone to fight, men from the towns were brought in to do the work. Most had no inclination for farm work or experience of work with horses, and many had been turned down by the Army on health grounds. The agricultural labour force was also augmented by allowing children of 13 to leave school in order to start work on the land. This had been permitted before the war, but only if the pupil attained a minimum standard of education and had attended a certain number of times in the last three years at school. The child was then awarded an exemption certificate enabling him or her to leave school before the statutory age of 14. But in the war, exemption certificates were waived. In September 1914, there were only three boys over the age of 12 in the school. The labour problem on farms also improved when the Women's Land Army was formed in 1917. School children's holidays had always been adjusted to fit in with harvest time, but in 1918 the harvest holiday had to be extended to 7 October because the school was 'in the hands of the Land Army'. Presumably it was being used as a hostel for Land Army girls, although many of them lived on the farms where they were working. The agricultural labour force was also supplemented by prisoners of war and by local women mostly working part-time. In order to conserve vital stocks of grain, older boys and girls were encouraged to join the Rat and Sparrow Club, which paid them a small amount for each rat's tail and dead sparrow they brought in. The killing of vermin had long been encouraged in this way, and continued to be so until the end of the Second World War.

The arrival in Holderness of army recruits coming to train was greeted with enthusiasm and when the King's Own Yorkshire Light Infantry passed through Keyingham, Mrs Susannah Westmorland cleared all the baking from her pantry and gave it to them. But the setting up of camps in Holderness caused many problems. The commanding officers were usually of the mind that the training of soldiers took precedence over everything else. The 'extensive cutting of trenches in Holderness' caused serious damage to growing crops, fences and land and prompted a letter of protest to be sent to the War Office by the Holderness Agricultural Club in February 1915. In December of that year the parish council wrote to the Commanding Officer of the KOYLI asking if the piece of trench between the road and the footpath opposite the vicarage on Ottringham Road could be filled in as it was dangerous to the public. William (Willam) Harness can recollect one of these trenches continuing down the east side of Eastfield Road as far as the cemetery. When the war was over claims amounting to thousands of pounds were made for the damage done by the Army in the Patrington Rural District.

The school had other wartime uses besides housing the Women's Land Army. Not all the uses were greeted with enthusiasm by those responsible for the school. In October 1916 the men who were using the building for the purposes of volunteer drill were told that they 'had to arrange for any extra cleaning and heating, as the Education Authority may not incur any expense'. The headmaster's attention was also called to 'a waste of cinders' - the drill was obviously insufficient to keep the volunteers warm without lighting the school fires. When the rationing of food was instituted early in 1918 it was from the schoolroom that food cards were distributed. A distribution of a happier kind occurred a year later when Herbert Francis, of Saltaugh Grange, sent a box of oranges to the school for an Armistice treat for the children. The holiday in commemoration of peace, however, was not until July.

When we think of Keyingham's involvement in the Great War, it is natural that our thoughts turn to Remembrance Day and the war memorial. Although the Armistice was signed on the 11 November 1918, it was not until April 1921 that the parish council applied to Major Chichester-Constable for permission to erect a war memorial

Keyingham war memorial, October 1921. *At the unveiling by Colonel R Hall of Kelsey Hill and the dedication by the Bishop of Hull. Almost everyone from the village was present. The picture shows the original statuette of a First World War soldier.* *From the Kathleen Stancer collection*

on Dan Hill, a site that he had granted to the council in 1911 for use as a recreation area. His permission was promptly granted and the memorial was erected that year. Fund-raising had started even before the war ended. A 'Keyingham War Memorial Fund' account was opened with the Halifax Banking Company on 8 February 1918 with a deposit of £53. Mention is made in the school log of 29 November 1918, soon after the Armistice was signed, that the school was to be used for a concert to be given on behalf of the Keyingham Memorial Scheme. The concert was performed by a party of men and officers of the KOYLI stationed at Winestead Camp.

The original memorial project had been to erect a parish hall, but escalating costs put this outside the resources of the village, especially as the war relief work was still proceeding enthusiastically. It was only through the energy and tenacity of the members of the committee that they realised their ambition to erect the memorial, described at its unveiling, as 'in design, unique; in situation, ideal; and in appearance, choice, ornate and striking.' The unveiling and dedication ceremony was reported in the *Hull Daily Mail* of 31 October 1921.

'STRIKING MEMORIAL UNVEILED -
The 16 feet tall Portland stone column stands on a square base, and has the names of Keyingham's war heroes inscribed in gold lettering on emerald pearl granite panels. The column is surmounted by a carving of a "khaki soldier, standing with bowed head on his reversed arms" executed by a Hull sculptor. The erection of the Memorial was entrusted to Messrs. Quibell & Son of Hull, and Colonel R. Hall of Kelsey Hill, Burstwick, performed the unveiling. Almost everyone from the village was present.'

On 14 December 1921 £236 was withdrawn from the Memorial Fund to pay the bills, and the account was closed.

The memorial contains not only the names of those who fell in the Great War but also the names of all Keyingham's servicemen (Appendix 1). At least two of them returned with decorations for gallantry. Private F W (Frank) Thompson gained the Military Medal, awarded to non-commissioned officers and men for bravery in battle, for his gallant action whilst fighting with the 25th Infantry Brigade of the Manchester Regiment in October 1918. Tom Guy also won the MM as a sergeant in the Royal Engineers. On a separate occasion he was mentioned in despatches. Frank Thompson returned to agricultural work after the war as a farm foreman at Cherry Cobb Sands. His medal was recently presented to the Manchester Regimental Museum by his daughter, Joyce Eyre. Tom Guy, who was seriously wounded in the war, returned to his joiner's bench in Keyingham. His medal was stolen from Patrington church vestry where he had left it whilst playing the organ at a commemorative service.

In the years between the wars, a two-minute silence was observed at eleven o'clock on Armistice Day, 11 November. Traffic stopped in the streets, the wireless was silent and all work ceased. The schoolchildren went from the school to the war memorial and observed the silence. Today we commemorate Remembrance Day on the nearest Sunday to 11 November, a date that was fixed after the end of World War II. In Keyingham on that day a service is held at the chapel and church alternately. The uniformed organisations of all ages attend and parade their standards. The service culminates with a two-minute silence at the memorial, during which traffic is halted in the street.

In 1921 the British Legion was formed. Its membership was open to ex-servicemen and

Remembrance Sunday, November 1998. Mrs Freda Lanham lays the British Legion's wreath at the Cenotaph. The priest is Rev W H McLaren. OBE. Mrs Joyce Eyre (holding a wreath) is wearing the Military Medal that was awarded to her father, Frank W Thompson, in the First World War.
Photo: Mrs Susie Kirkwood

women of all ranks who had served in the forces, including the merchant navy and Red Cross. A royal charter was granted in 1925 and the organisation became the Royal British Legion. The Keyingham branch of the British Legion was formed in 1921 and a separate women's section in 1945. The men's section was active for over 50 years, finally closing in 1978 owing to lack of support. There had at one time been as many as 120 members, but interest had unaccountably waned and latterly only three or four members had met at the home of Frank Howes. Two long-serving members and Great War veterans were awarded the Legion's Gold Badge. One was Mark Goundrill, who had been the president, and the other was Herbert Lound, who had been the standard bearer and Poppy Day organiser. Herbert Lound was accorded the honour of parading the

Keyingham Branch standard at the Royal Festival of Remembrance at the Albert Hall. It was his proudest memory. After the closure of the men's section permission was obtained from Legion headquarters for the standard to continue to be paraded at the annual Remembrance Service provided someone would carry it. It was then carried by a member of the women's section until it was laid up at a special ceremony at St Nicholas Church on 15 August 1999. The women's section, which has its own standard, is still active. Under the presidency of Rachel (Peggy) Clark, the ladies promote the sale of poppies for Remembrance Day and raise money in other ways for British Legion funds.

Although the intention of building a village hall had not been implemented by the Keyingham Memorial Project, it was not many years after the

unveiling of the war memorial that the village got its hall. The Keyingham Parish Institute came into being in 1930 when a group of people organised events and, with the help of the rest of the village, raised £150 to buy a barn that was part of the property now known as 'The Old Vicarage' but on the opposite side of Station Road. The barn was converted into a reading room and a billiards room. Later, the two rooms were made into the present small hall, and an army hut was bought and put at the north end where the kitchen now is. Half the hut was used as a kitchen, and the ERCC library was in the other half. It was the intention, when funds allowed, to extend the institute, but it was not until 1955 that further extensions were made.

- o -

At the Archbishop's visitation in 1919, in response to the question, 'What are the chief occupations in your parish?' Rev Ivor Griffiths, replied, 'Agricultural. A few business people connected with Hull.' Throughout the reign of George V agriculture continued to be the main occupation of the working population and it supported many ancillary trades, whose prosperity depended upon the success or otherwise of the farms. In *Kelly's Directory* for 1913, 11 farmers and a market gardener are listed. Tradesmen directly involved with farming included two blacksmiths, a farrier, a saddler, and a joiner and wheelwright. There was a brewer, two hay-and-straw dealers and a miller who would trade directly with the farmers, and a flour dealer to buy his stock-in-trade from the miller. The village was almost self-contained for its day-to-day needs. There was a tailor, a shoemaker, a boot repairer, a butcher, a greengrocer, two shopkeepers, a coal merchant, and two bricklayers. There were two carriers to transport goods in and out of the village. In the directory for 1937, although some of the names are different, most of the trades are still represented and the mill, which in 1913 was driven by a steam engine, has been converted to electric power. The farrier, the brewer and the boot repairer are no longer mentioned, but motor engineers and a petrol filling station, a cycle dealer, a poultry farmer, a haulage contractor, a monumental mason and even a fried-fish dealer have been added.

Three Keyingham tradesman and their transport.
Below: James Jackson of Rose Villa Brewery, Hull Road, delivering barrels of his 'Best Brew' on his brewer's dray. Jackson Ales were sold at several Holderness hostelries, and barrels were delivered to outlying farms, especially at harvest time. (From the Jackson family collection)
Top right: Herbert 'Butcher' Westmorland with his butcher's cart. He had the butcher's shop on the north side of Main Street and delivered meat to the farms in the Marsh. One day, when he was returning home in a howling gale, he climbed into the cart for shelter and let the horse find its own way home. (Courtesy of Mrs Gladys Cook)
Bottom Right: The miller's lorry. An early motor lorry. Note the encouraging advertisement and the logo showing the mill with its sails. Only the back wheels have pneumatic tyres.
(Courtesy of Ann Braithwaite)

FOR HEALTH. NUTRIMENT & APPETITE.

T.S. EYRE
& SON.
KEYINGHAM

British farming benefited greatly from the First World War. At the outbreak of the war something like three-quarters of Britain's food was imported. As the German submarine blockade increased, the country had to produce more of its own food. This required the ploughing up of grassland. It was estimated that 100 acres of land as pasture could feed nine people when devoted to stock rearing and 41 people if devoted to a dairy herd. Ploughed up, it could feed 208 people if wheat was grown and 418 if planted with potatoes. The War Agricultural Committee therefore compelled farmers to convert to arable, despite the fact that it required far more labour to cultivate it. In Keyingham, land that had gradually been converted to pasture over the years since the start of the agricultural depression in the 1870s was once again brought under the plough. The demand for labour meant that farm workers' wages rose, in this area to about £16 a year for a hired lad taking his first job and as high as £100 for an experienced wagoner - provided he could avoid conscription. There was, of course, an increase in the price of food during the war that partially offset the rise in wages, but on the whole the farm worker was better off. The farmer was certainly more prosperous than he had been for nearly half a century.

This well-being and prosperity seemed set to continue after the war when in 1920 the government decided to continue with the war-time measures of guaranteed minimum prices for wheat and potatoes and minimum wages for farm workers. Things looked well for the agricultural worker returning from the war. In 1919 Rev Ivor Griffiths, asked in the visitation articles if there was any poverty in the village, replied, 'No poor. All have done well in varying degrees out of the War Conditions. They are all better off financially than the Incumbent.' His last statement was ill-disguised irony. His income of about £250 a year may well have been low compared with that of other clergymen but it exceeded most incomes in the village by a long way. Any prosperity of the farming community expressed in Griffiths' statement was short-lived. The reopening of the world markets brought a collapse in farm prices and in 1922 the government abandoned both the minimum price and the minimum wage. Prices and wages were left to find their market levels, although the efforts of the National Union of Agricultural Workers managed to ensure a certain minimum wage for an approximately 49-hour basic week (longer in summer and shorter in winter), after which overtime was due. The wages stipulated in the East Riding by the Union in 1926 ranged from £12.10s a year for a lad just starting work to £33 for a wagoner. These were for men hired on a yearly basis and receiving their board and lodging while living-in on the farm. For men not living-in wages ranged from 15s (75p) a week for a lad under 15 to 35s for a man over 21. Martinmas week remained as an unpaid holiday for those hired on a yearly basis. The Martinmas hirings continued but wages were rarely negotiable, as they had been fixed by the Union, although the agreement for a year's work with the farmer was still sealed with a fest.

The 49-hour week was achieved in 1919 under an Act that reduced the daily working hours for agricultural labourers from 11 to nine and also gave the labourer Saturday afternoons off. Willam Harness says that when the free Saturday afternoon was obtained, 'the men stood around not knowing what to do with their time'. It was only a few years after this that the first football team, other than any school team, was formed in the village.

As farming began a decline into depression and farmers became impoverished, land was again put down to grass, partly to reduce the wages bill. Ken Hoe's recollection of the 1930s is of there being very little arable land on the higher ground in Keyingham. What there was, was to the east of Eastfield Road. The government took some steps to help the ailing farming industry in 1925 by introducing a subsidy for the cultivation of sugar beet, which provided a substitute for cane sugar imported from abroad. Harold Lowther was one Keyingham farmer who took up the offer and his daughter still has several of the weigh-bills received at the railway station, verifying the weights of sugar beet that had been shipped out by rail.

In 1933 the Milk Marketing Board was formed to encourage the consumption of milk, improve hygiene standards in its production and assist the dairy farmer by guaranteeing the price of milk. Harold Lowther had started his dairy farming business in 1924, buying his first cow when his wife won a prize of £100 in a Persil Soap competition. He kept his cows at the New Mill on Ottringham Road and leased the grazing on the verges of Dam Lane from the parish council under the old system of lane letting. He gradually increased his herd and, because he could get a higher price than he got from the Milk Marketing Board by selling direct to the customer, he started retailing milk. Mrs Lowther sterilised the churns and milk cooler, and later, when farm bottling started, the bottles were sterilised on the premises. The herd of pedigree Friesians was regularly tested for tuberculosis under the marketing board's scheme.

To help with milk deliveries, Harold bought a motorbike and sidecar, and sometimes, on Sundays, the whole family of wife and three daughters, Gladys, Evelyn and Freda, piled in for outings to visit Grandma at Roos. For transporting the churns and cans Harold built a special oblong sidecar, with a drop-down end. When his three daughters were old enough they delivered the milk on their bicycles, carrying two 2-gallon cans, one on each side of the handlebars. The milk was ladled from the bulk cans into customers' own containers at each house using half-pint or pint ladles that hung inside the cans. The local milk round covered most of the village. It extended as far as Bridge Bungalows to the west, and to the north as far as the railway gatehouse, down Eastfield Road. Daughter Gladys well remembers the severe winter of 1947, when the snow was six-foot deep in places, and they had to walk across submerged hedge tops and five-barred gates to deliver to Mrs Hargrave at the gatehouse. Any milk that was surplus to the village deliveries was left in churns at the roadside to be picked up by Rileys Dairies of Hull to be bottled up for the Hull delivery men. The price guaranteed by the Milk Marketing Board was obtained for this milk.

Besides milk, the Lowthers supplied home-made curd and fresh eggs, and the girls often had to return to a customer with half-a-dozen eggs and still be back promptly in time for school at nine o'clock. Harold also kept pigs and chickens. As on most farms in those days, the farmer's wife took charge of much of the care of the farmyard animals, and took her turn at milking. Mrs Lowther reared the chicks hatched in an incubator, about a hundred eggs at a time. The hatched chicks were kept warm under a 'brooder' heated by paraffin until they were strong enough to run about. Cockerels and geese were fattened up for the Christmas market. They were killed and plucked by hand on the farm and sold locally.

In 1938 the Lowther family left the mill and

moved to Jessamine Cottage in Ings Lane. The stock was kept on the land now occupied by the east side of Compton Drive and the bungalows towards Saltaugh Road. When new bungalows came to be built nearby, Harold realised there would be complaints about farm smells, so in 1972 he sold his herd, his pedigree bull and his pigs, and retired at the age of 72 after 48 years as one of the principal dairymen supplying milk to Keyingham.

There were several other dairymen in Keyingham. In 1946 W H Lanham of Bleak House was advertising as having been established 42 years. He offered 'Service with a smile by the WLA [Women's Land Army] - Bottled milk delivered daily'. Ken Hoe remembers several dairymen in Keyingham in the late 1930s: Lawrie Grant of Skeckling Farm, which was on the north side of Main Street, Wilkinson of Manor Farm, Chapel Lane, and C E (Ted) Westmorland of Elm Tree Farm, Waldby Garth Road.

Although there was some conversion to pasture on the large farms in the Marsh, the grass was mainly used for sheep rearing and beef fattening. Irish cattle were brought to Keyingham by rail. They were very thin and were driven on the hoof to the farms in herds of about 100. There was still sufficient arable in the Marsh, however, to warrant the need for draught horses and consequently the men living-in on the farms to look after them.

The tales the old men tell about their living conditions when they were hired out differ according to whether they worked at a 'good place' or one where provisions were poor, but the

Aerial view of the east end of Main Street before the development of the 1960s. In the foreground are Ferndale House, Harrison's joiner shop (now demolished) and the cottage that was formerly the Primitive Methodist chapel. The barns and piggeries were part of Skeckling Farm (left). Six bungalows and the former Police House now occupy the site. Willowfield House is the large house on the north side of the road and has since been divided into two houses. White lines are painted on the bend in the road.

Courtesy of Miss Muriel Guy

188

experiences of the late Frank (Bunny) Howes are perhaps typical of life on the farm in the years between the two wars. Bunny was hired on a farm about ten miles from Keyingham in 1929. His day started at half past five when he saw to the horses' feed and water, harnessed them up for the work of the day and then returned to the house at half past six for breakfast of cold meat, maybe beef or bacon, and bread, followed by apple pie. He would start in the fields by seven o'clock or, in winter, help with feeding and cleaning out the animals in the stockyard until it was daylight. Dinner was at twelve, with a cooked meal provided, then back to the fields by one o'clock and work until five. After tea, horses were fed and bedded down for the night. With such an early start to the day, Bunny was usually in bed by nine o'clock in winter. The bedrooms were sparsely furnished, with only a bed and the lad's 'box' that he had brought his belongings in. He would wash in the copper-house with cold water, but lads on some farms had only the pump and the horse trough in the yard in which to get washed. In wintertime, when the horses were stabled, the lads had to stay on the farm to see to them, but in summer, when the horses could be turned out into the fields and they could be left for the weekend, Bunny could come home. He had a bicycle, but some of the lads walked.

On some farms there was a communal room with a fireplace where on winter evenings the lads could meet others from neighbouring farms and they would roast potatoes or boil eggs. They were well able to provide their own entertainment. There was usually one who owned a harmonica or even a second-hand melodeon and could play popular tunes. There might also be a wind-up gramophone playing scratchy renderings of the popular tunes of the day.

Farm hands were paid at the end of their year's hire so it was not easy to buy even necessities during the year. It was possible, however, to obtain goods 'on tick' from Calico Jackson, a draper from Patrington who travelled round the villages with his horse and cart selling cloth and clothes. The customer paid when he got his wages at Martinmas. Another way to be able to buy essential clothing, such as a pair of working boots, was to obtain a 'sub' off the foreman, who would deduct it from the pay at the end of the year.

The hiring out of lads and putting girls into service at age fourteen helped to relieve overcrowded conditions in homes with the large families that were typical of the early part of the century. Opportunities were beginning to be afforded by the Education Acts to allow children from elementary schools to attain a scholarship to attend secondary school and go on to higher education and professional qualifications. There were openings for boys to learn a trade, but they were likely to be sons of tradesmen already in business in the village. Girls might consider nursing or dressmaking and more than one family in Keyingham can claim to have had a grandmother who worked for Madam Clapham, the Hull dressmaker who made high quality fashionable dresses for ladies in London and even for royalty. But for the most part the girls would go into service at some large house in the village, or a farmstead close to home or sometimes at a place as far away as London.

As with a hired farm boy, a girl's wage included board and lodging. There was no 'big' house in Keyingham with a system of domestic service as portrayed in the television programme *Upstairs, Downstairs* but several houses employed maids. These houses are remembered as Mount Pleasant, the Vicarage, Ellesmere House, the Mill, Ebor

House, the farms and the homes of the local professional people and tradesmen. Edith East (nee Marshall) was in service with Mrs William Clark at the Post Office, for instance. The work consisted of all the household chores, seeing to the fires, helping with preparing the vegetables and the cleaning in the kitchen. The girls who worked at the farms in Keyingham Marsh also helped to look after the hired men and the extra labour employed at threshing times. They would be the ones to take out 'lowance to the men in the fields. A can or bottle of tea and a cheese sandwich and a welcome ten-minute break were allowed to the men at nine o'clock and four o'clock. At busy times like harvest, the men would have half an hour for dinner, with a substantial meal of hot meat pie, served out in the field. All the meals were provided by the farmer's wife or the foreman's wife. The latter received a payment from the farmer to cover her expense, but the farmer's wife went unrewarded. Gladys Cook, whose husband John farmed at North End, says that at harvest time she did nothing but feed men and felt that she lived with a rolling pin in her hands.

Despite the efforts of the farm workers' union, wages in farming were poor compared with those in other industries. Farmers, trying to keep down their wages bill, would employ mainly men under the age of 21, so older men found it difficult to find a job in farming. Many of Keyingham's older residents will tell you that they were hired out when they were lads, but very few stayed in farming for the rest of their working lives. Fortunately, in the 1930s alternative work was to be found locally with the great building programme that occurred in Hull. Between 1930 and 1938 an average of nearly 1,900 houses a year were built in the city, both for corporation tenants and owner-occupiers, the latter taking advantage of the low deposits and low mortgages then available. Keyingham men, such as Jack Thompson, Cyril (Sid) Gardner, Albert Grant and Edwin (Ted) Roydhouse, found work in Hull in the building industry. Ted Roydhouse cycled fifteen miles to work on housing sites on Willerby Road in west Hull. He had to arrive there by 7 a.m., before labour was taken on for the day, as there were always plenty of men looking to be 'set on' and eager to step in. Other former farm workers, with their knowledge of horses, were equipped to take on jobs leading building materials. They continued to work in heavy haulage when motor lorries were introduced. The exodus of labour from farming continued into the 1940s and many former farm labourers obtained work at the installations at Saltend. Usually it was circumstances that dictated what they did. It was more often than not Hobson's choice!

Until 1947, if there was no work to be had, there was no national unemployment benefit to tide a man over until such times as he found a job. There was the possibility of applying to the Patrington Union for parish assistance, but this would have entailed the relieving officer, Mr Watkinson, coming to the house to ascertain if there were any non-essential goods that could be sold off to provide an income. Besides this, most able-bodied people were too proud to 'go on the parish'. In 1934, when her husband was out of work, Violet Roydhouse cycled to a farm on Cherry Cobb Sands to work for three shillings a day, to keep the family until he found work. When Albert Grant, who with his wife and three young daughters lived in one half of what is now called the Methodist Cottage in Chapel Lane, was laid off work, his wife Alice managed to obtain a few chickens to help bring a little extra food and income to the family.

There is a long tradition of using contractors to

do certain work on the farms, especially with equipment that needs a large capital outlay and is only used seasonally. There were threshing machine contractors in Keyingham in the 1860s and most farms continued to have their corn threshed by contractors. We are all familiar with the steam traction engines that can occasionally be seen trundling from steam fairs to Victorian threshing days around the country today, but as working machines on farms until the early 1940s, they were a common sight in the late-autumn and winter months. They were used to tow the threshing machines to the stackyards and there drive the machine. Some of the larger farms had their own threshing 'sets' - that is traction engine, threshing machine and sometimes straw elevator, which was used to raise the threshed straw on to a stack - but most farms hired one when required. After the end of the 19th century there were no threshing machine contractors in Keyingham, the nearest being Cornthwaite and Harness, both of Ottringham, and Wilkin of Welwick. The contractor provided two or three men, including the engine driver, towards the threshing team, but the other seven or so had to be provided by the farmer. A small farmer might have to hire extra men.

It was always an early start on threshing days as the engine took time to work up steam. Men would wait beside Keyingham Cross in the hope of being hired for the day. One character was notorious for being hired, taking the breakfast supplied before work started, and then finding he was indisposed. The farmer's or foreman's wife provided the food for the men, which meant an early start for her as she had to give them breakfast while the engine was heating up. The farmer was responsible for the coal and water for the engine. When the fire in the firebox had been stoked up hot enough to start the steam, the threshing machine was connected by a belt to the driving wheel. Each man had his own job to do. One pitched up the sheaves to two men on top, where one cut the bands and the other fed the sheaves into the hopper. Another man set the bags in place to catch the grain, and others cleared the straw away to a new stack if no elevator was being used. One of the least-liked jobs of the day was that of carrying the chaff away to be used later for animal feed. The chaff was collected on large square sheets that were picked up by taking hold of the corners and then slung over the shoulder. The bundles were very large, though they were not heavy, and it was a dusty, itchy job. It was the wagoner's job to carry away the full sacks of grain, as he was usually the strongest. Extra wages were usually paid for corn carrying. If the grain was to be stored in the granary the full sacks had to be carried up a ladder and there emptied out to save sacks being gnawed by rats. The sacks of grain destined for elsewhere were loaded on to rulleys ready to be led to the railway station. Because the grain was measured by volume in bushels, the sacks of grain had different weights. A 4-bushel sack held ten stone (63.5 kg) of oats, 16 stone (101 kg.) of barley or 18 stone (114 kg) of wheat.

Usually, only one day's threshing was done at each farm at a time, giving time for the threshed straw to be used up for feeding and bedding animals before the threshing set was sent for again. When tractors, running on paraffin or petrol, came to be used on farms they were used for driving the threshing machines and cut out all the time needed for building up steam that had previously been required.

Steam ploughing was another task carried out by contractors. The steam plough, invented in the 19th century, came more into use after the Great

Steam plough, circa 1935. The six-share plough was attached to steel cables and pulled back and forth between two stationary steam traction engines. This was achieved by a capstan arrangement underneath the engines. The plough was bi-directional and operated by two men. When it reached the end of the field, it was tipped and the men moved to the seats at the opposite end of the machine to face their new direction of travel. Courtesy of Ann Braithwaite

War, when deep cultivation of the land had been neglected. A horse plough ploughed to a depth of only six inches at the most. As the land had become compacted, it was too hard for even two or more horses yoked to a plough to do the work, so steam ploughs were used.

Two steam traction engines were needed. They were used as stationary engines, one at each end of the field. The six-furrow plough was attached to strong steel cables and pulled back and forth between capstans fitted beneath the engines. The ploughs were bi-directional and carried two men. When the plough reached the end of the field it was tilted to bring the other set of plough shares into operation, and the men moved to the seats at the opposite end of the machine to face their new direction of travel. The depth of the furrows could be varied to suit the soil to give the ground 'a good open up' and improve the drainage of the land. Other implements, such as a cultivator or a drainer, could replace the plough shares.

As in the case of contract threshing, coal and water for the engines were supplied by the farmer and were brought to the field in horse-drawn wagons. A crew of four men came with each set of ploughs. They arrived with their living van, which resembled a wooden shed on iron wheels. They cooked their own meals, or sometimes engaged a cook from the village. The local contracting team in the early 1930s was Bob East, the foreman, from

Bob East's steam ploughing team, circa 1935. (Left to right) Bob East, the foreman, Bill Ashmore (from Leeds), Bob Tarbotton and Edgar Walker. The wooden van in the background has small metal wheels and is where the team cooked, ate and slept when working away from home

Courtesy of G C East

Keyingham, Jack Rust, also of Keyingham, Arthur Dibnah from Burstwick and Joseph Taylor from York.

Albert Henry (Bob) East lived in a cottage near Hill Top, opposite the end of Church Lane, where his son George Clarence (Clarrie) was born in 1928. His employers were Kitchings, who came from Lincolnshire but operated on many Holderness farms. Clarrie recalls that living conditions for the steam ploughing teams were very basic and life was hard. He remembers spending some of his holidays with his father in the van when he was about five years old. Having to get himself washed outside in a large zinc bowl, and with no mother on hand to guide him, it seemed to him necessary to wash only his hands and just round his face.

The majority of steam ploughing was done between April and November on lands left fallow for the year. In the winter the equipment was taken to Crawshaw to be stripped down and made ready for the coming season.

In about 1936 'Gyrotillers' superseded steam ploughs. These tracked vehicles were driven by a diesel engine with, not a plough, but two slowly rotating spinners with large prongs at the rear. Like the steam ploughs, they could be set to work

The Gyrotiller. *In about 1936 gyrotillers superseded steam ploughs. Fully equipped, they carried shields around the tillers and a superstructure to carry powerful lamps for night work. Diesel driven and with caterpillar tracks they moved very slowly cultivating about six acres in 24 hours. When the war came, they were found to be ideal for levelling the land for airfields   Photo: G C East*

to any required depth, but Ken Hoe, who worked for contractors called de la Hope, where Bob East had moved to, remembers 14 inches as being most generally used. They were also suitable for rooting out hedgerows. The tillers moved extremely slowly, cultivating about six acres in 24 hours. Powerful lamps were fitted to the tillers so that eight-hour shifts could be worked round the clock from midnight Sunday to midnight Saturday. Sundays were set aside for maintenance.

De la Hope operated ten units in the Yorkshire area, with a crew of four men on each team. They did a lot of work on Holderness farms, but when war was declared in 1939 and gyrotillers were found to be suitable for levelling land for airfields they were diverted to that purpose. Jack Rust recalls their team working on airfields in the West

Riding and as far as the Scottish Borders. Gyrotillers were considered to be very successful in their operation, but Fred Rust remembers a year when one of W H Rodmell's fields was gyrotilled, and the next year's crop was a mass of runch (charlock). The deep tilling had stimulated dormant seed. Mr Rodmell, who farmed from Mount Airey, was furious!

Land draining was also a task carried out by contractors. Draining was very important in an area like Holderness, particularly in the former marshlands, which are mostly below high-water mark. The farmers let the field to contractors for either new drainpipes (pots) to be laid or old ones to be dug up, cleaned and replaced. Trenches were dug by hand by men receiving 2s.3d per chain (22 yards, the length of a cricket pitch). On the heavier soils of the higher ground a man was lucky if he earned 8s (40p) per day. On the siltlands he did better. The direction of slope of the trench was ascertained by trickling water on to the bottom and checking which way it flowed. The pots drained the water into the ditches that ran round the fields and carried the water away to the main drains and eventually to the River Humber at Stone Creek. These main drains were kept cleared by men employed by the Keyingham Level Drainage Board. A boat was kept at the board's boathouse, a barn now part of Applegarth on Waldby Garth Road. The boat was taken by horse and rulley to Keyingham drain where it was 'poled' or dragged along from Tunstall to Stone Creek, with the men leaning over the back to scythe the reeds. The reeds were also scythed from the banks. Harry Etherington had memories of his uncle working on the boat and bringing home great quantities of eels that he had speared with a weapon like Neptune's trident, with backward sloping indentations in its flat blades to prevent the eels from wriggling free. It was not until after the Second World War that an excavator began to be used for scouring the drain.

The recession of the 1920s and '30s slowed down advances in farming. The clearing of weeds from the land was still achieved by leaving fields fallow for a season and repeatedly ploughing, cross-ploughing, dragging and harrowing to kill off weeds and, in particular, couch grass. The Crown's agreement with its tenants on farms in this area required one-fifth of the arable to be left fallow each year. Twenty percent of arable land was thus totally out of production. Even in the Middle Ages the fallow fields had provided grazing for livestock. It was not until the use of selective weed killers that year-to-year cropping of the land was achieved.

The re-introduction in 1932 of subsidies and intervention prices on certain crops brought slight benefits to the farmer, but there was a world over-supply of foodstuffs and British agriculture was still depressed in the 1930s. The cost of labour and maintaining horses encouraged some mechanisation on farms, although conservatism and the capital outlay required slowed its introduction. Albert Walker, who was born in Keyingham in 1910, was a farm worker all his life and did not begin driving tractors until the Second World War. The replacement of horses was a slow process. When the stock of the 450-acre farm at Saltaugh was sold off in 1937 after the death of the tenant Thomas Cook, it included only a single tractor. On the other hand, 34 horses were put up for sale. As was usual in the history of British farming it took a war to hurry things along.

- o -

As seen in the previous chapter, church and chapel attendance in Keyingham on the eve of the Great War was probably as regular and as high as it had ever been. The war changed all that. Harry Verity in his book *Founded on the Rock*, dealing with Methodism in South Holderness, commented that the war 'changed irrevocably the pattern of Chapel life. A number of our men did not return alive from the battle fronts. Of those who did return some were never to resume their habits of Church attendance. The old certainties were shaken.' Unfortunately, there are no statistics to verify if this was the case in Keyingham although the comments of Ivor Griffiths in his Visitation return of 1919 suggest that it was true. Regarding Methodism in the village, he informed the archbishop that the chapels were not so well attended as they had formerly been. Regarding his own congregation, attendance had improved on what it was during the war (the average attendance at the most popular service, Evensong, was now 55) but 'they have little sense of their religious needs. The only appeal seems to be of a materialistic character. This has become more marked during the war.' He complained that there were five former churchwardens in the parish who no longer attended church except occasionally for a burial, 'to show respect'. The son of the previous vicar still lived in the village and 'uses Sunday for all sorts of Sabbath breaking'.

Aniron Ivor Griffiths was instituted as the Vicar of Keyingham on 7 January 1914, so he had some knowledge of the religious condition of Keyingham before the war. On the day he was instituted his first pastoral duty was to conduct the funeral service of Dr Compton, vicar's warden, who had died two days previously.

Several additions and improvements were made to the church and its surrounds during Ivor Griffith's incumbency. In 1914 the north aisle was taken down and rebuilt by Quibell & Green, builders, of Hull. The architect was John Bilson, also of Hull and a noted architectural historian. The restoration was dedicated by the Bishop of Hull in November 1914. The whole of the cost was borne by Anna Elletson, the widow of Job Elletson. Job was born at the Ship Inn, Keyingham, and emigrated to America during the agricultural depression of the 1870s. A bronze plaque in the north aisle records the restoration: 'To the Glory of God and in pious memory of Job Elletson, who was a native of the Parish of Keyingham, and died August 17th 1911, in Auburn, New York, U.S.A., this aisle was rebuilt by his devoted widow, Anna R. Elletson.' Anna Elletson, a Dutch-American, died in Auburn, New York, in the 88th year of her age in 1925. She also by her benefaction had the churchyard planted with various kinds of trees and the church path kerbed. Some of the trees still survive.

The commemorative oak reredos and side panels were erected at the end of the war. They bear the inscription: 'To the Glory of God, and in commemoration of those who fell in the Great War 1914-1918'. The work was executed by E Pickering, a wood carver and instructor at the Hull Municipal College of Art. The cost of the work at Keyingham was £62.6s, with a further £2.2s for the faculty, which was granted on 30 January 1917. As in the case of the village war memorial, preparations for the reredos began before the war ended. £59.17s of the required money was raised by subscriptions, with all but £5 of it donated by women. The deficit was made up by the churchwardens, Herbert Francis of Saltaugh Grange and Thomas Mook of Ebor House, who had initiated the project. The vicar paid the two guineas for the faculty.

In November 1926 an over-heated stovepipe set fire to the roof of the north aisle causing considerable damage to the woodwork. There was a service in progress at the time, otherwise the church might have burnt down. On this occasion, specialists King & Co. of Hull were brought in to thoroughly overhaul the stove so that it would be ready for use in the winter months. The chimneys of all three stoves, the one in the north aisle, one in the south aisle and one in the vestry, were reconstructed so as to pass through the stone walls rather than the wooden roofs. In 1927, no doubt as a result of the claim to the insurers for the fire damage, the value of the church building for insurance purposes was raised from £4,470 to £7,000. Today, the church is insured for well over £2m.

Ivor Griffiths died in March 1930, aged 65, after 16 years as vicar of Keyingham. He was buried at

Aldridge, Staffordshire. In the following year, when electric lighting was installed in the church, a bronze tablet was placed on the south wall of the chancel with the inscription, 'The electric lighting of this chancel was installed in memory of Ivor Griffiths, Vicar of this Parish, 1914-1930, by his friends M. E. and E. M. Goundrill.' He is remembered for wearing a mortarboard and leather gaiters with large brass buckles. He carried a large Gladstone bag on his journeys between the vicarage and the church. In the latter years of his life he commuted between Keyingham and the Midlands, where his wife lived. He left Keyingham on Mondays and returned for the weekends. Visiting his parishioners was perhaps not his first priority.

On 25 September 1930, Melville Leffler became vicar of St Nicholas. Leffler was a kindly man, who lived at the vicarage with his widowed sister. He had a speech defect, attributed to shouting at his eskimo-dog team when driving a sledge in Canada, so he assigned the reading of the lessons to laymen. It also meant that his sermons were not easily heard. What he lacked in preaching power, however, he more than made up for by his attention to his parishioners. He was a regular visitor to all members, whatever their denomination. He is remembered as someone 'who tended to have a short memory. He always seemed to have some coins in his waistcoat pocket and would give one to you if it was your birthday. Some of the lads pointed out to him at regular intervals that it was their birthday in order to get a present and usually succeeded.' His generosity was such that he occasionally had to borrow money from Albert Jackson, the vicar's warden. On Sundays Melville Leffler was kept very busy. There were three services and a Sunday school, at all of which he was present. His popularity might be judged by the collecting box. In the five years before his arrival (1925-6 to 1929-30) the annual collection had ranged from £54 to just over £58, the average being under £55. In the next five years (1930-31 to1934-5) the range was £59 to over £73, the average being over £68. Added to this is the fact that, owing to deflation, the buying power of the pound was about 15% higher in the early 1930s than it was in the late 1920s.

Shortly after Leffler's arrival, the state of the church spire gave cause for concern, and in November 1930 an estimate from D Berry & Sons, of Huddersfield, for £350, to do the work, was accepted. The specification was 'that they would pull down the spire to the top of the tower, rebuild and replace with new stones where required, put the finial into good condition and point the tower and fix new stone where needed'. A steeple fund was started and the money was raised by the usual fund-raising methods, the first being a carol service. Jumble sales and whist drives were also held, and the village's first church garden party took place in 1931 at Mount Pleasant, the home of Albert Jackson. The annual St Nicholas Church garden party has been a feature of village life ever since. The money for the steeple repairs was soon raised, although the repairs themselves were not totally successful. The rebuilding gave the spire a decidedly stumpy appearance and local opinion was that the men who built it had spent too long at their lunch hours in the Blue Bell. Thirty years later cracks appeared in the tower, and in 1969 it was thought prudent to remove the spire.

Further fund raising was required when the floor of the belfry was found to be in need of repair in 1933. Five years later an organ fund was set up in order to restore the organ, which had been installed in 1852. This organ was eventually replaced in 1957 by a larger one with electrically powered bellows. There always seems to have been someone to play the organ. The organists were paid £7 per annum from 1911 to 1926 and the blower received 10s. The first mention of Miss Kathleen Stancer playing the church organ was in 1923. Later she became the regular organist, giving her service free, until ill health compelled her to retire in 1987. Like the Anglicans the Primitive Methodists were well served by organists between the two World Wars and after. They, too, had their doyenne - Miss Edith Hart, who not only played the organ but taught others, such as Maurice Clark who later played at chapel services. Edith Hart was a small and fragile-looking woman who suffered terribly from arthritis but, despite this, she threw great energy into rehearsing the children for their parts in the anniversary, the harvest festival and the nativity plays, and brought them to a high musical standard. It is said that she bought dresses for any of the girls whose parents could not afford a new one for their child at the chapel anniversary.

The biggest change that occurred in Anglican church life in Keyingham during Melville Leffler's incumbency was the involvement of the laity in church government. This had been the intention of the Anglicans when, in 1919, they had introduced the electoral roll as the basis of lay participation in policy making. The electoral roll consisted of those who had been baptised and who declared themselves members of the Church of England. The electoral roll thus had a wide democratic basis, and members on the roll could serve on a number of representative bodies, ranging from the parochial church council to the National Assembly of the Church of England. This proved too democratic for some, and under Ivor Griffiths no electoral roll was drawn up or parochial church council formed. His only church meetings were the

annual Easter vestries, which were attended by never more than eight people, all men, and sometimes as few as four. Only in 1923, when Griffiths was absent from the parish with a long illness and presumably the rural dean took charge of parish affairs, was there a large annual meeting and 23 people, including 14 women, attended. On Griffiths' return the attendance dropped rapidly. In 1924 there were ten, including four women, at the annual meeting. Thereafter, until his death, the attendance varied between six and eight.

After Griffiths' death Keyingham's first electoral roll was drawn up, and a parochial church council was elected. There were 57 on the roll - 38 women and 19 men. Four men and four women were elected to the PCC. After that, and with the coming of Melville Leffler, there was far more lay involvement in church matters. There were 36 people at Leffler's first Easter vestry in 1931. In addition to the annual meeting the PCC usually held two or three meetings a year, but the minutes rarely, if ever, mention the discussion of spiritual matters - the concern is nearly always with the organising of events, usually in order to raise money for the latest repairs or renovations. Ivor Griffiths was perhaps right when he said in 1919, 'There is no interest here for conferences, except those for secular or materialistic purposes.'

The Methodists, particularly the Primitives, had always had lay involvement in the running of their affairs. At the highest level, Wesleyan government was in the hands of ordained ministers only. On the other hand, the ruling body of the Primitives had two lay representatives for every minister. At the local level, however, both denominations had far more lay control than the Anglicans had. Because each circuit of either denomination of Methodists was made up, in rural areas, of a dozen or more village chapels, overseen by perhaps only two ministers, the individual village chapels were very much used to organising their own affairs. Furthermore, ministers only stayed in a circuit for a few years, so chapels did not become minister-oriented. This was different from an Anglican church where a minister with a long incumbency, such as Ivor Griffiths, could impose his wishes on the parish. Chapel people had far more independence and intense local pride. It was in 1932 that this pride was put to the test, when the Wesleyans and the Primitive Methodists were called upon to unite by their respective governing bodies.

Union proceeded smoothly at the top level, but at the circuit level and village level it was a different matter. Some chapel-goers found it difficult to give up their old place of worship, which they had worked hard over many years to build and beautify, and attend the other chapel in the village. Instead of merging, the Withernsea Wesleyan circuit and the Patrington Primitive Methodist circuit continued side by side. As the Methodist authorities had a policy of not coercing local chapels into union, Keyingham and other South Holderness villages for a long time after 1932 had two groups of Methodists, although they shared the services of local ministers. It was not until 1950 that it was decided to amalgamate the two circuits in South Holderness, principally because of the shortage of ministers and the fall in rural population. The single circuit was known as the Withernsea Circuit. At that time Keyingham Wesleyans still had their own officers, with W H Rodmell and C Williams as society stewards, Miss J Goundrill as charities steward and Mrs J E Snelling as class leader. They, however, provided no local preachers and frequently had to ask for the help of the Primitive Methodist preachers. In Keyingham the two groups finally merged in 1952

and decided to use the Primitive Methodist chapel, which was larger and in a far better state of repair, the Wesleyan chapel having suffered blast damage during the Second World War. Emily Harness, a Sunday school teacher at the Wesleyan chapel, remembered the warm welcome she received when she moved to the Primitive chapel and helped to teach the children there. She was soon made to feel at home by Harriet Walker, the Sunday-school superintendent. Emily Harness herself became superintendent until her retirement in 1969. It was not long after 1952 that the Wesleyan chapel was sold off and pulled down.

- o -

At the beginning of the reign of George V, the school had provision for 156 scholars, from a total population in Keyingham of around 550. There were a good deal fewer than 156 children on the school roll, and the average attendance was well below 100. Mr Jefferson was the head teacher, assisted by Mrs Jefferson. In those days head teachers were expected to live in the school-house, adjacent to the school, and Mr and Mrs Jefferson did so throughout their service. Three pupil teachers were employed to assist with teaching the children. By 1911, new codes of practice in teaching were being issued by the Department of Education, and changes in the timetable mention music, drawing, transcription, composition and arithmetic. Mrs Jefferson had begun to teach the children to play the violin. Between 11.45 and 12.00 doesn't appear to allow much time for instruction, but the prize of a violin that was offered for the 'first pupil to play proficiently' was won by Grace Walker, later to become Mrs Harold Capes. School educational visits continued and in 1911 the children went up Eyre's Mill to see the process of making 'Standard Flour'.

In 1912, Mr Jefferson records using a Mirroscope, an early type of slide projector. The first picture show, given as part of a geography lesson, was of views of the East Yorkshire coast and Scottish houses. He hoped to continue to present history in this way when the slides became available. The successor to the Mirroscope was a Cinematograph, which was bought in 1927 with the proceeds of a jumble sale. The sum of £9.6s.7d was raised in the same way in 1928 to buy additional films and it is Charlie Chaplin who figures most often in the recollections of pupils of the early 1930s. They remember 'moving' pictures and a projector that had to be wound by hand. Any slowing down of the winding handle caused a similar reaction on the screen, and an accidental turn in the wrong direction sent the screen action into reverse. This was particularly amusing in a film of camels crossing the desert! Visits from His Majesty's Inspectors continued to shape the curriculum. In 1912, questions were asked about manual work done, and the suggestion was made that, if possible, gardening, housewifery and domestic subjects should be taught. It was not until 1919, however, that it was arranged for the older girls to attend a cookery course at Withernsea School. Eleven girls were chosen to attend and vouchers were issued for them to obtain their tickets to travel by rail. On the visit of the inspector in 1915, the need for handicraft work was spoken of, and experience of paper cutting and the use of plasticine in Standards 1 and 2 was enquired into. At this time, the school still consisted of two classrooms - the infants' room, for the under-seven-year olds, and the large room, which is now the Teachers' Centre, for the older children. The school admitted several three-year-old children in 1913.

Mrs Emily Harness started at Keyingham school as a five-year-old in 1915, and she remembered that the children were taught in 'ability groups'. Arithmetic was taught through counters and abacus, and times-tables by rote up to thirteen times. Tables were also learnt by heart for weights and measures and money.

The school managers were interested in encouraging the boys to play football and in 1911 a club was formed under an enthusiastic secretary, Walter Russell, son of John, of Sunthorp House. Hour-long practices took place every school day from 3.30 under the charge of Mr Russell. The girls played hockey in the schoolyard.

There is an instance in 1920 which foreshadows the National Curriculum, in operation in schools today, when a logbook entry in red ink states, 'The young lady organiser of physical culture informed me that the revised Government scheme would be advised to schools shortly. I was told to introduce a short period of 20 minutes each day for Exercises.' These were scheduled to be undertaken between scripture and arithmetic, and were to replace the three periods currently on the weekly timetable. 'The boys are also to take off their coats for the exercises and, *if possible*, their waistcoats.' If this new scheme *was* implemented, it must have had good effect, as by 1923 a team of two boys and two girls, Jennie Freeman and Jennie Ream with Edwin Roydhouse and Norman Ream, 'obtained the prizes at the Patrington Sports'. Joyce Eyre, nee Thompson, also remembers the Holderness schools' sports days when, one year, at Hornsea, the Keyingham team won most of the prizes. She recalls that 'the girls played cricket with the boys and Roy Whiting was a very good spin bowler'. Inter-school netball matches were played, with Joyce as shooter as she was the tallest. In her last year at school, she also helped Miss Middleton in the babies' class by pointing to words on a chart - at, bat, cat, etc. - to help the children with reading.

Keyingham school was fortunate that, during the Great War, there was no loss of staff to the war effort, and that provision was still being made for the supply of books. The proceeds from the Marritt-Ombler charity of about £22 per year was used to augment school funds. In July 1917 a set of 84 library books was supplied by the trustees of the charity. The books were kept separate from books supplied from other sources and were known as the Marritt-Ombler School Library. By the December of that year, arrangements had been made with the Education Authority and the Committee of the Union of Institutes and Village Libraries to supply 100 books, in sets of 25 books per quarter. As an experiment, the scheme was to be worked in conjunction with Ottringham. In February 1918, a set of books duly arrived from the Yorkshire Union of Village Libraries. Mr Jefferson commented, 'The selection is a good one and the books are clean and in good condition. Some of them set a rather high standard for village children under 14 years.'

As more provision was made for further education, pupils from Keyingham were able to transfer to Withernsea School at age eleven, but their parents were responsible for their travelling costs by rail or bus. A bus pass cost 11s (55p) for one month or 30s for three months in 1928. Other children went to schools in Hull - Hymers College, Craven Street (later Malet Lambert) and the Hull Technical School. Logbook entries in 1915 show that Florence Jackson, who had already 'satisfied the examiners in a written examination for a scholarship', had to pass a medical examination.

There were others who were successful in higher education, and Miss Lily Middleton recounted that 'for a small school, there were a fair number of successes, several later achieving school headships, for example, H Etherington at Pocklington and C W Howes at Hunmanby. W Coombe returned to Keyingham School as a teacher. He was very keen on sports and introduced circuit training and later became head teacher at a Hessle school. That the pupils had high aspirations is illustrated by a story of one boy's answer to a school inspector who asked what he was going to be when he grew up. "Prime Minister!" he replied. When questioned as to how he got that idea, he said that his teacher had told him that Lloyd George's mother had taken in washing, and if Lloyd George could rise from such humble surroundings, why shouldn't he? He became a head teacher.'

Childhood diseases continued to seriously affect school attendance. The schoolmaster recorded that there was an epidemic of measles in 1913 when children under five were excluded from school, and in 1920 an outbreak of measles reduced the attendance to 45 and the school was closed. Influenza closed the school in 1918 and 1920, and we find an indication that technology was beginning to arrive in Keyingham in November 1923 when notification that 'the school should be closed by order because of whooping cough' was sent by telegram. There were other reasons for low attendance. It was the weather on 9 July 1915, when thunderstorms kept the village children away for one day and the 'distance' children from Keyingham Marsh for two days. Throughout the war, warnings of Zeppelin raids during the night caused the children to stay away from school the next day. Church and chapel activities were often given as a reason for poor attendance at school. There were entries on 4 December 1914: 'Bishop of Hull at St. Nicholas. Many children away in consequence.' And on 1 Feb. 1918: 'Several boys away on Wednesday taking charge of stalls at Jumble Sale. Other children away on Thursday to take part in a concert at Thorngumbald.' Half-day holidays were taken on the afternoons of the Wesleyan Sunday school anniversary and, of course, there was the annual treat day when the Sunday school scholars from church and chapel enjoyed a day at the seaside.

It was still customary to give a half-day holiday on Empire Day, but in 1923, when a gramophone had been lent for the occasion, the children were able to listen to a recording of the speeches of King George and Queen Mary. Eleven years later, in 1934, a wireless set was installed and, as an experiment, the older children were allowed to listen to a talk on fruit growing. The verdict was 'that the broadcast would have been more useful if the children had possessed the accompanying handbooks'. When George V died on 22 January 1936, the children were able to listen first-hand to the funeral ceremonies and a talk about his life.

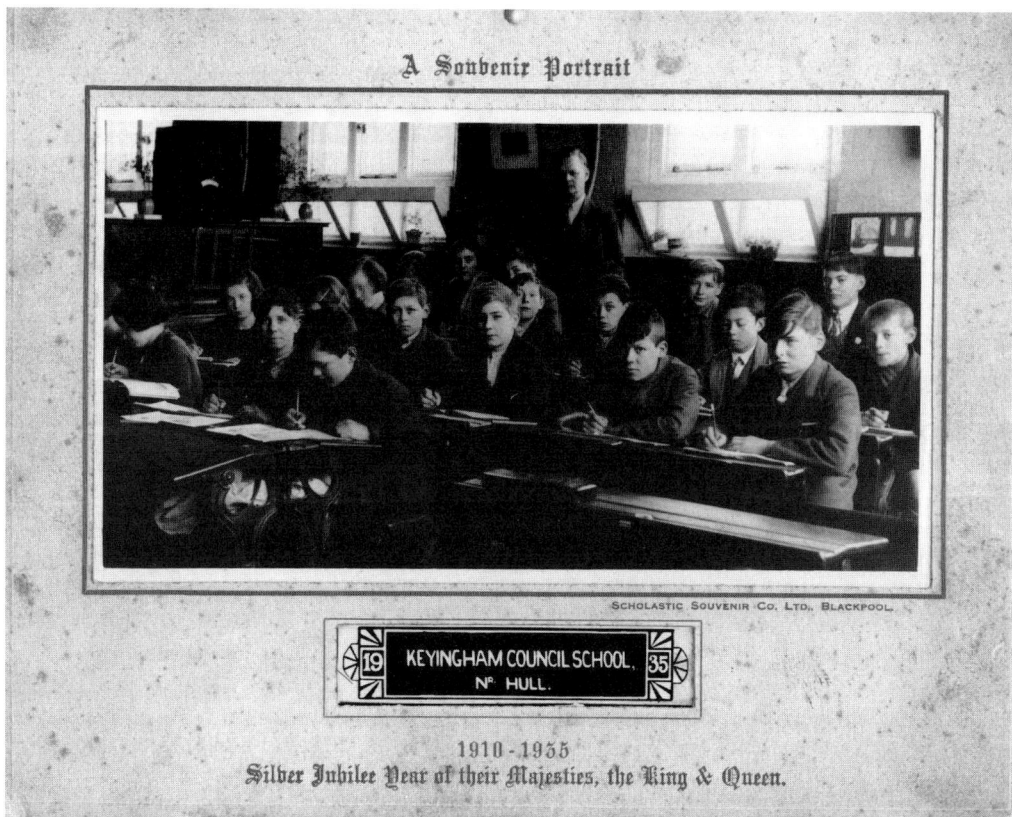

Class of '35. A Silver Jubilee souvenir photograph. Mr Jefferson supervises the children working at their desks. The wireless set sits uncomfortably on top of the piano. On the front row are (left to right): Frances Alderton, William Lowther and Alan Farmery; on the second row: Kathleen Gray, Doreen East, Charles Greenside, George Harness, George Downes and Clifford Guy; on the third row: Kathleen Bourne, Gordon Smith, Norman Dixon. James Wesley and Ernest Fox; and on the back row: Jessie Thompson, Frances Richardson, Roy Whiting and Arthur Kitching. Courtesy of Mrs Joyce Eyre

This was almost the last event recorded in the logbook by Mr Jefferson. He and his wife retired from the school on 26 February 1936 after 32 years' service. Many people in the village have memories of Mr and Mrs Jefferson's latter years at the school. There is a report of the release during a music lesson of 30 live mice by some of the older boys. The sight of hysterical girls jumping on desks remained a delightful memory of Frank Howes! Kathleen Braithwaite remembered, as many others did, Mr Jefferson marching up and down looking for his spectacles, which none of his pupils was prepared to tell him were safely resting on the top of his head. Jim Garsides recalled the outrage when Mrs Jefferson had an Eton crop - a new hair style of the 1920s. Until then she had worn her hair in a bun like most other women of her profession.

Leonard Scruton was appointed headmaster in March 1936. As Mr Jefferson had done in his early days, he brought the energies and thinking of a younger man into school. He saw the value of encouraging the children to learn from practical experience, and teaching was organised around not only giving the children a sound education in the three Rs but also in making learning a pleasurable activity based on first hand experiences. The curriculum became much broader based, with the introduction of gardening, country dancing (a doubtful pleasure for some of the boys!), Esperanto (quite revolutionary) and various musical activities. Theatre groups were brought into school to give the children experience of live theatre. Trips by train were organised with other Holderness schools to such places as the Lake District in 1937, London in 1938 and Wales in 1939. The war curtailed these excursions. Under Mr Scruton's guidance the sporting prowess of the school improved. Keyingham joined the Holderness Sports in 1936 and two years later won

the Maxwell Trophy, the Dr Jackson Cup and the British Legion Cup.

In those days competition was considered a desirable part of training for adult life, and a 'house system' was introduced in the school. The houses were named Kelsey, Kirncroft and Saltaugh, and there was great competition at the annual sports day when everyone tried to win the coveted trophies. A school uniform of green and white was introduced, helping to foster a feeling of pride in the school. The children were fully involved in the selection of the uniform. Several pamphlets were sent for and the pupils voiced their opinion as to the style and colour chosen. The girls chose green and white - green gymslips and white blouses in summer with light green jumpers in the winter. Miss Upshall taught the girls to knit their own jumpers. The girls' uniform was completed by green interlock knee-length knickers, green gaberdine coat and a little porkpie hat bearing the school badge, designed by the children. The boys' uniform consisted of ties and caps with badges. A blazer was also recommended. This uniform was not compulsory but many pupils attended school in part, if not full, uniform.

Before 1925 children had to walk to school, whatever the distance. Mrs Eva Levitt, who left the school in 1905 told of having to walk some two and a half miles to school each day. Transport for children who lived at the outlying farms at Saltaugh Sands and in the western part of Keyingham Marsh was introduced in June 1925, and the log records that 'Fifteen children are making use of the conveyance.' The first vehicle was a converted horse-drawn rulley over which a cover had been fitted. It somewhat resembled a gypsy caravan and was commonly called 'the van'. With only a canvas between the occupants and the

School transport, circa 1930. Clem Westmorland and 'Old Tom' crossing Sands Bridge, bringing the children to Keyingham school from the farms on Keyingham Marsh and Cherry Cobb Sands.   *Courtesy of Mrs Joyce Eyre*

elements it was an extremely cold ride in the winter. In mid-January 1929, heavy snow prompted an entry in the school logbook that 'no-one came to school in the van'. The first driver was Clem Westmorland and one of the users of the school van in those early days was Joyce Eyre. She lived at Sands Farm and had to be at the farm lane end by half-past seven in the morning. The cart picked up children from all the other farms, and then went along Marsh Road through six gates that had to be opened and closed, usually by the children. Her memories of Old Tom, the horse that

pulled the cart, was that he had only one speed and that was s-l-o-w. Another regular passenger, not a school child, was Eileen Laws from Rat Abbey who liked to wave to passers-by from the back of the cart. Rat Abbey was the name of a since-demolished black cottage that stood on the bank of Keyingham drain to the west of Sands House Farm.

- o -

At the start of George V's reign the railway was still the quickest and most convenient way of travelling to Hull from Keyingham. The North Eastern Railway Company ran the Hull-Withernsea Railway for 60 years until 1922, when the line was taken over by the London & North

Eastern Railway in the general consolidation of the country's railways. A dozen passenger trains were running daily and, apart from the 8.20 a.m. express from Withernsea to Hull and the 5.23 p.m. Hull-to-Withernsea express, they all stopped at Keyingham. As well as carrying day-trippers and commuters, the passenger trains brought the mail and the daily newspapers to Keyingham station. A goods train came through every day and dropped off goods on its way to Withernsea and picked up produce from a warehouse at the station on its return journey.

Besides the two platforms for passengers and small goods, there were also two separate sidings, one for coal delivery and one for livestock. The coal trains came in along a raised siding that ran over the top of the coal cells. The coal trucks stopped over the cells and the coal was released through the bottoms of the trucks. Each cell was marked with the different type of coal and the pit it came from. There was special 'steam' coal, hard and shiny and in big lumps, which was used to fire the steam engines used on the farms. The various grades of domestic coal were weighed out into eight-stone bags by the village coal-men, Walt Lanham and Clem Westmorland, to deliver to homes, mostly in Keyingham. Sometimes coal was collected by individuals, and lads could earn a few pennies fetching it for neighbours. Farmers from outlying farms collected coal in their wagons, drawn by two or three horses. The wagons were driven on to the weighbridge at the station to check the weight of the coal.

The other siding was the cattle dock. It was a raised platform, with a slope to drive the animals up to the level of the trucks. Cows, sheep and pigs were loaded into wagons to be sent to Hull cattle market every Monday. Cattle wagons could also be hired privately to move animals from village to village, although for short distances they would be walked.

In the 1920s the railway began to face serious competition from the road for passenger transport. At the start of the decade the Hedon-to-Withernsea road via Patrington was a Class II road maintained by the Patrington Rural District Council. Maintenance consisted of scraping off the surface of rolled-in gravel and replacing it with fresh gravel. A report in the local paper in 1915 described the condition of the roads in Keyingham as 'a sea of mud', probably the result of the thunderstorms that kept the children away from school that year. Usually in summer the roads were very dusty. In 1922 the RDC applied to the East Riding County Council for the road to be taken over as a main road by the ERCC. The ERCC agreed on condition that the road was brought up to the proper standard first. This meant tarmacking the 12.5 miles of road from Hedon to Withernsea (the Hull-Hedon road was already tarmacked and classified as a main road) at an estimated cost of nearly £54,000, towards which the Ministry of Transport made a 75% grant. The Ministry also contributed £51 towards the £154 required to purchase a tar sprayer. The work was completed, and by 1926 a Withernsea publicity brochure was proclaiming that the road from Hull had been completely remade with 'a smooth level service' and that the Automobile Association had certified the road to be 'good'. Ominously, for the railway company, the same brochure declared that the town was now served by buses.

A bus service from Withernsea to Hull, passing through Keyingham, had been started in 1922 by J J Symonds of Roos. This was before the road was upgraded, and the buses suffered much damage. Symonds sold out to W H Rea of Withernsea in 1924. The business soon passed to Lee & Beulah, who had been operating very successful services between Hull and villages on the west of the city since 1919. In 1926 Lee & Beulah merged with Hull & District Motor Services to form East Yorkshire Motor Services. In 1927 the EYMS timetable showed buses leaving Withernsea for Hull practically every half hour beginning at 6.45 a.m. and finishing at 9.30 p.m. The last bus from Hull left at 11 p.m. The company did not have the confidence to advertise the times of arrival. When the Keyingham Drama Group presented *The Mounteagle Letter* at the school in 1933, the programme announced that the bus to Withernsea left the village at 10 p.m. and 11 p.m. and the last bus for Hull left at 10.10 p.m. The last train for Hull left at 10.37 p.m.

Keyingham was also served by buses running from Easington to Hull. This service was started in 1921 by J H Graham and C Connor. As well as carrying the passengers, the buses brought newspapers to the village and operated a parcels service that connected to all bus depots in the country. Regular passengers on the Easington bus were never left behind in the mornings. The driver would go and knock on the door of anyone who was late.

Bicycles continued to be a regular way of getting about and cyclists had, by all accounts, a difficult time avoiding potholes on minor roads and even on the main road before 1923. Keeping the minor roads in repair does not seem to have been of paramount importance for in 1923 the RDC resolved that 'the roadmen be set at liberty for one month from 18 August for the purpose of helping with the harvest'. Maybe it was no coincidence that a few months later Major Chichester-Constable was complaining to the RDC about the state of the roads leading to his lands in Keyingham Marsh. Clarrie Thomlinson had a cycle shop at Hill Top opposite the end of Church Lane. A man's de luxe model bicycle with oil bath and gears cost about £8 in the 1920s, but there were models available at less than half this price. Violet Roydhouse remembers buying a cycle to enable her to travel from her place of work in Keyingham Marsh to her parents' home in Ottringham and back within the very short time she was allowed off from her work. Though much against her father's principles, she was allowed to buy a cycle by weekly instalments from Clarrie Thomlinson, but her father insisted on seeing the payment card every time she went home. Credit buying as we know it today was not widely approved of.

As more people began to drive motorcars and the demand for petrol for farm use increased, Clarrie Thomlinson installed a petrol pump near his shop, selling a brand named ROP (Russian Oil Products). The pump was operated by winding a handle and the delivery was very slow. Later, for safety reasons, he moved the petrol station down the hill, further away from the houses. It was some way from the shop and was not always manned, so it had a bell fixed so that customers could summon Clarrie or his wife to go and serve them.

The garage on Ottringham Road was built in 1922 on land formerly belonging to the vicarage. It was originally a service garage owned and run by Murdoch & Jackson, described as motor engineers in *Kelly's Directory* of 1929. The partnership was later dissolved, leaving William Kerr (Pat) Murdoch in sole control of the business. In the early days there were only the petrol pumps and an asbestos garage. The pumps had swing arms set on brick pillars four or five foot high, and the attendant had to climb steps to pump the petrol. Farm accounts show that petrol cost 1s (5p) a gallon in 1931, 1s.5d (7p) in 1933 and 1s.5½d in 1937. Besides being used in cars, petrol was also used in electricity generators. Both Thomlinson's garage and Eyre's Mill had generators and either of them would, for a small fee, charge up the accumulators needed to power wireless sets before electricity was installed in the houses in the village.

In the spring of 1935, a request was made by the parish council to the ERCC for a 15-mph speed limit through the village as Keyingham was considered to be one of the most dangerous villages in the East Riding. A year later a further request was made to the ERCC for a speed limit and for a white line to be painted along the centre of the road on the bend between the vicarage and the bus stop opposite the end of Saltaugh Road. This was a dangerous bend and cars were known to end up in Lawrie Grant's field at the corner of Eastfield Road. In 1937 it was the ERCC's turn to call for safety measures when they drew the attention of the parish council to the danger to traffic caused by the position of the stump of the ancient village cross encroaching on the public highway. The parish council replied that they 'preferred it where it was, but if found to be dangerous to traffic they would suggest it should be moved to the opposite side of the road and placed near the War Memorial'. Thirty years later, with the big increase in traffic, further discussion took place and in 1968, despite protests from organisations in the village, the cross was moved to its present position behind the war memorial. It has yet to be tested whether the legend, that whoever sat on the steps of the cross would always return to the village, still applied after the removal.

- o -

When Doctor Compton died in 1914 the village was left without a resident doctor. Reporting on an epidemic in Keyingham in 1915 the *Hull & Yorkshire Times* stated, 'that there is hardly a house which has not one or more inmates sick, and the need for a resident doctor is felt greatly'. In 1919, Ivor Griffiths noted, in his written return for the Visitation of the Archbishop of York, that, 'The nearest doctor lives five miles away. There is plenty of time for a case to prove fatal before medical aid can be obtained.'

At the time, Doctor James Soutter lived and practised in Hedon. His son, Doctor J Stewart Soutter, known as 'Young Doctor Soutter' or 'Doctor Stewart' opened a consulting room in Keyingham after he returned from his war service in the RAMC in the Great War. Doctors Soutter and Porteus' surgery was held in Mrs Tarbotton's front room (later Mrs. Levitt's) next door but one to the Blue Bell. The waiting room was in the back room and seated no more than four people. After all standing room had been occupied patients would have to queue down the passage between the 'surgery' and the house next door and sometimes into the street. Medicines were brought to Keyingham from Hedon by bus. They are recalled as being left with Mr Norris, the saddler, and at Mrs Levitt's. The medicines were wrapped in green paper and sealed with red sealing wax. It was quite usual for the doctor to dispense medicines himself and they would be labelled simply as 'The Mixture' or 'The Linctus'. Medicines for external use that were poisonous if taken were put into ribbed hexagonal bottles so they were easily distinguishable.

Doctor W H Coates, of Patrington, also attended patients in Keyingham. He was a colourful character who had owned first a motorcycle and then one of the first motor cars to be seen in the district. Doctors were among the earliest to take advantage of owning a car, as they were frequently needed in an emergency, and Old Doctor Soutter was another early possessor of a car. Doctor Coates died in 1924 and Doctor F R Cripps succeeded to the practice. Around 1935, Doctor Cripps opened a surgery at Prospect House in Chapel Lane, where it is today. He continued to live in Patrington and rented Prospect House to private tenants.

The ladies of the Keyingham Methodist Women's Group have memories of medical and, particularly, surgical treatment by local doctors in the 1920s and '30s. Operations for the removal of tonsils and adenoids, or even an appendix, were recalled as having been carried out on the kitchen table. Chloroform was used as a general anaesthetic but many people were very suspicious of its use, preferring to remain conscious while the operation was being carried out. Such operations may seem unusually primitive in these present days of micro-surgery and electronic monitoring, but the doctors were registered members of the Royal College of Surgeons, and Doctor Stewart Soutter would have been quite used to the crude conditions encountered during his service in the Great War.

A dentist visited Keyingham and took a room at the Ship Inn where he gave dental treatment, but there are many memories of teeth being pulled out by the doctors. Peggy Clark recalled having a tooth pulled by Doctor Soutter while she was sitting on the running board of his car. Another patient was laid on the floor and the doctor knelt on his chest whilst he pulled the teeth out with pliers, but in 1932, Violet Roydhouse, was able to have an anaesthetic when her teeth were extracted at home. For the presence of the doctor it cost £1, which had to be paid 'there and then'.

For the most part, the doctor was only called for a home visit in cases of serious illness, or he attended at difficult confinements where the midwife could not cope. The midwife in Keyingham was Granny Vickers, who lived in Station Road. She also laid out the dead. Most confinements took place in the home, but by the end of the 1920s, for mothers who could afford to pay, there were private maternity homes, the Humber View at Patrington and the Madeira at Withernsea. There were also two emergency maternity beds in the hospital wing of the Union workhouse at Patrington.

In the days before the National Health Service made medicine and treatment a free service, and when the arrival of a doctor's bill could deplete the finances of the poor beyond their meagre resources, home remedies were used for many illnesses and injuries. Camphorated oil or a mustard plaster, applied like a brown paper parcel, for chest infections, turpentine for head lice, camphorated oil on a handkerchief for colds, bread poultices for boils, tincture of iodine for cuts, stings and insect bites, butter or lard for bumps on the head, and raw onions rubbed on chilblains, were some of the treatments recalled by the ladies of the Methodist Group. Marie Westmorland remembered that as a little girl she was treated for a chest cold with a mixture of lard and turpentine mixed together and spread on flannel, which was wrapped around her chest and back and left on for several days.

School medical services are recorded in the logbook from 1915. In that year six children were recommended for special examination by the School Medical Officer. Dr Mitchell-Wilson was the MO at the time, and he made a suggestion regarding the provision of milk cocoa for the children who stayed at school for dinner, and records show that this was implemented. School milk was introduced into schools in 1935 at a cost of a halfpenny for a bottle holding one-third of a pint. In 1920 the dentist attended to the teeth of 12 children under seven years of age, out of 15 who had been examined. The school nurse is noted as making a special visit to the school in 1921 to examine the children for signs of scabies, an easily transmitted skin disease that affected the hands, particularly between the fingers.

As in the early part of the century, poor sanitation was blamed for many diseases. An outbreak of diphtheria in 1919 prompted complaints to the RDC about the stench from the open drain in School Lane. Ten years later, following a case of diphtheria, the parish council asked the sanitary inspector what steps he intended to take regarding the cleansing of the ditches in the back lanes. Raymond Kirkwood can remember that in the 1920s 'the dyke that ran to the corner of Beck Lane and then passed under the road near Fern Cottage at the bottom of Clay Hill, ran with bloody water when it was the butcher's killing day'. Further complaints to the sanitary inspector were to follow in 1930 regarding the 'insanitary condition of the ditch that ran behind the brewery and Boyes Lane'. The six recently built houses on Hull Road had bathrooms and water closets but the sewage from the houses was discharged into the open dyke down Boyes Lane.

Before mains water was available in the village, and until a sewerage system was laid, there could be no truly hygienic disposal of sewage. Mains water, usually referred to as 'Hull water', was a major factor in the improvement in the health of the people. As early as 1905, F J Bancroft, Hull's Water and Gas Engineer, was reporting that there was sufficient water produced at Hull's Springhead and Cottingham waterworks to be able to sell water to the surrounding area. The suggestion was for Hull Corporation to pipe the water to the city boundary and for the rural district councils to pipe it on from there. However this meant an increase in rates to the rural householder and in 1906 the county medical officer was having to reassure the Keyingham Parish Council that no public water supply had been suggested for Keyingham. The council was further able to take comfort in the fact that the most recently bored well in the village 'was 31 foot deep with 15 feet of water above the head of the bore.' It yielded good water and Hull water was not considered necessary.

Subsequent developments meant that Keyingham was by-passed by the mains water distributed from Hull. Pipes were laid to the urban centres of Hedon and Withernsea, but the pipe to Withernsea, completed in 1916, took the short route via Bilton, Preston, Burstwick and Halsham to the water tower at Rimswell, from where it was fed by gravity to Withernsea. At the same time the military authorities, who required water at the army camps and gun emplacements at Spurn and Sunk Island, laid pipes, using army personnel as labourers, from the tower at Rimswell. The pipe to Sunk Island went via Ottringham. Thus Keyingham was almost encircled by water mains, but at a distance. It must be stressed that the villages and farmhouses that were close to the main rarely took advantage of its proximity because of the cost of leading pipes from the main. However, they and Keyingham could not resist the march of progress for ever and in 1932 mains were laid to most of the villages in Holderness. An indication of the expected demand can be obtained from the fact that the main to Keyingham was only two inches in diameter, and it was well into the 1950s before nearly every house in Keyingham was connected, and even longer before homes had what the house sale advertisements described as 'hot and cold running water' on tap.

For housewives and farmers, having piped water available at the turn of a tap made a great difference to the daily workload. Farmers from Keyingham Marsh no longer had to bring water carts to the pump at the north end of Marsh Lane. In the home there was no more pumping of water from the well or carrying of water from the village pump. The water was delivered straight from the tap in the kitchen into the kettle or a glass, clean and pure. In houses like the vicarage, where a bathroom was already installed, the water no longer had to be pumped up to a storage tank in the roof. Some houses, however, still continued to collect rainwater in cisterns to use on washdays, as it was much softer than tap water. Some households persisted for a long time in the use of well water and avoided paying a water rate.

Mains electricity had already arrived in the village by the time water was being piped from Hull. In May 1928 the parish council was approached by the Holderness Trust Company, who wished to become distributors of electricity in the area. The council was in favour of the scheme proposed but wanted to be sure that it would also be supported by the RDC and the Withernsea Urban District Council. A month later the company explained its plans to the RDC. It would obtain its electricity in bulk from Hull Corporation and transmit it into South Holderness via Hedon and along the main road to Withernsea then back to Hedon via the Class II road through Halsham. They proposed charging 7d (3p) a unit for lighting and 2d a unit for power. However, the following year it was the South East Yorkshire Light & Power Company that was seeking permission from the Ministry of Transport to erect overhead wires in the area, and it was that company which was supplying electricity, taken in bulk from Hull Corporation, to the region in 1930.

Gradually, electricity was brought to almost every home in the village. Violet Roydhouse paid £3 for three electric lights to be installed by a local electrician at one of the Foresters cottages, where she lived. New houses were being built with water and electricity installed. Until electricity was installed in the houses, lighting in Keyingham homes, except for a couple of places that had their own generators, had been by oil lamps and candles. There was no gas available for lighting as there was at Hedon or Patrington, where gasworks had been built close to the railway, which delivered the necessary coke. The immediate advantages of electricity were that it was no longer necessary to spend time trimming and filling oil lamps, there was much better quality overall lighting for everyone in a room and there was a reduced fire risk. It took some time for people to get used to electric lighting and it was quite common for them to use very small wattage bulbs. There was concern from the electricity companies that their investment was not going to pay off and they offered electrical equipment to consumers to encourage them to use a stated minimum number of units each quarter. Violet Roydhouse benefited in this way and was given an electric iron, a cooker and electric kettle by the electricity company. Despite the obvious convenience of electricity it was a long time before houses in the village became all-electric. Many houses in Keyingham, including the vicarage, were not wired up for many years, even up to the 1950s, and the railway-crossing house in Eastfield Road had no mains electricity, as it had no mains water, right up to its demolition in 1967. There the Hargraves used paraffin lamps for lighting and a paraffin stove for cooking. A pump provided excellent sparkling drinking water, and rainwater from the roof was collected in butts for washing purposes.

When increases were made to the electricity charges in 1931, protests were made to the South East Yorkshire Light & Power Company by the parish council on behalf of the village. Edward Stancer of Station Road also complained about the increases and received the reply, 'The increase of 1s.5d in your fixed charge is due to a revision in our tariffs, viz, a reduction in the price of a unit from 1.5d to 1d and an increase of 5% in the standing charge. You will no doubt find that the saving of 0.5d on every unit consumed will compensate for the 5% increase on the standing charge, as your consumption increases during the winter months, *and should you install a cooker or radiator the saving would be considerable.*' The letter went on to say that for farms, to cover all supplies including domestic usage, there was an annual fixed charge based on acreage, with a minimum of £5 per annum, plus 1d per unit consumed. There were also special methods of charging for late shop-window lighting and businesses with electric motors up to 25 h.p. A pamphlet was enclosed showing hire charges for electrical goods: an electric wash boiler for 1s.4d per month; a Magnet electric vacuum cleaner or a Magnet electric floor polisher for 2s.6d (12.5p) per day, 5s (25p) per week; 7s.6d (37.5p) per month, or 12s per quarter. At the time a farm labourer's wage was £1.10s per week, so it was only the better off who could afford more than the basic electric lighting in their homes. It would seem also that householders were not expected to buy electrical appliances outright.

Not everything connected with electricity was considered to be an improvement. In February 1930 a letter of protest was sent from the parish council to the ERCC for allowing electricity transmission poles to be erected in the Main Street as they were considered to be a danger to both pedestrians and vehicular traffic.

- o -

In 1935, a year before his death, the country celebrated the silver jubilee of George V and Queen Mary. In Keyingham a jubilee committee was set up to arrange a programme of events, and funds were raised by voluntary subscription. There were 14 women and 23 men on the committee, under the chairmanship of the vicar, Melville Leffler. A printed programme for the day has been carefully preserved by Peggy Clark. The day was to start at the school in Saltaugh Road where the flag was hoisted and the assembled villagers joined in patriotic songs before processing to St Nicholas Church for a service. In the afternoon, children's sports were held in a field in Waldby Garth Road lent by Ted Westmorland. There were identical events for the boys and the girls in all the flat races and the comic obstacle race and high jump, but the boys ran three-legged-, sack- and potato races while the girls had egg-and-spoon and skipping races. The tug of war, however, was for boys versus girls, six a side. At half-past four, a children's tea and presentation of mugs took place in the Wesleyan school, while the adults had tea in the Foresters Hall. The menfolk, it appeared, organised the sports, and the ladies provided the tea. The day concluded with a dance in the school and a whist drive in the Foresters Hall. Both events started at eight o'clock and, very thoughtfully, the programme stated, 'A room will be set apart at the Council School for those not taking part in the Dance or the Whist.'

Royal occasions were not the only ones to be enjoyed in Keyingham. Sports days, gymkhanas, garden parties, bazaars all helped to fill the village calendar. In 1936, the circus came to Keyingham. There was a parade of elephants and other circus animals down Main Street. The big top was set up in Keldgarth. Much hilarity was caused when young Frank Howes attempted to ride a mule.

Between 1911 and 1931 Keyingham's population went up from 547 to 611. The increase appears to have been due to speculative house building in the 1920s and '30s, which attracted newcomers to the village. The six houses called Elm Villas in Ings Lane were built by A Lockwood in two phases in 1918 and 1921, but later building was along the main road. T F Steeksma built bungalows and houses along Hull Road in 1929 and '30, and James Welbourn bungalows on Ottringham Road in 1931. Wreathall Tuton, built bungalows to order in Church Lane from 1927 onwards. Cregagh, next to Murdoch's garage, was built for the proprietor in 1927. By 1937 James Welbourn had built a terrace of houses in Beck Lane and a terrace of houses and The Croft on Ottringham Road

This new development began to change the shape of the village. We saw in Chapter 4 how Keyingham was a long village stretching from north to south and how this shape had been moulded by agricultural pursuits. Now Keyingham was beginning to cater for people unconnected with agriculture. They were people with jobs in Hull, attracted by the amenities of mains water and electricity and who wanted to be close to what was now a good road with a convenient bus service. Consequently, the village began to spread east and west. The new shape of the village reflected the start of a long process whereby Keyingham became more a village of commuters than a community almost wholly connected with agriculture.

Keyingham Home Guard, circa 1940. Ready to defend their country and, allied with the AFS and the ARP, responsible for the safety of the people of Keyingham throughout the war years. Back row: Cyril Precious, Fred Barber, Roy Whiting, Norman Dixon, Les Barber, Gordon Smith, Frank Braithwaite. Middle row: Stanley Hooson, Albert Lanham, Fred Wilkinson, Gordon Sanderson, Philip Westmorland, George Beadle, Frank Simpson. Front row: Ted Westmorland, Rev H T Horrox, Frank (Bunny) Howes.
Courtesy of Ann Braithwaite

On 12 May 1937, with all the pomp and ceremony for which our country is famous, King George V1 and Queen Elizabeth were crowned in Westminster Abbey. People who had travelled from the furthest points of the Empire came to witness the event. The coronation did not go unheeded in Keyingham. The parish magazine recorded, 'as in all parts of the country, the spiritual appeal of the Coronation was strong and clear in Keyingham. Despite the weather a number of communicants appeared in church at 7.30 a.m. and the church was quite full for the special service of prayer and dedication at 9.15 a.m. The church had been most beautifully decorated for the occasion with masses of lovely flowers. Miss Stancer and the choir deserve a word of very special commendation for the excellence of their singing. The rendering of Parry's anthem *O Praise Ye the Lord* and the *Te Deum* inspired us all'. Two hundred and fifty leaflets were ordered for the service, and the collection, amounting to £3.4s was given to Hull Royal Infirmary, which was still a voluntary hospital relying on donations. The programme for the day's celebrations, organised by the George VI Coronation Committee, included an afternoon of children's sports in C E (Ted) Westmorland's field in Waldby Garth Road, followed by a celebration tea for the children in the Wesleyan schoolroom and for the adults in the Foresters Hall. The children had to take their own cups or mugs and the adults their own knives and forks. The evening was given over to entertainment for the adults, with sports, a whist drive in Foresters Hall and a dance in the school.

So began the reign of another sovereign. But even during the celebrations there were concerns about events in Nazi Germany and the possibility of war. Within 15 months of the coronation gas masks were issued in expectation of enemy attack and arrangements were being made to evacuate children from the cities. In Keyingham a searchlight battery was set up in the field behind Waldby Garth Villas with the crew camping in the field. The vicar took pity on them and gave them the use of the Church Room. When fears of war were temporarily allayed following Prime Minister Chamberlain's meeting with Hitler at Munich and his attempt at appeasement, the searchlight detachment was moved from Keyingham, and the Church Room benefited from the acquisition of an army tea urn and boiler. The respite was short-lived. On 1 September 1939 Hitler's troops marched into Poland, and Britain declared war on Germany two days later. In this chapter we shall see how the people of Keyingham responded to the demands of a second war within

25 years and the years of shortage and austerity that followed.

- o -

Despite the threat of war the parish council still had day-to-day matters to deal with. In the spring of 1938 there were complaints about the disposal of household refuse and the rubbish being dumped around dwellings and in the lanes. There was no local-authority provision for refuse collection, there being far less household refuse than there is today. Much of what there was could be burnt in the house grate as fuel. Food was bought with the minimum of packaging, and plastic containers had not been developed. A deposit was paid on lemonade and beer bottles and the children could make extra pocket money by returning them to the shop for re-use. Jam jars were kept to be refilled with homemade jam or pickles or they could be exchanged for goldfish from the 'jar man' who waited outside the school. Newspapers had few pages and many uses: lighting fires, wrapping fish and chips, and as toilet paper, to mention but a few. For the rubbish that could not be dealt with in these ways the parish council responded to demands and set up a scavenging scheme by arranging with Arthur Clark, the local carrier, to make a weekly collection with his horse and cart. He took the refuse to the 'tin dump' in Boyes Lane, but even the tins that gave the dump its name were not in such common use as they are today and most housewives scorned the use of the tin-opener.

There were other nuisances besides household rubbish. In January 1939 the Holderness Rural District Council, which had taken over from the Patrington RDC in 1935, was asked to cover in the open ditch at the end of Westmorland's paddock near the Village Institute as the area was considered to be 'unsafe for pedestrians on dark nights'. In the 1940s the parish council received a letter from a resident asking that the streets be swept at least once a week. This was probably more important than today, as there was still plenty of horse transport as well as herds of cows being driven twice daily through the village between pasture and milking shed. The request was answered by the East Riding County Council, who sent workers to sweep the roads and lanes of the village every Saturday morning.

With the outbreak of war, Keyingham, being close to the coastline, was very much involved in the country's plans to resist invasion either by sea or by airborne troops. In August 1939 large barriers were erected on the main road at the Ship Inn and at Hill Top at the west end of Main Street. The barriers each consisted of two thick stone walls (part of one such barrier is still to be seen in Station Road, Ottringham) placed in staggered fashion on opposite sides of the road so that traffic had to slow almost to a halt in order to weave through the gap. In the event of invasion, the road could be completely closed by rolling large concrete cylinders across the gap and standing them on end. Minnie Lound, of Hill Top Cottage (now Eastfield Cottage) on Ottringham Road, was responsible for placing red paraffin warning lamps at the end of each barrier every night at dusk and removing them the next morning. It is said that there were plans to block Saltaugh Road if necessary by dropping a large elm tree across the road near the Ship Inn, but in fact the elm was felled in 1940 when it was thought to be in danger of falling on the inn. Harry Hoe, who was in the Home Guard, remembers drums of an explosive liquid being buried in the vicarage garden close to Ottringham Road, ready to be blown up to block

the road in the event of invasion. He cannot remember them ever being removed! Concrete posts were erected in the fields to discourage enemy troop-carrying gliders or other aircraft from landing. All clues to the names of villages were removed. The word 'Keyingham' on the post office shop sign was painted over. Signposts were taken away. The milestone between Keyingham and Ottringham was buried and was not re-discovered until 1998.

A curfew operated for the region near the sea and Humber coast. At first it applied to those areas to the east of the main road running from Bridlington to Roos and so to Winestead, and to the south of the road running from Winestead to Thorngumbald. Everyone to the coastward side of that line had to be indoors by 10 p.m. This caused some confusion, as the road bisects many villages, including Keyingham, and whilst some villagers had to be in their houses by 10 o'clock, those at the other side of the road could move about freely. The order was soon altered to include the whole of any village through which the road passed. There were plenty of officials in Keyingham - the Home Guard, PC Fred Hensby and the Air Raid Precaution (ARP) wardens - to ensure the curfew was kept. Village dances ended at 9.30 p.m. to allow the dancers time to reach home. For many Keyingham girls it was a mad dash as they cycled home from dances at Patrington, where their partners were mostly RAF personnel. Nancy Wright said the curfew was a boon to mothers concerned about their daughters' welfare!

Terrible memories of poison gas on the battlefields of World War 1 prompted the issue of gas masks to civilians in the months leading up to the Second World War. In Keyingham the ARP wardens came to the school to fit the children with their masks and give them instructions on how to put them on. For children under three the masks were made of red and green rubber with the valve for exhaled air having the form of a nose. They became known as Mickey Mouse gas masks. For older children and adults the exhaled air passed out around the edges of the mask. Babies had gas-proof arrangements that completely enclosed them and air had to be pumped in. Children had to take their gas masks to school, usually in the cardboard box with shoulder string that had been provided on issue, although it was possible to buy a more substantial metal container. Emily Norris, the saddler's wife, made numerous covers for the cardboard containers. Gas mask drill at school was a weekly event.

Keyingham was on the direct route of German bombers attacking the docks and oil refineries at Hull and the aircraft works at Brough. The village itself was not a prime target, but might have suffered from the dropping of stray bombs and mines or misdirected anti-aircraft shells. The RDC advised the erection of communal air-raid shelters in the village. The parish council proposed various sites, and shelter accommodation was planned for 50% of the village population. In the event no communal shelters were built but several residents took their own precautions by building shelters in their gardens. Bob and May Dearlove built a dugout shelter behind their shop on the south side of Main Street (the site of the present Keyingham Hot Food). It contained furniture, including an easy chair. When the war was over Bob filled in the dugout, burying the furniture. Clarrie East

A Hull-bound train steams in to Keyingham station, circa 1950. The white borders to the platforms and flowerbeds were a blackout measure in World War II. The roof of the crossing-keeper's cottage at Eastfield Road shows over the top of the carriages. Diesel trains replaced steam locomotives on the line in January 1957.
Courtesy of Hedon Museum

remembers his father digging a hole in the garden and covering it with railway sleepers, which were also used to line the sides and provide a seat. This shelter was only used once, when enemy bombers were active for the first time in the area. Whilst the family sat in the darkness a landmine exploded somewhere between Keyingham and the Humber and caused a 'sandslide' of the walls, nearly burying the occupants. After this the dugout was filled in as it was deemed unsafe. The Easts had then to resort to what many other householders relied on when the air-raid warning sounded - an under-stairs cupboard or a makeshift shelter under the kitchen table.

There were, of course, restrictions on lighting after dark. All outdoor lights were turned off, railway carriages and buses were fitted with bulbs that gave off only a dim glow and householders were ordered to cover their windows with dark 'blackout curtains' so that not the slightest chink of light could escape. Clarrie East's mother made her curtains from very thick blankets, which were pinned up with his dad's darts. Public buildings used at night, such as dance halls and pubs, usually had some kind of unlit vestibule that people passed through a few at a time as they entered or left the building. The lights of all vehicles, including cycles, had to be shielded so they shone only downwards, and torches had to be taped to minimise the light emitted as people made their way round in the darkness. An immediate consequence of the blackout was a rise in road accidents, and people were urged by the Government to wear something white at night. Kerb edges, the edges of railway platforms and the rear mud flaps of vehicles of all description were painted white to aid visibility.

Although no houses or buildings in Keyingham sustained a direct hit during the bombing, plenty of missiles fell around the village as the following reports to the Civil Defence post at Hedon indicate:

'16.4.41. 03.19 hours - Telephone lines to Keyingham out of order, believed due to enemy action near Camerton Hall 0255 (1 HE - slight damage to Camerton Hall).'

'27.4.41. Message received 15.34. Keyingham Wardens report two UE AA shells W of village and N of Rose Villa in football field opposite the bungalows at the foot of the hill.' (Note added later: '1 May 16.38 hr 2 AA shells disposed of by BD squad.') 'Also 2 HE craters NE of village beyond railway station near E. Carr Rd. One HE crater 1/2 mile E. of village at the edge of Dam Lane. One HE crater 1/2 mile ESE of village, close to Dam Lane. All 4 craters in fields. No Damage. No casualties.'

'4.5.41 - 10 IBs and 4 bomb sticks or metal rods found in fields at Keyingham. Now in possession of Hedon Police. Date of occurrence - 26 April 1941.'

'17.7.41 - Three UE AA shells in grass field, Cemetery Lane, Keyingham. Time of occurrence NK. Reported dealt with by BDS 2nd August.'

'26.7.41 - UE AA shell 1/2 mile NE of constable's house, Keyingham, in grass field 5 yds. from hedge on E side and 30 yds. from hedge on S side. Hole in E corner of field. Dealt with 6.11.41.'

'1.9.41 - 2 HE Bombs dropped in field at Keyingham at 22.40 yesterday. No damage and no casualties beyond broken windows and ceilings. In grass field on N side of Hull-Withernsea road opposite constable's house. 250 yds. from road (Mill Hill field).'

[HE = high explosive; UE = unexploded; AA = anti-aircraft; BDS = bomb disposal squad; IB = incendiary bomb.]

Barbara Lindop, nee Williams, remembers a day of great excitement when a British Lysander aircraft landed in a field opposite the school and a soldier with his rifle could be seen guarding it. Few realised the important job these small aircraft did during the war. We now know that they were used to ferry agents to occupied territory. Gladys Beadle remembers, when she and her sister were in a field with their father, having to take cover in a ditch when a German aeroplane flew over, machine-gunning them as it went. Harry Hoe worked at Keyingham Grange where there was a searchlight battery with a crew of about 12. He recalls an event in August 1940 when the army came looking for a German parachutist who they suspected was hiding in a summerhouse in the orchard at the Grange. They asked his uncle to send in his three Alsations and a terrier but there was no one there. They later learned that the parachute had been attached to a magnetic mine intended for the Humber. It exploded in a field 30 yards from Wallis's farmhouse at Far Marsh, Ottringham, and blew every stook of corn out of the field. It dislodged the tiles and blew in the windows at the farmhouse and at Saltaugh Grange. Ted Osgerby was one of the farm lads living-in at Keyingham Grange. From the window of their quarters the lads were watching the fires burning in Hull during the blitz of 1941. Suddenly there was a terrific bang nearby. It was a mobile anti-aircraft gun that had been set up, unannounced, in the farmyard.

Enemy aircraft were not the only ones to be feared. About a year after the Americans came into the war at the end of 1941, Harry Hoe was with a group of men threshing in a field at Marsh Cottage. Suddenly he saw an aircraft flying low towards them and the stubble ahead of it erupting with shellfire. Everyone dived into the shelter of the straw stack. One shell hit and passed right through the hub of the rear wheel of the tractor that was driving the threshing set. It burst the tyre and stopped threshing operations for a day or two. The aeroplane was American. Some days later PC Hensby called at Marsh Cottage with a letter from the American commanding officer, explaining that the pilot had pressed the gun button by mistake for the one that operated a camera.

Although agriculture was a reserved occupation, many agricultural workers from Keyingham joined the forces and saw active service at Dunkirk and Normandy or in the desert campaign. Ken Hoe and Vic Lanham can probably lay claim to being the first Keyingham men to enlist. They happened to be called up for the militia three months before the war broke out. At first they trained in civilian clothing but on the declaration of war they were immediately transferred to the East Yorkshire Regiment and issued with uniforms. Keyingham saw the exodus to the forces of approximately 38 men, some of whom did not return. The plinth on the north side of the war memorial records the names of the seven men who were killed in the Second World War (Appendix 1). Inside the door of the blacksmith's shop at Bryn Ferra, Billy Beadle nailed a horseshoe, and some of the men who left Keyingham to join up each nailed a farthing inside it for luck. Every man who did so returned home to remove his farthing. Albert Beadle, one of Mr Beadle's sons, who was one of those who nailed a farthing to the door, remembers that the shoe was almost 'full'. The imprints of the horseshoe and the nails are still to be seen on the door. A number of young women from Keyingham joined the armed forces, many of them working in the Women's Auxiliary Air Force as barrage balloon technicians, control room operators etc.

Women also played their part in the war by doing jobs that had previously been done by the men who were now in the forces. One of their jobs was as bus conductresses, in the days when buses were operated by a crew of two. Lilian Thomlinson, wife of Clarrie, worked as a conductress during the war. There are no recollections of women driving buses. At Keyingham railway station Alice Grant and Alice Taylor became porter/signal women. They worked in shifts, one from early morning until noon and the other from noon until the last train of the day. When the war was over they had to give up their jobs to the men returning to civilian life.

Women worked in many voluntary capacities. They sold National Savings stamps and certificates, knitted socks, gloves and balaclavas for the soldiers and generally raised money for funds that had been set up to help the war effort. The Women's Red Cross, under the direction of Mrs Horrox, the vicar's wife, held their practices in the Church Room. Their job, in the absence of any resident doctor or nurse in the village, was to deal with accidents and provide first aid. The Red Cross hut was prominently sited on Hull Road near to Clarrie Thomlinson's petrol pumps. First-aid classes were also started in the village, with Dr Fouracre of Patrington and Bob Ellerby, a Connor and Graham bus driver, as instructors. Ken Suddaby can recall as a lad being called into the school to act as a casualty and bandages being wrapped round his bare muddy knees.

Fire watch, circa 1940. Members of Keyingham Auxiliary Fire Service (AFS) standing by the fire tender. In the background is Skeckling Farmhouse. The converted tractor was very difficult to start and was not kept in Keyingham for long. From left to right, the firemen are: John Harness, Mr Wright, (a schoolteacher), Arthur Clark, George Eastwood, Clive Guy, Fred Harness and Ted Thompson. Of the seven men, John Harness, George Eastwood, Mr Wright and Ted Thompson were called up, and Arthur Clark and Clive Guy joined the Royal Observer Corps.
Courtesy of Miss Muriel Guy

Men who could not be spared from their occupations or were too old to enlist played their part. In 1938 the East Riding County Council recommended the establishment of an ARP post in the village. Support was readily forthcoming and a unit was established. Frank Middleton was the Chief Air Raid Warden and together with a group of volunteers was the first to be summoned if a warning was received. These men kept a nightly watch on the village and made the initial move in an emergency and alerted the fire or other emergency services if necessary. Frank Middleton's daughter recalls a day 'when a man brought an object to our back door and my father told him to put it on the rubbish pile in the garden, saying, "Put it down gently, then come back here." The man thought it was a shell but my father explained it was an unexploded incendiary bomb. It was later removed without any mishap.'

The local knowledge of the ARP was extremely valuable, as they knew where everyone lived, how many there were in a family and whether they were likely to be at home during an air raid. Initially, warnings of air raids were telephoned through to Henry Norris, the saddler. He then rang the outlying farms and relayed the message to Frank Middleton who alerted the other wardens. It was their job to ride round the village on bicycles blowing whistles to alert people. This system was soon replaced by a siren sounded from Clarrie Thomlinson's garage on Hull Road. Parents were asked about their wishes for their children at school if an air-raid warning was sounded. The results are interesting in that 51 wanted them to go home, 41 wanted them to stay at school and 20 wanted them to go to another house near the school.

In 1940 the Local Defence Volunteers (LDV) were formed. They were soon renamed the Home Guard. Initially the Home Guard practised with all kinds of improvised weapons - shot guns, pitchforks and the like - until proper weapons were issued in early 1941. Regular NCOs helped with weapon training and at Keyingham Sergeant E Simms, stationed with a searchlight crew, was called on to help. The squad was about 18 strong and included older men and youths not yet 18, most of whom would eventually join the forces. Harry Hoe joined the Ottringham Home Guard at the age of 15 and transferred to the Keyingham Home Guard two years later when he went to work at Keyingham Grange. With a real threat of invasion everyone took his duty very seriously. In order to prepare the men for action, regular manoeuvres were held in the village. Everyone turned out to watch. The Ship Inn served as the casualty clearing station on such occasions, and no one minded being the first 'wounded hero' as it was more rewarding indulging in the host's hospitality than being out in the field. One of the first men to volunteer for the Home Guard was George Beadle. He with Gordon Sanderson had, in fact, joined the LDV. When George moved to Church Farm in 1940 it became the squad's headquarters. George's daughter Marjorie can remember the family hosting the squad in Church Farm kitchen when they were on night manoeuvres. She can also remember hand grenades and thousands of rounds of ammunition being stored in one of the barns. In addition there was a variety of weapons, one of which was in sections. Every weekend the squad took it to Kelsey Hill, assembled it and practised with live ammunition. In September 1940 the Home Guard throughout the country was stood to because it was thought there was a possibility of invasion. The alert lasted for 12 days. It was probably on this occasion that the Keyingham Home Guard were sent out one weekend to be prepared to blow up foot bridges if necessary. Mr Horrox the vicar, was one of the men on duty and after spending an extremely long time through the early hours of Sunday morning awaiting orders that never came he excused himself - 'Do you think you could manage without me, lads, while I go and take Matins?' Harold Thompson Horrox had become the vicar of Keyingham in the summer of 1939, and both he and his wife played a large part in the community. He helped many people although, from the stories heard, he had some idiosyncratic tendencies. His wife, Clarice, used to tell of how he once gave a whole week's meat ration to the cat for its dinner. Mrs Horrox was a gifted woman who had studied chemistry at Cambridge in the early years of the century. She had then become a teacher, had marched with the Suffragettes in 1911 but after her marriage had become, like many incumbents' wives, 'an unpaid curate'. The couple had two sons who both served in the RAF. Michael Horrox was killed during secret flying operations early in 1941, and Mr Horrox, to the end of his incumbency made a special point of commemorating Battle of Britain Week, the proceeds of the service going to the RAF Benevolent Association. The second son, Paul, was reprimanded on one occasion for making a diversion to fly his Spitfire over Keyingham after a mission.

Besides the ARP and the Home Guard there were also members of the Observer Corps in Keyingham. Some were paid and worked a 48-hour week, and others were unpaid, helping out in the evenings and at weekends. One of the volunteers was Mr Horrox, not a man to share a night duty with as his idiosyncrasies extended to eating all the breakfast rations while his companion was asleep. There were two observation posts, one down Dam Lane, close to where the aviation beacon now is, and the other in the soldiers' brick wash house near the mill on Ottringham Road where there was an anti-aircraft gun and searchlight battery.

Youth played its part in the defensive preparations. The Army Cadet Force, led by Mr Hoy, met in the Foresters Hall. Eight or nine of the local youths belonged to the Army Cadet Corps in Withernsea. They cycled to Withernsea each Sunday to parade with the corps there but in mid week joined in with the local Home Guard.

Members of the regular forces were stationed in and around Keyingham. Most of them manned the searchlight batteries or gun emplacements at Keyingham Grange and Ottringham Road mill. Soldiers were also billeted at Foresters Hall and one day water was found to be coming through the ceiling into the house below. When the cause was investigated it was found that the soldiers were swilling the floor with buckets of water and a yard brush. Soldiers on route marches through the village would be followed for a while by the lads mimicking them and attempting to keep in step. Mrs Gertrude Rodmell, a member of the Wesleyan chapel, ran a canteen for soldiers in the Wesleyan schoolroom. It was staffed by volunteers and was open several evenings a week. The men came from camps at Cherry Cobb Sands and Ryhill as well as Keyingham. The canteen provided an alternative to the pubs as a meeting place. Tea, coffee and refreshments were served, and soldiers could play cards and dominoes, write letters and have someone to talk to.

- o -

Contributions to the war effort from the people of Keyingham came in many ways. An early sacrifice demanded by the government for munitions-making was the iron railings from round the school, the war memorial, the entrance to the Foresters Hall and some private houses. Money to support the war effort was raised under different Government schemes. The people were asked to lend money to the country by investing in War Bonds and Defence Bonds, repayable after the war ended, and in Post Office and savings bank deposit accounts. A branch of the Hull Savings Bank was set up at the school and children were encouraged to save at least 6d per week. The bank was also open every Monday evening for adults' transactions, a facility that continued for many years. But for the majority of people, the War Savings Movement was their main way of contributing to war funds. The excellent support in Keyingham was noted in a newspaper report in January 1941: 'A typical illustration of the way villages are responding to the War Savings Movement by the formation of savings groups is afforded by the Holderness village of Keyingham. By June last year a total of £1,205.7s.3d had been invested. Six months later the total had risen to £2,171.18s.0d, an increase of nearly £1,000.' As the membership of the group was 172 'this gives an average of £6 per member invested in War Savings during the six months, which must be regarded as most creditable for a village that is mainly agricultural. Possibly this record could be equalled at other places in Holderness but I do not think it could be much exceeded. But Keyingham always was progressive.' By July 1941 membership of the savings group had risen to over 200 (more than a third of the village population) and the money invested had passed the £3,000 mark.

War Savings Week, 1941. A line of pennies is being laid along Main Street outside the Ship Inn. Clem Westmorland is the man bending over placing a coin, and the child on the path is Mick Thompson. Mrs.Horrox, the vicar's wife, is the Red Cross nurse on the right of the picture. There were 240 pennies in the £ in those days.
Courtesy of Ann Braithwaite

Special weeks were set aside for fund-raising for the different demands of the war. During War Weapons Week, in early October 1941, a garden party was held at Willowfield House, with the school children playing their part. They contributed £12 from raffles, bran tubs, etc. as well as depositing a total of £52 in the school bank. By the end of the week, the total raised in Keyingham was a staggering £10,940.

War Savings target, 1941. *Mr Len Scruton foots the ladder as 'Bunny' Howes raises the pointer to the top of the target board to show that £10,940 had been collected by Keyingham people for the war effort. The building is the (then) Post Office on the corner of Main Street and Ings Lane. Note the boarded-up windows. They are said to have been blown out when a landmine fell at Ryhill. The name KEYINGHAM has been obliterated for security reasons. Bunny later joined the Royal Engineers and whilst with an assault squadron lost a leg in a mine explosion when going to the help of an injured comrade.*

Courtesy of Ann Braithwaite

223

1943 was an especially busy year for raising funds. In February a Book Drive was held. The proceeds from the sale of books, after they had been sorted for salvage and school use, were given to the Merchant Navy Comfort Fund. The Merchant Navy was particularly chosen, as the school had adopted the merchant ship 'Widestone' commanded by Captain William Storm, a resident of Keyingham. Sadly, the ship was later torpedoed, and the captain and crew lost their lives. On Empire Day (24 May) 1943 a collection was made for the 'Tobacco for the Forces' fund. June saw the Wings for Victory Week, and Neville Dee remembers that during that week an RAF fighter plane was put on display in the school playground to encourage the children to raise £500 in the week. Although the school fell short of its target, raising £385, the village as a whole raised £8,710 through raffles, stalls, bank deposits, and National Savings certificates and stamps. The National Savings Committee congratulated Keyingham 'for the really excellent result. The sum obtained means more than just £sd and represents loyal and devoted service to the community by a splendid band of happy workers.' The year ended with a sale at the school in the December, with the proceeds going to various war charities.

Money was raised for other causes. In the early years of the war Lawrie Grant cleaned out the farm buildings at Skeckling Farm in Main Street, whitewashed the interiors, set up dartboards and held a darts competition for the surrounding villages. The money raised went to the Red Cross. At the end of the tournament there was an auction, and amongst the lots were two bananas, fruit that rarely reached Britain's shores in wartime. Lawrie outbid the competition and his three children shared the bananas.

Keyingham played its part in taking evacuees from Hull. There were two main periods when evacuees came to the village. The first began two days before war was declared when primary schoolchildren and their teachers and mothers of children under five moved into the country from areas of expected danger. Many of these evacuees returned home when the expected bombing did not occur. The next local period of evacuation started as the bombing of Hull began to be stepped up in early 1941. Then, people came out into the country each evening, often on foot, to avoid the nightly terror of the 'blitz'. The next day they would return to their homes, often to find them damaged or destroyed.

The plans for evacuation in September 1938 were postponed following Chamberlain's visit to Munich, but by January the following year the Holderness RDC and every other rural authority in the country were circularising households to find what accommodation would be available for children moved out from the cities. Payment by the government for taking evacuees was to be at the rate of 10s.6d a week where one child was taken and 8s.6d for each child where more than one was taken. School children were to be moved school by school accompanied by their teachers, and arrangements were to be made for the children to attend school in the districts to which they were taken. The Women's Voluntary Service, formed as part of the Civil Defence in 1939 before the outbreak of war, played an important role in organising evacuation. Gladys Cook joined the WVS in 1939, and one of her first jobs when war seemed imminent was to canvass every home in Keyingham for places to house evacuees although, as she said, she knew what accommodation everyone had available anyway. She worked with several others, one being Violet (Vi) Roydhouse who was appointed billeting officer for evacuees.

As a consequence of this early planning, when the time came on 1 September 1939 to evacuate children from the cities, a million and a half were moved with scarcely a hitch. At Keyingham there was one difficulty when a bus carrying children and parents arrived from Hull after dark and there was no accommodation left in Keyingham. The bus was therefore driven to a farm on Cherry Cobb Sands where the farmer and his wife said that in no way could they take the whole group. It was pointed out that they could not refuse, as the housing of evacuees was compulsory. They very reluctantly agreed and the bus was unloaded. The parting comment of the organiser was, 'Just wait until the morning when they find out where they are, they'll all want to be back in Hull'. She proved to be right - the isolated position of some of the farms did not appeal to many from the city.

Besides the children and parents evacuated under the government scheme, two million more people moved out privately to the country, and families from Hull moved to Keyingham to stay with relatives in the comparative safety of the village. In many cases the men had to return to Hull to work once their families were settled. Children evacuated without their parents missed their families but having access to open fields and the peace and quiet of rural surroundings left fond memories in the minds of many who made Keyingham their temporary home. Barbara Lindop remembers being impressed by seeing cows being brought in for milking and how she was kept out of the fold yard when a stallion was brought to cover the mare.

The evacuees who came from Hull during the blitz were mostly young women and older men who worked in Hull during the day. They slept the night in the Primitive Methodist chapel, where there was one room and one toilet. Before they left for Hull each morning they had breakfast, given by the villagers, who realised that the 'trekkers', as they came to be called, might find on their return home that their gas and electricity had been cut off or their house demolished by overnight bombing.

People kept in touch with the latest developments in the war through the newspapers or the radio, or wireless, as it was then called. Newspaper editors faced many difficulties in trying to produce a paper every day. The censors stopped them writing about certain items and often blocked out large sections of photographs in case the enemy gained information from them. Newsprint was in short supply and only limited numbers of the national newspapers could be printed each day. They consisted of only two or four pages and were passed round from house to house. Newspapers contained a lot of propaganda designed to make the people work together and believe in what they were fighting for. Propaganda slogans appeared in newspapers and on posters in public transport and in the streets. Such slogans as 'Careless talk costs lives', 'Be like dad - keep mum', 'Take care in the blackout', 'Dig for victory' and numerous others still ring a bell for many older people.

Most people tuned in to the radio at some time during the day to listen to the news and other programmes mostly designed to boost morale. Most radios in the village were still powered by accumulators and it was a good policy to have a second one already charged in case the first ran out. Ken Suddaby's father was very upset when the accumulator ran out in the middle of a boxing match being broadcast. Just before the war Clarrie East's father, home for the weekend, found he could not listen to his Saturday afternoon horse racing because of an exhausted accumulator, so he attached his wireless to a motor cycle battery. The set went up in smoke. 'Father swore and went to the Blue Bell to listen to his favourite sport.'

- o -

Once the war started the 'freedom of the seas' ceased and imported foodstuffs were in short supply. As in the First World War farmers had to rapidly increase food production and were required to change their land use from pasture to wheat and potato growing. The amount of arable land increased from 12 million acres in 1939 to 18 millions in 1944. Many hedges, no longer needed as barriers for livestock, were destroyed to maximise land area. Harry Hoe can remember the numerous owls that were disturbed when the hedgerows in Keyingham Marsh were rooted out. The gates across the roads in the Marsh, erected to keep cattle from straying, gradually disappeared, assisted by the efforts of the army personnel stationed at Keyingham Grange and Cherry Cobb Sands. They found it too much trouble to open and shut the gates for their vehicles to pass through. The first gate 'went' after a despatch rider crashed into it in darkness.

The control of the national farming effort was put into the hands of War Agricultural Executive Committees (War-Ags) set up on a county basis, although the three Yorkshire ridings each had its own. War-Ags were empowered to direct the type of cultivation, set up mobile groups of farm workers with the machinery to help the farmers, and inspect farms. They could terminate tenancies and take over properties where they thought the farming was bad. The East Riding War-Ag, made up mostly of farmers and ex-farmers (ironically, some of whom had failed in the 1920s and '30s), was based at Beverley. A preliminary survey of farms took place between June 1940 and spring 1941. This was followed by a more detailed inspection, which finished at the end of 1943. If a farm was considered to be badly managed the farmer could be 'turned off' his land. No Keyingham farmer suffered this indignity, although it was pointed out to Lawrie Grant that too much of his land was devoted to crops to feed his cows rather than to feed people. At least one Keyingham farmer, considered as inefficient by his peers, benefited by having to plough up long-standing pasture. The resulting land was so fertile and the price of corn so good that it saw him through to his retirement after the war.

Under the War-Ag's direction it became compulsory for the farmer to devote a proportion of land to sugar beet and potatoes, the latter producing more sustenance per acre than any other crop. Previously, few potatoes had been grown on the heavy lands of Holderness. Potato growing was labour intensive, requiring the use of women and children for planting in the spring and harvesting in the autumn. Keyingham people saw this as an opportunity to earn a bit of extra money, and school children were given a holiday to pick potatoes. They were taken down to Saltaugh Grange, complete with packed lunch, in Clem Westmorland's horse-drawn van.

The War-Ag had the use of powerful tractors, both wheeled and tracked, combine harvesters, and all the other implements necessary for rapid cultivation and harvesting. They were obtained from America through the Lend-Lease scheme. Farmers, most of whom were still using horses and the odd small tractor, could call on this equipment and its operators to help them out if necessary. Some Keyingham men, including Ted Roydhouse and George Kitchen worked for the War-Ag. One of their early tasks was ploughing up large tracts of grassland. Ted worked on the Wolds throughout the war and came home on his motor cycle each weekend.

Though it was possible for a private farmer to buy a large tractor, brought by convoy from America, they were in very short supply. Where farmers had tractors they were old, pre-war ones. They had no mudguards and no cab and were very uncomfortable to drive. Because of the shortage of petrol, most tractors were driven by paraffin. They were often difficult to start, the spark plug having to be warmed on the kitchen range on a cold day. They were started with petrol, then, when the manifold was 'just too hot to touch', they were switched to paraffin. The War-Ag took over commercial petrol pumps for the storage of paraffin for agricultural purposes. Pat Murdoch and Clarrie Thomlinson were therefore unable to supply petrol to lorry drivers or the few private drivers, who had to go to Airport Garage at Saltend for their fuel.

With the intensification of agriculture far more labour was required on the farms. Posters could be seen everywhere urging people to 'Lend a Hand on the Land'. As early as 1941, Keyingham farmers were asking for four boys to be released from school to help out, and the next year the school holidays were arranged round the farming needs. A week was allowed in July for haymaking and another for harvesting beans, then four weeks in August and September for the corn harvest and a week at the beginning of October for potato picking. Soldiers stationed locally were also called on to help the farmer, especially at harvest time, and former farm workers came out of retirement to lend a hand. Even with this extra help, the farmers needed more workers, and the Women's Land Army, which had been so important in the First World War, was re-established.

Land Army girls became the most important source of labour on the farms. Initially, the government relied on volunteers but in 1941 conscription was introduced. The pay was low and the hours were long. Vera Jackets (nee Chapman) was conscripted at the age of 18 and had the usual choice between joining the forces, working in a munitions factory or joining the Land Army. She chose the Land Army and left her job in the factory at Harlands the printers of Hull, where she was earning 32s.6d a week, to join the Land Army and earn 10s a week plus board and lodging (at that time a soldier in the Army was receiving basic pay of 14s a week). She was sent to work on a farm at North Cave, where she lived-in, the farmer receiving 27s.6d a week from the government for her board and lodging. It was a life of sheer drudgery working from 5.45 a.m. to 8 p.m. each day, and after four months she asked to be moved to a Land Army hostel and was sent to Keyingham, where a new building at the corner of Saltaugh Road had been erected for the accommodation of 50 girls. It was known as the Agricultural Hostel and was on the site of the present Horrox Court. Whilst she was at the hostel Vera worked on a farm at Ottringham, doing one of the most disliked jobs on a farm - carrying chaff from the threshing machine to the barn. To keep out the dust she was enveloped in sacking. Normally Land Army girls wore a uniform with strong fawn corduroy trousers, a green jumper and the distinctive Land Girl's hat. Gumboots, stout overalls and a heavy-duty coat protected them in the bad weather. It was when two girls, dressed in their best uniforms, turned up at the farm to catch rats that Vera decided to apply for a new job in the Land Army and became a rat-catcher. Her pay went up to 15s a week and she left Keyingham.

The Women's Land Army, circa 1942. Photo-call for the girls at the Land Girls' Hostel on Saltaugh Road. The girls came mostly from town and city backgrounds and jobs. They formed the main part of the labour force needed to keep the farms at their highest production levels while the menfolk were away at war. Courtesy of Mrs Vi Roydhouse

Dorothy Chilton (nee Perkins) signed up for the Land Army in 1942. She met up with a group of girls at Hull's Paragon Station and they travelled to Keyingham by train, arriving in the dark. On their arrival at the brand new hostel, Mr Derrick, the hostel's supervisor, showed them to their quarters. They slept in beds, arranged in groups of four, with little privacy. Jobs were allotted to them according to experience and aptitude. The girls sometimes worked as long as 14 hours a day, milking, ploughing, tree felling and at the many other jobs around the farm. Some of the girls, Dorothy and the future Mrs Barbara Jackson (nee Thompson) and Mrs Lilian Scotney (nee Taylor) for instance, married Keyingham men and lived in Keyingham after the war. When the war ended and the Land Army was disbanded the Agricultural Hostel was used for a while to house Italian prisoners of war, who were employed in organised labour groups on the farms. In their free time the Italians sat on the fallen elm in the grounds of the Ship Inn, talking to the schoolchildren and selling them their sweet coupons so that they could buy cigarettes. They also used to sell bracelets, rings and necklaces that they had made out of plastic-covered wire.

To help the food supply people were encouraged through the Dig for Victory campaign to grow as much of their own food as possible.

Lawns and flower beds were sacrificed and any spare land was turned into allotments. It was not always easy. Clarrie East, as a lad of 11, planted the major part of the family's garden at Hill Top with potatoes in the spring of 1940. He did the job because his father was away all week working with gyrotillers. Soon after he had completed the task there was an air-raid warning and people congregated at the top of the hill to watch the bombers flying towards Hull. Suddenly, there was the sound of an aircraft flying towards them along Church Lane. It was a low-flying German aeroplane, which passed immediately overhead and continued towards the Humber. Everyone rushed into Clarrie's garden to get a better view and trampled all over his precious potato patch. He spent all next day digging up potatoes and replanting them.

Basic foodstuffs began to be rationed in January 1940 when everyone was issued with a ration book and was required to register with a local grocer for their provisions, Lee's and Butler's being the two grocers in the village. The food items that were rationed were: butter, sugar, cheese, cooking fat, margarine, tea, bacon, jam, milk and eggs, with the amounts allowed varying throughout the war as the availability of foodstuffs was not constant. The meat ration was given as a money value, and not all meat was on ration. Many things were rationed simply by a shortage of supply, but in 1941, a system of 'points' was introduced for biscuits, dried egg, cereals, Spam, and tinned goods. When the word went round that a commodity that was in short supply was available in the village shops, the women left whatever they were doing and rushed to buy the precious item. It was sometimes possible to obtain luxury foods. Village women used to club together and at Christmas send to Southern Ireland, which was a neutral country, for ground almonds and dried fruit. The address is not known but it was a risk and sometimes the money got lost!

Continued rationing was frustrating, but there were ways of meeting the challenge of eking out meagre rations. Many householders kept hens and pigs, and a wartime pigsty survived at the bottom of one of the gardens of Waldby Garth Villas until the mid-1990s. The home-produced eggs and meat were often shared with friends and neighbours. In order to get a meal ration for pigs, a meat ration had to be given up but it was possible to fatten a pig on only kitchen waste and potatoes discarded by the farmers as 'pig potatoes'.

Snares were set to catch rabbits, which were made into a tasty pie or stew. Twice a week Mrs 'Butcher' Westmorland made a copper-full of soup which she sold to customers. They brought their own containers to collect this delicious off-the-ration addition to the wartime diet. Keyingham Women's Institute canned fruit in season from their gardens or bought in bulk from the Humber Street fruit wholesalers in Hull. They hired a canning machine, which they set up in the Methodist schoolroom. The cans were bought in bulk and when the fruit was sealed inside, they were boiled in a member's copper normally used for boiling the laundry.

Clothing coupons were introduced in 1940. An adult received 48 coupons a year, 11 coupons being required for a woollen frock and 24 for a man's suit. Like some foods, clothes were rationed simply by shortage, and it was shortage of material that was responsible for the wartime fashion of short skirts. It was often a case of 'mend and make do to avoid buying anything new'. This particularly applied to wartime weddings, which were very different from those of today. The wedding often took place while the groom, and perhaps the bride as well, was home on short leave from the forces. Because of clothes rationing the bridal gown may have been borrowed or made from parachute silk or material bought with coupons donated by generous friends and relatives. Many brides had to make do with an afternoon dress worn with a hat and gloves. Owing to the extreme shortage of ingredients some brides had a mock wedding cake made of cardboard.

- o -

The school, under the head-ship of Mr Scruton, played its part in the war effort. The children collected rose hips, which were sent off to make rose-hip syrup, a vitamin-C supplement for children. The children also collected nettles, which were used to make camouflage dye. Poultry- and rabbit-keeping were added to the school's gardening lessons. The poultry rearing was organised by the Children's Committee. Six pullets were purchased, the money being raised by the sale of 6d shares to the children. Shares were available for a limited period and once the closing date was reached they could only be bought from children who were leaving the school. The children, working in pairs, looked after the hens, each pair doing one week's duty. The Poultry Society met every Tuesday when the results of the past week were discussed. The eggs could be purchased only by members in strict rotation. A girl was appointed as record keeper and accounts were carefully kept.

The children were taught knitting and sewing in order to help with the war effort. In 1939 it was recorded in the school logbook that, 'Scholars and teachers worked hard to send comforts for the forces. Miss Upshall collected names and addresses of all ex-Keyingham-school men on active service. Each week the children brought small contributions varying from a halfpenny to six pence. With this money wool has been bought. The girls have knitted various garments and these together with cigarettes etc. have been sent to the men. A typical parcel contains: 1 woollen helmet or scarf, 1 pair of socks or gloves, 1 pair wristlets, 2 bars of chocolate, 1 packet of cigarettes.' No one escaped helping, and even the boys were recruited to knit squares which were later made into blankets.

In 1941 the senior children formed a salvage squad, and in 1942 the children took part in the Dig for Victory exhibition at York. The school gardens had been developed to help with this effort and were extended when evacuee children joined the school, Albert Jackson of Mount Pleasant lending a quarter of an acre of land in Chapel Lane for the purpose.

Materials at the school were scarce and every inch of space in exercise books had to be used, together with the front and back covers. No margins were allowed and even the spaces at the top and bottom of the page were written on. Woe betide anyone who was found wasting anything! All materials were counted out and counted in to make sure nothing went missing. Pupils had to write either with very thin, easily broken, pencils that had to be used down to the last inch or with scratchy pens dipped in inkwells. Very few textbooks and reading books were printed so if a book was torn or became worn it had to be repaired and much learning took place out of old, outdated books. All these problems meant that teachers had to draw on all their resources to keep up the standards in the basic subjects.

School numbers were augmented by the arrival of evacuees at the start of the war. The first evacuees to arrive in Keyingham on 1 September 1939 were 14 children from Beverley Road School in Hull. On 7 September there were 51 evacuee children in the village, the extra numbers being made up by those who had been privately evacuated from Hull. The number on roll at the school in the middle of September was, 'evacuees 51, Keyingham children 104'. The older evacuees were accommodated in the small classroom in the main school, and the juniors and infants were taught in the Wesleyan schoolroom in Chapel Lane, where trestle tables had to be used as makeshift desks. On 14 November, as the numbers diminished, plans were made to bring the evacuees from the Wesleyan schoolroom into the school. By the end of that month, with no bombing of cities having occurred, many evacuees returned to Hull, and only 16 remained.

During the war years the school closed at 3:15 p.m. in order to give the children time to get home before blackout time. Lighter evenings were achieved nation wide by applying British Summer Time throughout the year. In the summer months double Summer Time was applied and the clocks were two hours ahead of Greenwich Mean Time. If night raids or warnings had occurred, the school did not open until 9:30 the following morning but whenever possible normal routine was maintained. Several changes were made to the school building to make it safer. The porches were altered to make it easier to evacuate the children, and cloakrooms and corridors were strengthened and protected to form refuge rooms. Further measures were taken in 1940 when linen tape and anti-splinter solution was put on all windows, which had already been taped by the scholars.

As a supplement to wartime rations children were allowed one third of a pint of milk per day free of charge. Before the war milk had been available in schools but at a cost of $1/2$d per bottle. With many women taking on the work of men in wartime and being away from home during the school lunch hour, the need to provide school dinners was realised. In March 1942, after discussion between parents and teachers, a canteen was opened in the Primitive Methodist room. Miss Jessie Goundrill was in charge and provided meals for 41 children and two teachers at a charge of 4d a head. A large solid fuel stove was used to cook the food. The canteen was run as a commercial enterprise by parents, with the food being supplied by local traders. In 1943 the price of a meal was raised to 5d, a typical menu being shepherd's pie with greens and Bakewell tart and custard. On Thursdays all meal preparations had to be cleared away by 2 o'clock so that the Women's Bright Hour could meet at 2.30.

After the war a new school canteen was opened in a prefabricated hut in School Lane with Mrs Marjorie Dawson in charge. The on-site dining facilities were far more convenient than having to walk the children in procession up Clay Hill and along Ings Lane each day to the Methodist room, particularly if Farmer Rodmell's geese decided to attack. The new canteen also catered for other schools, and the school bus was used to take meals to Burstwick school.

The welfare of the children was taken care of with routine dental inspections and regular visits from the school nurse. Hand inspections, for signs of scabies, and inspections for head lice were held regularly. School attendance was very much depleted by the measles epidemic of 1941. In that year there was also a slight rise in the incidence of diphtheria, and 96 children at the school were immunised by Dr Cripps. In view of the fact that immunisation depended on the wishes of the parents and that some children may already have been immunised, this was a high percentage.

Throughout the war the school and the community worked closely together. On one occasion, when the school was producing a concert, the stage was erected by T & C Guy free of charge, the curtains were lent by Keyingham Drama Group and lighting, including overhead battens, front lights and focus lamps, were provided by Thomas Eyre. The costumes were made by Miss Upshall and the girls, and the scenery was built and the stage furnished by Mr Scruton and the boys. The concert was very successful and children were said to have shown a high standard of acting ability.

School plays were just one of the many forms of entertainment still available to the people of Keyingham during the war. Despite the restrictions, they had not forgotten how to enjoy themselves. Day trips to the seaside, however, came to an end as the beaches and promenades were closed off by barbed wire and guarded by sentries. There were tank traps on the beaches and pillboxes on the cliff tops. Surprisingly, in view of the blackout and the possibilities of air raids, there was plenty of social activity in the evenings. There were two drama groups besides the school group: one attached to the youth club and an adult group. The plays, always well attended, were presented in either the school hall or the Village Institute. Whist drives continued to be held every Saturday night in the Foresters Hall. There were dances at the Ottringham and Patrington village halls and at Keyingham school, where the music was provided by a group of soldiers from Cherry Cobb Sands. The journeys home, on foot or on bicycle, were through unlit streets and along dark roads, with plenty of horseplay *en route*. One young lady of the time remembers cycling home on a dark night and meeting a loose bull in the lane. She pedalled like

mad hoping it would remain where it was until she had reached a 'safety zone'. She is still here to tell the tale so the story has a happy ending! At a barn dance held in a farmer's granary in 1945 the music was provided by a wind-up gramophone, but the dancers enjoyed themselves all the same.

The Women's Institute party, held in the school on New Year's Eve, was one of the social events in the village calendar. Tickets were much sought after, as everyone knew that a good time, with plenty of home cooked food, would be had by all. After the feasting one of the local drama groups would present a play.

The St Nicholas annual garden parties were not held in the first two years of the war but were resumed in 1943, being held in the vicarage garden as they had been before the war. Except for 1944, when the party was in the grounds of Prospect House, they continued to be held at the vicarage until 1948, the year Charles Patchett became vicar's warden. He offered the use of his garden at Ebor House and the garden party was held there, weather permitting, with the enthusiastic permission of Mr Patchett and later his son Richard, every year until Ebor House was sold in 1995.

In the early years of the war, Albert Jackson the churchwarden continued the practice he had begun before the war of showing films in the Church Room on a Saturday afternoon. Admission was one penny. Films were also shown in the Land Girls' hostel on Tuesday and Thursday evenings. Film shows continued after the war in the late 1940s and early '50s when Charles Etherington gave shows in the Village Institute. These were evening performances of commercial films. Children sat in the front with adults behind, and there was always a watchful eye kept on the children and a painful poke for any child who disturbed the performance by making too much noise. Mrs Gertrude Rodmell produced concerts in the Wesleyan chapel to raise money for the war effort, the Red Cross etc. In the late 1940s the Gaiety Girls Concert Party, a group of young Methodists led by Gladys Cook, entertained not only the people of Keyingham but also the neighbouring villages.

In the summer time people would travel from miles around to attend the Keyingham gymkhana. Initially the event was held at Harry Lanham's Bleak House Farm but was later transferred to Bill Rodmell's field down Saltaugh Road. There were classes for heavy horses, decorated horses, hackneys and jumpers. A firm of carters from Hull used to bring several shire horses into Harold Lowther's yard, where his daughters helped decorate them with ribbons and brasses. The men braided the horses' manes and tails and they were a truly fine sight. Horses for the jumping classes came from a well known ice cream firm, Massarellas of Doncaster. There were cups to be won for many of the events and much pride was at stake in the winning of them. It was a great occasion. One year during the war, when the gymkhana was being held at Bleak House, Ted Eyre fixed up an amplifier system, which picked up the propaganda being broadcast to Germany from the Ottringham BBC wireless station!

Both the Ship Inn and the Blue Bell thrived during the war years. Although many of the regular customers were away at war, their places were taken by the troops, the land girls and other visitors billeted in or near the village.

For the youngsters there were plenty of outdoor activities, playing in the streets and fields and going for cycle rides, often on second-, third- or even fourth-hand bicycles. They explored ponds and ditches for wild life and, in the days before agricultural pesticides, caught newts and sticklebacks. Girls collected rose petals and shook them in a bottle with water to make perfume. The games played in the street were those that had been handed down through the years. Cowboys and Indians, rounders, cricket, football, hopscotch, skipping, marbles, cigarette cards, ball games, pig in the middle, queenie, tin-off, block and conkers all had their seasons. In summer the older boys made the trek over Mill Hill, across two fields and over the drain and the railway line to the ponds at Kelsey Hill in Burstwick parish. There they would play all day on improvised rafts. If they knew a train was coming when they were about to cross the railway line they would put a halfpenny on the rail, hoping it would be squashed to the size of a penny. In winter there was sledging in Clay Lane when it was icy. Girls began their run at the top of the lane near the gateway to Mount Pleasant. Boys started round the corner from in front of Prospect House. Nearly everyone finished in the ditch at the bottom of the hill, having worked up too much speed to negotiate the slight bend there. Henry Naylor, an adult who invariably smoked a pipe, once volunteered to have a go. He went down the hill lying prone on the sledge and still smoking his pipe. He ended in the ditch and they never did find his pipe. The war brought lads a new pastime - searching for war relics. This was true in town and country alike, a piece of shrapnel being a prized possession. Opportunities for such treasure hunting were not so numerous around Keyingham but Keyingham lads took full advantage to go souvenir hunting when a cluster of bombs was dropped near Camerton Hall and when a Junkers 88 was shot down at Ottringham in August 1940.

Children's activities were usually kept a friendly but authoritative eye on by PC Fred

Hensby, the village policeman. He lived in Keyingham at the police station at 2 Hull Road, although his beat included Burstwick and Ottringham. He was an imposing ruddy-faced man, who wore the peaked cap of the East Riding Constabulary. He patrolled his beat on cycle and when in Keyingham parked it near the village cross whilst he walked round the village. Children knew he was the boss and respected him although on one occasion when he had parked his cycle one of the Kitchen lads managed to lift it up the nearby telegraph pole and hang it from the first step used by repair men when working at the top of the pole. Mr Hensby was not the only one to wield authority; older boys would sometimes bring the younger ones into line by ducking them in the horse trough in Arthur Clark's yard at the corner of Main Street and Station Road.

Organised activities for the young were provided mostly by church and chapel. Which of the three Sunday schools a child attended often depended on circumstances. It might be the one your parents chose or the one your mates attended. Clarrie East's parents felt it incumbent on them to send him to the Wesleyan Methodists because their landlord was Joseph Langdale, a keen Wesleyan. Other lads were attracted into playing in the bazooka band trained by Rose Walker, the Primitive Methodist Sunday school superintendent, whilst shy girls might take the earliest opportunity to evade the strict discipline required to perform in one of Mrs Rodmell's Wesleyan Sunday school productions by attending one of the other Sunday schools. Both the church and the Primitive Methodist chapel had the attractive job for boys of pumping the organ. The boy sat, out of sight in the vestry, his mind often anywhere but on religious thoughts, with his foot attached to the pump handle by a piece of string.

Once the rhythm was established, thoughts could wander, only to be brought back to the job in hand by the heavy stamping of the organist's foot when more air was needed. At the church the pay for organ blowing was raised from £1 to £1.10s a year in 1938 at the same time as the organist's fee was raised from £8 to £10. For older girls Mrs Horrox ran a Girls' Friendly Society at the vicarage. Those who attended were given very good training in domestic and social skills as well as talks on first aid and child care by the Horrox's daughter, Marguerite, who was a nurse. They also played a lot of games, running riot round the vicarage. In the mid-1940s, the Primitive Methodist Chapel had a club for older children after the Sunday evening service.

There was an attempt just after the war to provide other indoor activities for youngsters. The British Legion hired the Church Room for recreation purposes and made an offer to purchase it from the churchwardens in 1947, although the offer was turned down. Legion members cleaned up the room, which had been sadly neglected during the war, and set up a snooker table, which they allowed youths to use one night a week. Unfortunately, they couldn't behave themselves and stuffed straw up the chimney and rifled the coin meter that supplied power to the lamps over the table. Naturally, the Legion discontinued the amenity. The youths were probably not the first, and certainly not the last, of a minority of numbskulls who have occasionally clouded the Keyingham scene over the years.

- o -

The war in Europe ended on 8 May 1945 and was celebrated as VE Day. In Keyingham streamers were strung across Main Street and effigies of Hitler were hung from the telegraph poles. A big bonfire with 'Hitler' on top was lit in the middle of the road opposite the village cross. There was another bonfire at Church Farm, with a feast of roast potatoes and mushy peas and a display of fireworks provided by Charles Couse. He was a Hull printer and shopkeeper, who at the start of the war when there was a general order to destroy fireworks, had buried his stock in tin boxes in the garden of his wooden bungalow in Eastfield Road. They were disinterred and worked perfectly. There were further celebrations on VJ Day, 2 September, following the surrender of Japan on 14 August. Everyone was given two days' holiday. With more time to prepare, the celebrations were perhaps more spectacular than on VE night. No doubt particularly celebrating on that night were those Keyingham soldiers who had fought in Europe and had been about to embark for the Far East. By the end of 1945 the Home Guard had been disbanded and the Keyingham branch of the Royal British Legion had begun to raise funds in order to welcome home the servicemen and women of the village.

The plaque dedicated to the seven Keyingham men who fell in the Second World War was added to the war memorial in 1951. The seven names perhaps indicate the difference between how the two world wars were fought. The seven Keyingham men who gave their lives in the First World War were all soldiers; the Second World

Welcome-Home party, 1946. *The British Legion raised funds to give a 'Welcome Home' party to the men who had returned from the war. The venue is the schoolroom facing Saltaugh Road.* Courtesy of Mrs Marjorie Stancer

War dead included two men from the Royal Navy, two from the Merchant Navy and one from the Royal Air Force. The unveiling ceremony took place early in 1952, and 16-year-old Michael Storm, whose father was commemorated on the plaque, cycled over from his new home in Sutton to witness the event. The original sculpture that surmounted the memorial had been damaged during the war and was replaced by a stone cross in 1945. To commemorate the Silver Jubilee of Queen Elizabeth II in 1977 a new statuette of a soldier was commissioned and dedicated. The money for all these projects and for remodelling the memorial garden was raised by the Keyingham Branch, both men's and women's sections, of the Royal British Legion.

In 1946 the St Nicholas Parochial Church Council decided as a war memorial to install a new organ, something which had been under consideration in 1938. An Organ Fund was started and joined the existing Church Expenses Fund, the Sunday School Fund, the Lighting in the Vicarage Fund and the soon-to-be-formed Choir Vestment Fund. However, the final amount of money in the Organ Fund did not run to a new instrument, and in 1957 it was decided to have the existing organ restored by Hall & Broadfield of Hull at a cost of £220. The organ was restored again in 1994 under a legacy left by John Charlton.

Once the euphoria of victory had faded it became clear how much the war had cost. The country needed rebuilding for life in peacetime. Lend-Lease by America came to an abrupt halt and Britain had to begin repaying the debt by exporting as much as possible and cutting down on imports. The late 1940s and early '50s continued to be years of austerity, something the people were prepared to put up with after the horrors of war. Farming continued to be under the direction of the War-Ag until about 1950. Rationing of some commodities became even tighter than it had been during the war, the bacon ration, for instance, being reduced from 6oz to 3oz in 1950. It was not until July 1954 that food rationing finally came to an end.

Rationed goods continued to be obtained from Lee's and Butler's grocers' shops where the customers had registered. Alfred Lee had owned the shop at the corner of Station Road and Main Street, next to the Blue Bell, since the middle of the 1920s, when he took over from Mrs Priscilla Adamson. Mrs Blanche Butler had run the shop adjacent to the war memorial since 1939. She was only the third person to own it since the beginning of the century, when it had belonged to James Tarbotton. In the 1920s the shop had passed to Mrs Emily Jackson, sister to Fred Butler the saddler. In early 1939 Fred and his wife Blanche moved into the shop. Mrs Butler took pride in giving good service and supplied a wide range of goods including drapery, wool, haberdashery, ironmongery, shoes, paraffin, stationery, shampoos, detergents, groceries and vegetables. At the end of the war the shop also sold, on rare occasions, ice cream, which arrived at 1 p.m. on a Saturday and by 2 p.m. was gone. It came as a block, and Mrs Butler cut off a slice and served it between wafers. The thickness of a penny ice cream varied with the child, whether he or she was in Mrs Butler's good books or not. Mrs Butler ran the shop until 1968, it having joined the Spar organisation in 1959. After 1968 the shop was rented to various concerns, such as Holderness Hardware and a succession of greengrocers. At the beginning of 2000 it is run by Mrs Sylvia Percy as Sylvia's Soft Furnishings, with the goods being made on the premises. What was the front room of Mrs Butler's house became a baker's shop, which at the end of 1999 was owned by Oliver's Bakery, which as well as bread and pastries, sold sandwiches and snacks.

The grocers delivered goods and Clarrie East can remember that at the start of the war he delivered groceries on Saturday mornings for Mr Lee, who was always smartly dressed and wore a white apron when serving in the shop. Clarrie was provided with an errand boy's bicycle with a large carrier in front. He also did a daily paper round for Mr Lee and for doing both jobs received 2s.6d (12.5p) a week and a bar of chocolate. Though packaged and tinned goods had been on the market for a very long while, basic provisions were still bought in bulk and Mr Lee would weigh them out into smaller quantities to the customers' requirements. Flour was weighed into pale-brown paper bags; sugar bags were blue. Butter was cut from a slab and patted into shape with patterned butter pats, salt was cut from a block and biscuits were sold loose, and a bargain could be had with a bag of broken biscuits. Herbert's son, A P (Percy) Lee, with his wife Vera, continued to trade at the shop as Keyingham Newsagency until 1995, after which it stood empty until converted to a hairdresser's shop in 1999.

Other shops in the village included Bob Dearlove's on the south side of Main Street to the east of Beck Lane. He sold sweets and fruit and vegetables and had started the business in about 1919, when poor eyesight prevented him from continuing as an apprentice shoemaker to Frank Middleton. He did his deliveries by horse and cart, travelling round the outlying farms and going as far as Sunk Island on Saturdays. His shop passed successively to Edmund (Ted) and Margaret (Marg) Thompson, John Roydhouse, Leslie and Eva Ounsworth, the Hornbys and the Sandersons, continuing all the while as a grocery. Latterly it

was known as County Stores. In 1988 David Cheng bought the shop and converted it to the present Chinese takeaway, known as Keyingham Hot Foods.

At the end of the war the butcher's shop, which was in Main Street near the end of Church Lane, was run by Philip Westmorland, son of Herbert Westmorland, who had a slaughterhouse behind the shop at the beginning of the century. At that time the shop was used by a saddler but Herbert took it over to use as a butcher's shop and Philip succeeded to it. The slaughterhouse, with its entry from Church Lane, was still used, Philip usually having assistance from his brother Ted on killing days. In 1955 Philip moved to Wray House to concentrate more on farming, although in time he found he needed another source of income and opened a cafe in the Humber Street area of Hull. After about ten years there he bought the new butcher's shop in Station Road, Keyingham, in 1974. The old butcher's shop in Main Street was taken over by another butcher, Mr Petty, but the business failed and in 1958 the shop and the adjoining house, The Chestnuts, were bought by John Smith the electrician. After a period as John's retail and repair shop the premises served as a chemist's, a printer's workshop and gift shop, and today is a video rental shop.

The post office was at the corner of Main Street and Ings Lane. It had moved to that position when Arthur William Clark took over the post office from James Tarbotton before 1920. Tarbotton continued as a grocer at his old shop, which later became Butler's. The post office was still with the Clark family at the end of the war and was being run by Mrs Rachel (Peggy) Clark. When only a few people in the village had telephones most urgent messages were relayed by telegram to the post office. The messages were written on the telegram form and delivered by hand. Good news and bad was received this way, and during the war it was often the postmistress who had to pass on the news of the death of a loved one. At a later date the post office and shop were run by another family of Clarks, Len and Madge, and in 1969 they transferred to the present site on the west corner of Station Road and Main Street following the demolition of Cross Cottage (so called because of its proximity to the village cross). The Clarks retired in 1983. The present postmaster is Denis Mills who at the beginning of 2000 is campaigning with his wife Cathleen to keep the post office open under the threat of closure posed by government policy on the payment of pensions and state benefits.

The Clarks' former post office continued as a grocery shop run by the Senior family and then for a short while by Mike Temple. In 1989 Harish and Lata Chauhan bought the shop, which they greatly extended in 1996. It is known as Keyingham Village Stores and, with the closure of the other grocery shops in the village, is a boon to folk who cannot travel to the super markets. Like Keyingham's grocers of earlier days, Harish provides a delivery service, but not by bicycle or horse and cart.

Supermarket shopping, February 2000. Mrs Joyce Eyre is served in Keyingham Stores by Lata Chauhan and Dawn Huntley. The shop is the former post office set up by Arthur Clark in the 1920s. It has been considerably extended and is arranged in the modern supermarket style, but maintains a friendly village tradition.

The first fish-and-chip shop in the village may have been the one opened in about 1925 by John Crawforth, although there is an earlier record of there being a fish shop, which may have sold wet or fried fish, belonging to John Woodhouse who had the shop which later became Adamson's and then Lee's. Crawforth's shop was in an outhouse to the rear of the cottage at the eastern corner of Chapel Lane and Main Street. The fish and chips were cooked in pans heated by a coal-fired oven that could be temperamental when the wind was in the wrong direction. Clarrie East remembers the price being 1d for fish and 1/2d for chips at the start of the war, but later the price was 'two and one' and Cyril Beadle could recall being sent out with half a crown (2s.6d) to buy fish and chips for the family of ten. In January 1950 Ben Drury opened a fish-and-chip shop opposite the school in Saltaugh Road. He later moved to a shop on the north side of Main Street next door to the present post office. In the early years of the century the shop had been occupied by Joseph Tong the tailor, who worked sitting cross-legged in the window as he stitched the garment he was making. In 1956 the fish shop was purchased by Ted and Marg Thompson, who gave up the greengrocer's shop. The coal for the frying range, and the fish, were both brought from the railway station by Ted's brother Jack on his coal lorry. As the shop had no refrigeration facilities the decision on the correct amount of fish to buy was an important one. There was an electric 'rumbler' that cleaned the potatoes but it was prone to breaking down and two hundredweight of potatoes might have to be peeled by hand. Chipping was done, one potato at a time, through a hand operated chipper. In 1956 the price for a 'standard-sized' fish and chips was a shilling (5p). Except for soft drinks, only fish and chips were sold - there were no patties, sausages, chicken nuggets or mushy peas. A good example of the benefit of local services in a village is provided by an occasion when one of the pans sprang a leak. Ted and his son disconnected it, took it on a barrow to Harry Beadle the blacksmith who repaired it and barrowed it back. It was re-connected and back in service within two hours of the fault being discovered. One feature of the shop was the long wooden bench along the wall. Some of the local lads would eat their fish and chips there whilst passing comments about the quality and quantity to Marg and Ted as well as any potential customers. Fortunately, Marg could easily hold her own in any exchange of banter. Regular customers at harvest times were the Irish who came to work on the farms. They came to the shop with huge appetites after quenching even huger thirsts at the Ship or the Blue Bell. The pubs in the area were themselves customers and would ring up with orders of upwards of 30 suppers for their clientele. Passengers on the Connor and Graham bus were often impromptu customers when in an evening the driver would stop at the shop and order his supper. More often than not he was followed by his passengers who would eat their purchases on the bus while the driver finished his meal. Marg and Ted sold up in 1968, by which time Ted had been one of the village postmen for a couple of years. The shop continued in business under the proprietorship of the Briglin Brothers, Tom and Betty Cuerden, Peter and Leslie Noonan, Bob and Jean Turner and finally Akbal and Gurvinder Bhati. At the end of 1999 the shop was put up for sale.

- o -

When the war ended, Keyingham was able to concentrate more on its own affairs and work began on the long-held desire of providing the village with a playing field. A four-acre field on Saltaugh Road had been purchased for that purpose in 1937 at a cost of £200. The money came from a grant of £50 and a loan of £150 from the East Riding Playing Fields Association. Keyingham Parish Council became trustees of the land and arranged for it to be drained. Work was halted when the war started and the field was let to Harold Lowther for grazing, although the school continued to use it for their annual sports. In 1949 and 1950 the field was ploughed and two crops taken off under the direction of the War-Ag. After the harvest of 1950, the field was levelled by ploughing and bull-dozing using War-Ag equipment driven by Ted Roydhouse, a treatment that removed all evidence of the ancient ridge and furrow that had hitherto added an interesting dimension to any ball games played on the field. A vast amount of voluntary labour, especially on the part of farmers like George Beadle, Lawrie Grant, William Lanham and Harold Lowther, was put in and by the autumn the field had been sown with grass. In the next two years crops of hay were taken off and sold, helping to reduce the debt to the EYPFA. The playing field was officially declared open on August bank holiday 1952, the opening being performed by Neil Franklin, centre half for Hull City Football Club and a former England international.

- o -

At the school in the years immediately following the war there were very few improvements in the school building. The teachers still had the job of stoking the stoves and fireplaces that heated the classrooms. A familiar sight on a wet or snowy day was the fireguard festooned with wet coats, scarves and gloves, with shoes nearby and, if it was frosty, the milk crate positioned close by to help the milk to thaw. In 1947 technology reached the school when the first telephone was installed, but only as an extension from the telephone in the schoolhouse. Water closets replaced the old earth closets in 1949. The only drawback was when they froze in winter. Maybe the old earth closets had some advantages after all.

Educational visits began again after the end of the war, the children going to Hull to a concert given by the Yorkshire Symphony Orchestra and performances at the New Theatre, for instance. In 1948 they visited the Royal Show at York. These occasions helped to develop the children's experience of life outside their own Holderness village, although there was excitement nearer to home when children were taken to the Ken Hill gravel pit in 1948 to examine pottery and a human skeleton that had been excavated from 15 feet below the surface.

One thing that came to light during the war was the unfairness of the education system. For most children a secondary education was difficult to obtain. With financial support through scholarships, some children went to Hull schools for secondary education after taking the 'eleven plus' exam. A few scholarships were gained before 1938, although the present honours board contains only the names of those gaining awards from that year onwards. Each year saw an equal or increased number of scholarships being awarded to pupils from the school, and many Keyingham boys and girls came to be grateful for the efforts made by Mr Scruton on their behalf to get them into schools and colleges in Hull or even further afield. However, most children received no secondary education of any kind.

With the majority of children continuing their

education at Keyingham after the age of 11, there came to be problems. Mr Scruton's son recalls, 'The post-war population increase known as "the Bulge" was a problem for my father as the school was not large enough to accommodate the increased numbers. He negotiated with the Wesleyan trustees to use their schoolroom as an overflow classroom. By this time the chapel was no longer in use as a place of worship as it was structurally unsafe, with the ceiling sagging dangerously. Classes continued to be held on the premises until the numbers started to decline and the old canteen was used as an overflow classroom instead.'

The Education Act of 1944 granted to all children free secondary education in one of three types of school - grammar, technical or secondary modern. The Act also provided for the raising of the school-leaving age to 15 and then to 16 at some time in the future, and the school log for October 1944 records that 'if the school-leaving age was raised to 15 years the school would need accommodation for a further 12 children'. In 1947, the age of leaving school was raised to 15 in accordance with the Act. That year, in order to cater for the pupils staying at school for a further year, Withernsea Senior School began to admit children from the surrounding villages, and five boys and three girls were transferred from Keyingham to the Withernsea school - the first mention in the school log of automatic secondary education for Keyingham children. However, it was not until the Withernsea school was enlarged that it could accommodate all the 11-year-olds and upwards from the surrounding villages, so it was not until 1954 that the headmaster at Keyingham was able to report, 'as from 30th of July 1954 Keyingham School became a true Primary School providing education only up to the age of eleven'.

Withernsea High School was a comprehensive school giving both grammar and secondary modern education and, except in special circumstances, all Keyingham children progressed to Withernsea.

With village schools now only providing for children under the age of 11, pupil numbers declined, leading to the closure of some schools. Halsham and Ottringham schools closed in 1947 and 1948 respectively and the pupils from those villages now attend Keyingham school. For Keyingham an era came to an end when in December 1952 Mr Scruton left the school to become headmaster of Withernsea Junior School. On 1 January 1953 Mr W A Butterfield, BSc, assumed charge. The school number on roll was about 180.

Throughout the war the children from the Marsh and Cherry Cobb Sands had continued to be transported to and from school. Clem Westmorland retired from transporting the school children in about 1948. He had begun using a motor van instead of his original horse-drawn van when petrol became more easily available after the war. Harold Capes took over the job using an ex-army field ambulance with bench seats in the back. Harold was one of the village carriers and once had to bring a coffin from Hull to Keyingham. Percy and Vera Lee, from the newsagent's shop, took over the school contract from Harold and used a half-ton Ford van, with slatted seats and side windows, which was quickly replaced by an Austin Mini-bus, the first of two. Jack Thompson then took over and by the time he retired in 1977, the number of pupils requiring transport to school from Cherry Cobb Sands and Saltaugh Grange had decreased. His daughter-in-law Edwina was the driver until 1995 when Humberside County Council began to put the contract out to tender to local taxi firms.

Another school transport run came into being when Halsham school was closed and the children were transferred to Keyingham School. Grace Capes was the driver and her first vehicle was a pre-war timber-bodied shooting brake. When Ottringham children began attending Keyingham school the number of children requiring transport to Keyingham increased and the contract was passed to various bus companies. In recent years there have been as many as forty children bussed in on this service.

Operation Salvage, July 1955. Two tractors typical of the 1950s. The smaller is a 23 h.p. Ferguson, the larger a 40 h.p. Fordson Super Major. Modern farm tractors vary from about 180 to 250 h.p. The two tractors, fitted with buck rakes, have been sent by local farmers to help move smouldering hay from the stack yard of Lawrie Grant's farm in Main Street, after firemen had fought an unavailing battle to save a 25-ton stack ravaged by fire. David Beadle is driving the Ferguson, sent by his father from Church Farm. Bill Harness drives the Fordson, sent by his employer, Jim Jackson of White House Farm. Lawrie Grant is immediately behind Bill Harness, and Lawrie's son, Bill, is on the extreme left of the picture. The picture sums up the community spirit amongst farmers because, besides the tractors and the drivers sent from other farms, also lending a hand on the stack are six other men, including Harold Lowther (second from left) and Fred Stephenson (far right). Looking on is Vic Lanham in his postman's uniform. The fire was probably caused by spontaneous combustion, and Bill Harness recalls a similar stack fire at Medforth's at Bleak House Farm at around the same time. By permission of Hull Daily Mail

Other transport services developed from the school runs. Both Grace Capes and Vera Lee transported school meals to Burstwick school from the Keyingham school kitchens, and Percy and Vera Lee started a local taxi and private hire business with their mini-bus. One of their unusual jobs was when the Vicar of Ottringham paid them to pick up worshippers from Ottringham Marsh and Sunk Island on Sundays and take them to church.

- o -

During and immediately after the war the large and powerful machines used by the War-Ag emphatically demonstrated to farmers the advantages that mechanisation could bring. However, the cost of its introduction, with many pieces of equipment having to be replaced or converted so that they could be drawn by a tractor, meant that the use of the horse went on for a long time after the first use of tractors. Some Keyingham farms had tractors before the war. Chris Jackson at White House Farm is said to have been the first farmer in Keyingham to have one, and, as mentioned in the previous chapter, there was a Fordson tractor at Saltaugh Grange when it was sold up in 1937. These tractors were small and capable only of pulling a two-furrow plough, something within the capability of a three-horse plough team. In the 1930s, with farming in depression, the farmer had to weigh up many

Bill Johnson with his horse ready for work at Keyingham Grange, circa 1935. Horses continued to be used on the farms throughout the war years and after. Bill is wearing 'rat-bands' - in local dialect they were known as 'yorracks' - tied below his knees, said to prevent rats from running up inside trouser legs, but more probably to prevent the strain of heavy corduroy trousers, especially in wet conditions, causing the worker's braces to snap!
Courtesy of Mrs Joyce Eyre

things before deciding to buy a tractor. Maintenance was cheaper than for horses, but a Fordson tractor cost him at least as much as two good horses and had only half the working life. Many farmers believed that the iron-rimmed wheels fitted to most tractors 'puddled' the land. So horses continued to be kept. When Mr Chichester Constable began leasing Keyingham Grange to Charles Patchett in 1943, 53 horses of all kinds were put up for sale. Four of them were unbroken and quite wild, and Harry Hoe was obliged to crawl along the rafters over the loose box in order to put halters over their heads.

Milking by hand was a time-consuming task so when a milking machine was installed at Bleak House Farm in 1942 it attracted many interested spectators. A milking machine meant that a farmer could deal with more cows. During the war, despite the fact that there was a reduction in the acreage of grassland, there was an increase in milk production owing to the use of more milking machines and the chemical fertilising of grass at the direction of the War-Ag.

The first time combine harvesters were used by a Keyingham farmer was in 1944 when Charles Patchett used two to thresh a field of dry cut peas at Ken Hill. The combines had engines that drove the threshing gear but they had to be towed by tractors. A second man was required on the combine in order to collect the bagged peas and slide them off on a chute. Because the combine was offset behind the tractor and occupied quite a width PC Hensby had to cycle ahead from Ebor Farm to halt the traffic at the top of the hill until the miniature convoy had made its way to the field. These combines were incapable of cutting wheat, which in those days had a very long stalk, and had a cut only about six or eight foot wide, whereas the American combines used soon after by the War-Ag

had a cut of at least ten foot, were self driven and could deal with wheat.

Gradually, farms became more mechanised and for a while new practices and old ran side by side. As late as 1960 John Cook at North End Farm was using both a reaper binder, pulled by a tractor, and a combine harvester. The corn cut with the reaper had to be threshed separately and a threshing set was hired from Burnham's of Burstwick. The threshing set was powered by a tractor driven by Edgar Walker, a Keyingham man. For small farmers the tractor proved a blessing and in 1950, the year that petrol rationing ended, Harold Lowther bought a petrol tractor from the Holderness Plough Company at Burton Pidsea for £333.

Beef and dairy farming received a setback in 1949 when the country was hit by foot and mouth disease, and restrictions on the movement of cattle were put in force. Harold Lowther built a temporary stall in his field south of the playing field in Saltaugh Road where he chained the cows up for milking as they were not allowed to walk the short distance to his farmyard in Ings Lane. A special licence had to be obtained from the police if animals were being transported to market.

In the 1950s most of the farmers in the village had only small farms, although some of the Marsh farmers had considerable acreages. The village farmers at that time were George Beadle at Church Farm, John Cook at North End Farm, Lawrie Grant at Skeckling Farm, Harold Lowther at Jessamine House, Len Medforth at Bleak House, Bill Rodmell at Mount Airey, Ted Westmorland at Elm Tree Farm and Philip Westmorland at Wray House. Of these only John Cook had over 200 acres. There were 400 acres of land attached to Ebor House Farm, which Charles Patchett bought from the Church Commissioners in 1953. Mr Patchett also leased Keyingham Grange and Marsh Farm, as well as Westlands Farm in Winestead, which together totalled about 1,000 acres. Most of the small farms were mixed, with livestock and arable, and most of the farmers had a second business interest, such as haulage, butchering, dairy rounds or underwriting.

- o -

During the war years church and chapel services had been held in the afternoons instead of the evenings because of the blackout. As one of the warnings of invasion was the ringing of the church bells, their regular use to indicate service times was forbidden. Both church and chapel had their women's groups. Gladys Cook began the Women's Bright Hour in 1941, and Mrs Horrox ran the Mothers' Union. At St Nicholas there was also a very active Women's Guild whose members worked hard to improve the interior of the church. They were responsible for its cleaning and they raised funds for carpets and other soft furnishings within the church.

After the war there seems to have been a decline in regular church attendance. In his report to the Easter vestry meeting in 1947 Mr Horrox described the ordinary church service congregations as 'discouragingly small' although he estimated there were some 200 acknowledged members of the Church of England in Keyingham. It was only at the special services of the year that there were good attendances. At Easter nearly all the 100 communicants in the village were present, and the collection, which was given to the vicar in the days before fixed stipends, was large. There were also good congregations at harvest festivals, with usually the largest collection of the year when the farmers made up for their absence at other times. Church and chapel were always beautifully decorated with farm and garden produce at harvest festival. Someone from the farming community read the lesson and the harvest hymns were sung with gusto, although some might be a little hesitant in singing *All is safely gathered in* if they were late with the harvest. The St Nicholas Sunday school nativity play could be counted on to attract many parents and relatives of the performers. The play was produced each Christmas throughout Mr Horrox's incumbency, including during the war. The stage was erected over the chancel choir stalls. It was an ambitious production with good lighting effects and carefully thought-out continuity. The finale was the stable scene with the youngest children, who for most of the performance had been looked after at Ebor House, entering the church, carrying lanterns and singing *Away in a manger*. There were equally ambitious productions by the Primitives and the Wesleyans, and from the late 1930s right up to the '70s one of the highlights of the Primitive Methodist year was the crowning of the May Queen. Traditionally the 'Queen' wore a dress with a long pink train and was accompanied by two attendants.

- o -

Motor transport had begun to be an accepted part of everyday life just before the war. Most of the big farmers had cars and Clarrie East can remember Mr Leffler, the vicar, having one. Just before the war, Mr Scruton bought a new Morris 8, and Mr Lee, the grocer, bought a new Vauxhall 10, which, collected by one of Murdoch's mechanics and delivered to his door, cost £175. When the country's resources were channelled into the war effort the manufacture of vehicles for the home market was halted. For all motorists, driving was restricted because of petrol rationing.

The two bus companies that served the village, Connor & Graham and East Yorkshire Motor Services, carried many passengers. It was not uncommon to see three Connor & Graham buses full of passengers passing through Keyingham to Hull in the mornings. On the EYMS service from Withernsea to Hull in the early 1950s there would be five double-deckers and a single-decker bus, already laden with commuters from Withernsea, calling at Keyingham at 8 a.m. The frequency and convenience of the motor buses created strong competition for the railway and though it still continued to carry passengers and goods between Withernsea and Hull, its days were numbered. Following nationalisation of the railways in 1947 improved services were hoped for but did not materialise. A request by the parish council in 1948 for cheaper rail fares in line with bus fares went unheeded, and in 1953 a reduced winter service was introduced.

- o -

Some of Keyingham's old health hazards still persisted both during and after the war. In 1943 the parish council resolved that the pond known as Bewell's Well be filled up 'as it is of no further use, and was being used only as a dumping ground for old tins and other rubbish'. Bewell's Well was a horse wash at the bottom of Ings Lane near 'Sunnyside' and it had caused the parish council problems and some expenditure on cleaning out since the beginning of the century. It was finally filled in with road rubbish in 1945. In 1946 the parish council asked the Holderness RDC for a night-soil collection 'as there was a number of houses with no means of disposal and some unknown persons were developing the habit of emptying night-soil receptacles on the grass verges

Bewell's Well, circa 1900. The well was a horse-wash and a watering place for animals being driven on the hoof to farms in neighbouring villages. Carts and wagons could also be drawn into it to ensure that the wood of the wheels stayed swollen and tight fitting. The council spent a great deal of money over the years keeping the well in repair, but after the arrival of mains water in Keyinngham it became an unofficial rubbish dump. In 1945 the council finally filled it in. The house is Sunnyside, with Peace Cottage behind. Also, in the distance is South View before it was rebuilt.
Courtesy of Ann Braithwaite

in some of the lanes'. In 1948 there was a request that the four semi-detached bungalows on Ottringham Road, next to Murdoch's Garage, be included in the weekly collection of night soil.

Newly built houses of the 1930s and '40s were provided with water closets and septic tanks rather than earth closets, so the removal of night soil was not a problem. However, few, if any, private houses were built in Keyingham during the reign of George VI. Some of the private houses built in the 1920s and early '30s had benefited from a subsidy granted under the Conservatives in 1923 whereby a builder received a grant of £6 a year for 20 years, or a lump sum of £75, for every house built at a cost below £525. In 1924 the Labour government granted subsidies to local authorities that built houses for rent. Both pieces of legislation stemmed from Lloyd George's promise at the end of the First World War to build houses for the heroes returning from the war. However, under the Patrington RDC no local-authority houses were built in South Holderness. It was not until after Patrington RDC merged with Skirlaugh RDC in 1935 to form Holderness RDC that anything seems to have been done about the matter, and in 1937 there was a move in parallel with other rural areas to demolish old properties and replace them with modern council houses. John Guy can remember as a lad hearing the Liberal candidate for the 1937 general election being closely questioned on the matter by landlords of cottages in the village. They pointed out that their properties were perfectly habitable and they would lose revenue if the houses were demolished (it may be significant that some of these landlords had served on the Patrington RDC). Their protests were to no avail and council houses began to be built in Holderness in 1937. The six houses of Waldby Garth Villas in Eastfield Road were built the following year. They were substantial two-storey houses with three bedrooms (one with a fireplace) and a bathroom with hot water coming from a tank heated by the Yorkist range in the living room. There was a boiler in the kitchen and a water closet outside the back door, with a single septic tank serving all six houses. Soon after the houses were built the row of old cottages next to Wray House in Station Road were knocked down. However, it was not until the 1960s that any other old properties in Keyingham were knocked down. The subsidised rents of the council houses were 7s.6d (37.5p) a week, but a farm worker earning 30s (£1.50) a week might be stretched to find even that amount and might prefer to stay in one of the old rented cottages, such as the Foresters cottages, where the rent was 25s a quarter, or the cottages owned by Joseph Langdale. He lived at Beacon Hill opposite the end of Church Lane, and owned the row of cottages between his home and Chapel Lane. The rent of one occupied by the East family in 1932 was 16s.8d (83p) a month. Of the first occupiers of Waldby Garth Villas, only one was a farm worker. The others included a builder's labourer, two railway workers, a worker from Saltend and a dock labourer who cycled to his work at Hull docks.

In 1944 the parish council were considering plans for the erection of more council houses in Keyingham. After due deliberation the council submitted their opinions as to the best layout to the Holderness RDC surveyor, and in 1945 a sub-committee was formed. In January 1947 the council notified the surveyor of their strong preference for permanent brick houses although they would not object to a dozen prefabricated homes provided these could be erected in the next few months.

Prefabricated homes (prefabs) were considered as the solution to Britain's post-war housing problem. The parts for prefabs were made in the factory and could be quickly assembled on site. By April 1947 land in Station Road had been purchased and provisional plans had been made for the building of ten traditional brick houses and 28 prefabricated houses made by Spooners of Hull and with a life expectancy of 60 years. By September, erection of the Spooner houses had begun and it became a favourite Sunday afternoon walk to go and see the progress being made. The bottom storeys of the houses were built of brick, with the upper storeys and roofs being of prefabricated asbestos. At the parish council meeting in April 1948 it was unanimously agreed that the estate should be called Northfield. A year later the brick council houses on Station Road had been completed. All the houses were three bed-roomed and had large gardens. The houses had water closets with one large septic tank, emptied two or three times a week by the RDC, in the centre of the green. The Spooner houses had the neat arrangement of the oven in the kitchen backing on to the fireplace in the living room and being heated by it. The only trouble was that to bake bread in the summertime there had to be a roaring fire in the living room.

Before the council houses were built it had been stated that the parish council had no power to select tenants but recommendation to the Holderness RDC could be made. Many Keyingham people, especially workers from the farms in the village, became tenants, but there were a few from other parts of Holderness. The rents, which included the RDC rate, were 15s.5d a week, although for tenants who were agricultural workers, the rents were 2s.2d less, an

Northfield, during upgrading in 1984. Built by the Holderness Rural District Council in 1947, the houses were upgraded in 1984. The picture shows a block in the original design and one that has been improved.

Photo: D G Smith

acknowledgement that, as for over a century, farm workers' wages were lower than in other industries. At about that time the rent for one of the cottages in Station Road, opposite where the butcher's shop now is, was 5s. It was probably because of the comparatively high rents of the houses in Northfield that the Foresters thought it opportune to raise the rents of Foresters Cottages from 25s a quarter to 32s.6d, which they did at the end of 1947. Waldby Garth Villas and the houses in Northfield were upgraded in the 1980s, the Spooner houses having the bottom storeys clad in new brick and the upper storeys rebuilt in brick and timber. The roofs were given a steeper pitch and tiled. In both the Villas and Northfield there are people living today who were there as tenants or the children of tenants when the houses were first built.

- o -

The middle of the century was reached with Britain still suffering from the aftermath of the war. Some goods were still rationed, imports were restricted, building activity was directed almost wholly to council housing and schools. Men were still conscripted to serve with the forces in Germany, different regions of the British Empire and Korea. For most people the austerities imposed during the war continued. A break in the monotony came with the holding of the Festival of Britain in 1951. The festival was national in its scope and in Keyingham was celebrated by the presentation of a two-day pageant, *Home of the Chaine Folk*, undoubtedly the biggest drama spectacle ever produced by the people of Keyingham and certainly something that has lived on in the memories of all those who took part or who watched it. The pageant told the history of the village from its early beginnings up to the start of the 20th century. It had begun as an idea taken from the school's winning entry in a BBC *Children's Hour* competition. The pageant, written by Mr Horrox and described as 'a dramatic history of the ancient village of Keyingham in Holderness', consisted of a series of playlets presented in the open air over two evenings in July. The play was produced by the school staff, past and present scholars and friends of the school. It was held in the grounds of Ebor House on a stage built of flooring from ex-Army huts supported on four rulleys, and surrounded by a framework of tubular scaffolding covered by sacking. There was seating for over 500 people. There were over 300 acting parts performed by a cast of nearly 140 men, women and children, all from Keyingham. There were 50 helpers ranging from the production team to the car park attendants, and the whole project was planned and controlled by a very large committee. Twenty-five years later the script was published and parts of the play, performed by a new generation of Keyingham people, were broadcast in serial form on BBC Radio Humberside.

The 1951 Festival of Britain, intended to demonstrate the solidarity and industrial achievements of the British Empire, also aimed at restoring faith and confidence to the people of the country, and seems to have succeeded. 'A real family party,' Archbishop Fisher of Canterbury declared at the closing ceremony. It certainly produced an event that was long remembered in Keyingham.

A year later, events took a sombre turn when in February 1952 King George V1 died - a monarch who had become the people's king, who with his family had lived through the war supporting his people. During his reign there were aspects of

The upper photograph shows some of the cast: Standing, left to right: Gladys Clark, Wendy Gordon, Madge Lanham, Marguerite Horrox, Marianne Patchett, Leo Cartwright, Kathleen Stancer, Gladys Beadle, Elsie Pashby, Catherine Ness, Elizabeth Eyre, F Robinson, Jack Thompson, Harry Hargrave, Colin Precious, John Hargrave, Frederick Stephenson; Kneeling: David Scruton, Shirley Storm, Jean Hodgson, Michael Thomlinson, Margaret Clark, LilianThomlinson, Kathleen Hoe, Sally Worsnop, Florence Thompson.
The lower photograph gives an indication of the size of the audience.
By permission of Hull Daily Mail.

The Pageant, July 1951. *Keyingham's contribution to the Festival of Britain in 1951 was the production of a Pageant.* Home of the Chaine Folk *was performed in one of Charles Patchett's fields over two evenings and had a cast of 150. It depicted the history of Keyingham and was written by the Vicar, Rev H T Horrox. The finale on the last night was illuminated by a spotlight shining from the Old Mill about 80 yards away.*

250

Keyingham life that had changed greatly, especially the outlook of the people. Young men, who had fought in Europe and North Africa and the Far East and met others from all walks of life, had new ideas about social justice. Women had experienced a great deal of independence, and children, like their elders, had learned to save and economise and go without. The war had jerked farming into being an efficient industry, receptive to new ideas and technology and well able to maintain its edge on European competition for many years, unlike the situation after the First World War. Physically, however, the village, except for the outlying farmlands, had changed little. Two groups of council houses had been built on the edges of the village and a few old properties had been knocked down but the population had changed little and the number of inhabitants connected with agriculture was still about the same as at the start of the reign. There were just as many shops and workshops in the village, and they were still operated by the same families and patronised by all the village. There were the same old leafy lanes and ponds where children could go fishing. Television was something watched by people in the south of the country: in Keyingham people provided their own evening entertainment. At the end of the reign Keyingham could still be considered as a mainly rural, self-contained community.

Disused Railway Track

Playing Field

Footpath

Old Mill

Footpath

Cemetery

Gravel Pits

Nurseries

Nurseries

Nurseries

Nurseries

Nurseries

New Mill

Allotments

Playing Field

Extension to Playing Field

Footpath

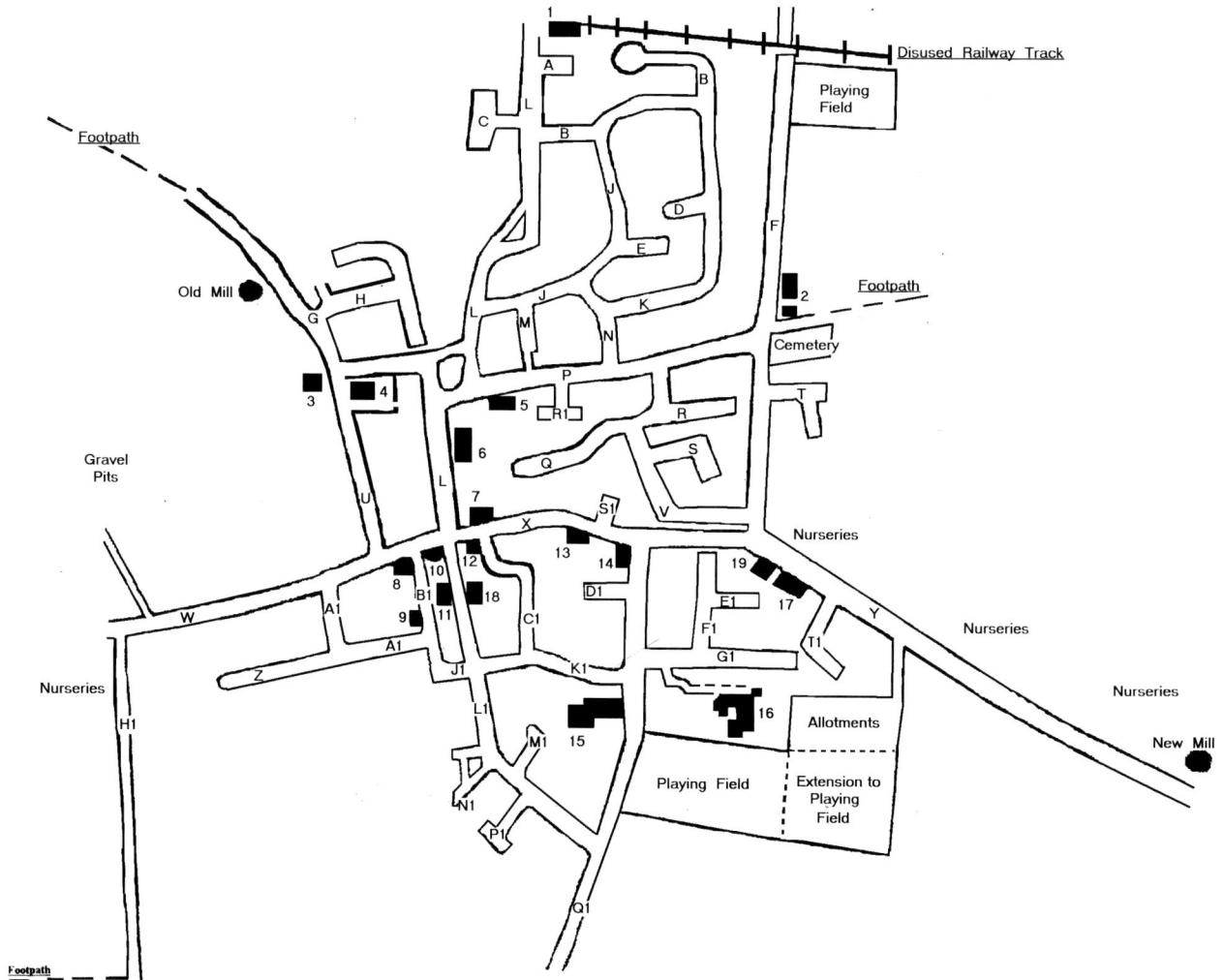

Keyingham in the year 2000. The difference in layout between the old village and the new housing estates is quite evident from this map. The houses of the old village were laid out along roads and lanes that led to the various open fields and pastures (see map on page 10) whereas the roads of the new estates serve as a means of access to closely packed houses and are typically winding or end in cul de sacs.

KEY. Buildings

1. Former Railway Station
2. Waldby Garth Villas
3. Ebor House
4. St. Nicholas Church
5. Former Wesleyan Chapel
6. Village Institute
7. Blue Bell Inn
8. Surgery
9. Surgery (Prospect House)
10. War Memorial
11. Methodist Chapel
12. Foresters Hall
13. Former Primitive Methodist Chapel
14. Ship Inn
15. Junior School
16. Infant School
17. Garage and Filling Station
18. Church Room
19. Vicarage

Streets

A. The Ridings
B. St Philips Road
C. Northfield
D. Etherington Close
E. Langdale Drive
F. Eastfield Road
G. Mill Road
H. Ebor Manor
J. Albermarle Road
K. Owst Road
L. Station Road
M. Kelsey Drive
N. Seymour Road
P. Waldby Garth Road
Q. Westerdale Close
R. Maude Close
S. Ombler Close
T. Broadacres
U. Church Lane
V. Marritt Way
W. Hull Road
X. Main Street
Y. Ottringham Road
Z. Manor Garth
A1. Maister Road
B1. Chapel Lane
C1. Beck Lane
D1. Jellison Walk
E1. Melville Close
F1. Griffiths Way
G1. Russell Drive
H1. Boyes Lane
J1. Clay Lane
K1. School Lane
L1. Ings Lane
M1. Kirncroft
N1. Elm Villas
P1. Compton Drive
Q1. Saltaugh Road
R1. Elm Tree Close
S1. Willowfiel Drive
T1. Osbourne Drive

Map by Rob Brown, Len Haxby and Mike Smith

The coronation of Elizabeth II, on Tuesday, 2 June 1953, was celebrated· by the people of Keyingham with the same enthusiasm as had been shown on coronation days earlier in the century. A celebrations committee of nearly 60 people had been formed nine months previously following a public meeting called by the parish council. It included at least half a dozen who had served on the committee at the coronation of George VI. The funds necessary to carry through the programme had been raised by house-to-house collections and different social events.

The celebrations and entertainments took the form that had become almost a tradition since the time of Victoria's golden jubilee. On the eve of the great day souvenir mugs were presented in the Village Institute to all the children. The day itself began with a united service conducted by the Anglican and Methodist ministers in the parish church. The souvenir programme tells us that the afternoon was to be occupied with children's fancy dress and sports on the playing field, and tea parties for children and the over-60s. In the evening there were to be sports for the adults and the day was to end with a whist drive and a dance in the school. As the programme put it, no one was to feel excluded, 'for this day Keyingham speaks with one voice acclaiming the Crowned Queen and uniting in joyful approbation'.

Unfortunately the programme could not be followed in its entirety. It was a rainy day, and some of the outdoor events had to be cancelled or postponed until the evening. There was, however, one treat for the people of Keyingham in 1953 that had not been available at previous celebrations of coronations and jubilees: for the first time the coronation was televised. Very few people in Keyingham had television at that time, but on the great day they could view the coronation on small black-and-white sets in the Methodist schoolroom, the Village Institute and the primary school. The sets were provided by John Cook, Philip Westmorland and local electricians, Maurice Clark and Sydney Dalby. Viewing Elizabeth's coronation is the first recollection many people have of watching television.

It was in the year of the coronation that the Village Institute Committee decided they were in a position to extend the Institute, as had been the intention from the time it was first converted from a barn. In 1953 the main hall of the Institute consisted of what is now the small hall at the west end of the building, so that some of the major village events, the coronation dance for instance, had to be held in the school. For the extension the Ministry of Education gave a grant towards the cost of materials, but the work was done by voluntary labour. It was a truly communal enterprise. Used bricks were brought by the tipper load from demolished properties in Hull, and the village youngsters, boys and girls, were set on with hammers and chisels to clean them up. Bricklaying was done by volunteers under the direction of Wreathall Tuton, a retired builder in his 70s. Reg Scarlett, a bricklayer from Burstwick, was employed to give the work a professional finish. He was paid by the local farmers, each giving one week's wage in turn. Cyril (Sid) Gardner, when not working shifts at Saltend, acted as his labourer. Charles Patchett, of Ebor House, also lent one of his men, Dennis Medforth, to act as labourer.

When the time came to put the metal roof trusses in position it was done manually, mostly by men lent by the farmers. It was one of those jobs where everyone was in charge with no overall direction. The consequence was that on one occasion ten-year-old Ray Thompson was left by himself holding a rope to steady a truss until a tractor was brought to anchor the rope. That problem was sorted out but no lessons were learnt, for there are recollections of a steel girder later falling and missing Maurice Clark by inches. It was then that builder Jim Howes thought it wise for him to oversee all building operations.

The new extension was opened on Saturday evening, 29 January 1959. The total cost had been about £2,500 and £300 was still owing. It was hoped to raise some of the money from the events to be held in the Institute during the opening week. Beginning with the Saturday there was entertainment on every weekday evening up to the following Friday. To most events the admission was two shillings (10p) for adults but at the culminating event - a supper and dance (on the newly installed sprung floor) to music by Tommy Fisher and his band - admission was 10 shillings. No doubt a large part of the debt was removed in that week and within a year the whole debt had been paid.

In 1960 the kitchen was added, and central heating was installed soon afterwards. As there was no surplus from the hire charges for the Institute, the money for all the improvements was raised by the people of the village supporting the events arranged by the management committee. Further major extensions took place in about 1990. The funding for these came about as a result of a village lottery called the Keyingham Rainbow Draw, the first of which took place in April 1985. People in the village took a number and paid for it weekly, their contributions being collected at Carole's newsagents and by the two milkmen, Ray Lawton and Dave Westmorland. Part of the money went towards prizes and the remainder was put into a fund to provide a facility in the village for everyone to use. By the 20th week of the draw

there were 1,300 participants and there was £1,000 in the fund. The fund continued to increase and by early 1986 there were plans to use the money to build a community centre on the Saltaugh Road playing field. The plan fell through as the proposed building would have encroached on the existing playing facilities. Gradually the draw lost its attraction, and the committee set up to administer the fund dwindled. The remaining committee members had the problem of how to use the money to best benefit the residents of Keyingham. After much debate, it was given to the Village Institute Committee who, with the aid of a further grant, used it to build a comfortable meeting room behind the main hall of the Village Institute. It was named the Rainbow Room in recognition of the hard work and dedication of all the people concerned in setting up and running the draw. At the same time as the Rainbow Room was added the old toilets were replaced with up-to-date facilities.

In 1975 the parish council became trustees of the Institute, although as before, it is still run by a management committee with no financial help from the rates. One name that became synonymous with the Institute was that of Dorrie Clark. She, with the help of her husband Dick, was caretaker of the building for 50 years from September 1946. In all that time she could be relied on to have all the chairs and tables set out for whichever group was about to use the rooms. Dorrie retired from duties in 1996 but in 2000 is still a member of the Institute Committee.

- o -

At the start of Elizabeth's reign Keyingham retained much of its old rural character. Twice a day Lawrie Grant's cows moved at their own pace

Waldby Garth Road, before the development of the 1960s. Still a very rural scene with geese running freely on the the road. The picture shows the house that is now known as Applegarth, the old Drainage Board boat-shed and Elm Tree Farm. The grass patch in the foreground is the site of the old pinfold, moved in 1855. The far (eastern) end of the road was so narrow that in 1955 the parish council asked the county surveyor to have a passing point for vehicles made in it. Courtesy of Ann Braithwaite

between his farm in Main Street and their pasture in the field at the corner of Eastfield Road. There were still people in the village who kept chickens, or who had a sty in the back garden with a pig or two in it, a practice that had been encouraged during the war. On certain Saturdays, Cyril Beadle went round the village with his truck and collected the animals that were to be slaughtered by 'Butcher' Westmorland. The joints would be ready for collection the following morning and they would be taken home and prepared for eating. The hams would be hung from hooks in the kitchen with a pillowcase over them to keep off the flies. The village boys usually begged the pigs' bladders from the butcher, blew them up, dried them in the oven and used them for footballs.

Only two years before the coronation the herbage in Keyingham's lanes was still being leased out, a custom going back 150 years in the village's history. The roads that had been laid out at the enclosure in 1805 were as yet virtually devoid of houses. Waldby Garth Villas and a wooden bungalow were the only houses in Eastfield Road. The eastern half of Waldby Garth Road was so narrow that in 1955 the parish council requested the county surveyor to have a passing point made for vehicles. In the 1950s the parish council was frequently requesting the county surveyor to provide footpaths along the various roads in the village. Street lighting was still a thing of the future. With the building of a few private houses and of Waldby Garth Villas (1938) and Northfield (1947-8) the population had risen from 611 in 1931 to 793 in 1951, the first time it had topped 700 since the middle of the previous century.

Keyingham's rural nature was soon to disappear. At the end of the 1950s great changes were heralded. This was hinted at in March 1957 when Frank Middleton, chairman of the parish council, commented to a reporter from the *Yorkshire Times*, 'There is a possibility that in the future houses will be erected in the village, but this depends on the progress that can be made with a sewerage scheme.' In fact, as early as 1955, the Minister for Housing and Local Government had approved plans for a sewage treatment works to the south of Hull Road close to Keyingham Drain into which the treated effluent would be discharged, and this was where the works were built.

The effect of the new scheme was dramatic. Old houses had their earth toilets replaced by water closets, usually with the aid of a 50% grant from the local authority, and new housing estates, linked directly to the sewers, were built with great rapidity. In 1961, the council bungalows in Kirncroft were completed. In 1962 St Philips Road, Albemarle Road and Owst Road were laid out, and by 1964 Marritt Way, Ombler Close, Westerdale Close, Maude Close, Kelsey Drive, Langdale Drive and Etherington Close were completed or were in the course of construction. All these were new roads laid out on fields to the northeast of the village centre. Other development took place along the established roads and lanes, such as Eastfield Road and Waldby Garth Road, in the northeast quarter, and Ings Lane to the south of the main road through the village. In the early 1970s Maister Road and Manor Garth were laid out on what in early times was known as South Hill.

The building of the 13 council bungalows in Kirncroft Close led to the demolition of some of the old privately owned, low-rent cottages, and by 1963 Extoby Row, Slated Row in Saltaugh Road and the Georgian houses at the corner of Chapel Lane and Main Street, together with the saddler's shop, had been knocked down.

The policy in naming the new roads was that the builder could suggest a name to the parish council for approval. Otherwise the parish council decided on the name. Many of the names given were connected with the history of Keyingham. For example, those built on or close to the former vicarage land were named after vicars of Keyingham - Robert Jellison, Ivor Griffiths and Melville Leffler. Others were named after men, such as Charles Etherington, Frederick Maude, John Russell and James Langdale, who had served the village well in a variety of capacities.

The new estates were built by local builders. Wilkinsons and Barkers were Hull firms. Coulsons came from Hornsea. Ben Hooson, who built Jellison Walk and The Woodlands, was a former porter/signalman at Keyingham railway station. When the railway was closed he used his redundancy money and his savings to set up as a building contractor. After building 17 houses in Keyingham and over 80 in Market Weighton, he made a reputation for himself in restoring 18th- and early-19th-century buildings in Hull, receiving awards from the Hull Civic Society for converting warehouses in High Street into flats and renovating houses in Prince Street and Worship Street.

Brian Dillon of Keyingham, in partnership with Charles Hunter of Patrington, built Compton Drive and houses in Ings Lane and Saltaugh Road. But it was the Keyingham firm of Howes & Clark that played the major part in the new development, building more than half the new houses of the 1960s and '70s. Jim Howes started his business with capital of £3.10s and a motorbike-and-sidecar to carry his equipment. The 'firm' consisted of himself and his labourer, Charlie

Whiting. Jim had a family background of building in Keyingham going back to the early part of the 19th century. His great-grandfather, Thomas Tuton, is listed in *Pigot's Commercial Directory* for 1834 as a bricklayer of Keyingham. Tuton's son and grandson, both named Wreathall, continued in the trade and it was the grandson who, in his later years, helped to supervise the extending of the Village Institute in 1953. His name with the date 1909 is signed on a rafter in the house, Hazeldene, in Main Street, and again in 1919 he scratched his name on the repaired sill of a clerestory window in St Nicholas Church. He later built the first bungalows in Church Lane. Wreathall Tuton junior had no children so the family building licence passed to his nephew, Jim Howes. Jim later formed a partnership with his brother-in-law, Maurice Clark, a man who served the community as both parish and rural district councillor. Howes & Clark had the distinction of taking down the spire of St Nicholas Church and also rebuilding the Church of St Margaret at Hilston that had been bombed during the war. The rebuilding of Keyingham's Methodist chapel in 1973 was their work. Jim Howes' sons, Ray and Barrie, continue the family building tradition as R and E B Howes. They, too, have built houses in Keyingham, including some in Osbourne Drive, Osbourne being their mother's middle name. When the rate of house building slowed in Keyingham it meant a reduction in work for local builders unless they had sufficient capital to invest in building-land elsewhere. At one time Howes & Clark employed 40 men on a permanent basis but today Keyingham's builders have few permanent employees and subcontract work, such as plumbing, plastering and electrical work to self-employed craftsmen.

At the same time as the new houses were being built, new shops were erected in Keyingham, three in Albemarle Road and a butcher's shop close by in Station Road. The butcher's shop was first occupied by John Hughes but in 1974 Philip Westmorland, who had once had the old butcher's shop in Main Street, bought it. It was later run by his son Michael, from whom it passed to Julian St Quinton in 1995 and then to the present owner, Graham Marshall in 1997. The shops in Albemarle Road were completed in 1965 despite objections that they would create two 'village centres'. All three shops were quickly occupied, the last being the shop at number 38, which Clifford Dunkerly opened as a grocery in April 1966. It was a time when supermarkets were still in their infancy, Clifford Dunn having opened the first one in Hull earlier in the decade, and Keyingham was easily able to support another grocer's shop in addition to Mrs Butler's and the Ounsworths' in Main Street. When Mr Dunkerly died in 1979 his wife Dorothy continued with the shop for a short while, before selling up. There were then two brief occupancies before Harry and Pat Boxall took over in 1982. They managed to survive the ever-increasing competition of supermarkets until 1994, when the introduction of a business rate of £800 on the shop, in addition to the council tax on the flat, caused them to sell up. As Pat said, a small shop has to sell a hell of a lot of beans to make up £800. Their departure left Keyingham Village Stores in Main Street as Keyingham's only grocery. There, Harish and Lata Chauhan survive by dint of hard work, long opening hours (6 a.m. to 9.30 p.m. Mondays to Saturdays, 7 a.m. to 9 p.m. on Sundays) and the provision of a delivery service.

Number 38 Albemarle Road is now the studio of the Holderness Performing Arts, which was started by Debbie Wastling, Donna Blackman and Helen Redhead. Debbie Wastling had begun teaching children all aspects of the performing arts in the Church Room in 1979. When she moved to Keyingham, she began teaching drama to her more dedicated students on a one-to-one basis at her home at Elm Tree Farmhouse. In the early '80s she set up a production company called Hull Musical Youth. This was a group of multi-talented children and adults that performed in big musicals, such as *Grease*, *Bugsy Malone*, *Chicago* and *Blondel*, all round the country. When the group disbanded in 1989 owing to lack of sponsorship and patrons Debbie formed the Holderness Performing Arts Guild with the assistance of Donna and Helen, two of her trainee student teachers. The three teachers each taught the performing arts in village halls in different parts of Holderness. When Debbie emigrated to America in 1995 she left the school to Donna, who changed the name to Holderness Performing Arts and set up the studio in Boxall's former shop where Donna and Helen teach singing, movement and drama to children and adults who go on to take examinations and perform in shows and competitions.

The shop at number 40 Albemarle Road was opened as 'Small Talk', which sold baby clothes. The owners were Irene and Stanley Kingette, an ex-trawler man, who had the shop for about two years. The shop was then bought by Mrs Elizabeth (Betty) Lambie who retained the name, but added knitting wool and women's fashions to her stock in trade. Knitting and sewing clothes for the family were still practical crafts that women enjoyed, and there was room in the village for a second shop selling knitting and sewing materials. In 1970 Mrs Val Coatham bought a shop on the north side of the Garth and opened it as 'Knit and Sew'. The premises had been Maurice Wilson's plumber's shop until Malcolm Bray, a builder, bought it in 1965, installed a shop window and started selling do-it-yourself materials. Despite the many new houses in Keyingham the venture did not flourish and Jan Overvoorde took over the shop to sell fruit and vegetables, including salads from his nurseries. The venture lasted until Val Coatham's purchase in 1970. Both 'Small Talk' and 'Knit and Sew' did well, and Betty Lambie stayed in business until about 1989 and Val Coatham until 1990. 'Small Talk' was bought by Malcolm Taylor and continued as a dress shop for a while. There was then a brief period when the shop was used as a sun-bed parlour, and then second-hand goods were sold at the shop before Malcolm converted it to a sweet shop and off-licence in 1995 after he had taken over the Boxall's licence. The business continues as such in 2000. At 'Knit and Sew' the new proprietor, Mrs Iris Ratcliffe concentrated more on the sewing side of the business, displaying her beautiful bridal gowns in the windows of the shop. The business closed in 1998 and the shop is due to be converted to a private garage.

Number 42 Albemarle Road began life as a sweet shop under the ownership of Charles Taylor, an ex-trawler skipper, who in 1955 had won Hull's Silver Cod Trophy, awarded to the skipper with biggest aggregate catch of fish in the year. The shop is called 'Carole's' after Mr Taylor's daughter. Mr Taylor had the shop for about two years, before it passed successively to two more ex-trawler men (it was a time when Hull's fishing fleet was declining as countries, particularly Iceland, extended their fishing limits, and the available fishing grounds dwindled). There were other short tenancies before Eric and Evelyn Headspith took over in about 1977 and added a newsagency to the business. In 1981 the present owners, Michael and Pat Beacock, bought the shop and it was during their time as proprietors that the shop was extended to give an area where cards and stationery are sold. A modern facility, lately provided, is the sale of National Lottery tickets.

- o -

The building of the new estates brought many new families to the village, mostly from Hull. Some came because of the ease of reaching the breadwinner's place of work at factories at Saltend or east Hull. At that time there was no Myton Bridge crossing the River Hull and, with river traffic far busier than it is today, there could be great delays in getting from one side of the city to the other when the existing bridges were 'up'. Add to this the fact that there were numerous railway level-crossings in Hull, almost all on the west of the river, and one can understand why many people chose to move east of the city. Other newcomers to the village came because they wanted to live in the country and, with building land cheaper and the rates lower than in the older established dormitory villages to the north and west of Hull, Keyingham was a less costly option.

Whatever the attractions of Keyingham the fact is that by 1971 its population had risen to 2,263, nearly treble its 1961 figure of 818. Since then building development and the rise in population have slowed: in 1991 the village had 2,522 inhabitants. It may be higher in 2001 because of the building of a few houses since 1991, although it is possible that the increase will be counterbalanced by the departure from the village of the grown-up children of the earlier incomers.

For those who worked in Hull there was a good choice of transport at the beginning of the 1960s. The railway was still operating, there were two companies running buses to Hull and practically every new house had the option of a garage.

(When a two-bedroom bungalow could be bought for as low as £2,000 a brick-built garage could be added for an extra £200-£300.)

On each weekday six trains (11 in summer), 20 East Yorkshire Motor Service (EYMS) buses and seven Connor & Graham buses stopped to pick up passengers at Keyingham on their way from Withernsea or Easington to Hull. The fares were 1s.9d by train and 1s.8d by bus (approximately 8.5p). Advertised journey times were from 26 to 30 minutes by train and 40 to 45 minutes by bus. For workers whose destination was one of the factories, such as Reckitts, east of the River Hull, the journey time was much shorter: it took only 17 minutes for the train to reach Southcoates Station on Holderness Road in Hull. For factory workers travelling to Hull there were three buses and one train leaving the village before 7 a.m. After that, for the office workers, there were two buses and one train that arrived at Hull before 8.45 a.m.

One mode of travel to Hull did not last long into the '60s. The Hull-Withernsea railway was one that Dr Beeching, head of British Rail, envisaged cutting in his effort to make the national system profitable. In 1962 a survey was made of the number of people using the Hull-Withernsea line. In the week ending June 23 only two or three people joined the 6.50 two-coach diesel as it trundled into Keyingham each weekday morning. At 8.05 a.m. the number joining was usually between 12 and 16, although on the Tuesday and the Friday around 20 people got on - Hull's two market days still had their attraction. There was no cheery stationmaster or porter to greet Keyingham's rail travellers as, by that time, the station platform was one of those on the line that was unmanned. Keyingham's official stationmaster was William Newby but he was also stationmaster at Hedon, where he lived. The guard on the train collected the fares. Previously tickets had been issued by the signalmen/porters at the ticket office. There is a story that John Harness, on his way to his work in Hull, collected the fares and issued the tickets before he boarded the train, leaving the signalman/porter free to operate the signals. In 1963 the staff at Keyingham consisted of two signalmen and five maintenance men. One of the maintenance men was William (Willam) Harness, who remembers that they were on a system of 'PBR' - payment by results. They were paid for the number of bolts they tightened, or the number of sleepers they had adjusted or the number of square yards of herbage at the side of the track that they had scythed. The last was a source of great amusement to Willam, as in his time as farm worker he had frequently been paid for mowing by the acre, but never in units as small as a square yard. Two of the staff had also been responsible for opening and shutting the level-crossing gates on Eastfield Road and Station Road. In 1955 and 1959, respectively, these had been closed permanently to road traffic, although farmers with lands or farmhouses to the north of the line had been allowed keys to the main gates. Pedestrians could still pass through the small side gates. For many years the gatekeeper at Eastfield Road was Elsie Hargrave, whose husband Harry was a track walker. His job was to walk the line from Ryhill to Wilmington station in Hull, knocking in the 'keys' that secured the line tightly to the sleepers. It was a contemplative occupation that greatly suited Harry. For one thing he could rehearse his lines for any plays the Keyingham Drama Group was presenting.

The 1962 survey showed the unprofitability of the Hull-Withernsea line. Although on sunny summer weekends Withernsea could expect over 3,000 people arriving by rail, the annual earnings from the line were only £37,000 whilst the costs were £78,000. Plans were made to close it. There were, of course, numerous objections. Keyingham Parish Council sent a letter of protest in July 1963. Private objectors pointed out the limitations of the bus services. The buses would not be able to deal with the weekend holiday traffic; they were not as comfortable as trains; they were inconvenient for the disabled; and they could not carry perambulators, invalid chairs or cycles. There were no bus shelters (it was not until 1974 that Keyingham had its two bus shelters). Keyingham folk pointed out that new houses (St Philips Road) were being built near the railway station and they would bring an increase in rail passengers. British Rail thought it extremely doubtful. An objector in Northfield said he was a 'good distance from the main road' and hence from the bus route. British Rail offered no comment.

Inevitably, the decision was taken to bring the Beeching axe to bear on the Hull-Withernsea line. A public meeting at Withernsea on 6 January 1964 and a special meeting called by Keyingham Parish Council on 9 September had no effect. On 19 October the line was closed to passengers and the following May to goods traffic. The rails were taken for scrap very soon afterwards and the old track became the ideal place to walk the dog or ride a horse. The stationmaster's house and the booking office survive as a private house, and on the west of Station Road can still be discerned the ramp to the cattle dock where cattle and sheep were held before being driven into cattle trucks. Nearby, a last fragment of the crossing gate is quietly rotting away.

One of the stationmaster's perquisites had been the right to sell coal delivered to the station. He sold it to the coal delivery men as well as to private individuals who came and collected their own.

Ray Thompson at the wheel of his cab, early 1999. Ray runs his transport business from the old station coal-yard. His father, Jack Thompson, took over the local coal deliveries in 1954 from Fred Harness who had delivered coal with a horse and rulley. Ray's work is mostly for local farmers and the greenhouse industry and takes him all over the country.

Photo: J A McLeod

The last coal man was Jack Thompson who took over from Fred Harness. Fred had delivered by horse and rulley, keeping his horse at the stables that still stand close to the old crossing gates. Jack used a motor lorry when he took over deliveries in about 1954. When the railway closed he continued to run the business from the station yard, collecting the coal by lorry from the West Riding. His son Ray succeeded him. The coal delivery business declined rapidly after mains gas was brought to Keyingham in 1987, and Ray changed to the haulage business, which he still runs from the old station yard.

The closure of the railway was compensated for by the bus services and the increased use of the car. As the number of cars rose the number of buses at peak periods fell (there were as many as five EYMS buses on the rush-hour runs in the 1960s).

Today the company runs 31 buses through Keyingham to Hull each weekday, seven of them reaching Hull before 8.45 a.m. The advertised journey times are exactly the same as in 1964. At the end of 1999 the single fare was £1.45. However, the car is now the favoured mode of transport. From a 10% sampling of Keyingham's population at the 1991 census it appeared that 84% of households owned at least one car. A limited survey (based on 98 replies received from questionnaires circulated to 300 households in Keyingham) conducted in 1998 by Matthew Rees for his geography coursework, showed that 86 of the 98 owned a car. Of the 12 who were not car owners, ten were retired. Matthew's figures indicated that in Keyingham 97% of the households where someone was working owned a car. More than a third of these households had more than one car. Some of the new houses built in Keyingham are provided with two garages and, although the Connor & Graham service is now defunct, (the last bus ran on 26 October 1996) there is no need for extra buses in the rush hour. What the journey time to Hull by car is in the rush hour we would not like to state.

The people coming to live in Keyingham's new houses in the 1960s were mainly couples with young families and one of the first consequences of Keyingham's rapid rise in population was the need for increased accommodation at the school. When William Butterfield was appointed headmaster of Keyingham school in 1952 the school was still small enough for the head to be able to remember the names of all the pupils. This was not to continue for much longer as the school grew quickly in numbers, and for nearly all Mr Butterfield's years as head, classroom space was to lag behind the number of pupils that had to be accommodated.

The first of the many additions to the school buildings was undertaken in 1958 when two large classrooms and a corridor were added to the original building. These classrooms had large windows and were light airy rooms. Storerooms were added and a new boiler house was built to provide oil-fired central heating, a much-appreciated luxury after the old open fires and stoves. In 1965, when the number on roll had risen slightly to just over 200 and the forecast was for a much more rapid rise, two more classrooms were added, and interior toilets, cloakrooms, a staff-room and a headmaster's room were built. By 1968 the school had outgrown these facilities. The regulatory daily assembly could not be held, as the old hall was no longer large enough to hold the whole school. The canteen facilities, still in a temporary hut, were inadequate, because, not only

were there extra pupils, but more mothers were going out to work and their children were staying for school dinners.

In 1968 a new school hall, kitchen and open-plan infant unit were built on the south side of the school grounds. This unit was quite revolutionary for its day and was designed to cater for the new teaching methods. It consisted of one large area, subdivided by screens, to house 90 infants, and two smaller open areas and one closed classroom. Although the new extension provided considerable further accommodation it was not long before the old canteen was in use as an extra classroom, and in 1972 it was necessary to erect two temporary classrooms in the orchard. When, in 1975, the number on roll had risen to 450 a further temporary classroom was added, giving a total of 13 classrooms. Classes were also being held in the corridors and the hall. In the canteen there had to be two sittings at dinner, and playtimes also had to be staggered. By this time a new infant school had been in the planning stage for five years. Sadly, Mr Butterfield, who had battled for nearly 20 years with ever increasing numbers of pupils and inadequate accommodation, never saw the plans come to fruition, although he had been involved in the early stages of planning. In June 1975 he died suddenly in the garden of his new home in Thorngumbald, where he had moved from the schoolhouse in preparation for his retirement. He had been very much involved in village life and was an active member of the parish council. The school lost a caring headmaster who negotiated the school through many changes in methods of teaching and systems of organisation and administration. His place as head teacher was taken by Mrs Rosalie Haxby, who had been deputy head and head of infants.

The long-awaited infant school in Russell Drive

was opened on 6 September 1977. Mrs Haxby became head of the new school and James Stead was appointed head of the junior school, numbering at that time about 270. The temporary classrooms at the junior school were removed, although the old canteen continued in use for some years as a scout hut and as the Humberside Leisure Services lending library. The new infants' school, which began with eight staff and 180 children, was of quite original design. Built round a sheltered courtyard with an open playground and grassed area on three sides and gardened approaches it was a far cry from traditionally built schools. The building consisted of an assembly hall, three teaching units and an administration area. By now it was being accepted that quiet areas were needed for learning, and each unit contained a closed classroom. But open-plan teaching was not yet to be relinquished and within each unit was a large area for more active learning and an area divided from this by a curtain. It was a plan that could lend itself to a variety of teaching methods.

During all these·changes in the school buildings there had been equally far-reaching changes in teaching methods. Although from the beginning of the century Keyingham's teachers had used observation and inquiry as part of the learning process, much of the basic teaching was by rote. After the constraints that had hit every walk of life during and immediately after the war came freedom - freedom of thought, action and way of life - and some educators began to question the restraints that had been put on children, the strict social rules they were expected to adhere to, the competitive element fostered in schools and the formality of organisation within the classroom. It was advocated that learning should be through experiences that were to be fostered and nurtured to bring about understanding. A child's confidence must be developed: no child must experience failure. This philosophy led to extensive changes in methods and organisation. Class teaching was abandoned and children were taught in social groups or as individuals. The role of the teacher changed to that of an enabler. Children were encouraged to develop at their individual levels according to ability and aptitude. No longer were children seated in rows of desks facing the blackboard or contained in one room for teaching. Instead, within a large open area there were smaller working areas for the various curriculum topics - a number area, a maths area, an art area etc. Teachers no longer sat at their desks with children coming to them and waiting in queues for attention. Instead, the teacher continually moved from group to group and from area to area. Quite a feat of endurance, both physically and mentally, as within a short period of time the teacher could be moving round four areas covering a variety of topics at many different levels of learning.

Anyone entering a classroom in those times would hear plenty of noise and see lots of movement, as children discussed with their peers the work being undertaken, or moved around the classroom in search of the materials they needed. Spelling and grammar went uncorrected because creativity was considered to be the important aspect in writing. Children did not struggle with the correct formation of letters as it was considered that this would inhibit the flow of the children's thoughts. Schools were quite autonomous establishments with each head devising the curriculum to be followed. Where no curriculum was given each teacher devised his or her own subject content. The result was very haphazard teaching patterns, a decided disadvantage when teachers, with widening job opportunities, were moving around the country with their work and ideas. There was no local consistency of method and curriculum content, let alone national consistency. The methods advocated meant that more resources were needed to provide children with the apparatus and equipment for learning. Young children were encouraged to develop mathematical concepts through handling mathematical apparatus, a sand tray and water tray being an essential part of every classroom, as was a Wendy house to develop social and role-play. Through play activities children developed the necessary motor, auditory, visual and intellectual skills necessary for learning.

Although informal methods were advocated, the teachers at Keyingham used what they thought were the good points of the old system whilst allowing for some of the freer thinking that the new system offered, and the children had a carefully structured programme in the basic subjects. Open-plan teaching was in its infancy and one wonders if there was any truth in the story that the system was used because it was cheaper to build schools without interior walls.

To help run the system teacher's aides were used and Keyingham was one of the first schools in the area to employ a teacher's aide who, under the direction of the teacher, undertook work with the children not requiring professional training. There was also a national recommendation that parents should be more involved in education and should be brought in to help in the classroom. At Keyingham parents helped to run the school bank, organised the library and made apparatus for use in the classroom. A change in the system for the teaching of children with special needs meant that Keyingham school was able to integrate into mainstream education those children who would formerly have been educated in special schools.

After the 1960s and '70s, years when the teachers at Keyingham had struggled to cope with inadequate accommodation, both schools began to be affected by the drop in numbers of pupils. School numbers had, in fact, reached a peak at about the time the new infants' school was opened. Thereafter they fell, as young families, where the fathers were employed at Saltend or the gas and oil installations at Easington, moved out of the village because the breadwinners were being re-located by their employers. By 1982 the number of children at the junior school had fallen to 200 from the figure of 270 in 1977. Rather than shortage of space there was now the problem of too much accommodation and over-staffing. For the first time the words, 'voluntary retirement' and 'redundancy', were to be heard in the teaching profession, and staff numbers at Keyingham had to be reduced on more than one occasion.

In 1991 a new entry system was introduced into the school. Previously the children had entered the school at the beginning of the *term* in which they attained their fifth birthday. This meant that there were three admissions per year - one at the start of each term. The alternative was an early-admissions policy, whereby children were admitted at the beginning of the school *year* in which they attained their fifth birthday. Keyingham school had kept the three-term entry in the hope that it might be allowed a state nursery school. However, the school was considered to be in too privileged an area for a state nursery school, so in 1991 it decided to adopt an early admission policy. This meant the intake of younger children, some of whom had just passed their fourth birthday, so that nursery-age children now had to be catered for.

A hotly debated issue arose in the village when the system of grant maintained schools was introduced at the end of the 1980s. A meeting of parents, governors, teachers, the local education authority and other interested bodies was held in the Village Institute where the case was put by the authority, the governors and the teachers that Keyingham schools should be grant maintained. This would have meant the schools becoming completely free from control by the local authority and receiving finance direct from the Government, with the schools setting their own budgets covering salaries, heating, repairs, equipment etc. All expenses would have come from the Government grant except the salaries of those who supported children with special educational needs. The governors, working with the head, would have held the ultimate responsibility for the school, with the participation of parents being encouraged through their presence on the governing body, which would contain teaching and non-teaching representatives. However, on a vote the meeting decided that the schools should remain under local authority control, which is how they continue today.

In the late 1980s the term 'National Curriculum' began to hit the headlines. Instead of schools working on their initiative and using their own methods, it was the Ministry of Education that prescribed the methods and curriculum to be followed by every school in the country. Goals were set for each year level and children were tested at certain ages. The new system was introduced into the infants' school in about 1988 with the first testing in about 1990. Modifications to the system are being continually made and at

Keyingham Junior School, Class of '99. The Year 5 children at work in the classroom that was added to the school in 1905.

Photo: J A McLeod

the turn of the century testing for three-years-olds at nursery schools is being introduced. In order to monitor standards the Government, through OFSTED, introduced a system of inspection whereby schools are assessed every four years by external assessors. The assessors' report is used to devise an achievements programme to improve the future development of the school. The first OFSTED inspection took place at Keyingham School in 1996. The wheel has thus come full circle. At the beginning of the 20th century and before, the fate of the school depended very much on the report of Her Majesty's Inspector, in that the size of the government grant was proportional to the ability and attendance of the pupils. In the year 2000 the fate of the school depends on the report of the OFSTED inspectors, whose arrival is no doubt awaited with as much trepidation as was that of the old Victorian inspectors. In the same way as the HMI reports were available to the public, so are the OFSTED reports, and it is heartening to read parts of the latest reports on Keyingham's two schools:

'Keyingham Junior School - Moral values are constantly reinforced and pupils have a good understanding of right and wrong, and conduct themselves well around the school. They show respect to each other and to adults working in the school, and they respond in a friendly and courteous manner to visitors.'

'Keyingham Infant School provides a very supportive and caring environment in which individuals are valued and respected. Pupils enjoy coming to school and this encourages positive attitudes to learning. The behaviour and attitudes of most of the pupils contribute positively to the life and ethos of the school. Pupils'

attitudes to work are good - they show an interest in their lessons and, in most cases, are attentive.'

In 1993, after 27 years of being involved in the education of Keyingham children, Mrs Haxby took early retirement from the infant school. For a term Mrs P Tweddle, deputy head, took over the running of the school until Mrs A Mawson became head teacher in January 1994. After four years in the post she also took early retirement and was succeeded by Mrs Sandra Edmiston, who is the head in 2000. Mr Stead who, like many of the staff of both schools, has given over 20 years' service to the education of Keyingham's children, continues as head of the junior school.

In the last century education in Keyingham has come a long way. In the early part of the 20th century, when Mr Jefferson was head of the school, he was no doubt happy to turn out pupils with a good grounding in the 3 Rs, although even in his day it was possible for the brighter scholars to take a scholarship and gain a grant to be educated in a town grammar school. In later years Mr Scruton encouraged children to progress not only to grammar schools but also to institutions like Hull's College of Commerce. Many Keyingham parents were proud of children who were able to obtain clerical posts rather than the low-paid farm-worker's or housemaid's jobs that they themselves had had. Today, those clerical workers take pride in the fact that their grandchildren have gone on to university and have a whole range of occupations and professions open to them. With the broadening of educational opportunities Keyingham's young people have been fortunate that many doors have been open to them, and we have people from the village today working in the fields of medicine, science, engineering, education, telecommunications and a diversity of other jobs and professions, not only at home but in every corner of the world.

- o -

In the same way that the school population rose in the 1960s, there was an increase in the number of children under school age, and in 1967 a number of young mothers, who had been teachers before they came to Keyingham, decided to form a playgroup to help prepare children for starting school. The founding members, including June Hudspith, Gillian King and Pauline Oliver, formed the committee to oversee the running of the group, which met one morning a week in the Village Institute. The first supervisor was Phyllis Sadler, a member of a long-established Keyingham family. She was assisted by other volunteers, who provided the refreshments, washed up and set out the toys for the children. Phyllis was succeeded by Sheila Mayes, under whose enthusiastic supervision the number of meetings increased to five half days a week, and a second supervisor, Margaret Easingwood, was appointed. By this time the funds, made up of the shilling or two received for each child at each meeting, were sufficient for the supervisors to be paid. Also out of the funds play equipment was bought, although a lot of toys were given and others were made. Ron Whincup made a Wendy house, for example. Different firms sent discarded stationery for use as drawing paper, and name badges for the children came from BP at Saltend. The children were usually admitted about a year before they were due to start school and in their last term were taken along to the infants' school for half a day. The playgroup continues today, with a paid staff of half a dozen ladies under the management of Sharon Towse. The group still follows the original

principle of providing a safe and secure environment where children can learn through play and learn to mix with others. There are now four half-day sessions a week, the fee for each session being £2.25, although children over four can receive free nursery education under the Department of Education and Employment scheme. The group is part of the Early Years Development and Childcare Partnership, introduced by the Government about three years ago, and works towards nationally agreed learning goals for pre-school children. It is subject to inspection by OFSTED. The sessions are still at the Village Institute, although during the term before the summer holiday one session per week is held at the infants' school.

In 1973 the Holderness Department of Adult Education was seeking to expand its community work and invited suggestions from some Keyingham residents on how this could be done. Mrs Doreen Rotherham suggested that a group should be set up whereby mothers with young children could have the opportunity to learn non-vocational skills whilst still having their children with them. The proposal was given a six-week trial, with Mrs Rotherham in charge of a group that met each Friday in the Methodist schoolroom. She helped both the mothers and the children with art and craft work, with the children working separately from their mothers. A lending library for both the parents and the children was begun with books provided by the East Riding Library Services. The trial was a success, and Mrs Rotherham continued the project for a year before returning to teaching. The group was supported financially by the Department of Adult Education. After Mrs Rotherham's departure the group does not seem to have lasted long, and in 1978 Mrs Maureen Drescher, the Humberside Health

Authority health visitor, suggested to some Keyingham mothers that a mother and toddler group should be formed. The result was the group that has lasted to the present time. It is officially named the Keyingham Mother and Toddler Group, although it is now open to fathers as well as mothers, and meets on Fridays in the Village Institute. It is less formal than its predecessor, the idea being for the parents to have a break, a chat and a 'cuppa' while the children play. The children have educational toys and role-play equipment, and there is a craft table where children and parents can be creative together. The group is self-supporting and is financed by the weekly fees of £1.30 per child and some fund-raising activities.

A professional child-minding facility became available in the village in 1988 when Sally Smith opened Chestnut Nursery. Sally had gained a qualification in family and community care but was disappointed with the kind of work that it offered and when her father, John, suggested she start her own nursery she jumped at the chance. John converted part of his electrician's workshop in Church Lane to a play room, and Sally began her venture with facilities for ten children. Today, Chestnut Nursery, run by Sally with the help of her mother and other trained helpers, can accommodate 15 children between the ages of one and five. The nursery's clients come from all points between Easington and Hull.

The increase in the number of children in the village led to calls for greater road safety measures, and in 1965 the education authority appointed the first crossing warden, Beatrice Duffy, whose duty

Chestnut Nursery, early 1999. Sally and Jean Smith (seated) provide professional childcare in Keyingham for children under school age.

Photo: J A McLeod

it was to conduct the children across the main road at the Ship Inn. Street lights were erected at the end of 1965 following a parish meeting in February 1964, at which the people of the village had voted for street lighting. Long before this, however, in 1930, the year that mains electricity came to Keyingham, the parish council had discussed the possibility of street lighting. In 1950 the council had asked the electricity board for an estimate for installing and maintaining 20 street lamps, but it was not until the village began to expand and new residents, used to town amenities, voiced their desires, that street lighting was finally introduced. A speed limit of 30 mph through the village was imposed in the 1970s. Requests from the parish council for such a measure began in May 1964. Earlier than this there had been a public meeting calling for a speed limit following the death of one child and the injury to another in two separate road accidents in the village. The outcome was the erection by the WI of signs saying, 'Spare Our Children, Drive Carefully,' at each end of the village. Later safety measures have included the introduction of the zebra crossing on Main Street near Station Road and the installation of speed cameras.

The requests for all the above measures were channelled through the parish council, which often had controversial matters to deal with. One which raised particular ire in the village was the use of the old Ken Hill gravel pit as a tip by council refuse-collection lorries. As the tip became filled to capacity, rubbish was blown across the village and littered the roads. It was said that prospective house buyers entering the village from the west saw the mess and promptly turned round and began looking elsewhere for a new house. Beginning in 1977 there were many protests, which the parish council had to direct to the appropriate authorities, but the nuisance persisted despite the erection of high wire-mesh fences round the site. It was not until the tip closed in 1983 that the problem was finally solved. Although a new tip was opened close by at Burstwick, as near to the village as the Ken Hill tip had been, there were few further problems thanks to the lessons learned at Ken Hill.

Ken Hill had been first opened up for gravel excavation in the 1940s. In 1942 Arthur Stanley Whittaker leased the site from the Church Commissioners, who had taken over the rectorial estate previously belonging to the Archbishops of York, and in 1945 the first gravel was sold. The pit was in constant use until 1973, when the plant was moved to the Mill Hill site. After that the Ken Hill pit was used for rubbish disposal by Humberside County Council until the closure when the site was grassed over. It is now used for grazing sheep. Mill Hill had been opened for gravel extraction by Mr Whittaker in 1951 and was used until 1964. Extraction began again after the closure of the Ken Hill pit. The Holderness Sand and Gravel Company, under the direction of Mr Whittaker's son, Stephen, continues to work the site. Some notable uses of gravel from the two sites have been for making concrete at the RAF radar station at Holmpton and the RAF station at Patrington Haven and repairing the sea-breaches at Spurn. In the 1980s, clay was taken from Mill Hill to raise ten miles of the Humber bank in order to protect Sunk Island from increasing sea levels and to make good deteriorating banks. Clay was later taken to improve the bank between Paull and Saltend.

- o -

The influx of newcomers to Keyingham had a great effect on the social activities of the village.

There were already a number of clubs and associations in existence. The Keyingham Women's Institute was formed in 1930, when it held its meetings in the Foresters Hall. In 1980, when the group celebrated its golden jubilee, three of the founder members - Kathleen Braithwaite, Nellie Lowther and Kathleen Stancer - were present. The Keyingham WI contributed to many village amenities. They paid for the bus shelter at Hill Top, the road safety signs at the approach to the village and the safety barriers at danger points along the footpaths. WI members helped during the early days of the baby clinic in the village and, when Gladys Cook started the Meals on Wheels service in 1968 during her presidency of the WI, the members were quick to volunteer their cars and their services. They sometimes had to do more than provide a meal. On one occasion a helper was greeted by a voice from the toilet saying, 'Can you pass me my knickers, please? They're warming in the oven by the fire.' New helpers visiting old Mr Branton in Main Street had to get over the initial surprise of hearing a wolf whistle when they entered the house. They only relaxed when they discovered that he had a mynah bird that was a remarkable mimic. The twice-a-week delivery of meals continued to be organised by Gladys Cook until her retirement in 1984. Soon afterwards she received the BEM for her many services to the community.

In the 1960s and '70s many of the newcomers to the village joined the WI and the membership reached over 70. Other newcomers got together to form a Keyingham Townswomen's Guild. At its formation in 1970 the TWG had more than 40 members, and the membership of the two women's groups was high enough for both of them to be viable. However, when membership began to decline owing to changing outlooks there was naturally competition for membership as well as for speakers. Each group had to pay for the cost of hiring a meeting place, so running costs were more than they need have been. Eventually the WI found difficulty in recruiting officers, and they met for the last time in 1996. The Townswomen's Guild, now with a membership of 12, including founder member Marcia Atkinson, continues to meet once a month and in the year 2000 celebrated its 30th anniversary.

The Keyingham branch of the Royal British Legion had a membership of about 120 in 1957. Meetings of the men's section were held monthly in the Blue Bell. The monthly meetings of the women's section were held in the Institute, where the annual dinner of the branch was held. The increase in Keyingham's population did not bring about a concurrent increase in the branch membership and, as recounted in a previous chapter, the men's section disbanded, although there is still a women's section.

In the 1950s, whist drives were popular in Keyingham as they had been for several decades. There was a travelling band of enthusiasts, who would play whist in Keyingham on one night of the week, in Ottringham on another night and in other villages on other nights. In Keyingham the venue was the small room in the Village Institute. However, the pastime declined in popularity and the most popular weekly gathering at the Institute came to be at the Wednesday-night bingo, which began in 1970. Bingo evenings were very successful, with people from all parts of South Holderness attending. With the profits the organisers were able to assist other Keyingham associations, such as the Darby and Joan Club, the Village Institute and the Good Neighbours. Bingo evenings continue at Keyingham but the attendance has declined to about 50.

The Darby and Joan Club was formed in 1963 by Violet Roydhouse, to whom the idea was suggested by the WVS of which Violet was a member. Barbara Gardner took over the running of the club in 1966 and, with the help of Dorothy Chilton, Celia Dunn, Joyce Eyre, Marjorie Kitchen and Freda Lanham, continues to organise the weekly meetings, the Christmas dinner, trips to the theatre and other outings for Keyingham's senior citizens.

The Good Neighbours was formed in 1965 by six couples, led by Geoffrey and Ivy Edwards. They realised that in the past when the village was small there had been a strong community spirit and much good-neighbourliness. They wanted this spirit to continue now that the village was growing. Their main aims were to visit the sick at home or in hospital, if they would otherwise be without visitors, and generally help the community, particularly the older members, in emergency or crisis. Other people were recruited to the Good Neighbours. They provided a nursery service, where children could be left for a while, shopped for the aged and infirm, did the washing for people temporarily incapacitated, looked after families when Mum was ill, or baby-sat if Dad had to visit Mum in hospital. They would visit the sick and sit up at night with people who were ill. They provided an emergency service for the elderly, who could, in the days before the telephone was so widely available, summon assistance if needed by placing a prominent yellow and red 'GN' sign in their window. In this the group was very ably assisted by David Westmorland the milkman and Vic Lanham the postman, who on their rounds would keep an eye open for the GN signs. Besides simply notifying the Good Neighbours, David and Vic usually found out what the problem was there and then, and it was not unknown for Vic to cycle round to the person's relatives, if they lived in the village, and tell them of the situation.

The Good Neighbours raised money with an annual nearly-new sale in order to provide everyone over the age of 65 with a food parcel at Christmas. Friends and relatives of the Good Neighbours gave clothes for the sale, and there were often some very good clothes at low prices. Ivy Edwards remembers a large lady coming to the sale and falling in love with a suit that was a real bargain, but which looked rather small for the customer. She and her friend took the suit into the fitting room to try it on. The helpers could not help but hear the struggling and heavy breathing and the conversation: 'I think I'll take it. The colour's lovely, and it will just do for Arthur's wedding.' 'Well, as long as you don't sit down or try to reach anything off the top shelf, you'll be all right.' Substantial sums were raised by the sales. In 1981, for instance, £400 was available for spending at the local shops on goods to make up the Christmas parcels. Much discretion was exercised in discovering who had reached the qualifying age to receive a parcel, and even with pointers from the postmaster and the doctor, there were some people who had to be asked outright. Mrs Edwards remembers plucking up courage to ask one lady, who replied, 'Don't worry, love. I'm only 70 but if there's owt going for nowt I'll ev it.' In the first year of the scheme 83 parcels were given out. By 1988 the number had risen to 157. Part of the increase was due to the fact that older people were coming to the village to live near their sons or daughters. Because of the increase, combined with the rise in prices of groceries and the fact that the members were realising they were beginning to provide parcels for folk younger than they themselves were, it was reluctantly decided to make Christmas 1989 the last one for the distribution of parcels. The following year the Good Neighbours disbanded, their role, but perhaps not the spirit, having been largely replaced by more official groups and bodies. The surplus funds of the group were used to buy a seat in the garden of rest in Keyingham cemetery.

As the Good Neighbours ceased another group began. Neighbourhood Watch had somewhat different objectives from those of the Good Neighbours but still aimed at bringing the community together. Following a national initiative a meeting was held in April 1989 with the result that a Neighbourhood Watch Scheme for the south side of the village was formed. The area beat officer at that time was PC Forth and he worked with Len Haxby, the area co-ordinator. In the months that followed a meeting was set up to assess the interest of people on the north side of the village with similar results and Dennis Green was elected area co-ordinator of Keyingham (North) Neighbourhood Watch. It was soon agreed that both areas should amalgamate. Villagers were asked to give a one-off donation towards Keyingham Neighbourhood Watch funds and the majority of houses joined the scheme. Signs were erected to indicate that Keyingham was a Neighbourhood Watch area and various steps were taken to make the homes of the elderly more secure. Neighbourhood Watch is a community care organisation whose objectives are to work with the police and villagers in order to maintain Keyingham as a pleasant village in which to live. It also acts as a support organisation for anyone needing assistance. It is an active group that meets monthly to be updated by the police on criminal activity in the area. Problems of the village and other matters of interest are also discussed. Events are held to make villagers more aware of personal and home security. A free Neighbourhood Watch magazine, *Keywatch*, is delivered bimonthly to every house in the village by about 35 volunteers. It acts as a means of communication between villagers and keeps people informed about village events. Advertisements and sponsorship from various sources finance the magazine.

The Keyingham Drama Group, formed in 1931 following a drama and literature course held in the village by Hull University College, had folded in 1956. With the exception of the war years, there seems to have been productions in all the years from 1931 to 1955. Performances were originally at the school. Then, following the success of *Home of the Chaine Folk* held outdoors in Festival of Britain year, two productions were held in a field belonging to Charles Patchett in 1952 and '53. The final production was in the newly extended Village Institute in 1955. Throughout those years, Harry Hargrave had been a leading figure as actor, producer, make-up man and painter of scenery. The arrival of new people in the village did not immediately bring about a restoration of the drama group, and it was not until 1979 that a new drama group was formed on the initiative of Joan England, landlady of the Blue Bell. Her advertisement for interested people initially aroused only the interest of Kay Dearnley, Marlene Whitelam, Rosalie Haxby and Sheila Storey, but others soon joined and the first production, *Happy Christmas Dear Edward*, was put on by an all-female cast in the Methodist rooms with no stage or stage lighting. After that the group grew, with the recruitment of men as well as women, and now has 16 members. They produce a play and a pantomime each year on the Village Institute stage. The group has bought lighting and sound equipment and has 'toured' some of the Holderness villages as well as Hull venues. The proceeds of the pantomimes are donated to various charities.

The earliest organised outdoor sport in Keyingham, other than when the Holderness Hunt met in the village or children's races were organised on treat days, was cricket. Although there was little opportunity for farm workers to play football when they worked on Saturday afternoons, it was possible for them to play cricket on weekday summer evenings. The first record of the cricket club occurs in September 1902 when the parish council gave it permission to use the Church Room, at that time called the Council Chamber, for a meeting. The month suggests that it was an end-of-season meeting and that the club was already in existence, rather than that it was a group of people contemplating starting up a new club the following season. The next we know of the club is from recollections of a team in the 1930s playing on Harold Lowther's field to the south of the present playing field on Saltaugh Road. The changing room can just be discerned on an RAF aerial photograph of 1946. Just after the war Keyingham fielded two cricket teams, the second one being of younger players brought together by the enthusiasm of Lionel Cartwright, a man who had moved to the village during the war and stayed on. In 1948 the first team won the Burstwick Cup for the first time in the club's history.

On match days the players' teas were provided by wives and mothers. They usually also had the task of laundering their beloved ones' flannels and were no doubt delighted when in 1952 the pitch was moved to the newly completed playing field from Harold Lowther's field which, when not being used for cricket, was used for grazing cows. The move was made before the official opening of the playing field in August 1952. Thereafter, the history of cricket in Keyingham is intermittent. There seems to have been difficulties in fielding teams in the 1950s, probably because, up to 1960, all young men had to do two years' National Service, and at some time between 1958 and 1960 the club disbanded. When the village began to expand, and with ending of National Service, there were more players to call on, and the club was re-formed in 1964. A photograph of the team of that period shows it to be made up of newcomers to the village and Keyingham folk, born and bred. In 1965 the club secretary and playing member was Trevor Salton, who had moved to Keyingham in 1963. At that time the team played on weekday evenings and Saturday afternoons. By the early '70s the club had once again folded, but by the end of the decade a local Sunday cricket league had been formed with teams from both the Ship Inn and the Blue Bell taking part. The Ship team did particularly well and won the league, which included teams from a wide area. In 1988 the playing field was extended to the east by renting the Marritt-Ombler land that had been part of the allotments, and a cricket square was laid out on the new ground. A few years later the Halsham cricket club, which played on Saturdays, had to give up their pitch in Halsham, and one of their members, Brian Foster of Keyingham, got permission from the parish council to use the Keyingham pitch. Members of the Halsham and Ship Inn teams re-laid the square and made a very good pitch, which was well maintained by Ken Shepherd under contract from the parish council. After two seasons the Saturday team was re-named the Keyingham and District Cricket Club and continued playing in the East Riding Amateur League. However, with cricket no longer being played at either of the local secondary schools, recruitment of new members practically dried up and in 1997 the club was disbanded. By this time Sunday cricket in Keyingham had become a little less competitive with the formation of a gentlemen's league in

which both the Bell and the Ship participated. Both teams, however, suffered a demise so that in 1998 there was no cricket in the village. The Blue Bell cricket team was re-started in 1999 after a one-year break. The team plays in the Gentlemen's League in competition with other pub teams on Sunday mornings in limited-overs games that leave ample time for a lunch-time drink and sandwiches provided by the pubs.

Tennis was available for some Keyingham residents from as early as 1911 when the *Hull News* reported the formation of a tennis club in the village. There were tennis courts at both Mount Pleasant and Bleak House up to the Second World War, and at Bleak House there was also a bowling green. Neither tennis courts nor bowling greens exist in Keyingham today, although there was a suggestion that the Garth should be made into a bowling green when the parish council bought it from the Church in 1978.

The earliest we know of a men's football club in Keyingham is a photograph of a team taken at the end of the 1925-6 season, although well before that time boys at the school were being encouraged to play football, and in 1912 the *Hull News* mentioned a concert being held in aid of the Keyingham Junior Football Club. It was not until 1920, however, when farm workers were granted Saturday afternoons off, that there were sufficient men available in the villages to make up regular teams and so form a league. It was not only farm workers who were released by the change for, up to 1920, other workers in the country worked longer hours than their counterparts in the town.

Keyingham Football Club, 1925-26. *The names were recorded by Vic Lanham as: Back row: Bob Tarbotton, Bert Dunn, Jack Thompson, ? Davey, Sid Gardner, Ted Roydhouse, E C Lawton. Front row: Tom Drury, Dick Howes, Jack Dixon, Ted Thompson, F Danby. Courtesy of Ces Gardner*

Patrington RDC roadmen, for instance worked until 4 p.m. on Saturdays whereas roadmen in the towns finished at midday. Keyingham's team was no doubt formed soon after 1920. The team, which won the South Holderness Cup in 1930 and '31, played in the South Holderness Association Football League, which was disbanded at the start of World War II. During the war occasional Keyingham sides were raised to play against military teams stationed in the area. In 1946 the club joined the South Holderness League on its re-formation. The league re-introduced its cup competition, and in 1948 Keyingham reached the final. They drew with Thorngumbald and shared the cup for the next year. By 1951 the club had joined the Church League, a Hull league originating in the early years of the century. In 1951 the team included Edwin (Ted) Roydhouse,

the only player remaining from the team whose photograph was taken in 1926. Playing alongside Ted in 1951 was his elder son John. Ted's second son Bruce later played for the team. There was a longer family connection with the team of 1926: one of the team members on the photograph was Sid Gardner, and both his son Ces and grandson Paul played for later Keyingham teams.

With other local teams joining Hull leagues in the early 1950s, and others disbanding, the South Holderness League folded in 1954, although the organisers continued with the cup competition, which Keyingham occasionally entered up to the 1960s with no success.

In the 1930s the football pitch was on the north side of Hull Road, opposite the last bungalows on the road to Hull. After the war the team played for a couple of seasons on one of Lawrie Grant's fields on the north side of Ottringham Road, before moving to Ings Field, south of the field where the cricket pitch was. The final move was to the village playing field after its opening in 1952. At that time there were no dressing-room facilities, and whilst the home team was able to turn up ready kitted out, the referee and away players, who mostly arrived by the service bus or bicycle, had to change in the Ship Inn or the vestibule of the Foresters Hall.

The team's progress at this time, with only a limited number of players to call on, was what might be called halting, particularly as National Service had to be completed by the younger players. The club seems to have disbanded by the early 1960s. With the expansion of the village, however, a new club was formed, playing football on Sundays. The club may have existed before Sunday football was recognised by the FA in 1965 because in March 1959 the parish council was discussing the question of the 'official use of the playing field on a Sunday'. In 1965 Hull Sunday Football League, which had been in existence unofficially for 15 years, was affiliated to the County FA. Keyingham joined Division 8 of the league, with players drawn mostly from newcomers to the village and from Patrington, where there were Saturday players who wished to play Sunday football. The club did not enter a team the following season but re-entered Division 8 in 1967 and thereafter, with only the occasional setback, progressed through the divisions and also won the Aldbrough Cup. By 1971 the team had reached Division 1 and the Premier Division in 1992. Teams do not necessarily have to win their division to gain promotion to the next, and can rise by more than one division, but in 1969 the Keyingham team was top of Division 7, and in 1986 won Division 4, in 1987 Division 3 and in 1992

Division 1. In 1969 a second eleven was formed, which started off in Division 14, won it and progressed to Division 5 by 1974. In 1999 the Hull Sunday League was divided into two districts, Wyke and Myton, and currently Keyingham's first team is in Division 1 and the second team in Division 3 of Myton District. The teams now have the benefit of a dressing room and floodlights for use in the evening training sessions, the erection of the standards for the floodlights being a novel addition to training sprung on the players by the coach one evening.

Like the old Keyingham Saturday team the Sunday football club has its long-serving members. Dave Thompson began playing for the second eleven in 1970 at the age of 15. He progressed to the first team and since 1988 has served the club as secretary or treasurer, and sometimes both. Paul Waites began playing for the club in about 1975 and was still playing at the start of the 1999 season. He and Kenny Harrison were instrumental in 1999 in forming a Keyingham Saturday football team. Paul's three brothers have all played for the Sunday side, and on occasions the four Waites brothers were in the same team. For one family's contribution to Keyingham soccer, it is probably a toss-up between the Roydhouse, the Gardner and the Waites families.

In 1964 a badminton club started in Keyingham, more by chance than as a result of a demand by the increasing population. A group that played at the South Holderness school included Dr and Mrs Wilkie, the only two members from Keyingham. It was in about 1964 that the group decided to move to the Village Institute and played on Tuesday evenings. However, there was soon a lot more interest in the game and by 1965 there were groups playing on Monday and Thursday evenings, the Thursday group having about 25 members. The

Thursday evening group has survived into the year 2000, though with reduced membership. A small group also plays badminton in the Institute on Thursday afternoons.

Horse riding has expanded greatly over recent years. In the days before the motor car there were many horses, besides working farm horses, kept in the village. Some were used for pulling tradesmen's carts, others for traps, but some were ridden. Ted Westmorland, who lived at Elm Tree Farm in Waldby Garth Road had a reputation not only as a rider, but also as a horse breaker. Apparently there was often great sport at his farm, lassoing either bullocks for his brother's butcher's shop or horses for breaking in. In the years either side of, and during, the Second World War a gymkhana, attracting horse riders from all round the district, was held at Keyingham. In the early 1950s nearly £1,000 was raised by the event towards the cost of extending the Village Institute. By 1957 the gymkhana had come to an end. At the start of the '60s there was accommodation for a few riding horses at the old stables near the former railway station. Since then, there has been an increase in stable accommodation with land to the north of the Old Mill being divided into paddocks and stables built on them. There are now about 25 horses kept in the village for pleasure riding.

Before 1983 no organised rugby of any kind had been played in Keyingham. It was in that year that Mike Bullock, the new landlord of the Ship Inn, started a Rugby League club. He was a former player and together with Peter Giddings began training sessions on Sunday mornings with local

Mill Hill stables, January 2000.
Alison and Laura Smith 'mucking out' the new stables. Horse riding has become a popular pastime in Keyingham in recent years.

youngsters. After signing on five former soccer players a team, the 'Ship Inn', was formed, playing on Sunday mornings. After a year Mike Bullock moved on and his place as landlord was taken by Kevin Harvey, another Rugby League enthusiast. He merged the team with one from the Crooked Billet at Ryhill and the team began to play in the Hull & District Amateur Rugby League on Saturdays. Under the coaching of Joe Tripp and then Dave Chester it became one of the leading amateur sides in the area and progressed from Division 3 to the Premier League. The team included a number of former professionals and brought to the fore players like Steve Morrod and Dean Ralph who both gained international recognition in the amateur code. Today, with the departure of interested Ship Inn landlords, the team is known as Keyingham Rugby Club.

It is thanks to the rugby club that Keyingham can boast first-class changing facilities at the playing field on Saltaugh Road. The building of the changing rooms, which began when the team was preparing to enter the Saturday Rugby League, is another good example of voluntary effort and local fund-raising in Keyingham. Water, electricity and sewage disposal had to be laid on with most of the work being done by members of the club. The basic structure consists of two former prefabricated bungalows with two subsequent extensions. Together they contain two changing rooms, a weight-training room, a shower area, kitchen and toilets. They provide facilities not only for the rugby team but also for the soccer club. Floodlights were erected round the rugby pitch to facilitate evening training in the winter months. It was probably the success of the rugby club that

Keyingham Vikings Under 12s, 1998. Back Row: James Kennedy, Samuel Barker-Platt, Steven Norris, Joe Taylor, Marc Clark, Jamie Walton. Front row: Karl Beardshaw, Simon Wilson, Ian Hudson, Oliver Miskin, Ben Purdue, Andrew Taylor.... and this was when they had lost!

Photo: Paul Beardshaw

sparked off the formation of the junior teams, although there is no official connection between the two. In 1991 two parents asked Joe Tripp if he would coach a group of lads and start a village team. After some training a team was formed and, in borrowed kit, played its first game against Orchard Park, a team from North Hull. So Keyingham Vikings were born. Within a few years and with help from Wayne Smith, Gary Beacock and Paul Beardshaw, more teams in different age groups were formed, so that by 1996 the club was fielding six teams, including an under-14 girls' team. The object of the club is as much one of character building as of producing rugby players and, although the different teams have won a number of trophies since their formation, their proudest achievement was the award to the club of the Humberside Fair Play Trophy in 1997. There is a policy of giving a game to all those committed enough to pay their subs and turn up for training, rather than producing teams of stars.

Unfortunately it has resulted in some of the improving players moving to clubs of a higher standard, and at the start of the 1999 season the club fielded only four teams. The club, now called Holderness Vikings, has support from local sponsors, but the chief sources of finance are the players' subscriptions and the proceeds of draws run by the club. This income has allowed the club to provide kit for the players and also to erect Portakabins as changing rooms.

Keyingham's two public houses were the natural meeting places for the officials, selection committees etc. of the different clubs and associations. Before the expansion of the village in the 1960s both pubs were simple affairs. Both had a central passage opening from the front door with one or two rooms, including private rooms, at either side. Both pubs served their beer from barrels standing near a hatch opening into the passage. The landlady at the Ship Inn was Mrs Bertha Elmsley-Midgley who had been the

The Ship Inn, circa 1950. - when Mrs Bertha Elmsley-Midgley was the landlady
Photo: S Maddra

licensee since the mid-1930s. She was a member of the Linsley family of Linsley Breweries who at that time owned the pub. Her son was killed in the Second World War and his name is on the war memorial. At the Ship there was only one public room, on the right of the passage and about ten foot by eight foot in size, although overflow customers could be accommodated in Mrs Elmsley-Midgley's private parlour. The regulars had their own seats and woe betide anyone else who occupied one of them. One regular customer was Rev Harold Horrox who called every Monday lunchtime for his weekly ration of 200 Craven 'A' and stayed supping Guinness until the afternoon closing time. At harvest time Irishmen engaged on the farms in the Marsh were regular customers, and ten Irishmen drinking ten pints each a night could considerably increase the profits. Pig-men also came in direct from work and as there was always a roaring fire in the room whatever the weather they could cause the gradual exodus of the other customers.

Shortly before Mrs Elmsley-Midgley gave up the licence the Ship was altered. The parlour and small room on the left of the passage, where the barrels had been stored, were made into a new bar, and inside toilets were built to replace the ones that had stood close to Saltaugh Road (the gents' toilet had no roof and users were easily visible from passing double-decker buses). In 1966 John (Gig) and Muriel Hart took over the running of the pub until 1968 when George Marshall became the licensee. By this time the village was beginning to expand and, with the help of his wife Ena, George ran a very successful establishment until the couple retired in 1982. During their occupancy further extensions were made to the Ship. The Marshalls were followed by a number of fairly short-lived tenancies, two of which have been mentioned in connection with the rugby club. In May 1999 Alan Platten became the manager and the Ship has since been extensively renovated inside and out.

In 1960 Jack Burrell had just become the landlord of the Blue Bell. Like most village pub landlords of those days, he needed a second occupation in order to make a living and he was senior representative for a brick making company at Gilberdyke. He was succeeded in 1965 by Austin Clappison whose second occupation was farming at Marsh House. Austin and his wife Dorothy managed the Blue Bell until 1977, during which time it was modernised. Further improvements were made during the time of Joan England in the 1980s. Besides hosting the meetings of the different sports clubs and sponsoring others, both the Ship and the Bell had their own organised sports. Both had tug-of-war teams and both had darts, although George Marshall at the Ship stopped having darts teams in order to give casual players more opportunity to play. At the Bell darts flourished greatly as the village expanded. When Austin Clappison became landlord there was only one team based at the Bell. When he left there were eleven teams, including four women's teams, playing on three nights of the week. Today the Bell, run for the last five years by David and Pauline Stiggants, has six darts teams - two men's, three ladies' and one mixed - as well as two pool teams. At the Ship there are two men's darts teams, one women's team and a pool team.

There have been many regular annual events that have come and gone in Keyingham over the last century - the Sunday school outing, the annual sports, the gymkhana, the pig roast of the 1970s, to name but some. Two events that have become established in the Keyingham calendar are the village show and the Keyingham Gala. Keyingham

WI inaugurated the Keyingham Village Show in 1978. The committee consisted of 17 people who were responsible for the organisation and administration of 79 classes covering vegetables, fruit, flowers, wines and beers, cookery, handicrafts, floral art, jams and preserves and a children's section. Thirteen cups and trophies were presented. The show quickly established itself as one of Keyingham's annual events and in 1999 celebrated its 21st birthday. As interests have expanded or changed, classes have been extended and 100 classes are now staged, and the number of cups and trophies has risen to 19. Among the 31 on the present committee are four of the original members - Ann Braithwaite, Jean Overvoorde, Yvonne Stone and Rob Brown.

The Keyingham Gala was the idea of John and Edith Edmands who realised that Keyingham was one of the few local villages without its gala. With the help of Paul Field and Ernie Oldfield they organised the first one in 1991. Held every August, the gala has continued to the present time. John, Edith, Paul and Ernie are still involved in what is a popular event. The preparations by the strongly committed members of the committee begin each February. Proceeds of the gala are donated to groups within the village.

- o -

In June 1977 the silver jubilee of Queen Elizabeth II was celebrated. Since Elizabeth's accession the population of Keyingham had almost trebled and two thirds of the village could be said to be newcomers and they were well represented on the 25-strong committee established to organise the celebrations in Keyingham. However, the committee still contained many who had lived in the village before the building of the new houses. Two of them had been on the coronation committee 24 years earlier. Money to finance the celebrations was raised in a number of ways, including a jubilee prize draw and a ladies-versus-gentlemen football match on the playing field on the Easter Monday at which a collection was taken. In all, over £1,000 was raised.

The celebrations lasted three days, beginning on Sunday 5 June, when there was a special church service in the evening. A parade, which included the British Legion and the boy scouts, led by the Salvation Army band, marched from the school to the church. The church was packed, with every seat occupied, including the Sunday school children's chairs and 30 extra ones brought from the Institute on Ray Thompson's lorry. After the service the congregation proceeded to the war memorial where the newly carved figure on the column was dedicated. The following day was the Spring Holiday, which culminated with the lighting of bonfires all over the country to coincide with the one lit at Windsor at 10 p.m. Unfortunately, Keyingham's bonfire remained unlit owing to two days of rain.

The main celebrations took place on the Tuesday. In Keyingham in the morning there was a boys-versus-dads soccer match, where the dads were at a decided disadvantage in not being allowed to wear football boots in wet conditions. All the same, a three-all draw was neatly contrived by a referee with loyalties to both sides. After that souvenir mugs were distributed to the children of the village. In the afternoon there was a tug-of-war competition, children's sports and fancy dress. The prizes were presented by Susan Thompson, the Jubilee Queen. In the early evening there was a tea for the senior citizens at the Village Institute and a disco (music by Slipped Disc Oh) and Fred Duffy's pig roast on the playing field. The last official event of the day was the Jubilee Disco in the Institute with music by Kinetic Energy.

The war memorial, June 1977. To celebrate the silver jubilee of Queen Elizabeth II, the Keyingham British Legion commissioned a new statuette of a World War II soldier to grace the memorial column. It replaced a cross that had surmounted the memorial in place of the original figure of a World War I soldier that had suffered damage.

Courtesy of Kevern Thompson

Five years after the jubilee there were celebrations of a different kind when three Keyingham men who had served in the Falklands war returned safely to the village. The celebrations were part of a gala held on 14 August 1982 to raise money for the South Atlantic Task Force Fund, which was to provide support for the families of those killed or injured during the war. The driving force behind the Keyingham event was Rodina (Dena) Wood whose son Nicholas was serving on the aircraft carrier Hermes. Ex-RAF man Jim Rowe, who served on the parish council at the time, was chairman of the organising committee. The gala was held in the centre of the village - in the Village Institute, and on the Blue Bell car park and the Garth, which at that time had no shrubs or trees on it. The weather was fine and, following a giant jumble sale and refreshment stalls run by the WI in the morning, the afternoon events were begun by Captain Garnons-Williams RN, the local organiser of the South Atlantic Fund, presenting inscribed tankards to Nicholas Wood, Ron Whincup and John Lilley. Ron had served on the North Sea Ferries vessel Norland, which had been commandeered for the campaign and manned by North Sea Ferries volunteers. John, who like Nicholas was in the Royal Navy, had been seconded to serve as wireless operator on another ferry vessel, Stena Seaspread. The afternoon was a great success with the Humberside Majorettes, plenty of stalls, a coconut shy, 'drench the wench', swings, children's rides, a 'lunar walk' and a wheel of fortune. The events in the Institute were accompanied by the playing of favourite tunes from World War II by Mrs Gladys Beadle on a particularly fine organ loaned by Gough & Davy of Hull. In the evening Mrs D J Richardson, the Mayor of Holderness, opened the 'Grand Variety Show' in the Institute, where it was standing room

only for latecomers. The show ended with *Land of Hope and Glory* sung 'magnificently', as a local diarist noted, by Maureen Van Bruggen standing in front of a huge Union Jack, before the National Anthem was sung and the audience departed. The whole event, together with door-to-door collections made by the youth club under the direction of Dennis Roe, made £1,050, which was later presented to Captain Garnons-Williams at a ceremony at the Blue Bell. At the same time Joan England, the landlady, presented a cheque for £75 raised at a Caribbean evening held at the pub.

- o -

Keyingham's rise in population brought about an increase in attendance at both church and chapel. At the Anglican church Mr Horrox, who had charge of only the one parish, conducted three services each Sunday. Communion was held at both the morning services and a record was kept of the number of communicants on each occasion. In 1963 the total number of people taking communion during the year was 761, the average for the years 1960-63 being 757. In 1964 the number was 1228 and in the following year 1458. In two years church attendance had almost doubled. 1965 represented the peak for the number of people taking communion at St Nicholas. At the midnight service on Christmas Eve that year 140 communicants were recorded. After Mr Horrox's retirement there began to be a shift in emphasis in the type of service, with some of the morning communions being replaced by family services, and it is difficult to make a statistical comparison of the trend in church attendance immediately after 1966. Today the church registers of services record the total attendance as well as the number of people taking communion. As for nearly everywhere else in the country, attendance has declined over the last 30 years, and at the midnight service on Christmas Eve 1999 the number taking communion was 39.

It was during Mr Horrox's incumbency that Keyingham had its first woman churchwarden when Kathleen Stancer was elected as people's warden in 1960. Miss Stancer was a very retiring person and only accepted the position because the previous people's warden had left the village. She no doubt gladly gave up the post when Geoffrey Edwards became available the following year. There had been an occasion earlier in Mr Horrox's time when a woman churchwarden was elected in Keyingham but, because of objections, she had had to stand down. This occurred at the annual vestry meeting in 1948 when Mrs Brenda Lawson was elected. However, she lived in temporary accommodation near Crawshaw, and so was not counted as a householder and therefore not entitled to stand for election. Alfred Goundrill was chosen in her place. It caused a minor storm in the village with complaints about how the electoral roll was compiled. The storm rumbled on for two years before the Bishop of Hull called a meeting in September 1950 in order to restore calm.

Harold Thompson Horrox vicar of Keyingham, 1939 to 1966. In 1951, he wrote a pageant, Home of the Chaine Folk, *a Keyingham celebration of the Festival of Britain. He was a member of the Civil Defence Movement and the Home Guard during World War II.   Courtesy of Denis Rourke*

Mr Horrox retired as vicar of Keyingham in 1966, although he and his wife continued to live in the village. He was succeeded by David Edward Ashforth, a young and energetic man, during whose six-year stay many changes in worship and of a practical nature took place. He introduced the family service at which he used a glove puppet, 'Freddy', to help put over his message to children. He ran discos for teenagers in the Village Institute, and it was on his initiative that the scout and cub groups were begun in Keyingham. Up to that time there had been no scout or cub pack in the village, although in 1959, Joan McCurdy and Barbara Cobb had started a brownie pack which had a consistently high membership of about 24 girls. Later, Elva Whincup was able to form the Second Keyingham Brownies, which had quite a long existence until falling numbers reduced the Keyingham brownie representation to one pack. An attempt to found a guide company in Keyingham initially failed, but in 1969 one was formed under the leadership of Alma Stretton. A second company was later begun by Ann Webb but it was short-lived. By this time a cub pack had been formed following a meeting chaired by Mr Ashforth. Elaine Phillips and Barbara Dale agreed to run the pack, and 24 boys joined. Soon it was possible to expand and by 1973 there were two cub packs as well as a scout troop with John Fairbank as group scout leader. At one time, in the early 1980s, the village had two brownie packs, two cub packs, two guide companies and a scout group. The position in 2000 is that there is one brownie pack, with a full complement of 28 girls, and a guide company of 14 girls. There is a very active troop of 14 scouts under the leadership of Ian Spencer and, although there has been no cub pack in the village for three years, there is an arrangement whereby Keyingham lads are encouraged to join the Burstwick pack with the cubs from Burstwick progressing to the Keyingham scouts.

Over the years many parents have helped with the children's organisations, either as uniformed leaders or as unit helpers. Many have given long service, including Barbara Dale, Geraldine Moor and Norman Staniforth with the cubs, John Kirkwood and father and son Bob and Tony Bell with the scouts, Joan Bell, Pauline Boynton, Jennie Redhead, Jean Smith and Elaine Sparks with the brownies, Sheila Tindall and Lynne Malinder with the guides, and Val Duffy with both brownies and guides. For her services to guiding Val Duffy has recently been appointed one of the vice-presidents of the Guide Association of the East Riding. The commitment of the leaders and their helpers has meant that over the years the different groups have benefited from weekend camps and pack holidays in many parts of England, and in the year 2000 the scouts are planning to go to Poland.

One of Mr Ashforth's last contributions to village affairs came after he heard that someone was leaving the village because there was nothing to do here. He suggested the publication of a newsletter to let people know just how many groups and events there were in the village. The first issue of the *Keyingham Newsletter* was in February 1973 the month that Mr Ashforth left the village and, in it, it was pointed out that there were some 20 organisations in Keyingham. All that was lacking was a means of notifying people of their existence and activities. Hence the newsletter, which would be issued monthly and would print articles of interest and a diary of forthcoming events. With only a short break in 1982, the *Newsletter* continued to be published until September 1986. In the days before cheap photocopying the *Newsletter* was printed by

duplicator, initially hand operated, but later by one electrically operated. The 850 copies were delivered free to every household in the village by 25 schoolchildren. The production was funded by annual subscriptions from the village organisations, initially of £1, but later £2.50. The function of the *Newsletter* has now been taken by the Neighbourhood Watch magazine *Keywatch*.

On the practical side of church affairs Mr Ashforth drove forward the removal of the church spire, the clearance of gravestones to one side of the churchyard and the building of a new vicarage. Cracks had been noted in the church tower, and glass tell-tales, placed there at the architect's direction, showed that there were definite signs of movement. The spire had to be taken down. There were suggestions that it should be replaced with a lighter copper or fibre-glass spire, but in the end costs dictated that the tower should be simply covered with a flat roof and finished off with a parapet and that the work should be in concrete and not in stone. The scheme cost about £2,500. Except for a grant of £150 from the York Diocesan Board of Finance, all the money was raised locally by numerous events and appeals. Mr Ashforth proved a great fund raiser and it was during the appeal that covenanted giving was introduced. The work, in which about 100 ton of stone was removed, was carried out in 1969.

The gravestones were moved preparatory to the parish council taking over the care of the churchyard. Before removal the vicar's wife, Joan Ashforth, made a careful record of the original position of the stones and their inscriptions. The inscriptions have been published by the East Yorkshire Family History Society. The task of

The removal of the church spire.

Above: View from the north, early 1969. Note the stumpy appearance of the spire after the repair of 1931.

Top right: View from the east, 1969. The spire in the course of removal by Howes & Clark.

Bottom right: View from the north, January 1976.

moving the stones to the south side of the churchyard began in 1967 and was carried out by church members and anyone else Mr Ashforth could recruit. A start at pulling out some of the gravestones was attempted using a tractor borrowed from David Beadle at the adjoining Church Farm. However, the tractor became stuck and Ray Thompson, the coal man, was called in. He offered to do the job with a large machine used for loading coal, on condition that the vicar would marry him or bury him, whichever came first, 'for nowt'. A bargain was struck and Ray pulled the stones out with his machine. Two years later Ray married Edwina and asked Mr Ashforth for the return of the fee. As he handed it over, David Ashforth nodded towards the box appealing for donations for the spire-removal fund. Despite his strong Yorkshire instincts, Ray put the money in the box.

The Victorian vicarage, designed for large families and attendant maidservants, was far too big for David and Joan Ashforth. The old vicarage was pulled down and a new house built on the site. Some of the grounds and the stable block were sold off. The stable block was incorporated into the new property built next door, and Griffiths Way and Melville Close were built on the former grounds by Howes & Clark. During the building of the new house 17 Marritt Way was bought for use as the vicarage.

David Ashforth resigned the living at Keyingham to become chaplain to the University of London. He was succeeded in 1973 by John Yates, a gentle man, who had spent 25 years of his career in South Africa, ministering to the black population. He introduced a midweek communion into the church's programme. He himself went up to the church every day to conduct the daily office. It was during his ministry that the oak panelling at the front of the altar was made by Clive Guy. A few years previously Clive had made the panels and doors to the vestry, the doors being dedicated to the memory of Mr Horrox. John Yates was nearing retiring age when he came to Keyingham and at the end of July 1975, two years after his arrival, he conducted his last service here. He and his wife retired to Kegworth in Leicestershire.

Geoffrey Owen Wilbourne, was inducted in April 1976. It was during Mr Wilbourne's incumbency that the Church Room, which had served the village in many capacities for 140 years, was restored and extended. The room was in a dilapidated condition, with rotting doors and wainscot and corroded metal window frames. The driving force behind the restoration was Kathleen Charlton, ably assisted by Robert (Bob) Bell, one of the churchwardens. They enlisted the help of Community Industry, a body that used otherwise unemployed youngsters to do the work under the direction of trained craftsmen. The result was the outline of the building that we have today, with its two toilets and a kitchen added to the simple rectangle of the original building. One of the most laborious tasks during the restoration was re-fitting nearly 800 diamond-shaped pieces of glass into the cast-iron window frames. An outstanding feature of the Church Room, on its reopening in October 1978, was the sculpture of the Dove of Peace on the north wall executed in fibreglass and resin by Kathleen Charlton's husband, John. In 1998 and '99 more improvements were made. The Church Room was re-roofed and gas central heating and new kitchen facilities were installed. The room is now a very comfortable meeting place, one of its uses being for the regular Thursday morning 'Pop-in' organised by members of St Nicholas Church.

The Church Room before and after its refurbishment in 1978. The pictures show the original (1835) cast iron window frames. The poor state of the wainscotting can be seen in the first photograph. The sculpture on the north wall executed by John Charlton in 1978 can be seen in the second photograph.
Photos: Mrs F K Charlton

During Mr Wilbourne's term as vicar the piece of glebe land at the junction of Station Road and Waldby Garth Road was sold to the parish council with the condition that it should not be used for building. Previously the rent from the land had contributed a small amount towards the vicar's salary, and in the '60s had had pigs on it. Since being taken over by the parish council it has been grassed and planted with shrubs and trees and is now known as The Garth.

Geoffrey Wilbourne was the last vicar to preside over Keyingham as a single parish. Even before he moved to the parish of Hemingbrough in October 1985, plans had been drawn up to unite the parishes of Halsham, Keyingham, Ottringham and Sunk Island into a single benefice. It was as rector of this united benefice that Ian R S Walker arrived in March 1986. Until Sunk Island church was closed in June 1988 Ian had four churches in his care but even with three it was difficult to fit in services for each church every Sunday. Fortunately for the benefice Ian's wife Susan was a deacon, and with her help it was possible to have a Sunday morning service at all three churches. Susan later became a priest and was amongst the first group of women priests ordained at York Minster in May 1994. During Ian Walker's incumbency the election of women churchwardens became a regular affair. Eileen Holmes became a churchwarden in 1988 and she has been followed by many other women who, like their male counterparts, have put a lot of their time into fund raising and keeping the church in good repair. In particular, St Nicholas owes a debt of gratitude to Denis Rourke, who after some years as churchwarden continued to serve the church as odd-job man, guardian of the fabric and clerk of works whenever any major repairs were needed.

Despite his busy Sunday morning schedule, Ian Walker reintroduced evensong with some success.

His duties were increased when he was appointed rural dean, which amongst other things meant that on occasions he had to take services in other churches in the South Holderness Deanery when they were without a minister. He must have perhaps felt some pangs of envy for the Keyingham parsons of earlier in the century who had the cure of only one parish with a fifth of its present population and a far higher percentage of churchgoers.

Ian and Susan Walker conducted their last service at Keyingham on 24 May 1998 before they moved to Scartho near Grimsby. Ian has the

Ian and Susan Walker at their farewell service, 24 May 1998. Ian Walker was Keyingham's last incumbent of the millennium and also served the cures of All Saints, Halsham, and St. Wilfrid's, Ottringham. Susan was one of the first women ordained into the Anglican priesthood.

distinction of being Keyingham's last incumbent of the millennium. At the start of the year 2000 the benefice is without a rector. However, the village is fortunate in that Rev Bill McLaren, former rural dean and vicar of Hedon and Paull, has 'retired' to Keyingham and has maintained a full programme of Sunday morning and Wednesday morning services during the interregnum.

Primitive Methodism had been strong in Keyingham from before the start of the 20th century. In 1950 it was one of only three chapels in the Patrington Circuit to have services both Sunday mornings and evenings. In 1952 the membership increased slightly following amalgamation with the Wesleyans. With the expansion of Keyingham in the 1960s, there was an increase in chapel attendance, with the Sunday school having about 80 scholars and eight or nine teachers in charge. For most of the '60s Rev Ronald Brierley was the circuit minister. He was a forward-looking man and when David Ashforth arrived as vicar of St Nicholas Church in 1967 there were soon moves to have united services, culminating in a joint communion service of Methodists and Anglicans in the parish church some time before Ron Brierley left in 1969. Since that time there have been many services where Methodists and Anglicans have worshipped in each other's church.

The larger congregations of the late 1960s prompted the move to have the chapel enlarged, and the plans were set in motion in 1972. The building was extended to the north by the erection of a foyer projecting about 12 foot. The original entrance in Ings Lane was blocked and the tower that had stood above the entrance was taken down. A new, imposing gable was added to the north end of the old chapel and the interior was rearranged so that the congregation faced south instead of north as they had done previously. The architect was Bernard W Blanchard who had designed the Methodist chapels at Willerby, Hunmanby and Willerby Road, Hull. Substantial financial support came from the Joseph Rank Benevolent Trust. The new chapel was opened in July 1973 with £5,000 of the total cost of over £26,000 still owing for the rebuilding and the installation of an electronic organ, which took place at the same time. The debt was soon paid off following a vigorous fund-raising campaign.

Over the years Keyingham's Methodists have formed a number of groups welcoming people of all denominations. As early as 1941 Gladys Cook formed the Women's Bright Hour on the suggestion of Mrs Ablett and Mrs Waller from Lincolnshire, who were staying in Keyingham during the war. In the early days there were only about seven or eight women in the group, but today the membership is about 45. They meet every Thursday afternoon. In 1954 Maureen Precious began a youth club under the auspices of the Methodist Association of Youth Clubs. The club was open to all youngsters in the village and there were 18 members at the first meeting. There were plenty of outdoor activities and with help from Norman Clark and Joh Overvoorde it was a successful venture. In 1961, Maureen's mother, Gertrude Precious, started the Young Wives, which met in her home. About ten years later the meetings were moved to the chapel room, with some of the Methodist women members looking after the young wives' children.

Soon after the rebuilding of the chapel the idea of welcoming newcomers to the village with flowers was introduced. The scheme was run in conjunction with the Anglicans although the organisation was almost totally a Methodist affair. Two Methodists, Len and Madge Clark, ran the post office and were able to note new householders very promptly. Flowers were bought out of church and chapel funds and someone would take them to an often surprised but delighted new resident. One of the chief bearers of flowers was Anita Wakefield until failing health caused her to resign in 1983. The scheme has since been discontinued, mostly owing to the greater size of the village and the rate at which houses change hands.

Although in the early days of Methodism women had played a part as local preachers, by the time the Wesleyans had begun to set up their own ministry they had conformed to the general outlook regarding women preachers. When the Wesleyans and the Primitives united in 1932 it was the Wesleyan view that prevailed, although the Primitives themselves appear to have had no women ministers and only few women local preachers. It was not until 1973 that women ministers were recognised. However, before that, beginning in the 1950s, Methodist Home Missions had a policy of appointing Wesley deaconesses to new housing estates and rural areas. In 1954 Sister Blanche Baker was appointed to an area covering Keyingham, Ottringham, Burstwick, Ryhill Thorngumbald and Cherry Cobb Sands. She was succeeded by Sister Winifred Woolman, who was provided with a motor scooter on which to cover her round. Her successor, Sister Gwen Catley, chose to use a bicycle. When Gwen married she had to leave the Wesley Deaconess Order, as before 1970 married women were not allowed to serve, it being thought that you cannot do two jobs at once! At that time the Withernsea Circuit, to which Keyingham belonged, was served by two ministers but, in 1977, because of a shortage of ministers, the number was reduced to one. In order to assist the minister, lay pastoral assistants were used, and Stanley Kerman of Withernsea was given oversight of Keyingham until succeeded by Joan Johnson in 1981. In 1985 she was succeeded by Gwen Catley, now Mrs Agar, who had been re-instated into the Wesley Deaconess Order. The name of the order was changed to the Methodist Diaconal Order when men began to be employed, and the title 'Sister' has been replaced by 'Deacon'. When Sister Gwen Agar retired in 1995 she was replaced by Deacon Kate Barrett, who is still the Methodist minister at Keyingham.

As with the Anglicans, there has been a decline in chapel attendance in recent years. The Methodists make statistical returns of the average attendance at the morning services during the month of October each year. At Keyingham the figure was 65 in 1985, 60 in 1990, and 50 in 1995. The average attendance at morning services in October 1999 was 44. There is still an evening service attended by about 15 people. In 1993 there were 47 children in the Sunday school. At present there are about 20 children. Although the youth club had a membership of 35 in 1979, there having been a large increase in the village population since the founding of the club, it closed in that year, principally owing to a lack of leaders.

- o -

When Queen Elizabeth was crowned in 1953 the National Health Service had been in operation for five years. Although prescriptions were not to be made free until 1965, people were more prepared to take their illnesses to the doctor instead of treating them with home remedies. Doctors' surgeries became very crowded and doctors were called out far more frequently than previously. Jeanne Wilkie well remembers those times. Her husband, Dr John Wilkie, came to Keyingham as an assistant to Dr F R Cripps in August 1952. Two years later he became a partner in the practice. The Wilkies lived at Prospect House, which was attached to Dr Cripps' Keyingham surgery but with no direct access between the two. Life was very hectic. There were morning and evening surgeries most weekdays. On Tuesday evenings Dr Wilkie stood in at the Withernsea and Patrington surgeries when it was Dr Cripps' half day. With often a few house calls to do afterwards, it was usually 10 p.m. when Dr Wilkie arrived home. On Saturdays there was a surgery at Keyingham between 2 p.m. and 3 p.m. After that it was the Wilkies' half day until midnight, when Dr Wilkie was again on call. One Saturday night the Wilkies went visiting friends and returned home at 11.30 p.m. On the way home they were spotted by Dr Cripps, who rang next day to say that half days were not for going out and enjoying oneself but for resting up for the week's work ahead. When Dr Wilkie became a partner he changed the Saturday surgery to a morning one as he and Jeanne realised the patients were putting them on the weekend's shopping list!

The surgery was much smaller than at present, and there was no ancillary staff, no appointments system and no telephone. Telephone messages were taken in the house by Mrs Wilkie, who in surgery hours also acted as receptionist and assistant, being a fully qualified nurse. If any telephone messages came during surgeries then she had to run out of the surgery and round into the house to take them.

The practice covered an area from the Hull boundary to Withernsea and Spurn Point, including Hedon, Burstwick, Coniston and Halsham. The surgeries were at Withernsea, Patrington and Keyingham. Later, Dr Wilkie began the practice's first surgery in Hedon, initially in the front room of a patient's house in Church Lane. Doctor Cripps was Medical Officer for the lifeboat at Spurn, and occasionally Dr Wilkie had to cover for this duty. One wild night he was called out to accompany the lifeboat to a Dutch ship where a seaman had broken all his fingers when a hatch cover fell on his hand. They took the man off but had to go to Grimsby because of the tide. For some reason the lifeboat had to remain at Grimsby so, after taking the man to hospital, Dr Wilkie had the problem of returning to Keyingham in time for the 9 a.m. surgery. He had just sufficient money in his pocket to catch a train to New Holland and then the ferry to Hull. With no money for the train fare to Keyingham he had to take a taxi, with the driver being very doubtful about getting his fare from a somewhat bleary-eyed and scruffy passenger. He arrived home at 8.30. Jeanne talked him into having a decent breakfast rather than a bath and a shave, so it was a dishevelled and unshaven doctor who called his first patient in at 9 a.m. As he did so, two ladies in the waiting room turned to each other and said, 'Well, it's easy to see he's just got out of bed.'

Because so few people had cars, house visits by the doctor were a frequent occurrence, and Dr Wilkie usually fitted in 20-30 visits a day between the morning and evening surgeries. On occasions he had to leave patients sitting in the waiting room whilst he went out to an emergency, and sometimes he continued his visiting after the evening surgery. Elderly patients were visited every 4-6 weeks, with one or two villages being dealt with at a time. Because of the lack of private transport people preferred going to the surgery, rather than the casualty department at the Hull Infirmary, for the treatment of burns, scalds or sprains or the stitching of cuts. The doctor also performed minor surgery, such as the removal of cysts, although the days of tonsillectomies on the kitchen table were over. In 1953 vaccination against smallpox was routine, but the polio vaccine was not introduced until 1956, and the measles vaccine in 1966. Up to that time measles epidemics occurred every two years, and their effect on school attendances have already been mentioned in earlier chapters. Penicillin was available in 1953 but only by injection, administered three or four times a day by the GP or by District Nurses Evelyn (Peggy) Beal or Irene Derving, who both lived in Keyingham and were also the District Midwives. Penicillin injections were usually given at home as the patient was often too poorly to come to the surgery.

The first secretary to the practice was Mrs Jessie Rourke who joined in 1969 after the surgery had been enlarged and a telephone installed. Jessie was joined in 1972 by Mrs Pamela Samwell, and shortly after that the appointment system was introduced. When Jessie retired in 1977 she was replaced by Mrs Elizabeth (Liz) Tilby who is still with the practice. In her time Liz has seen the introduction of a practice nurse, the holding of the baby clinic in the surgery and the linking of the Keyingham and Hedon surgeries by computer.

After Dr Cripps' retirement, Dr Wilkie became head of the practice, which in 1976 was divided, with Patrington and Withernsea forming one practice and Keyingham and Hedon the other. When Dr Wilkie retired in 1982, he and Jeanne left Prospect House, which is again a private house although the surgery is attached to it.

The Hedon practice of Drs Marshall and Clark had a surgery in Keyingham in the house next door but one to the Blue Bell, where Hedon doctors had had a surgery since just after the First World War. Since then the practice, now known as the Hedon Group Practice, has had a new surgery built at the corner of Chapel Lane and Main Street. One afternoon, soon after the Wilkies had arrived in Keyingham, their car was standing in the drive. A man in a rather old and grubby raincoat knocked at the door and asked if the doctor was in. 'Yes,' said Jeanne, 'but it's his half day off.' 'Well, tell him to get his bloody car in the garage so no one knows he's in. I'm Dr Marshall come to introduce myself!' Evidence of the small operations done by GPs is provided by the story of when Harry Webster, landlord of the Blue Bell, went to Dr Marshall's surgery to take a telephone message, the surgery itself having no telephone. Whilst Harry was there Dr Marshall had occasion to put his hand in his pocket to take out his handkerchief and a finger end fell on the floor. Doctor Marshall had forgotten to dispose of it after an operation.

It was under the health service that the former Agricultural Hostel in Saltaugh Road was taken over in the 1950s for use by patients with learning difficulties from Winestead Hospital. Mr Wilson was the first warden, with 30 men in his charge living in the barrack-like accommodation formerly occupied by Land Army girls and then by prisoners of war. The intention was to give the men more independence and they became a familiar sight in the village, going to the shops, working on the farms, growing vegetables in the hostel garden, doing work round the village and joining in cricket and football on the playing field. The parish council often had occasion to thank them, for example, on the cleaning of the school playground in 1958. In January 1959, when the council discussed snow clearance, the clerk minuted that 'much more could be done by the RDC workmen than was being done in these trying times and Mr Wilson, Agricultural Hostel Supervisor, would be pleased to loan some of his

boys for this task'. Although the 'boys' or the 'lads', as they were also known, received only low pay, or no pay at all on occasions, they did their work cheerfully and often lent a hand in other situations, such as putting out the chairs etc. for the playgroup in the Village Institute. In 1981 the accommodation at the hostel was improved greatly when the concrete huts were replaced by four complexes of two-storey flats, with each man having his own apartment. In 1992 the running of the hostel was taken over by Humberside Independent Care Association Ltd (HICA), a 'not for profit' organisation that manages 24 residential and nursing homes in the region. The flats were divided into two complexes, one, Horrox Court, which has accommodation for 16 adults who require a minimum amount of help and support, and a second, The Orchard, for eight adults needing additional support. Some of the men at Horrox Court have lived on the site since the old 'hostel' days and have seen many changes in the village in their time.

Horrox Court. Care Assistant Sheila Waites reads with Irene Pawson, a resident at The Orchard.

By kind permission of HICA

- o -

When Keyingham expanded and became a commuter village, agriculture and the associated trades were no longer the major employers of labour. Agriculture itself, as it became more and more efficient, required less and less manpower. The official analysis of the 1991 census did not even class agricultural employment under a separate heading - it was grouped with 'Other' occupations, which formed 6% of Keyingham's working population. The trades in the village associated with agriculture disappeared. Wheelwrights, saddlers and blacksmiths were no longer required to make or repair farm equipment. The selling of hay and straw, which George Beadle of Church Farm had taken over from W H (Harry) Lanham of Bleak House, came to an end with the demise of horse transport for short deliveries in Hull.

At the very beginning of Elizabeth II's reign the saddler's shop on Hill Top opposite the end of Church Lane was being operated by Fred Butler, who had succeeded Henry Norris for whom Fred had worked. In the Great War Fred had served with the Royal Scots Greys and Bays, maintaining the harness for the cavalry. The shop, as it had probably done since the very start of a bus service to the village, provided shelter on wet and windy mornings for waiting passengers, with time passing quickly as they watched the craftsmen at work. In the old days the work was making and repairing horse harness, including the collars for draught horses. The collars were stuffed with horsehair, and boys would collect hair from horses' manes and tails and trade it with the saddler for horse brasses, brushes or currycombs. In Henry Norris's day it had been a popular place to visit, especially during workmen's lunchtime, as

Harry, in the days when off-course betting was illegal, was willing to place a bet on a horse for any one who fancied his luck. Since those times there had been much diversification in the saddler's work at Keyingham. Horse harness was still produced but other leather goods, such as school satchels, shopping bags, purses, wallets and dog collars were also made. The upholstery of furniture was carried out, but one of the chief jobs was going out to the farms to repair the canvas in reaper binders. The business ceased when Fred Butler died in 1954. The shop was demolished in the early 1960s along with the cottages that extended to and round Chapel Lane corner.

Until the 1970s there was still a working blacksmith's shop at Bryn Ferra in Saltaugh Road. It had been built by Herbert Francis of Saltaugh Grange in 1916 for William Beadle, following the closure of the blacksmith's shop in Main Street. Mr Francis wanted to ensure that there was a smith in the village to carry out the repairs to machinery and the shoeing of horses on his farm. When William died in 1955 he was succeeded in the business by his son, Harry, although the time was fast disappearing when children on their way to school would watch in wonderment as he or his father shoed a farm horse or fitted hot iron rims to the wooden wheels made by Clive Guy the joiner. Much of the work was still for the farmers, however, and there were always harrows stacked up outside the shop awaiting repairs. Clive Mason, who worked as a blacksmith for Hull Corporation, often helped Harry in his spare time and devised an economic way of replacing the broken teeth on harrows. In order to supplement the work he did for farmers, Harry did welding repairs on cars, usually sent over from Murdoch's garage. He retired in 1972, but the blacksmith's shop still stands. Harry Beadle's place as farrier for the increasing number of horses ridden for leisure has been taken by mobile blacksmiths, who use a metal that needs no forging to shape it. The repair of farm machinery is now done on the spot by contractors. Locally, Peter McCurdy has set up a workshop at Keyingham Grange. Besides repairing farm machinery he erects steel-frame farm buildings.

The village elders outside the shoemaker's shop in Main Street, circa 1920. From left to right: Harry Guy; George Robinson, driver of the RDC steam roller that parked at Bryn Ferra when working in Keyingham; Richard Westmorland; Herbert Walker, the father of Albert Walker and Grace Capes; and Jack Gray who was blind. The shoemaker's shop, with its warm stove, was a popular meeting place for old men to discuss the events of the day and it is no coincidence that

Frank Middleton, who had succeeded Richard Westmorland at the shoemaker's shop in Main Street opposite the end of Beck Lane in 1917, was still working at the shop in 1960. Up to the start of the Second World War he had made shoes but then decided to do repairs only, in order to save the trouble of handling clothing coupons. The cobbler's shop, the smithy and the saddler's shop, where the proprietor was usually confined to his work place and there was a warm stove or forge,

shoemakers were often active in local politics. The shop had previously belonged to Richard Westmorland who was a parish councillor and rural district councillor, positions that his successor at the shop, Frank Middleton, also occupied.

Courtesy of Miss Phyllis Middleton

were the traditional places for old men to meet and talk. Here, there were many discussions of local problems and how they should be put to right, and it is no coincidence that Frank Middleton and his predecessor, Richard Westmorland, like many other shoemakers, were closely involved in local affairs. Both were Foresters, school managers, parish councillors, rural district councillors and Primitive Methodist local preachers. Frank's delivery from the pulpit was in the old style of Primitive Methodist preaching, and his daughter says that on one occasion when she arrived early by car to pick him up from Thorngumbald chapel she could hear him inside with the doors shut. His days as a preacher were ended when he won the pools and was thus discovered to be indulging in games of chance. He continued to attend chapel and it is said that on one occasion when the preacher failed to turn up and there was no local preacher in the congregation, he was invited to preach. He could not resist choosing as his text the passage from the *Book of Jonah* in which *lots were drawn* to decide who was to blame for the storm encountered by the ship in which Jonah was sailing. Frank Middleton retired from his shop in 1969 at the age of 81 and all his shoe-making equipment was donated to Hull Museums. The shop has had several uses since, including antiques shop, art shop and an estate agent's office. In 1990 it was bought by Raymond and Jacqueline Curtis and run as 'The Clothes Shop', selling ladies', children's and some men's wear. The shop, which now also hires out ladies' hats, is still run by Mrs Curtis.

Clive Guy, onetime wheelwright, was concentrating on the joinery side of his business in 1960, and in the early days of Keyingham's housing boom was, amongst other things, making window frames, doors and kitchen cupboards for the new houses. He was also the village undertaker, and there was often a coffin, resting on trestles, in the process of being made in his workshop. Everything for local delivery was transported on a handcart, even the coffins. At one time the workshop had been the place where the weights and measures inspectors regularly checked all the weights and volumetric measures used by the local shopkeepers, farmers and milkmen. Clive's daughter remembers the occasions when the workshop was cleaned out and made ready for the inspector's visit and the posters announcing the day of the inspection were circulated round the village. Clive was succeeded by his son John, who eventually gave up the business in 1978, when the mass production of house fittings proved too competitive. In the latter years his workshop had become the meeting place of the old men of the village after the closing of the smithy and the retirement of Frank Middleton from his shop across the road. The joiner's shop has since been demolished and two houses have been built on the site.

With the closure of the joiner's shop all the ancient crafts and craftsmen's shops had vanished from Keyingham. However, modern skills were still needed, and the repair of cars begun by Murdoch's garage between the wars continued. During World War II William (Pat) Murdoch, the owner of the garage on Ottringham Road, had gone to work for an engineering firm in Hull when his pumps were taken over by the War-Ag and when there were few private car repairs to be done. When the war was over he continued working in Hull and asked Albert (Horace) Beadle to work at the garage. Horace already had a lot of experience with vehicles. Before the war he had on several occasions, at the age of 14, driven Harry Lanham's lorry, laden with hay and straw, into

Hull, using Harry's driving licence and wearing his trilby hat to make him look older. From 1940 to 1946 Horace served with the motor transport section in the Royal Engineers, most of the time in North Africa. In 1946 there were no more than half a dozen cars in Keyingham, and most of Horace's work was as petrol pump attendant. As more people came to own cars and petrol rationing ended, the business flourished. Pat Murdoch left his job in Hull and joined Horace at the garage, and in the 1950s there was a staff of nine mechanics and two office staff. Work increased further with the expansion of the village, and many people will recall the air of activity that the forecourt presented under Horace's direction. To many he was a knight in shining armour as he accepted all cars for repair on the day, if the emergency seemed great enough, ('Aye, leave it ovver there and it'll be ready tonight.') and he would be at the garage long after all the other workmen had gone home. There is many a thankful motorist who has watched anxiously as Horace peered under the bonnet and listened to a faulty engine before slowly taking a screw driver from the top pocket of his overalls, turning a hidden carburettor screw a quarter turn and putting everything right. Unfortunately, the firm got into financial difficulties and closed in 1982. The garage was later bought by Bob Willie and his family, who already had a garage and repair station at Burton Pidsea. It is now run by two of Mr Willie's sons, Charles and Trevor, who have followed in the tradition of helpfulness set by Horace. The forecourt is not as busy as in the '50s and '60s, however, because of strong competition for the petrol trade from the supermarkets and the fact that modern cars are more reliable and need less servicing.

Keyingham Garage, circa 1960.
A busy forecourt scene with the old style petrol pumps. Pat Murdoch, the owner, chats to Harold Harness (in the white coat) as Horace Beadle prepares to serve petrol to Mrs. Murdoch. Bill Bromwich, the garage accountant, is behind the car.

From the Vic Lanham collection

When Murdoch's closed in 1982 one of the mechanics, Andrew Metcalf, who had served some of his apprenticeship with Horace, went into business on his own, doing car repairs from a mobile van. In 1984 he bought land in Boyes Lane, built a workshop and bungalow there and opened Boyes Lane Engineering at the end of 1985. He repairs and services all types of vehicle, which provides work for himself and another mechanic. Andrew also has half ownership in Riverside Karting on St Andrew's Quay in Hull and participates in endurance go-karting with his 13-year-old son Lee. In 1999 they finished fourth out of over 50 in the Kartsport Enduro Championship, the highest position of any private team in a competition dominated by works teams.

When Frank Middleton found that he wasn't getting enough work mending shoes he became a part-time postman, joining a distinguished band of men and women who have cycled round the village cheerfully delivering the mail in all weathers. The postmen also delivered telegrams received at the post office. If one arrived in Frank's day it was taken to his shop. He would shut up the premises and deliver the telegram on his own bicycle, a huge 'sit-up-and-beg' with 28-inch wheels, which he could ride at quite some speed. He gave up the postman's job at the age of 79.

Amongst the ranks of postmen was Clive Guy who, during the early years of the First World War when he had just left school and the regular postman had joined the Army, delivered the mail in between learning his father's trade of joiner and wheelwright. The round covered the farms in the Marsh as well as Sands Farm, which was reached from Saltaugh Grange by a footbridge over Keyingham Drain. The postmen's bicycles were fitted with extra wide tyres, known as marsh tyres, which were supposed to cope with the tricky conditions in the Marsh, and it was normal for the postman to cycle over the bridge. One day, however, when young Clive descended the bank to the bridge at speed, the cycle slithered in the mud and he was precipitated into the drain. He managed to clamber out and was given dry clothes, a hot drink and food at the farm.

Harold Whiting, who was postman in the late 1940s and the '50s, also had adventure near the drain. He used to set snares for rabbits on his rounds and one day was emerging over the drain bank with two rabbits in his hand when Mr Chichester-Constable, owner of Keyingham Marsh, came upon him and asked him what he was up to. He replied that he was teaching the rabbits to swim. Harold was quite a character. He lived in Peace Cottage in Ings Lane and regularly 'swept' his chimney on Sunday mornings by firing his shotgun up it, and on at least one occasion Jim Howes was called on to mend a broken chimney pot. One morning Harold was delivering mail at the Hull Road bungalows when a lorry travelling from the direction of Hull knocked down and killed two geese that had wandered into the road. The driver stopped to ask Harold who the owner was so that he could apologise. Harold told him not to worry, but to throw the geese in the ditch at the roadside. The driver threw the geese in the ditch, from where Harold later retrieved them for his next dinner or two. Harold made his own funeral arrangements. All the mourners were to have a drink on him at the Ship Inn on their way to the cemetery from the burial service at the chapel. Only Clive Guy, the undertaker, was to wait outside with the hearse and Harold. This all came to pass in about 1959, and Ray Thompson can well remember seeing Clive standing by the funeral car outside the Ship Inn in his shining top hat and black suit while the rest of the party was inside imbibing.

Letter delivery in Keyingham is not a full-time occupation, and most of the village's postmen have had other occupations, no better exemplified than by Vic Lanham. At his house, with its outbuildings and large orchard, he kept pigs, chickens, pigeons and Jacob's sheep. He did a bit of men's hairdressing and kept a small museum, open to anyone who was interested. In it were bygones and old photographs of Keyingham. He painted pictures of the village as he remembered it and wrote articles for *Keywatch*, some of which have been used as a source of information for this book.

Vic Lanham with a group of children from Keyingham Infant School, 1992. He has just shown them round his museum. Born in Keyingham, Vic was known throughout the village for his many talents - artist, author, barber, chorister, farmer, keeper of pigs, chickens and Jacobs sheep, Methodist, model-maker, philosopher, photographer, postman, soldier, and village chronicler.   Photo: Mrs A M Foster

- o -

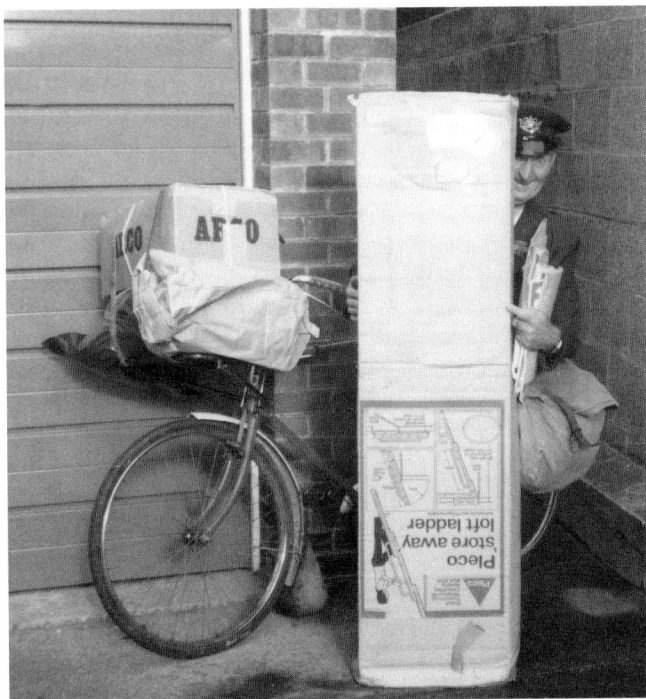

Village postman, circa 1980. Vic Lanham with one of the packages he was required to deliver. It contained a stepladder that was taller than he was!

Courtesy of Mrs Freda Lanham

Although agriculture is no longer a big employer in Keyingham, farmland still covers the major part of the parish, only about 200 of Keyingham's three and a half thousand acres having houses built on them. An increasing amount of land, however, is being covered by greenhouses.

Some of the small dairy farms near the centre of the village were still selling their own milk at the beginning of the 1950s, but they either changed use or were sold off for the housing development of the 1960s. The fate of Harold Lowther's land has been mentioned in an earlier chapter. Len Medforth did not continue with dairy cattle when he bought Bleak House from Harry Lanham in

1951. Lawrie Grant sold Skeckling Farm, which extended from the farm house on the north side of Main Street to almost as far as the windmill on Ottringham Road, to Howes and Clark and it was used for housing and greenhouses. Ted Westmorland sold milk from Elm Tree Farm in Waldby Garth Road, and in 1953 Ted's 17-year-old son David was delivering milk from the farm. He carried the containers and ladles in a carrier mounted on a tricycle. In time David became the sole dairyman in the village. By this time the Westmorland cow pastures, which were on the north side of Waldby Garth Road, had been sold for housing development and the milk was obtained in bottles from Hull. When the new estates were built and the milk round expanded, David was joined by Ray Lawton, who had already been helping him with a window-cleaning round. In the late 1980s, Ray Lawton took over the whole of the business, and is now helped by his son, Peter. Owing to competition from supermarkets, the size of the round is now greatly reduced.

Some of the smaller farms in and close to the village have survived but are constantly having to adapt to the demands of world trade and new regulations. Mike and Leslie Galtrey run about 90 acres of land from Bleak House. The family came to Keyingham when Les and Mike's father, William, bought three acres of land attached to The Croft on Ottringham Road in 1939. There he hatched chicks for sale and for rearing to the pullet stage. In 1959 he bought Bleak House Farm from Len Medforth, who had run a small mixed farm of arable, sheep and pigs. Mr Galtrey established a dairy herd there. The milk was sold directly to Riley's Dairies of Hull. At one time the Galtreys had 60 Friesians and their calves, and many former Keyingham schoolchildren will remember being taken round the farm to see newborn calves and the milking operation. When milk quotas were introduced in 1997 in order to limit the supply of milk, Mike and Les gave up the dairy herd. The pastures were ploughed out and given over to corn, oil seed rape and vining peas, the harvesting of which is done by contractors. The cowsheds at Bleak House and The Croft (chick hatching was discontinued in 1963) are now used for pig fattening. Pigs are brought in at 35 kg weight and sold for bacon 10-12 weeks later at 86 kg.

Mike Westmorland runs the 30 acres of Wray House Farm inherited from his father Philip. The farm was larger but land to the east of Eastfield Road was sold for housing in the 1960s and for the recent extension of Mill Nurseries. Philip Westmorland ran a mixed farm but today Mike has the 30 acres under the plough. In the farm buildings he raises poultry for the table.

The larger farms in Keyingham have tended to become even larger as farm machinery has become more efficient and capable of dealing with greater acreages. Keyingham Marsh, which covered more than 1,400 acres, was tenanted by farmers at Keyingham Grange, Marsh Farm, Marsh House and Marsh Cottage when it was sold in 1948 by R C T Chichester-Constable, descendant of the lords of the manor, to J Marr & Son Ltd, the Hull trawler firm. Soon after, Charles Patchett took on the tenancy of Keyingham Grange and Marsh Farm as well as Westlands Farm at Winestead so that he was farming 1,000 acres in addition to the 400 acres of Ebor House Farm, which he bought from the Church Commissioners in 1953. In those days he employed 50 staff to run the whole enterprise, which included piggeries, general farming and market gardening. Later, Mr Patchett relinquished most of Ebor House Farm, some for gravel extraction and some by sale to other farmers. He also gave up the tenancies, so that by the early 1980s he had only 100 acres, mostly devoted to pigs. This land was subsequently sold off for use as horse paddocks and for the building of the houses in Ebor Manor.

The tenancy of the 520-acre Keyingham Grange, these days usually referred to as Grange Farm, was taken on in the early 1970s by Jim Jackson and his sons Martin and Graham. They already owned the 385-acre White House Farm in Saltaugh Road. Later, the 365-acre Poplar Farm in Ottringham was added to the acreage. After Jim's death in 1977 Graham and Martin bought Grange Farm from Marr's trustees. The Keyingham and Ottringham lands are run as one farm and, by contrast with the 50 staff required by Mr Patchett for his 1,400 acres in the 1950s, employed seven men at the beginning of the year 2000 to work 1,370 acres. This included four men looking after a pig unit. A similar enlargement in acreage has occurred elsewhere in Keyingham Marsh, where David Kirkwood of Sands House Farm on Cherry Cobb Sands is tenant of both Marsh Cottage and Marsh Farm. At the opposite end of the village, North End Farm, which Neville Sadler bought from his father-in-law John Cook in 1962, has been increased from 270 acres to 387 acres by purchase. The farm is now run in conjunction with Thorpe Farm in Halsham and Stockholm Farm near Hedon. The whole 1,100-acre holding is run by Matthew and Howard Sadler and employs five men, some of them for managing pigs.

There has been much specialisation in farming over the last half-century. At North End Farm in 1950, John Cook, besides growing crops - wheat, barley, oats, and peas for drying - also raised cattle, sheep, pigs and chickens. As on many Holderness farms there came to be a strong emphasis on pigs, although at North End there was still provision for the Christmas poultry trade up to 1986. At White House Farm in 1973, Jim Jackson devoted some of his 900 acres to livestock. There was a flock of 300 breeding ewes and a pig herd of 180 sows. He usually fattened up 40 or 50 bullocks a year for local butchers. In the 1970s the growing of oilseed rape was being encouraged and Jim had 20 acres of rape growing in 1973, being one of the first in the area to grow the crop on any scale. In that year the intervention price for rape seed in Hull was £70 a ton and was expected to go up to £98 in the next five years. Residents in Holderness over the last 20 years would have noticed the ever-increasing patches of yellow in the landscape during springtime. However, there has been a decline in the growth of rape in recent years. As has already been recounted in these pages, agriculture in Britain has been affected by events well beyond its shores for over two centuries, and the reason for the decline in rape growing in England is the cheaper production of soya oil in South America. Consequently Holderness farmers have to use other crops as a break in corn growing. Currently peas, for freezing, are being grown. On North End Farm borage, a source of oil for health treatments, has been tried out over the last few years, and potatoes, grown in large amounts during the war years, are once again being turned to.

Not all the difficulties faced by the British farmer at the turn of the millennium are due to events beyond our shores. When the animal-feed manufacturers decided to include meat offal in the diets of cattle and sheep they began a train of events leading to the spread of BSE, the slaughter of millions of cattle and the loss of the sale of British beef around the world. Because of the BSE crisis and the reduction in milk quotas there are now very few cattle to be seen on Keyingham's fields. Neville Dee keeps half a dozen bullocks on the four acres behind his bungalow on Hull Road, and Kevern Thompson and Peter Boardley have two Highland cows in the field on the west of Church Lane. The cows produce one or two calves between them each year and add to the rural scene as one enters the village from the west. But the only herd of significant size is at Marsh House. There the tenant of the 280 acres is Leonard (Jack) Clappison. He has 52 acres at grass, with a 30-cow suckling herd as well as 90 sheep reared for meat. The rest of the land is arable, some of which is used to produce fodder for the animals. Jack works the farm single-handed except in the springtime, when he needs help with lambing, and at harvest when extra hands are needed.

Jack Clappison with his beef cattle at Marsh House Farm, January 2000. Jack is the only farmer in Keyingham in the year 2000 to keep cattle.

Another internally produced crisis was caused by legislation to improve the hygiene and welfare of pigs. Restrictions were put on what could be included in the diet. Practices, such as tethering pregnant sows in stalls and rearing piglets in cramped conditions, were banned. Pig breeders spent thousands of pounds in order to comply with the regulations and the traceability schemes demanded by supermarkets, processors and caterers. Unfortunately, it was only in this country that such standards were insisted on, so that foreign pork and bacon were cheaper. Buyers forgot about traceability and kindness to animals and went for the lower prices. Consequently, at the end of 1999, the pig industry in Britain was in crisis, and many farmers in Holderness who concentrated on pig breeding went bankrupt. At White House Farm in November 1999 the Jacksons were spending over £1,100 a week on keeping pigs they were unable to sell, and the jobs of men working in Keyingham's pig units were in jeopardy.

In Keyingham the loss of jobs in agriculture over the years has been offset by the growth of the horticultural industry, which from the 1950s onward has had quite an impact on the village landscape. It was in 1954 that Ottringham Nurseries were seeking to transfer their greenhouses to better-drained land. They purchased an 8.5-acre site in Marsh Lane, where the land was light and free draining and conveniently on the route between Ottringham and the vegetable wholesalers in Hull. The glasshouses from Ottringham were transferred to Marsh Lane, and Berrygate Hill Nurseries began.

Ottringham Nurseries had been formed by Edward Hinchliffe, farmer and vegetable-and-fruit wholesaler with a business in Wellington Lane, Hull. It was in 1948 that he took the decision to grow some of his own vegetables and salads for sale. Managing the business in 1949 was Dutchman Johannes (Joh) Overvoorde. He had learned some of his horticulture in Holland before the Germans invaded his country when he was a youth of 16. He was a member of the resistance movement until the war ended and then spent thirty months as a soldier in the Dutch East Indies. On demobilisation in 1948 he was on the point of seeking a new life in Australia when a friend in the Dutch wholesale vegetable business told him of a job as greenhouse manager in England. So Joh arrived in Ottringham in March 1949. A year later he met his future wife Jean Westmorland, a Keyingham girl.

Joh went into partnership with Edward Hinchliffe and another Dutchman, William Verhoef. After the move to Berrygate there were difficulties. For the first year there was no piped water so it had to be brought in milk churns from the Ken Hill gravel pit on the opposite side of Hull Road. When Edward Hinchliffe retired in 1959 Joh bought out the business and in 1972 built a new range of oil-heated greenhouses. The production of earlier crops that this should have brought was set back when the price of oil shot up owing to the war in the Middle East, but the storm was eventually weathered and many other improvements followed.

Joh kept in close touch with the horticultural research conducted in Holland and was the first in this area to use a greenhouse built with aluminium framing. The narrow glazing bars allowed in more light than did the old wooden frames, and the weight of the glass gave the structure its stability. The greenhouse was bought from the Kemp Brothers, a Dutch firm. The company wanted to expand its sales in Britain, but needed skilled erectors to build its product. One of the brothers, Dick Kemp, therefore came to Keyingham and formed a partnership with Charles Howard and Joh Overvoorde for the purpose of erecting greenhouses. The company, HOK (the initials of the three partners), was formed in 1969. East End Nurseries were built as a show nursery for HOK, using the most up-to-date construction and environment-control technology of the day. In 1978 HOK was sold to a Dutch company, Gakon. East End Nurseries was not part of the sale, however, and continues independently.

Glasshouse under construction, July 1999. Six-and-a-half acres of new aluminium framed glasshouses being erected by HOK for Mill Nurseries. Older greenhouses can be seen in the background. Ten months after this photograph was taken tomatoes were being harvested from the new houses. Also since the photograph was taken nearly 1,000 young trees have been planted round the site by the De Langs of Mill Nurseries.

In 1959 one of Joh Overvoorde's brothers, Jan, joined him in Holderness. Jan initially worked at Ebor House Farm for Charles Patchett, in charge of poultry. In the stackyard Jan began some nursery growing. Later, when Mr Patchett sold off some of his land he insisted that part should go to Jan in order to develop his sideline and so Keyingham Nurseries came into being. Later, Jan's brother-in-law, Gerrit de Lang, came to Keyingham and in partnership with Joh Overvoorde founded Marsh Lane Nurseries. Two years later the partners went their own ways. When Gerrit's brother, Gerard, came to England in 1971 the brothers purchased land on Ottringham Road and began the nurseries near the mill. The mill, which was derelict, was renovated by the two brothers and local craftsmen and converted to a home, which Gerard and his family moved into. After Gerard's early death Gerrit and his sons took over the running of the nurseries, which are now known as Mill Nurseries.

Jan de Groot, brought over from Holland by Joh Overvoorde to run East End Nurseries, eventually went into business on his own and built Grooton Nurseries on Ottringham Road. These nurseries are now Natural Salads Ltd. Thus, the Dutch, with their industry and technical knowledge, have, over the last half-century, contributed greatly to the development of the greenhouse industry in Keyingham. They have also taken part in the life of the village. The Overvoordes and the de Langs are active members of the Methodist chapel, and Joh Overvoorde served as a school governor and was on both the parish council and the Holderness Borough Council. In 1985 he was made Mayor of Holderness.

When Joh Overvoorde was managing the greenhouses at Ottringham Norman Clark used to cycle over in his school holidays to work there. When he left school he began work full-time at the new Berrygate Hill site. The first greenhouses there were unheated and the growing season was short. Cauliflowers, lettuce, cucumbers, tomatoes, celery and gladioli were brought on in greenhouses and Dutch frames. After work he did his own growing for the market in frames set up in part of Howes & Clark's builder's yard in Main Street. In the transplanting season he paid two women 3s.6d (17.5p) an hour to prick out plants. After three years working for Mr Hinchliffe, he bought three acres of land, formerly part of Skeckling Farm, on Ottringham Road and transferred his frames from the builder's yard. Two years later he was able to buy the adjacent six acres. With the aid of Government grants the business, Village Nurseries, was built up and at the end of the '80s the site was thoroughly modernised.

Today there is much specialisation in the greenhouse industry, with nurseries concentrating on cucumbers or tomatoes or on raising young plants from seeds for selling on to other growers to bring to maturity. The technology has advanced tremendously since 1954. New sites for greenhouses are made absolutely level so that there is a constant head of liquid feed throughout the greenhouse and so that warm air does not rise to one end. In the greenhouses heating, humidity, carbon dioxide levels, irrigation and ventilation are all computer controlled. Each individual tomato or cucumber plant can be watered and fed by computer to the nearest millilitre. Bumble bees are used to pollinate tomato plants and a whole range of predator insects are used to combat pest infestations so eliminating the need for chemical sprays on tomatoes or cucumbers. Greenhouses are heated with oil- or gas-fired boilers, and the flue gases, which are rich in carbon dioxide, are pumped into the greenhouse to aid photosynthesis. The latest hi-tech innovation, now used at Mill Nurseries, is carbon dioxide generation using combined heat and power. Gas-driven generators are run to produce electricity, which is sold to the National Grid, and the heat and carbon dioxide produced are used in the greenhouses. Harvested tomatoes are sorted into the appropriate packaging according to the colour, size and weight of each individual tomato by computerised grading machines. Cucumber and tomato plants are grown on clean rock fibre made from volcanic rock that helps to keep the plants free from disease. For plants that are grown for selling on, as at Premier Plant Producers at Berrygate Hill, the humus is bought in. It is interesting to reflect that, although the first greenhouses were brought to Keyingham because of the suitable soil conditions, now no particle of Keyingham soil is used in the growing process.

The original 8.5 acres of Keyingham has greatly expanded since 1954. By 1976 there were 23 acres under glass, and at the beginning of 2000 the figure is 63 acres with plans for another seven acres by the end of the year. Despite the technological advances the nurseries are quite labour-intensive, requiring a work force of about two persons per acre, so that the greenhouse industry is the village's largest employer, providing work for 130 people full-time and between 50 and 100 part-time.

- o -

It is fitting to end this chapter on a note of advancement in technology and the development of new ideas because they have formed the thread of Keyingham's history for over a thousand years, but particularly over the last 100 years. The embanking of the Marsh, the digging of drains, medieval wool production, the enclosure of the open fields, the use of fertilisers and agricultural machinery, and the building of the railway were all technical advances that had occurred before the 20th century opened. During the last century there have been continuing advances in agriculture, improvement in roads and communications of all kinds, the provision of water, electricity and gas, improvements in health and hygiene and the development of the greenhouse industry. These many private, communal and public initiatives have, for better or for worse, made the village what it is today.

Epilogue

Keyingham is now a village of over 2,500 inhabitants living in 900 houses. In place of the traditional basic country cottage, lacking the facilities that are now considered essential, the village has a wide variety of modern housing ranging from four-bedroomed detached houses to single-person flats. Some old cottages built in previous centuries have been tastefully modernised and, since mains gas was brought to the village, almost everyone has some kind of central heating. New houses are often built without chimneys, but most houses have television aerials and satellite dishes.

The increase in population over the last 40 years has greatly altered the character of the village. The strong community feeling of the past has inevitably faded with so many inhabitants commuting from the village each day to their education or work. Television, a long working day and the strain of modern living tend to lead to insularity, and the ownership of cars and the opportunities for more sophisticated entertainment outside the village contribute to a lack of interest and involvement in village affairs.

There is still, however, a nucleus of village life, and there are groups of dedicated people who organise village societies and events that maintain a community spirit. Activities abound for those who seek social contact outside the home, and every day of the week there is an event of some kind at which people can meet and exchange views. Whist drives, bingo, Women's Bright Hour, Darby and Joan and Pop-In are but a few of the regular activities that people can enjoy. Annual events like the Village Show, Gala, Church Garden Party, Flower Festival and Autumn Fair also bring the village together. Young people gather near the cross as they did in years gone by, although they are at present working hard in conjunction with the police and other authorities to provide an indoor meeting place.

The village has an excellent playing field, provided by the foresight of an earlier generation, with up-to-date changing facilities and floodlights added in the 1990s by the rugby and football teams. At the same time the playing area was almost doubled in area to accommodate extra sports pitches and a permanently maintained cricket square. In the 1960s the sports teams in the village were a great unifier when 'incomers' arrived on the new estates. The football team and the cricket team were reinstated when enthusiasts from the newcomers joined with former village players. Rugby League teams have come and gone, but the junior teams - the Vikings - field players from all around the area and play on a regular basis.

The two public houses, the Blue Bell and the Ship Inn, have served the village for two hundred years. Though the structures are old, both are modern in outlook and provide 21st-century entertainment with satellite television, games machines and karaoke alongside the more traditional pursuits of darts, pool and dominoes.

The parish council provides the local administration for the village as it has done for over a century and its responsibilities include the cemetery, the allotments and the playing fields. Over the years the powers of the council have diminished and its decisions on planning, arrived at with local knowledge, are at times over-ruled at county council level, to the detriment of the village. The parish council has little money to use but by careful husbandry of its resources has managed to bring amenities and improvements to the village. In the early months of the year 2000, new swings and slides were erected on the Saltaugh Road and Eastfield Road playing fields and trees were planted on roadside verges.

Keyingham school has changed greatly in character in the last half-century. Instead of providing education for children of the village up to the age of 14, it now educates children from three villages up to the age of 11, and there are now two school buildings instead of one. Few, if any, of the teachers live in Keyingham. The children no longer walk to school with brothers and sisters and friends, enjoying the delights of becks and hedgerows on the way, but are brought to school by parents on foot or in cars, a reflection of the worries of a modern society about the safety of its children. After the age of 11, children begin to attend school at Withernsea or Preston. A few travel into Hull to Hymers College, Hull Grammar School or Trinity House. Daily, during term time, double-decker school buses can be seen leaving the village taking most of the older children to Withernsea High School. From the age of 16 they have the choice of staying on at Withernsea or attending a sixth-form college in Hull.

The country's future, September 1999. Twenty-four children were admitted to Keyingham Infant School in September 1999, the last intake of the 20th century. Whose future lies in Keyingham? By kind permission of The Holderness Gazette.

Diminishing congregations at both the Methodist chapel and St Nicholas Church reflect a countrywide trend. However both are supported by hard-working groups of volunteers who strive to maintain the buildings and services. The Methodist chapel has a minister, Deacon Kate Barrett, but St Nicholas has been without a minister for more than a year.

Most of the small farms in the village have disappeared, their lands taken up by housing or absorbed into larger farms. The larger farms need less manpower than in the past owing to the introduction of high-technology machinery and equipment that requires fewer men but with different skills. Farmers who kept pigs and beef or dairy cattle have been devastated by the effects of regulations imposed by the EEC and the national government and have had to diversify into other areas of farming. The land continues to provide employment for Keyingham people, but the emphasis is now on horticulture rather than agriculture. The continuing increase in acreage of glasshouses has made Keyingham one of the largest producers of salad crops in the UK. Supermarkets all over the country are supplied with Keyingham tomatoes and cucumbers. An ancillary industry that has grown up alongside the growing of salad crops is that of producing plants for the industry and bedding plants for gardeners.

Craftsmen and tradesmen have always been a part of Keyingham village life and this is true today. A 'Year 2000' directory would still include builders, electricians, plumbers and metalworkers, a petrol station, with vehicle repair facilities, and also a motor engineer and an undertaker. Window installers, kitchen fitters, and home decor in curtains and upholstery are newer industries that can be found here.

Keyingham is well served with shops. The

smaller grocers gradually ceased trading as the out-of-town supermarkets took their customers, but Keyingham Stores increased its floor area and, though it operates in the style of a modern self-service supermarket, it maintains the village tradition of offering free delivery and personal service and stocks most of the goods that people require. Keyingham Post Office is at present under threat of closure because of proposed legislation to have pensions and benefits paid directly into bank accounts - a move that could adversely affect the trading in the village. There is a unisex hairdressing salon, a clothes shop, a newsagent and an off-licence. The fish and chip shop has gone, but the Chinese Hot Food Shop caters for the present day taste for cosmopolitan food and instant take-away meals. The Video Shop provides entertainment for those requiring an alternative to television programmes.

The village is fortunate in having two up-to-date surgeries; each served by a team of doctors. They both have facilities at Hedon for full health care and operate an appointments system that shortens the time of waiting for attention. Keyingham no longer has a resident village 'bobby' covering Keyingham and one or two neighbouring villages but is policed by a Neighbourhood Beat Officer responsible for several other villages as well as performing general policing duties. He is stationed in Hedon. There is a strong possibility that even this kind of policing will have to be removed in the near future.

The village enjoys a half-hourly bus service to Hull or Withernsea throughout the day but cars are the main means of transport. Most households have at least one car, and many have two. Most of the working population travel out of the village to their jobs and many people shop outside the village. Main Street carries a large volume of traffic, and the increasing size of lorries and the speed at which traffic passes through the village has caused concern for those walking the narrow pavement, although the speed camera, with or without a film, has proved a deterrent to speeding. A bypass was discussed in the recent past, but present thinking is that bypasses simply encourage more traffic. At times the noise of low-flying military aeroplanes can be heard as they swoop across the village using the radar mast in Dam Lane as a navigation point. A new feature of the landscape is the mobile-phone mast. There is one within the boundaries of Keyingham and others within viewing distance. Plans are in hand to take Keyingham into the era of communication technology and e-mail by the provision of a computer centre for use by villagers. Through advances in media and communication the village is more than ever before influenced by, and part of, the outside world.

There has always been a degree of mobility amongst Keyingham's population, as a reading of these pages will show, but in the past there was some stability lent by the fact that some men had a piece of land, or a shop with its custom, or a craft and its workshop to pass on to a son. There were, therefore, families who continued in the village for generations. But with small farms disappearing, retailing in a village becoming more precarious and many craftsmen no longer needing a central workshop from which to run their business, there are now fewer ties to hold families to the village. Moreover, with ever widening educational opportunities, the children of the village are able to attain levels of qualification that enable them to work in many parts of the world. Consequently, Keyingham has become more a village of residents who stay for a while and then move on, others who use it as a dormitory village and some as a place for their retirement. Let us hope that, no matter how short their stay, they are imbued with something of the community spirit of Keyingham's past.

Appendix 1 - The Inscription on the War Memorial

On the north side of the memorial facing Main Street is the inscription, 'TO THE GLORIOUS MEMORY OF THE MEN OF KEYINGHAM WHO MADE THE SUPREME SACRIFICE IN THE GREAT WAR 1914-1918'. It is followed by the names:

2nd Lieutenant T H EYRE, Yorkshire Regiment
Lance Corporal G SIMPSON, Cheshire Regiment
Driver T CARR, Army Service Corps
Gunner C E COX, Machine Gun Corps
Private D GOUNDRILL, Yorkshire Regiment
Gunner H ROYDHOUSE, Royal Garrison Artillery
Gunner G SMITH, Royal Field Artillery

On the other three sides are the names of the remaining Keyingham men who served in the war

W H ATKINSON, H BARNABY, G BIGGINS, G BILLANEY, W E BILLANEY, A T BLANCHARD, G H BLANCHARD, W BLANCHARD, J G BLASHILL, F BUTLER, H CARTER, T DUNN, T W ETHERINGTON, F C EYRE, J FAIRBANK, A FORD, T FOX, A H FREEMAN, H GARSIDES, A GOUNDRILL, C GUY, C GUY, T GUY, H HARNESS, W HOLMES, W. HOWES, F P LANGDALE, H LANGDALE, A. LANHAM, H LANHAM, J LANHAM, W LANHAM, A E LOWTHER, H J LOWTHER, C W LOCKWOOD, F LORENZ, F MIDDLETON, C J REAM, S B REAM, T ROYDHOUSE, S RUSSELL, W D RUSSELL, F E SMITH, G T SMITH, T W G SMITH, R T TARBOTTON, F THOMPSON, F W THOMPSON, W TUTON, R VICKERS, T H VICKERS, C L WALKER, S H WALKER, T H WALKER, W WHATLING, L W WHATLING, H WHITING.

The plinth on the north side of the memorial records only the names of Keyingham men killed in the Second World War:

H EMSLEY-MIDGLEY, Merchant Navy
Private J M HOOSON, Royal West Kent Regiment
Pilot Officer J M HORROX, Royal Air Force
Trooper D MARRITT, Royal Armoured Corps
Chief Petty Officer F E SMITH, Royal Navy
Petty Officer J H SMITH, Royal Navy
Captain W STORM, Merchant Navy

Bibliography

This story of Keyingham and its people covers a thousand years, and it will be appreciated that this has meant the consultation of many records. We cannot give a list here; we can merely give an indication of the trail that was followed in finding information.

One of the chief starting points was the *Victoria County History of York, East Riding, Vol 5*, pages 55-65, which gives numerous references, many of which can be followed up in the local libraries and archives. These services - the Local Studies Library at Hull's Central Library, the Brynmor Jones Library at the University of Hull, The East Riding of Yorkshire Record Office at Beverley and the Borthwick Institute at York - also have comprehensive index systems that lead to further information. In addition they all have very helpful staff. The Brynmor Jones Library and the Borthwick Institute provided us with illustrative material to use in this book.

The works of Barbara English, David Neave and N Denholm-Young proved to be very valuable sources on Keyingham's history and in these days of computer searches should be easily located. The many booklets of the East Yorkshire Local History Society give useful background on East Yorkshire. Local-newspaper references to Keyingham can be found in an index compiled by the University of Hull Department of Adult Education for the years 1794 to 1825 and in two volumes of the *Meadley Index* published by the Humberside College of Higher Education and covering the years 1826 to 1857. Both sets of indexes are at the Hull Local Studies Library as are copies of the newspapers. John Meadley continued his index of local newspapers up to the year 1929, and references to Keyingham were taken from the manuscript of this index in the 1970s when it was in the custody of Dr Joyce Bellamy at the University of Hull.

One last source of information that should be mentioned is the material given out to students at Workers' Educational Association local-history classes conducted in Keyingham by Dr David Neave and later by Dr Graham Kent. Quite a few of the group that compiled this book had kept the material, and it proved to be very useful, particularly Graham Kent's translations from medieval documents in Latin.

Index

The index is not complete with regard to persons. As a rule we have included the names of: 1) national figures whose activities to some degree or other affected events in Keyingham; 2) prominent local people; and 3) people or families whose names occur in more than one place in the text. The villages listed in the index are in Holderness, and streets, buildings and other locations are in Keyingham, unless otherwise stated.